**Fodor's** First E

# Argentina

*Les possibilidades*
*Go for it!*
*Love,*
*Dad & Mom*

**The complete guide, thoroughly up-to-date**

Packed with details that will make your trip

**The must-see sights, off and on the beaten path**

What to see, what to skip

**Mix-and-match vacation itineraries**

City strolls, countryside adventures

**Smart lodging and dining options**

Essential local do's and taboos

**Transportation tips, distances and directions**

Key contacts, savvy travel tips

**When to go, what to pack**

Clear, accurate, easy-to-use maps

Fodor's Travel Publications • New York, Toronto, London, Sydney, Auckland

# Fodor's Argentina

**EDITOR:** Natasha Lesser

**Editorial Contributors:** Eddy Ancinas, Amy Karafin, Laura Kidder, Kristen Masick, Chelsea Mauldin, Lauren Myers, Mary Reed, Robert P. Walzer, Brad Weiss, Susan Winsten

**Production Editorial:** Tom Holton

**Maps:** David Lindroth, *cartographer;* Mapping Specialists Ltd., *cartographers;* Bob Blake and Rebecca Baer, *map editors*

**Design:** Fabrizio La Rocca, *creative director;* Guido Caroti, *art director;* Jolie Novak, *photo editor*

**Cover Design:** Pentagram

**Production/Manufacturing:** Bob Shields

**Cover Photograph:** Richard Pasley

## Copyright

First Edition

ISBN 0–679–00458–0

ISSN 1526–1360

## Special Sales

Fodor's Travel Publications are available at special discounts for bulk purchases for sales promotions or premiums. Special editions, including personalized covers, excerpts of existing guides, and corporate imprints, can be created in large quantities for special needs. For more information, contact your local bookseller or write to Special Markets, Fodor's Travel Publications, 201 East 50th Street, New York, NY 10022. Inquiries from Canada should be directed to your local Canadian bookseller or sent to Random House of Canada, Ltd., Marketing Department, 2775 Matheson Boulevard East, Mississauga, Ontario L4W 4P7. Inquiries from the United Kingdom should be sent to Fodor's Travel Publications, 20 Vauxhall Bridge Road, London SW1V 2SA, England.

PRINTED IN THE UNITED STATES OF AMERICA

10 9 8 7 6 5 4 3 2 1

## Important Tip

Although all prices, opening times, and other details in this book are based on information supplied to us at press time, changes occur all the time in the travel world, and Fodor's cannot accept responsibility for facts that become outdated or for inadvertent errors or omissions. So **always confirm information when it matters,** especially if you're making a detour to visit a specific place.

# CONTENTS

## Maps

# ON THE ROAD WITH FODOR'S

**T**HE TRIPS YOU TAKE this year and next are going to be significant trips, if only because they'll be your first in the new millennium. Acutely aware of that fact, we've pulled out all stops in preparing *Fodor's Argentina*. To guide you in putting together your Argentine experience, we've created multiday itineraries and neighborhood walks. And to direct you to the places that are truly worth your time and money in these important years, we've rallied the team of endearingly picky know-it-alls we're pleased to call our writers. Having seen all corners of the regions they cover for us, they're real experts. If you knew them, you'd poll them for tips yourself.

**Eddy Ancinas,** who wrote the introduction, the Andean Patagonia section of the Patagonia chapter, and the Cuyo and Northwest chapters, met an Argentine ski racer at the 1960 Winter Olympics in Squaw Valley, California. After they were married in 1962, they traveled and lived in Argentina. Since then, Eddy has led ski and horseback trips in Peru, Argentina, and Chile, and written about skiing and adventure travel in those countries.

After graduating from Boston University with a degree in International Studies, **Kristen Masick** set off for Latin America. She ended up living in Buenos Aires for two years, managing press relations for the Embassy of Nigeria. While there, she also wrote the Buenos Aires and Las Pampas chapters of this guide.

**Robert P. Walzer** is a journalist who has spent most of the past decade living and working in the Caribbean and Latin America. After returning to his native New York from a year in Milan, he couldn't pass up the opportunity of visiting the world's southernmost post office in Ushuaia while writing the Atlantic Patagonia section of the Patagonia chapter.

Fluent in both Spanish and Portuguese, English-teacher, translator, and intrepid traveler **Brad Weiss** put his language skills to work on the Argentine Litoral chapter. Until recently, Brad lived in São Paulo, Brazil, where he worked for the financial newspaper *Gazeta Mercantil* and was a weekend tour guide. He has since made New York City home.

## Don't Forget to Write

Keeping a travel guide fresh and up-to-date is a big job. So we love your feedback—positive and negative—and follow up on all suggestions. Contact the Argentina editor at editors@fodors.com or c/o Fodor's, 201 East 50th Street, New York, New York 10022. And have a wonderful trip!

*Karen Cure*

Karen Cure
*Editorial Director*

# South America

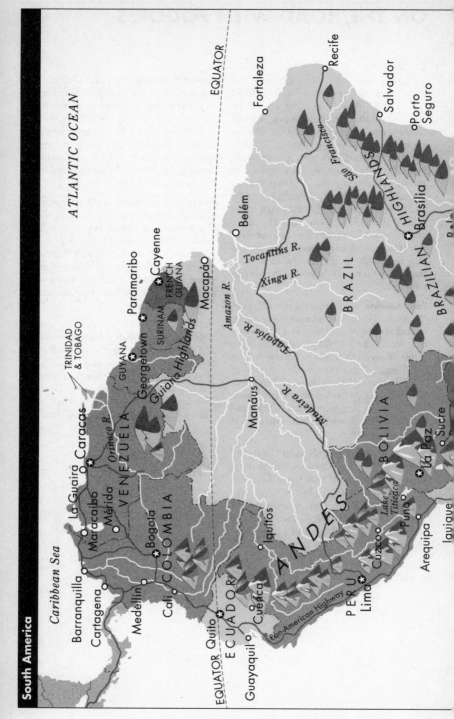

ATLANTIC OCEAN

Caribbean Sea

Barranquilla
Cartagena
Maracaibo
Mérida
La Guaira
Caracas
Medellín
Bogotá
Cali
COLOMBIA
Orinoco R.
VENEZUELA
GUYANA
Georgetown
Guyana Highlands
Paramaribo
SURINAM
Cayenne
FRENCH GUIANA
TRINIDAD & TOBAGO
Macapáo

EQUATOR
Quito
ECUADOR
Guayaquil
Cuenca
Iquitos
Pan-American Highway

Manáus
Madeira R.
Amazon R.
Tapajós R.
Xingu R.
Tocantins R.
Belém

Recife
Fortaleza

BRAZIL
São Francisco
Brasília
BRAZILIAN HIGHLANDS
Salvador
Porto Seguro

ANDES
PERU
Lima
Cuzco
Lake Titicaca
Puno
BOLIVIA
La Paz
Sucre
Arequipa
Iquique

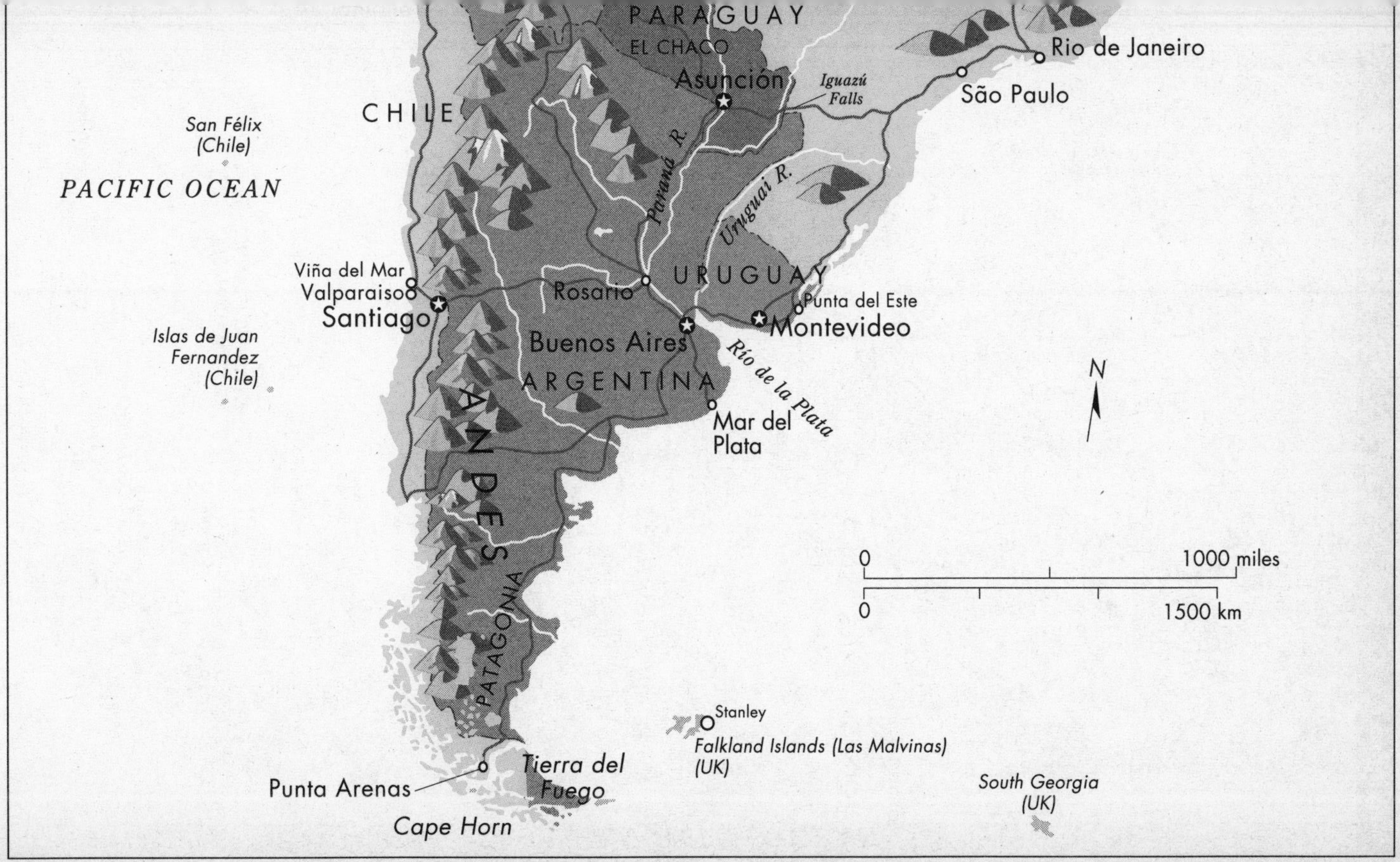

Rio de Janeiro

São Paulo

PARAGUAY

Iguazú Falls

EL CHACO

Asunción

Uruguay R.

Paraná R.

CHILE

San Félix
(Chile)

PACIFIC OCEAN

Islas de Juan
Fernandez
(Chile)

Viña del Mar
Valparaíso
Santiago

Rosario

Buenos Aires

URUGUAY

Punta del Este
Montevideo

Río de la Plata

Mar del
Plata

ARGENTINA

ANDES

PATAGONIA

Punta Arenas

Tierra del
Fuego

Cape Horn

Stanley
Falkland Islands (Las Malvinas)
(UK)

South Georgia
(UK)

N

1000 miles

1500 km

0

0

# Argentina

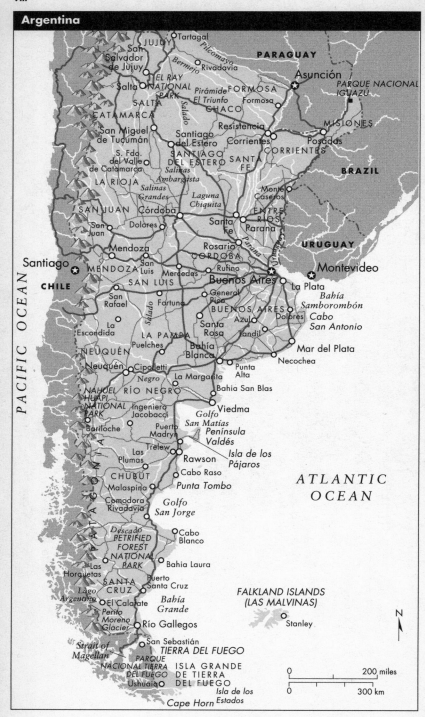

PARAGUAY

Tartagal
JUJUY
Pilcomayo
San Salvador de Jujuy
Bermejo
Rivadavia
Asunción
PARQUE NACIONAL IGUAZÚ
EL RAY NATIONAL PARK
Salta
Pirámide
El Triunfo
FORMOSA
Formosa
SALTA
CHACO
CATAMARCA
Salado
Resistencia
MISIONES
San Miguel de Tucumán
Santiago del Estero
Corrientes
Posadas
S. Fdo. del Valle de Catamarca
SANTIAGO DEL ESTERO
SANTA FE
CORRIENTES
Salinas Ambargasta
BRAZIL
LA RIOJA
Salinas Grandes
Laguna Chiquita
Monte Caseros
SAN JUAN
Córdoba
Santa Fe
Paraná
ENTRE RÍOS
San Juan
Dolores
Rosario
URUGUAY
Santiago
MENDOZA
CÓRDOBA
Montevideo
CHILE
Mendoza
San Luis
Mercedes
Rufino
Buenos Aires
La Plata
PACIFIC OCEAN
San Luis
SAN LUIS
General Pico
Bahía Samborombón
San Rafael
Fortuna
BUENOS AIRES
Azul
Dolores
Cabo San Antonio
La Escondida
Salado
Santa Rosa
Tandil
LA PAMPA
Puelches
Bahía Blanca
Mar del Plata
Neuquén
Cipolletti
Punta Alta
Necochea
NEUQUÉN
Negro
La Margarita
NAHUEL HUAPI NATIONAL PARK
RÍO NEGRO
Bahía San Blas
Ingeniero Jacobacci
Viedma
Bariloche
Golfo San Matías
Puerto Madryn
Península Valdés
Trelew
Isla de los Pájaros
Las Plumas
Rawson
ATLANTIC OCEAN
Cabo Raso
CHUBUT
Punta Tombo
Malaspina
Comodora Rivadavia
Golfo San Jorge
Deseado
PETRIFIED FOREST NATIONAL PARK
Cabo Blanco
Las Horquetas
Bahía Laura
SANTA CRUZ
Puerto Santa Cruz
Lago Argentino
FALKLAND ISLANDS (LAS MALVINAS)
El Calafate
Bahía Grande
Perito Moreno Glacier
Río Gallegos
Stanley
Strait of Magellan
San Sebastián
TIERRA DEL FUEGO
PARQUE NACIONAL TIERRA DEL FUEGO
ISLA GRANDE DE TIERRA DEL FUEGO
Ushuaia
Isla de los Estados
Cape Horn

N

0        200 miles
0        300 km

# SMART TRAVEL TIPS A TO Z

*Basic Information on Traveling in Argentina, Savvy Tips to Make Your Trip a Breeze, and Companies and Organizations to Contact*

## AIR TRAVEL

For international flights, **the major gateway to Argentina is Buenos Aires's Ezeiza International Airport,** 34 km (21 mi) and 45 minutes from the city center. Ezeiza International Airport is served by a variety of foreign airlines, as well as domestic airlines that run international routes. Though Argentina has other international airports, they generally only serve flights from other South American countries. If your national airline does not fly directly into Buenos Aires, it's often possible to fly into Brazil, and take a 2–3 hour flight on Aerolíneas Argentinas into Ezeiza. Miami and New York are the primary departure points for flights to Argentina from the United States.

Major sights in Argentina are often very far apart and long-distance transportation overland can be slow, so you'll probably be traveling around the country by plane, especially if you're short on time. Note that it's often necessary to fly back to Buenos Aires in order to get to your next point (even if it's in the same region as the place you departed from).

Keep in mind that **flights from Buenos Aires to other points within Argentina depart from Aeroparque Jorge Newbury,** which is a 15-minute cab ride from downtown and more than 60 km (38 mi) from the international airport. In winter the number of flights to tourist destinations is greatly reduced.

### CARRIERS

➤ DOMESTIC AIRLINES: **Aerolíneas Argentinas** (☎ 11/4340–3777 in Buenos Aires, ☎ 800/333–0276 in U.S.). **Austral** (☎ 11/4317–3605 in Buenos Aires). **LAPA** (☎ 11/4912–1008 in Buenos Aires).

➤ INTERNATIONAL AIRLINES: **Aerolíneas Argentinas** (☎ 800/333–0276 in U.S.; ☎ 11/4961–9361 in Buenos Aires) to Buenos Aires. **Aeroperu** (☎ 800/777–7717) Buenos Aires, via Lima. **American Airlines** (☎ 800/433–7300 in U.S.; ☎ 11/4480–0366 in Buenos Aires) to Buenos Aires. **LanChile** (☎ 800/735–5526 in U.S.; ☎ 11/4312–8161 in Buenos Aires) to Buenos Aires, via Santiago. **United Airlines** (☎ 800/538–2929 in U.S.; ☎ 11/4316–0777 in Buenos Aires) to Rio de Janeiro, São Paulo, Montevideo, Buenos Aires, Santiago, Lima, Belo Horizonte, Caracas. **Varig Brasil** (☎ 800/468–2744 in U.S.; ☎ 11/4342–4420 in Buenos Aires) to Buenos Aires via Rio de Janeiro and São Paulo. **Vasp** (☎ 800/732–8277 in U.S.; ☎ 11/4311–1135) to Buenos Aires via São Paulo and Rio de Janeiro.

➤ U.K. TO ARGENTINA: **American Airlines** (☎ 0345/789–789) from London Heathrow via Miami or New York. **British Airways** (☎ 0345/222–111) from London Gatwick. **Iberia** (☎ 0171/830–0011 in U.K.; 11/4327–2739 in Buenos Aires) via Madrid. **Virgin Atlantic** (☎ 01293/747–747) from Gatwick to Miami, with connections there.

### CHECK-IN & BOARDING

Remember to **bring your passport.** You'll be asked to show it when you check in and at customs in Argentina and upon your return home.

### CUTTING COSTS

Always **check different routings** and look into using different airports. Travel agents, especially low-fare specialists (☞ Discounts & Deals, *below*), are helpful.

Consolidators are another good source. Carefully read the fine print detailing penalties for changes and cancellations, and **confirm your consolidator reservation with the airline.**

➤ CONSOLIDATORS: **Cheap Tickets** (☎ 800/377–1000). **Discount Airline**

Ticket Service (☎ 800/576–1600). Unitravel (☎ 800/325–2222). Up & Away Travel (☎ 212/889–2345). World Travel Network (☎ 800/409–6753).

## ENJOYING THE FLIGHT

Traveling between the Americas is a bit less tiring than to Europe or Asia because there's less of a time difference and thus less jet lag. New York, for instance, is only one time zone behind Buenos Aires in summer (it's two in winter, as Argentina does not observe American daylight savings time), and there's only a four-hour difference between Los Angeles and Buenos Aires. Flights are generally overnight to Buenos Aires, so you can plan on sleeping while flying.

If you happen to be taking LanChile from the United States, you must change planes in Santiago, which means you'll probably get a lovely view of the Andes on your connecting flight to Buenos Aires. Southbound, the best views are usually out the windows on the left side of the plane.

For more legroom **request an emergency-aisle seat.** Don't sit in the row in front of the emergency aisle or in front of a bulkhead, where seats may not recline. If you have dietary concerns, **ask for special meals when booking.**

Most carriers prohibit smoking throughout their systems; others allow smoking only on certain routes or even certain departures from that route, so **contact your carrier regarding its smoking policy.** Note that smoking is common throughout Latin America, so be sure to ask especially when flying a Latin-American carrier.

## FLYING TIMES

Flying times to Buenos Aires are 11–12 hours from New York and 8½ hours from Miami. Flights from Los Angeles are often routed through either Lima, Bogotá, or Miami.

## HOW TO COMPLAIN

If your baggage goes astray or your flight goes awry, complain right away. Most carriers require that you **file a claim immediately.**

➤ AIRLINE COMPLAINTS: U.S. Department of Transportation **Aviation Consumer Protection Division** (✉ C-75, Room 4107, Washington, DC 20590, ☎ 202/366–2220). **Federal Aviation Administration Consumer Hotline** (☎ 800/322–7873).

## RECONFIRMING

Always **reconfirm your flight,** even if you have a ticket and a reservation. On the majority of routes in Argentina, flights are fully booked—usually with passengers with a lot of baggage to check-in. Many Argentinians arrive at the airport minutes before takeoff—you're best off avoiding this custom. Always **arrive at the airport well in advance of takeoff** to allow for the lengthy check-in. When leaving Argentina, you'll need to show your passport and pay a departure tax of about $20, either in pesos or dollars.

## AIRPORTS & TRANSFERS

### TRANSFERS

Bus, taxi, and *remis* (a kind of taxi or car service for which the price of a ride is pre-arranged) service is available from Buenos Aires's Ezeiza International Airport. Remis tickets can be purchased from the well-marked transportation counter in the airport. Regular taxi service from the airport to downtown costs at least $35. City buses ($2) operate on a regular schedule, but the ride takes close to two hours and there's a limit of two bags. A 24-hour, private bus service is run by Mañuel Tienda León to all downtown hotels ($15); buses depart from the airport on scheduled intervals throughout the day. For the trip to the airport, Tienda León provides frequent van service from its office in front of the Obelisk and from other locations throughout the city.

➤ BUS SERVICE: **Manuel Tienda León** (✉ Santa Fe 790, Buenos Aires, ☎ 11/4383–4454).

## BIKE TRAVEL

Bikes are sometimes used for innercity travel in Argentina, but traveling around the country by bike is not common. You're most likely to find bikes—and places to rent them—in the beach towns of Las Pampas (☞ Chapter 3).

### BIKES IN FLIGHT

Most airlines accommodate bikes as luggage, provided they are dismantled and boxed. International travelers can sometimes substitute a bike for a piece of checked luggage at no charge; otherwise, the cost is about $100. Domestic and Canadian airlines charge $25–$50.

### BOAT & FERRY TRAVEL

There is extensive and frequent ferry service between Argentina and Uruguay; the best ferries are run by Buquebus. American cruiseliners occasionally continue on to Argentina from Brazil. Yachting is extremely popular along the coast, though boat rentals are difficult to find.

➤ BOAT & FERRY INFORMATION: **Buquebus** (✉ Av. Córdoba and Av. Madero; ✉ in Patio Bullrich shopping mall, ☎ 11/4317–1001).

### BUS TRAVEL

Frequent and dependable bus service links Buenos Aires with all the provinces of the country and with neighboring countries.

There are generally two types of buses: *comun* and *diferencial*. On comun buses, the cheaper option, you'll usually get a seat, but it may not be that comfortable and there may not be air-conditioning or heating. Diferencial, only marginally more expensive, usually have reclining seats (some even have *coche-camas*, bedlike seats), an attendant, and snacks. To get between neighboring towns, you can generally get a local city bus.

Buenos Aires's Estación Terminal de Omnibus is the main gateway for long-distance and international bus travel in Argentina. Over 60 bus companies are housed in the station, which may seem overwhelming and confusing at first. But there's a logic to what appears to be chaos: Bus-company stands are arranged not in order of company name, but by destinations served. In general, different companies serving the same destination are clumped together, making it easy to compare times and prices.

Tickets can be purchased at bus terminals right up until departure time. Note that in larger cities there may be different terminals for buses to different destinations. Arrive early to get a ticket, and **be prepared to pay cash.** On holidays, buy your ticket as far in advance as possible and arrive at the station extra early.

When traveling by bus, **bring your own food and beverages,** though food stops are usually made en route. Travel light, dress comfortably, and **keep a close eye on your belongings.** On many long-distance trips, videos are shown.

### FARES & SCHEDULES

Purchase tickets in the bus terminal before boarding. Ticket prices depend on the bus company and destination.

For longer trips, **it's worth comparing bus prices with air fares,** as it's not always that much cheaper to take the bus (a roundtrip ticket to Paraguay, 18 hours each way, for instance, costs about $170; a roundtrip airfare for the same route may be available for the same price).

➤ BUS INFORMATION: **Estación Terminal de Omnibus** (✉ Av. Ramos Mejía 1680, Buenos Aires, ☎ 11/43100700). ☞ Individual chapters' A to Z sections for information about local bus stations.

### RESERVATIONS

You can make reservations on buses, though it's not really necessary (except on holiday weekends); there are always plenty of bus companies going to the same destinations.

### BUSINESS HOURS

Official business hours are 9 AM–7 PM for offices and 9 AM–4 PM for banks. That said, don't count on anyone actually being in the office before 10 AM. Note, too, that the lunch hour is long, generally at least and hour and a half.

### GAS STATIONS

The majority of gas stations in Buenos Aires, other cities, resort areas, and along the highway close at midnight and open again early in the morning, though it's possible to find

SMART TRAVEL TIPS A TO Z

some stations open 24 hours. In the suburbs, gas stations are generally open until about 9 PM. In rural areas, gas station hours are much less consistent. So **when traveling in the country, it's a good idea to start looking for station when your tank is half empty.**

### MUSEUMS & SIGHTS

Most museums are open only five days a week, generally from Tuesday to Saturday, though sometimes from Wednesday to Sunday.

### POST OFFICES AND TELECENTROS

Post offices are open weekdays 8–6 and Saturdays 8–1. Most Telecentros, offices where you can make long-distance calls or send faxes, are open 7:30 AM–midnight.

### SHOPS

In Buenos Aires shops are open late (from 10 AM often until 9 PM) and on Sunday to compete with the malls. In the rest of the country, stores tend to be open from 10 AM until 6 or 7 PM and close for the week from 1 PM Saturday through Sunday (including food shops).

## CAMERAS & PHOTOGRAPHY

### EQUIPMENT PRECAUTIONS

Before departing, you may want to **register your foreign-made camera or laptop with U.S. Customs** (☞ Customs & Duties, *below*). At the very least, if you plan to use your equipment in Argentina, it's a good idea to register it at customs upon entering the country.

Always **be prepared to turn on your camera or camcorder** to prove to security personnel that the device is real. It's a good idea to ask for hand inspection of film, which becomes clouded after successive exposures to airport X-ray machines, and **keep videotapes away from metal detectors.**

Carry an extra supply of batteries. Also, traveling in the jungle poses other problems such as dampness, so it's a good idea to **keep your equipment in resealable plastic bags.**

### FILM & DEVELOPING

It's very easy to find places to purchase and develop film in Buenos Aires and other major cities and resort areas, including one-hour photo shops. Out of these areas, film and developing facilities may be more difficult to find. Prices and quality are about equal to those in the United States.

### PHOTO ADVICE

The higher the altitude, the greater the proportion of ultraviolet rays. Light meters do not read these rays and consequently, except for close-ups or full-frame portraits where the reading is taken directly off the subject, photos may be overexposed. If you'll be visiting the Andes, **get a skylight (81B or 81C) or polarizing filter to minimize haze and light problems.** These filters may also help with the glare caused by white adobe buildings and sandy beaches.

Taking pictures in the jungle poses problems such as low light, so it's a good idea to **bring high-speed film to compensate.**

➤ PHOTO HELP: Kodak Information Center (☎ 800/242–2424). *Kodak Guide to Shooting Great Travel Pictures,* available in bookstores or from Fodor's Travel Publications (☎ 800/533–6478; $16.50 plus $4 shipping).

### VIDEOS

Note that the N-PAL video system is used in Argentina, whereas the NTSC system is used in the United States.

## CAR RENTAL

Renting a car in Argentina is expensive ($95 per day for a medium-size car, $475–$600 per week), but having a car gives you much more flexibility. Ask about special rates; generally a better price can be negotiated.

All cities and most areas that attract tourists have car rental agencies. If the company has a branch in another town, arrangements can generally be made for a one-way drop off. Offices in Buenos Aires can make reservations in other locations; provincial government tourist offices also have information on car rental agencies.

Another option is to **hire a *remise*, a car with a driver,** especially for day outings. Hotels can arrange this service for you. Remises usually end up being quite a bit cheaper than taxis for long rides, and at least marginally less expensive for rides within cities. You have to pay cash—but you'll often spend less than you would for a rental car. In cities, remises cost about $20–$25 per hour; sometimes there's a 3-hour minimum and an additional charge per kilometer when you go outside the city limits. In smaller towns, the rate is often much less (perhaps $20–$25 for the entire day). Note that when traveling by remise between two cities, it's always cheaper to get a remise from the more rural city.

➤ LOCAL AGENCIES: **Annie Millet** (✉ Paraguay 1122, Buenos Aires, ☎ 11/4816–8001, FAX 11/4815–6899). **Primer Mundo** (✉ Av. Libertador 6553, Buenos Aires, ☎ 11/4787–2140).

➤ MAJOR AGENCIES: **Alamo** (☎ 800/522–9696; ☎ 0181/759–6200 in the U.K.). **Avis** (☎ 800/331–1084; ☎ 800/879–2847 in Canada; ☎ 02/9353–9000 in Australia; ☎ 09/525–1982 in New Zealand; ☎ 11/43265542 in Buenos Aires). **Budget** (☎ 800/527–0700; ☎ 0144/227–6266 in the U.K.; ☎ 11/43119870 in Buenos Aires). **Dollar** (☎ 800/800–6000; ☎ ; 0181/897–0811 in the U.K., where it is known as Eurodollar; ☎ 02/9223–1444 in Australia). **Hertz** (☎ 800/654–3001; ☎ 800/263–0600 in Canada; ☎ 0181/897–2072 in the U.K.; ☎ 02/9669–2444 in Australia; ☎ 03/358–6777 in New Zealand). **National InterRent** (☎ 800/227–3876; 0345/222525 in the U.K., where it is known as Europcar InterRent).

## CUTTING COSTS

For car rentals in Argentina, it doesn't necessarily cut costs to book before you leave home. But you should reserve ahead if you plan to rent during a holiday period, when vehicles may be in short supply. If you're willing to wait, you can probably get the best rate by renting upon arrival, particularly from a smaller, local company.

Do **look into wholesalers,** companies that do not own fleets but rent in bulk from those that do and often offer better rates than traditional car-rental operations. Payment must be made before you leave home.

➤ WHOLESALERS: **Auto Europe** (☎ 207/842–2000 or 800/223–5555, FAX 800/235–6321).

## INSURANCE

When driving a rented car you are generally responsible for any damage to or loss of the vehicle as well as for any property damage or personal injury that you may cause. Before you rent **see what coverage your personal auto-insurance policy and credit cards already provide** and try to obtain the broadest coverage possible before your arrival in Argentina. Argentine car insurance prices are often significantly higher than in the United States, and the industry has only recently become truly regulated.

## REQUIREMENTS & RESTRICTIONS

In Argentina, **your own driver's license is acceptable,** though an International Driver's Permit, available from the American or Canadian Automobile Association, is always a good idea. The minimum driving age is 18, and unlike in some other areas in Latin America, this is enforced via road blocks and spot checks.

## SURCHARGES

Before you pick up a car in one city and leave it in another **ask about drop-off charges or one-way service fees,** which can be substantial. Note, too, that some rental agencies charge extra if you return the car before the time specified in your contract. To avoid a hefty refueling fee **fill the tank just before you turn in the car,** but be aware that gas stations near the rental outlet may overcharge.

## CAR TRAVEL

### AUTO CLUBS

The Automovil Club Argentino operates gas stations, motels, and campgrounds; sends tow trucks and mechanics in case of breakdowns; and provides detailed maps and expert advice (often in English). If you rent a car, the ACA can help you plan your itinerary, give you gas coupons, and make accommodation arrangements. Bring your auto club membership card for free advice and discounts.

➤ IN ARGENTINA: **Automovil Club Argentino** (ACA, ✉ Av. del Libertador 1850, ☎ 11/48026061).

➤ IN AUSTRALIA: **Australian Automobile Association** (☎ 02/6247–7311).

➤ IN CANADA: **Canadian Automobile Association** (CAA, ☎ 613/247–0117).

➤ IN NEW ZEALAND: **New Zealand Automobile Association** (☎ 09/377–4660).

➤ IN THE U.K.: **Automobile Association** (AA, ☎ 0990/500–600). **Royal Automobile Club** (RAC, ☎ 0990/722–722 for membership; 0345/121–345 for insurance).

➤ IN THE U.S.: **American Automobile Association** (☎ 800/564–6222).

## EMERGENCIES

In emergencies, call the ACA (☞ Auto Clubs, *above*).

## GASOLINE

Gas stations are easy to find in Buenos Aires and other cities and along the highway outside of major cities. Farther along the highway and in rural areas, locating a gas station is hit or miss; **don't let your tank get too low.** For gas station hours, *see* Business Hours, *above*.

Gas is expensive (at least $1 per liter, or about $4 per gallon). There are no regulations on leaded versus unleaded gas and most consumers choose the cheaper, leaded option. Many vehicles also use diesel.

## INTERNATIONAL TRAVEL

Paved highways run from Argentina to the Chilean, Bolivian, Paraguayan, and Brazilian borders. It's unlikely, however, that you would enter Argentina by car from another country. If you do, you'll be stopped at the border, asked for your passport, your visa, and any documents you may have about ownership of the car. It's

also very common for cars and bags to be searched.

## ROAD CONDITIONS

Ultramodern multilane highways exist in Argentina, but typically immediately surrounding the major cities. Gradually these highways become narrower routes, and then county roads. Many of these rural roads are not divided and not in particularly good condition.

Highways have been privatized, so you must pay tolls on many more roads. Tolls come frequently and can be steep (one toll, for instance, on the 5-hour drive between Buenos Aires and Mar del Plata is $13).

Night driving can be hazardous, as highways and routes typically cut through the center of towns. Cattle often get onto the roads and trucks seldom have all their lights working.

## ROAD MAPS

The ACA (☞ Auto Clubs, *above*) has the best road maps of Argentina.

## RULES OF THE ROAD

Some common-sense rules of the road: Plan your daily driving distances conservatively. **Don't drive after dark.** Ask before you leave about gas station locations. Obey speed limits (given in kilometers per hour) and traffic regulations. And above all, if you get a traffic ticket, don't argue, whatever a cop may ask for—it's generally not worth it. In the not so distant past, Argentina was a military state, and the police are still treated as though they wield quite a bit of power. Although you'll see Argentines offering cash on the spot to avoid getting a written ticket, this is probably not a good idea.

Seat belts are required by law but are not often used; it's a good idea, however, to wear one (if the car has them) as accidents are very common. Turning left on avenues is prohibited unless there's a traffic-light arrow showing that it's okay. Note that **traffic lights are not always observed, so you should proceed with care.** Also note that traffic lights not only turn yellow when they are about to turn red, but also when they are about to turn green. In Buenos Aires, give everyone else on the road priority, especially aggressive colectivo and taxi drivers who think they're race-car drivers.

In towns and cities, a 40 kph (25 mph) speed limit applies on streets, and a 60-kph limit is in effect on avenues. On expressways the limit is 120 kph (75 mph), and on other roads and highways out of town it's 80 kph (50 mph), although this is rarely enforced.

## CHILDREN IN ARGENTINA

Argentines generally adore children, and having yours along may prove to be your ticket to meeting locals. Many Argentines prefer to take their children along for a late evening out rather than leave them with a babysitter. As a result, **children are welcome at restaurants** and it's not uncommon to see kids eating midnight dinners with their parents.

Children should have had all their inoculations before leaving home.

### FLYING

If your children are two or older **ask about children's airfares.** As a general rule, infants under two not occupying a seat fly at greatly reduced fares or even for free. When booking **confirm carry-on allowances** if you're traveling with infants. In general, for babies charged 10% of the adult fare, you are allowed one carry-on bag and a collapsible stroller; if the flight is full the stroller may have to be checked or you may be limited to less.

Experts agree that it's a good idea to use safety seats aloft for children weighing less than 40 pounds. Airlines set their own policies: U.S. carriers usually require that the child be ticketed, even if he or she is young enough to ride free, since the seats must be strapped into regular seats. Do **check your airline's policy about using safety seats during takeoff and landing.** And since safety seats are not allowed just everywhere in the plane, get your seat assignments early.

When reserving, **request children's meals or a freestanding bassinet** if you need them. But note that bulk-head seats, where you must sit to use the bassinet, may lack an overhead bin or storage space on the floor.

### LODGING

Most hotels in Argentina allow children under a certain age to stay in their parents' room at no extra charge, but others charge for them as extra adults; be sure to **find out the cutoff age for children's discounts.**

### SIGHTS & ATTRACTIONS

On weekends, Argentine families can be found in droves on day-long outings to the mall, the zoo, or other kid-friendly sights. Places that are especially good for children are indicated by a rubber duckie icon in the margin.

### SUPPLIES & EQUIPMENT

It's a good idea to **bring books from home** as literature for kids in English is hard to find in Argentina. If you're traveling outside of Buenos Aires, you may want to stock up beforehand on items that you're familiar with such as disposable diapers and baby food.

### TRANSPORTATION

If you are renting a car don't forget to **arrange for a car seat** when you reserve.

## COMPUTERS ON THE ROAD

You are supposed to declare your computer upon arrival and pay a tax, though this isn't always the case. However, if you're going to be in Argentina for any extended period of time and plan to get Internet access, declare your computer at customs when you enter the country—you'll need to produce either the document from customs or a receipt to get service. If you've declared your computer on the way in, be sure to declare it on the way out also (hold onto the receipt for this purpose as well).

## CONSUMER PROTECTION

Whenever shopping or buying travel services in Argentina, **pay with a major credit card** so you can cancel payment or get reimbursed if there's a problem. If you're doing business with a particular company for the first time, **contact your local Better**

Business Bureau and the attorney general's offices in your state and the company's home state, as well. Have any complaints been filed? Finally, if you're buying a package or tour, always consider travel insurance that includes default coverage (☞ Insurance, *below*).

➤ BBBs: Council of Better Business Bureaus (✉ 4200 Wilson Blvd., Suite 800, Arlington, VA 22203, ☎ 703/276–0100, FAX 703/525–8277).

## CUSTOMS & DUTIES

When shopping, keep receipts for all purchases. Upon reentering your country, be ready to show customs officials what you've bought. If you feel a duty is incorrect or object to the way your clearance was handled, note the inspector's badge number and ask to see a supervisor. If the problem isn't resolved, write to the appropriate authorities, beginning with the port director at your point of entry.

### IN ARGENTINA

If you come directly to Buenos Aires by air or ship, you'll find that customs officials usually wave you through without any inspection. Also, the international airports have introduced a customs system for those with "nothing to declare," which has streamlined the arrival process. Foreign bus passengers usually have their suitcases opened, as do all other passengers.

Personal clothing and effects are admitted free of duty, provided they have been used, as are personal jewelry and professional equipment. You are suppposed to declare your computer and pay a tax on it, however this isn't always the case. However, if you are going to be in Argentina for any extended period of time and plan to get Internet access for your laptop or hook up your cellular phone, declare them both at customs as you enter the country—you'll need to produce either the document from customs or a receipt to get service. Fishing gear presents no problems. Up to 2 liters of alcoholic beverages, 400 cigarettes, and 50 cigars are admitted duty-free.

Note that you must pay a $20 departure tax upon leaving the country.

### IN AUSTRALIA

Australia residents who are 18 or older may bring home $A400 worth of souvenirs and gifts (including jewelry), 250 cigarettes or 250 grams of tobacco, and 1,125 ml of alcohol (including wine, beer, and spirits). Residents under 18 may bring back $A200 worth of goods. Prohibited items include meat products. Seeds, plants, and fruits need to be declared upon arrival.

➤ INFORMATION: Australian Customs Service (Regional Director, ✉ Box 8, Sydney, NSW 2001, ☎ 02/9213–2000, FAX 02/9213–4000).

### IN CANADA

Canadian residents who have been out of Canada for at least 7 days may bring home C$500 worth of goods duty-free. If you've been away less than 7 days but more than 48 hours, the duty-free allowance drops to C$200; if your trip lasts 24–48 hours, the allowance is C$50. You may not pool allowances with family members. Goods claimed under the C$500 exemption may follow you by mail; those claimed under the lesser exemptions must accompany you. Alcohol and tobacco products may be included in the 7-day and 48-hour exemptions but not in the 24-hour exemption. If you meet the age requirements of the province or territory through which you reenter Canada, you may bring in, duty-free, 1.14 liters (40 imperial ounces) of wine or liquor *or* 24 12-ounce cans or bottles of beer or ale. If you are 16 or older you may bring in, duty-free, 200 cigarettes and 50 cigars. Check ahead of time with Revenue Canada or the Department of Agriculture for policies regarding meat products, seeds, plants, and fruits.

You may send an unlimited number of gifts worth up to C$60 each duty-free to Canada. Label the package UNSOLICITED GIFT—VALUE UNDER $60. Alcohol and tobacco are excluded.

➤ INFORMATION: Revenue Canada (✉ 2265 St. Laurent Blvd. S, Ottawa,

Ontario K1G 4K3, ☎ 613/993–0534; 800/461–9999 in Canada).

### IN NEW ZEALAND

Homeward-bound residents 17 or older may bring back $700 worth of souvenirs and gifts. Your duty-free allowance also includes 4.5 liters of wine or beer; one 1,125-ml bottle of spirits; and either 200 cigarettes, 250 grams of tobacco, 50 cigars, or a combination of the three up to 250 grams. Prohibited items include meat products, seeds, plants, and fruits.

➤ INFORMATION: **New Zealand Customs** (Custom House, ✉ 50 Anzac Ave., Box 29, Auckland, New Zealand, ☎ 09/359–6655, FAX 09/359–6732).

### IN THE U.K.

From countries outside the EU, including Argentina, you may bring home, duty-free, 200 cigarettes or 50 cigars; 1 liter of spirits or 2 liters of fortified or sparkling wine or liqueurs; 2 liters of still table wine; 60 ml of perfume; 250 ml of toilet water; plus £136 worth of other goods, including gifts and souvenirs. If returning from outside the EU, prohibited items include meat products, seeds, plants, and fruits.

➤ INFORMATION: **HM Customs and Excise** (✉ Dorset House, Stamford St., Bromley Kent BR1 1XX, ☎ 0171/202–4227).

### IN THE U.S.

U.S. residents who have been out of the country for at least 48 hours (and who have not used the $400 allowance or any part of it in the past 30 days) may bring home $400 worth of foreign goods duty-free.U.S. residents 21 and older may bring back 1 liter of alcohol duty-free. In addition, regardless of your age, you are allowed 200 cigarettes and 100 non-Cuban cigars. Antiques, which the U.S. Customs Service defines as objects more than 100 years old, enter duty-free, as do original works of art done entirely by hand, including paintings, drawings, and sculptures.

You may also send packages home duty-free: up to $200 worth of goods for personal use, with a limit of one parcel per addressee per day (and no alcohol or tobacco products or perfume worth more than $5); label the package PERSONAL USE and attach a list of its contents and their retail value. Do not label the package UNSOLICITED GIFT or your duty-free exemption will drop to $100. Mailed items do not affect your duty-free allowance on your return.

➤ INFORMATION: **U.S. Customs Service** (inquiries, ✉ 1300 Pennsylvania Ave. NW, Washington, DC 20229, ☎ 202/927–6724; complaints, ✉ Office of Regulations and Rulings, 1300 Pennsylvania Ave. NW, Washington, DC 20229; registration of equipment, ✉ Resource Management, 1300 Pennsylvania Ave. NW, Washington, DC 20229, ☎ 202/927–0540).

## DINING

The restaurants we list are the cream of the crop in each price category. Properties indicated by a ✕🏠 are lodging establishments whose restaurant warrants a special trip.

| CATEGORY | COST* |
|---|---|
| $$$$ | over $35 |
| $$$ | $25–$35 |
| $$ | $15–$25 |
| $ | $5–$15 |
| ¢ | under $5 |

*per person for an appetizer, entrée, and dessert, excluding tax, tip, and beverages*

### MEALS & SPECIALTIES

Meat is still the center of Argentine cuisine. *Asado* (barbeque) is both a style of grilled meat and an event. If you eat at an asado restaurant, are invited to an asado, or go to one at an *estancia* (ranch), be prepared for countless courses of meat, interrupted only by the pouring of wine. *Parrillas* (grills) are also common and are great for casual Argentine fare. All this meat is usually accompanied by a salad and red wine. Pasta (often homemade) and pizza are also frequently available. For more about food in Argentina, *see* Chapter 1.

### MEALTIMES

Breakfast is usually served until 10 AM; lunch runs from 12:30 to 2:30; dinner is from 9 to midnight. Several restaurants in Buenos Aires and other large cities stay open all night, or at least well into the morning, catering to the after-theater and nightclub crowd.

### RESERVATIONS & DRESS

Reservations are always a good idea; we mention them only when they're essential or are not accepted. Book as far ahead as you can, and reconfirm as soon as you arrive.

Jacket and tie are suggested for evening dining at more formal restaurants in the top price category, but casual chic or informal dress is acceptable at most restaurants. Daytime clothing should be fashionable and on the conservative side. Dress is mentioned in reviews only when men are required to wear a jacket and tie.

## DISABILITIES & ACCESSIBILITY

Although international chain hotels in large cities have some suitable rooms, and it's easy to hire private cars with drivers for excursions, Argentina is not well equipped to handle travelers with disabilities. On only a few streets in Buenos Aires, for instance, are there ramps and curb cuts. It takes effort and planning to negotiate museums and other buildings (many have steps that are unfortunately almost entirely unnegotiable with a wheelchair), and to explore the countryside.

➤ COMPLAINTS: **Disability Rights Section** (✉ U.S. Department of Justice, Civil Rights Division, Box 66738, Washington, DC 20035-6738, ☎ 202/514–0301; 800/514–0301; 202/514–0301 TTY; 800/514–0301 TTY, ℻ 202/307–1198) for general complaints. **Aviation Consumer Protection Division** (☞ Air Travel, *above*) for airline-related problems. **Civil Rights Office** (✉ U.S. Department of Transportation, Departmental Office of Civil Rights, S-30, 400 7th St. SW, Room 10215, Washington, DC 20590, ☎ 202/366–4648, ℻ 202/366–9371) for problems with surface transportation.

### LODGING

When discussing accessibility with an operator or reservations agent **ask hard questions.** Are there any stairs, inside *or* out? Are there grab bars next to the toilet *and* in the shower/tub? How wide is the doorway to the room? To the bathroom? For the most extensive facilities meeting the latest legal specifications **opt for newer accommodations.**

### TRAVEL AGENCIES

In the United States, although the Americans with Disabilities Act requires that travel firms serve the needs of all travelers, some agencies specialize in working with people with disabilities.

➤ TRAVELERS WITH MOBILITY PROBLEMS: **Access Adventures** (✉ 206 Chestnut Ridge Rd., Rochester, NY 14624, ☎ 716/889–9096), run by a former physical-rehabilitation counselor. **CareVacations** (✉ 5-5110 50th Ave., Leduc, Alberta T9E 6V4, ☎ 780/986–6404 or 780/986–8332) has group tours and is especially helpful with cruise vacations. **Flying Wheels Travel** (✉ 143 W. Bridge St., Box 382, Owatonna, MN 55060, ☎ 507/451–5005 or 800/535–6790, ℻ 507/451–1685). **Hinsdale Travel Service** (✉ 201 E. Ogden Ave., Suite 100, Hinsdale, IL 60521, ☎ 630/325–1335).

## DISCOUNTS & DEALS

Be a smart shopper and **compare all your options** before making decisions. A plane ticket bought with a promotional coupon from travel clubs, coupon books, and direct-mail offers may not be cheaper than the least expensive fare from a discount ticket agency. And always keep in mind that what you get is just as important as what you save.

Note that **most museums are free one morning or afternoon per week** and that movies are often half price on Wednesday.

### DISCOUNT RESERVATIONS

To save money **look into discount-reservations services** with toll-free numbers, which use their buying power to get a better price on hotels, airline tickets, even car rentals. When booking a room, always **call the hotel's local toll-free number** (if one is available) rather than the central reservations number—you'll often get a better price. Always ask about special packages or corporate rates.

When shopping for the best deal on hotels and car rentals **look for guaranteed exchange rates,** which protect you against a falling dollar. With your rate locked in, you won't pay more, even if the price goes up in the local currency.

The Automovil Club Argentino, the Argentine version of the AAA, will usually recognize AAA cards for discounts within Argentina.

➤ AIRLINE TICKETS: ☎ **800/FLY–4–LESS.**

➤ HOTEL ROOMS: **Steigenberger Reservation Service** (☎ 800/223–5652).

## PACKAGE DEALS

Don't confuse packages and guided tours. When you buy a package, you travel on your own, just as though you had planned the trip yourself. Fly/drive packages, which combine airfare and car rental, are often a good deal.

## ELECTRICITY

To use your U.S.-purchased electric-powered equipment, **bring a converter and adapter.** The current in Argentina is 220 volts, 50 cycles alternating current (AC); wall outlets usually take Continental-type plugs, with two round prongs.

If your appliances are dual-voltage you'll need only an adapter. Don't use 110-volt outlets, marked FOR SHAVERS ONLY, for high-wattage appliances such as blow-dryers. Most laptops operate equally well on 110 and 220 volts and so require only an adapter.

## EMBASSIES AND CONSULATES

Besides providing assistance, each of the following embassies and consulates also hosts a Thursday evening cocktail party (call any embassy to find out the location of the next event).

➤ AUSTRALIA: **Australia** (✉ Villanueva 1400, Buenos Aires, ☎ 11/4777–6580).

➤ CANADA: **Canada** (✉ Tagle 2828, Buenos Aires, ☎ 11/4805–3032).

➤ NEW ZEALAND: **New Zealand** (✉ Echeverria 2140, Buenos Aires, ☎ 11/4787–0593).

➤ SOUTH AFRICA: **South Africa** (✉ Marcelo T. de Alvear 590, Buenos Aires, ☎ 11/43172900).

➤ UNITED KINGDOM: **Ireland** (✉ Suipacha 1280, 2nd floor, Buenos Aires, ☎ 11/43258588). **United Kingdom** (✉ Luis Agote 2412, Buenos Aires, ☎ 11/48036021).

➤ UNITED STATES: **United States** (✉ Colombia 4300, Buenos Aires, ☎ 11/47774533).

## EMERGENCIES

All over the country you can call the same numbers in case of emergencies. Each place also has local emergency numbers ☞ Emergencies *in* individual chapters' A to Z sections). Also *see* Health, *below.*

➤ CONTACTS: **Ambulance** (☎ 107). **Fire** (☎ 1100). **Police** (☎ 101).

## GAY & LESBIAN TRAVEL

In many parts of Buenos Aires, particularly Rosario, gay and lesbian couples mingle with the crowd, relatively unnoticed. However, in more traditional neighborhoods of Buenos Aires, and in smaller towns and rural areas, people are often far less open minded.

➤ GAY- AND LESBIAN-FRIENDLY TRAVEL AGENCIES: **Different Roads Travel** (✉ 8383 Wilshire Blvd., Suite 902, Beverly Hills, CA 90211, ☎ 323/651–5557 or 800/429–8747, 𝔽𝔸𝕏 323/651–3678). **Kennedy Travel** (✉ 314 Jericho Turnpike, Floral Park, NY 11001, ☎ 516/352–4888 or 800/237–7433, 𝔽𝔸𝕏 516/354–8849). **Now Voyager** (✉ 4406 18th St., San Francisco, CA 94114, ☎ 415/626–1169 or 800/255–6951, 𝔽𝔸𝕏 415/626–8626). **Yellowbrick Road** (✉ 1500 W. Balmoral Ave., Chicago, IL 60640, ☎ 773/561–1800 or 800/642–2488, 𝔽𝔸𝕏 773/561–4497). **Skylink Travel and Tour** (✉ 1006 Mendocino Ave., Santa Rosa, CA 95401, ☎ 707/546–9888 or 800/225–5759, 𝔽𝔸𝕏 707/546–9891), serving lesbian travelers.

## HEALTH

### ALTITUDE SICKNESS

*Soroche,* or altitude sickness, which results in shortness of breath and headaches, may be a problem when you visit the Andes. To remedy any discomfort, walk slowly, eat lightly, and drink plenty of fluids (avoid alcohol). If you have high blood pressure and a history of heart trouble, **check with your doctor before traveling to high Andes elevations.**

### DIVERS' ALERT

Scuba divers take note: **Do not fly within 24 hours of scuba diving.** Neophyte divers should have a complete physical exam before undertaking a dive. If you have travel insurance that covers evacuations, **make sure your policy applies to scuba-related injuries,** as not all companies provide this coverage.

### FOOD & DRINK

Drinking tap water and eating uncooked greens is considered safe in Buenos Aires. However, if you've got just two weeks, you don't want to waste a minute of it in your hotel room, so be scrupulously careful about what you eat and drink—on as well as off the beaten path. If you have any doubt at all, drink bottled water. The water may be fine, but you have a greater chance of running into contamination outside of metropolitan Buenos Aires.

Each year there are several hundred cases of cholera in the northern part of Argentina, mostly in the indigenous communities near the Bolivian border; your best protection is to avoid eating raw seafood.

### MEDICAL SERVICE

Medical service is generally quite adequate and readily accessible in Buenos Aires and other major cities. It's also free for basic services at public hospitals, though private clinics are usually not nearly as expensive as in the United States.

No one plans to get sick while traveling, but it happens, so **consider signing up with a medical-assistance company.** Members get doctor referrals, emergency evacuation or repatriation, hot lines for medical consultation, cash for emergencies, and other assistance.

➤ MEDICAL-ASSISTANCE COMPANIES: **International SOS Assistance** (✉ 8 Neshaminy Interplex, Suite 207, Trevose, PA 19053, ☎ 215/245–4707 or 800/523–6586, ℻ 215/244–9617; ✉ 12 Chemin Riantbosson, 1217 Meyrin 1, Geneva, Switzerland, ☎ 4122/785–6464, ℻ 4122/785–6424; ✉ 331 N. Bridge Rd., 17-00, Odeon Towers, Singapore 188720, ☎ 65/338–7800, ℻ 65/338–7611).

### SHOTS & MEDICATIONS

No specific vaccinations are required for travel to Argentina. According to the Centers for Disease Control (CDC), however, there's a limited risk of cholera, hepatitis B, and dengue. If you plan to visit remote regions or stay for more than six weeks, **check with the CDC's International Travelers Hot Line.** In areas with malaria (in Argentina, you are at risk for malaria only in northern rural areas bordering Bolivia and Paraguay) and dengue, which are both carried by mosquitoes, take mosquito nets, wear clothing that covers the body, apply repellent containing DEET, and use a spray against flying insects in living and sleeping areas. The hot line recommends chloroquine (analen) as an antimalarial agent; no vaccine exists against dengue.

Children traveling to Argentina should have current inoculations against measles, mumps, rubella, and polio.

A major health risk is Montezuma's Revenge, or traveler's diarrhea, caused by eating unfamiliar foods or contaminated fruit or vegetables or drinking contaminated water. Mild cases may respond to Imodium (known generically as loperamide) or Pepto-Bismol (not as strong), both of which can be purchased over the counter; paregoric, another antidiarrheal agent, does not require a doctor's prescription in Argentina. Drink plenty of purified water or tea—chamomile is a good folk remedy. In severe cases, rehydrate yourself with a salt–sugar solution (½ teaspoon salt and 4 tablespoons sugar per quart of water).

Note that many medications that require a prescription in the United States and elsewhere, such as antibiotics, are available over the counter in Argentina.

➤ HEALTH WARNINGS: **National Centers for Disease Control** (CDC, National Center for Infectious Diseases, Division of Quarantine, Traveler's Health Section, ✉ 1600 Clifton Rd. NE, M/S E-03, Atlanta, GA 30333, ☎ 888/232–3228, FAX 888/232–3299).

## HOLIDAYS

Dates for 2000: New Year's Day (Jan. 1); Labor Day (May 1); Anniversary of the 1810 Revolution (May 25); National Sovereignty Day (June 10); Flag Day (June 20); Independence Day (July 9); Anniversary of San Martín's Death (Aug. 17); Columbus Day (Oct. 9); and Christmas (Dec. 25).

## INSURANCE

The most useful travel insurance plan is a comprehensive policy that includes coverage for trip cancellation and interruption, default, trip delay, and medical expenses (with a waiver for preexisting conditions).

Without insurance you will lose all or most of your money if you cancel your trip, regardless of the reason. Default insurance covers you if your tour operator, airline, or cruise line goes out of business. Trip-delay covers expenses that arise because of bad weather or mechanical delays. Study the fine print when comparing policies.

If you're traveling internationally, a key component of travel insurance is coverage for medical bills incurred if you get sick on the road. Such expenses are not generally covered by Medicare or private policies. U.K. residents can buy a travel-insurance policy valid for most vacations taken during the year in which it's purchased (but check pre-existing-condition coverage). British and Australian citizens need extra medical coverage when traveling overseas. Always **buy travel policies directly from the insur-ance company**; if you buy it from a cruise line, airline, or tour operator that goes out of business you probably will not be covered for the agency or operator's default, a major risk. Before you make any purchase **review your existing health and home-owner's policies** to find what they cover away from home.

➤ TRAVEL INSURERS: In the U.S. **Access America** (✉ 6600 W. Broad St., Richmond, VA 23230, ☎ 804/285–3300 or 800/284–8300), **Travel Guard International** (✉ 1145 Clark St., Stevens Point, WI 54481, ☎ 715/345–0505 or 800/826–1300). In Canada **Voyager Insurance** (✉ 44 Peel Center Dr., Brampton, Ontario L6T 4M8, ☎ 905/791–8700; 800/668–4342 in Canada).

➤ INSURANCE INFORMATION: In the U.K. the **Association of British Insurers** (✉ 51–55 Gresham St., London EC2V 7HQ, ☎ 0171/600–3333, FAX 0171/696–8999). In Australia the **Insurance Council of Australia** (☎ 03/9614–1077, FAX 03/9614–7924).

## LANGUAGE

Argentines speak Spanish (commonly referred to as Castellano). There are a few important differences between Argentine Spanish and that of the rest of Latin America. For example, the informal *tu* form is replaced by *vos* (with some different conjugations). Also, the double L found in words like *pollo* is pronounced with a J-sound rather than a Y-sound. English replaced French as the country's second language in the 1960s, although most people still have a very limited knowledge of it. Luckily, many hotels, restaurants, and shops employ someone who speaks English.

### LANGUAGE SCHOOLS

A wide selection of language courses can be found in the classifieds of Argentina's English-language daily newspaper, the *Buenos Aires Herald*. The list includes schools as well as a large selection of private tutors.

If you you prefer to arrange your Spanish classes prior to your arrival in Argentina, try the Instituto de Lengua Española para Extranjeros (ILEE), which specializes in teaching

SMART TRAVEL TIPS A TO Z

Spanish to foreigners and has classes beginning every week. The school can help you find a place to stay.

➤ INFORMATION: **Instituto de Lengua Española para Extranjeros** (ILEE, ✉ Lavalle 1619, 7th Floor, Unit C, and 4th Floor, Unit A, Buenos Aires, ☎ FAX 11/43750730).

### SPANISH FOR TRAVELERS

A phrase book and language-tape set can help get you started.

➤ PHRASE BOOKS & LANGUAGE-TAPE SETS: *Fodor's Spanish for Travelers* (☎ 800/733–3000 in the U.S.; 800/668–4247 in Canada; $7 for phrasebook, $16.95 for audio set).

## LODGING

The lodgings we list are the cream of the crop in each price category. We always list the facilities that are available—but we don't specify whether they cost extra: When pricing accommodations, always ask what's included and what costs extra. Properties indicated by a ✕🏠 are lodging establishments whose restaurant warrants a special trip.

| CATEGORY | COST* |
|---|---|
| $$$$ | over $150 |
| $$$ | $100–$150 |
| $$ | $50–$100 |
| $ | $25–$50 |
| ¢ | under $25 |

*for a double room in high season, excluding taxes*

Assume that hotels operate on the European Plan (EP, with no meals) unless we specify that they use the Continental Plan (CP, with a Continental breakfast daily), Breakfast Plan (BP, with a full breakfast daily), Modified American Plan (MAP, with breakfast and dinner daily), or are all-inclusive (including all meals and most activities).

### ALBERGUES TRANSITORIOS

*Albergues transitorios* (temporary lodgings) is the euphemism name for drive-in hotels, which are generally used for romantic trysts. Very common in this country where people often live with their parents until marriage, they are easily recognizable

by their hourly rates and purple and orange exterior lights.

Real motels can be found through the Automovil Club Argentino (☞ Automobile Clubs *in* Car Travel, *above*). Generally these motels are inexpensive ($35–$45 a night) and more than adequate.

### APARTMENT & VILLA RENTALS

If you want a home base that's roomy enough for a family and comes with cooking facilities **consider a furnished rental.** These can save you money, especially if you're traveling with a group.

➤ INTERNATIONAL AGENT: **Hideaways International** (✉ 767 Islington St., Portsmouth, NH 03801, ☎ 603/430–4433 or 800/843–4433, FAX 603/430–4444; membership $99).

### CAMPING

Campgrounds can be found in popular tourist destinations, including some beach areas. Usually they have running water, electricity, and bathroom facilities with toilets and showers. The **Automovil Club Argentino** (☞ Auto Clubs *in* Car Travel, *above*) can provide a list of campgrounds nationwide. Provincial tourist offices in Buenos Aires have lists of campgrounds in their regions. Some have telephones so that you can make reservations.

### ESTANCIAS

In Las Pampas (☞ Chapter 3), the Argentine Litoral (☞ Chapter 4), and the Northwest (☞ Chapter 5) you can stay at *estancias* (working ranches). Some are more rustic than others.

### HOME EXCHANGES

If you would like to exchange your home for someone else's **join a home-exchange organization,** which will send you its updated listings of available exchanges for a year and will include your own listing in at least one of them. It's up to you to make specific arrangements.

➤ EXCHANGE CLUBS: **HomeLink International** (✉ Box 650, Key West, FL 33041, ☎ 305/294–7766 or 800/638–3841, FAX 305/294–1448; $88 per year). **Intervac U.S.** (✉ Box 590504, San Francisco, CA 94159, ☎ 800/756–4663, FAX 415/435–7440; $83 per year).

## HOSTELS

No matter what your age you can **save on lodging costs by staying at hostels.** Hostelling International (HI), the umbrella group for a number of national youth-hostel associations, offers single-sex, dorm-style beds and, at many hostels, couples rooms and family accommodations. Membership in any HI national hostel association, open to travelers of all ages, allows you to stay in HI-affiliated hostels at member rates (one-year membership is about $25 for adults; hostels run about $10–$25 per night). Members also have priority if the hostel is full.

➤ INTERNATIONAL ORGANIZATIONS: **Australian Youth Hostel Association** (✉ 10 Mallett St., Camperdown, NSW 2050, ☎ 02/9565–1699, FAX 02/9565–1325). **Hostelling International—American Youth Hostels** (✉ 733 15th St. NW, Suite 840, Washington, DC 20005, ☎ 202/783–6161, FAX 202/783–6171). **Hostelling International—Canada** (✉ 400–205 Catherine St., Ottawa, Ontario K2P 1C3, ☎ 613/237–7884, FAX 613/237–7868). **Youth Hostel Association of England and Wales** (✉ Trevelyan House, 8 St. Stephen's Hill, St. Albans, Hertfordshire AL1 2DY, ☎ 01727/855215 or 01727/845047, FAX 01727/844126). **Youth Hostels Association of New Zealand** (✉ Box 436, Christchurch, New Zealand, ☎ 03/379–9970, FAX 03/365–4476). Membership in the U.S. $25, in Canada C$26.75, in the U.K. £9.30, in Australia $44, in New Zealand $24.

➤ LOCAL ORGANIZATIONS: **Buenos Aires Hostel** (✉ Av. Brasil 675, Buenos Aires, ☎ 11/4362–9133). **Youth Hostel Association** (✉ Talcahuano 214, 2nd Floor, Buenos Aires, ☎ 11/4372–1001).

## HOTELS

Amenities in most nice hotels— private baths, 24-hour room service, heating and air-conditioning, cable TV, dry cleaning, and restaurants— are above average. The less expensive the hotel, the fewer amenities you get, though you can still find charm, cleanliness, and hospitality. You may or may not have television and a phone in your room, though you will find them somewhere in the hotel. Rooms that have a private bath may only have a shower, and in some cases, there will be a shared bath in the hall. In all but the most upscale hotels, you may be asked to leave your key at the reception desk whenever you leave, and many hotels have a curfew, so if you arrive after the reception desk closes, you may not be able to get your key. Most hotels in all categories offer breakfast, whether or not there is a full restaurant in the hotel.

## RESIDENCIALES

*Residenciales* can be either family-run pensions or bed-and-breakfasts. These are generally found in smaller towns.

## MAIL & SHIPPING

When delivery is normal and there are no strikes or postal vacations, mail takes 6–15 days to get from Buenos Aires to the United States and 10–15 days to the United Kingdom. Put postcards in envelopes and they will arrive more quickly.

### EXPRESS MAIL

Express mail takes 3–5 days for all international destinations and the cost can be steep (for instance, a letter to the United States via FedEx costs $28).

➤ COMPANIES: **DHL** (✉ Moreno 631, Buenos Aires, ☎ 11/43470600). **Federal Express** (✉ Maipu 753, Buenos Aires, ☎ 11/46300300). **UPS** (✉ Bernardo de Yrigoyen 974, Buenos Aires, ☎ 11/43072174).

### POSTAL RATES

An international airmail letter costs $1.

### RECEIVING MAIL

You can receive mail in Buenos Aires at the Correo Central (Central Post Office). Letters should be addressed to Lista/Poste Restante, Correo Central, 1000 Buenos Aires, Argentina. American Express cardholders can have mail sent to American Express.

➤ LOCATIONS: **American Express** (✉ c/o American Express, Arenales 707,

1061 Buenos Aires, ☎ 11/43120900). **Buenos Aires Correo Central** (✉ Sarmiento 151, 1st Floor, Buenos Aires, ☎ 11/43115030 or 11/43115040).

## MONEY MATTERS

Prices throughout this guide are given for adults. Substantially reduced fees are almost always available for children, students, and senior citizens. For information on taxes, *see* Taxes, *below*.

### ATMS

Before leaving home, **make sure that your credit cards have been programmed for ATM use in Argentina.** Note that Discover is accepted mostly in the United States. Local bank cards often do not work overseas or may access only your checking account; **ask your bank about a MasterCard/Cirrus or Visa debit card,** which works like a bank card but can be used at any ATM displaying a MasterCard/Cirrus or Visa logo. These cards, too, may tap only your checking account; check with your bank about their policy.

Although fees charged for ATM transactions may be higher, Cirrus and Plus exchange rates are excellent, because they are based on wholesale rates offered only by major banks. ATMs are getting easier to find, especially in Buenos Aires, Cordóba, Mar del Plata, and other major cities and resort towns.

➤ ATM LOCATIONS: **Cirrus** (☎ 800/424–7787). A list of **Plus** locations is available at your local bank.

### COSTS

For decades Argentina had one of the most volatile economies in the world, a boom-bust seesaw driven by inflation that sometimes rose several percentage points in a day. For the past few years inflation has been tamed, however, making it more likely that costs can be predicted with some degree of accuracy.

Argentina is not inexpensive, though occasional bargains can be found. The most sumptuous dinners, particularly in French restaurants, can run as high as $100 per person with wine

and tip. But a thick slab of rare, wood-grilled sirloin with salad, potatoes, a house wine, and an espresso will cost around $20 at steak houses in Buenos Aires and less in the hinterlands.

When ordering drinks, ask for Argentine liquors or you'll be paying for the tremendous import fees. A bottle of the national favorite, Chivas Regal, costs $75–$100 in shops, for instance. Simply ask for *"whiskey nacional, por favor"* or *"vodka nacional."*

**Sample Prices:** A cup of coffee in a café, $2.50; with milk, $3. A bottle of soda, $1. A taxi ride in central Buenos Aires, $4–$8. A tango show with a couple of drinks, about $60. A double room in a moderately priced, well-situated hotel, including taxes, $100–$130.

### CREDIT CARDS

If you choose to bring just one card, Visa is recommended, as it is the most readily accepted. American Express, Diners Club, and MasterCard are the most commonly accepted after Visa. It may be easiest to use your credit card whenever possible—the exchange rate only varies by a fraction of a cent, so you won't need to worry whether your purchase is charged on the day of purchase or at some point in the future. Note, however that you may get a better deal if you pay with cash.

Throughout this guide, the following abbreviations are used: **AE**, American Express; **DC**, Diner's Club; **MC**, MasterCard; and **V**, Visa.

➤ REPORTING LOST CARDS: **American Express** (☎ 11/4312–1661). **Diners Club** (☎ 11/4708–2484). **MasterCard** (☎ 11/4331–2555). **Visa** (☎ 11/4379–3333).

### CURRENCY

In the past, dramatic value swings occurred during periods of hyperinflation. In fact, during a bleak but brief period, a cup of coffee cost twice as much in local currency after dinner as it did for breakfast. But greater economic stability was acheived in the early 1990s and at press time the currency appeared to be more stable than it had been in the past.

One peso (P) equals 100 centavos. Peso notes are in denominations of P100, 50, 20, 10, 5, and 2. Coins are in denominations of P1, and 50, 25, 10, 5, and 1 centavos.

## CURRENCY EXCHANGE

For the past few years, the Argentine peso has been pegged to the U.S. dollar (although it's overvalued and worth less on the international market, the Argentine peso and U.S. dollar funtion interchangeably in Argentina).

Dollars are readily accepted throughout Buenos Aires and other large cities. Cabs, hotels, and most restaurants and shops accept dollars; often places that accept dollars will post a sign say so. Be sure that bills are not torn or dirty; **dollars in poor condition won't be accepted.**

Residents of countries other than the U.S. are advised to change their currencies to dollars before their journey, as dollars are the easiest to use and exchange. At press time (spring 2000), 1 U.S. dollar equaled 1 peso, 1 Canadian dollar equaled roughly.70 pesos, and 1 pound sterling equaled roughly 1.65 pesos.

You can change money at your hotel, at banks, or at *casas de cambio* (money changers), which offer competitive variations on rates. There's an exchange desk at Buenos Aires's Ezeiza Airport, right near the exit to the parking lot. Pesos can also generally be obtained by making a purchase in dollars and requesting the change in pesos. Exchange fees are better at banks, but not significantly so—and there are lines. Though you'll get a few pesos less by exchanging at your hotel, you'll save yourself time. Plan ahead, since it's often hard to change large amounts of money at hotels on weekends, even in cities.

Even if you do pay for items primarily in dollars, it's a good idea to have some pesos with you. Also, in rural areas, dollars are less likely to be accepted, so you'll want to have pesos. You may not be able to change currency in rural areas at all, so **don't leave the city**

**without adequate amounts of pesos** in small denominations.

➤ EXCHANGE SERVICES: **International Currency Express** (☎ 888/842–0880 on East Coast; 888/278–6628 on West Coast). **Thomas Cook Currency Services** (☎ 800/287–7362 for telephone orders and retail locations).

## TRAVELER'S CHECKS

Larger stores in Buenos Aires will occasionally accept traveler's checks, but smaller shops and restaurants are leery of them. You'll probably have to go to the bank or the American Express office to change your checks.

The benefit of traveler's checks is that lost or stolen checks can usually be replaced within 24 hours. To ensure a speedy refund, buy your own traveler's checks—don't let someone else pay for them: irregularities like this can cause delays.

## PACKING

Argentines in general are very fashion and appearance conscious.

If you're doing business in Argentina, bring the same attire you would wear in U.S. and European cities: for men, suits and ties; for women, suits for day wear and cocktail dresses or other suitable dinner clothes.

For sightseeing and leisure, casual clothing and good walking shoes are desirable and appropriate, although **shorts should be avoided by both men and women,** especially out of the city. In the smaller towns and villages, dress especially conservatively—no short skirts or halters.

Getting dressed up for dinner is not required in most cities, though more than jeans are expected in Buenos Aires.

For beach vacations, bring lightweight sportswear, a bathing suit, a sun hat, and sunscreen. Travel in the tropical rain forest requires long-sleeve shirts, long pants, socks, sneakers, a hat, a light waterproof jacket, a bathing suit, and insect repellent. If you're visiting high altitudes or Patagonian areas in the south, bring a light jacket and sweater, or plan to purchase one of the hand-knit sweaters

**SMART TRAVEL TIPS A TO Z**

or ponchos sold in the markets. In winter, bring much more.

In your carry-on luggage **bring an extra pair of eyeglasses or contact lenses** and **enough of any medication you take** to last the entire trip. You may also want your doctor to write a spare prescription using the drug's generic name, since brand names may vary from country to country. In luggage to be checked, **never pack prescription drugs or valuables.** To avoid customs delays, carry medications in their original packaging. And don't forget to copy down and carry addresses of offices that handle refunds of lost traveler's checks.

Other useful items include a screw-top water bottle, a money pouch, a travel flashlight, extra batteries, a pocket knife with a bottle opener, a medical kit, binoculars, and a pocket calculator to help with currency conversions. Take more film than you ever thought you would use and extra batteries for your camera. If you're traveling with children, take books and games—they're hard to find in English in Argentina.

### CHECKING LUGGAGE

How many carry-on bags you can bring with you is up to the airline. Most allow two, but not always, so make sure that everything you carry aboard will fit under your seat, and get to the gate early. Note that if you have a seat at the back of the plane, you'll probably board first, while the overhead bins are still empty.

If you are flying internationally, note that baggage allowances may be determined not by piece but by weight—generally 88 pounds (40 kilograms) in first class, 66 pounds (30 kilograms) in business class, and 44 pounds (20 kilograms) in economy.

Airline liability for baggage is limited to $1,250 per person on flights within the United States. On international flights it amounts to $9.07 per pound or $20 per kilogram for checked baggage (roughly $640 per 70-pound bag) and $400 per passenger for unchecked baggage. You can buy additional coverage at check-in for about $10 per $1,000 of coverage,

but it excludes a rather extensive list of items, shown on your airline ticket.

Before departure **itemize your bags' contents** and their worth, and label the bags with your name, address, and phone number. (If you use your home address, cover it so that potential thieves can't see it readily.) Inside each bag **pack a copy of your itinerary.** At check-in **make sure that each bag is correctly tagged** with the destination airport's three-letter code. If your bags arrive damaged or fail to arrive at all, file a written report with the airline before leaving the airport.

### PASSPORTS & VISAS

It's a good idea to **make two photocopies of your passport** (one for someone at home and another for you, carried separately from your passport). If you lose your passport promptly call the nearest embassy or consulate and the local police.

### ENTERING ARGENTINA

U.S., Canadian, and British citizens do not need a visa for visits of up to 90 days, though they must **carry a passport.** Upon entering Argentina, you'll receive a tourist visa stamp on your passport valid for 90 days. If you need to stay longer, exit the country for one night, and upon re-entering Argentina, your passport will be stamped with an additional 90 days. The fine for overstaying your tourist visa is $50, payable upon departure at the airport. If you do overstay your visa, plan to arrive at the airport several hours in advance of your flight so that you have ample time to take care of the fine.

### CANADIANS

Canadian citizens need only a valid passport to enter Argentina.

➤ CANADIAN CITIZENS: **Passport Office** (☎ 819/994–3500 or 800/567–6868).

### U.K. CITIZENS

Citizens of the United Kingdom need only a valid passport to enter Argentina.

➤ U.K. CITIZENS: **London Passport Office** (☎ 0990/210–410) for fees and documentation requirements and to request an emergency passport.

## U.S. CITIZENS

All U.S. citizens, even infants, need only a valid passport to enter Argentina. The tourist visa for U.S. citizens is valid for 90 days.

➤ U.S. CITIZENS: **National Passport Information Center** (☎ 900/225–5674; calls are 35¢ per minute for automated service, $1.05 per minute for operator service). **Office of Passport Services** (☎ 202/647–0518).

➤ AUSTRALIAN CITIZENS: **Australian Passport Office** (☎ 131–232).

➤ NEW ZEALAND CITIZENS: **New Zealand Passport Office** (☎ 04/494–0700 for information on how to apply; 04/474–8000 or 0800/225–050 in New Zealand for information on applications already submitted).

### SAFETY

Buenos Aires is one of the safest cities in the world. At any time of night, you'll see young children and little old ladies strolling around, apparently unconcerned about the hour or the darkness. Police constantly patrol any areas where tourists are likely to be, and violent crime is rare.

Smaller towns and villages in Argentina are even safer, so much so that you may find yourself in a room in a small country inn where the door doesn't have a lock.

That said, keep in mind that there are terrible incidents and crazy people everywhere, and Argentina is no exception. At night, **go out in pairs, or preferably in groups,** and remember that Buenos Aires is the ninth largest city in the world. When in doubt, follow local advice on whether or not it's safe to walk at night and where.

At all times, **keep documents, money, and credit cards hidden in a waist money belt or in zipped pockets.** Don't carry valuables swinging from your shoulder or hanging around your neck. Always **remain alert for pickpockets.** Passports, tickets, and other valuables are best left in hotel safes, when available.

Wear the simplest of watches and **do not wear any jewelry you're not willing to lose**—stories of travelers having chains and even earrings yanked off of them are not uncommon. Keep cameras in a secure camera bag, preferably one with a chain or wire embedded in the strap.

Generally you'll find that the local people are friendly and helpful and that the biggest crime you're likely to encounter is the exorbitant price of a gaucho poncho.

### WOMEN IN ARGENTINA

Women are safer in Buenos Aires than in many other major cities in the world, but violent crimes still occur. It's best not to over or under dress, or to flash jewelry on the street in Buenos Aires or elsewhere. Above all, just act as if you know what you're doing and take normal precautions and you should have no problems.

### SENIOR-CITIZEN TRAVEL

Senior citizens are highly revered in Argentina and are generally treated with the greatest of respect. There's no reason that active, well-traveled senior citizens should not visit Argentina, whether on an independent (but prebooked) vacation, an escorted tour, or an adventure vacation. Argentina has plenty of good hotels and competent ground operators who can meet your flights and organize your sightseeing.

To qualify for age-related discounts, **mention your senior-citizen status up front** when booking hotel reservations (not when checking out) and before you're seated in restaurants (not when paying the bill). Note that discounts may be limited to certain menus, days, or hours. When renting a car, ask about promotional car-rental discounts, which can be cheaper than senior-citizen rates.

Before you leave home, however, **determine what medical services your health insurance will cover.** Note that Medicare does not provide for payment of hospital and medical services outside the United States. If you need additional travel insurance, buy it (☞ Insurance, *above*).

**S M A R T   T R A V E L   T I P S   A   T O   Z**

➤ EDUCATIONAL PROGRAMS: **Elderhostel** (✉ 75 Federal St., 3rd fl., Boston, MA 02110, ☎ 877/426–8056, FAX 877/426–2166).

## SHOPPING

Buenos Aires is a great place to buy clothing, leather goods, and furs. Paintings, engravings, and fine local wine are other good options. In any case, just looking at the displays—of Tierra del Fuego fox in the latest Yves St. Laurent styles, butter-soft leathers, evening gowns with snakeskin appliqués, cashmere sweaters, loafers, boots, briefcases, and bags—can be a window-shopper's delight. Look for *liquidaciones* (sale) signs in the window. Argentine shops have fixed prices but often give discounts for cash (in the smaller shops, you can often begin a bargaining session by asking, "So, how much is the cash price?").

## STUDENTS IN ARGENTINA

To save money, **look into deals available through student-oriented travel agencies.** To qualify you'll need a bona fide student ID card. Members of international student groups are also eligible.

➤ STUDENT IDs & SERVICES: **Council on International Educational Exchange** (CIEE, ✉ 205 E. 42nd St., 14th fl., New York, NY 10017, ☎ 212/822–2600 or 888/268–6245, FAX 212/822–2699) for mail orders only, in the U.S. **Travel Cuts** (✉ 187 College St., Toronto, Ontario M5T 1P7, ☎ 416/979–2406 or 800/667–2887) in Canada.

## TAXES

Sales tax in Argentina is 21%. The tax is usually included in the price that you see.

## TELEPHONES

Using a phone anywhere in the country can be a frustrating experience, despite the privatization of ENTEL, the formerly government-run telephone company. Phone numbers change frequently and it's common to get the message "*equivocado*" ("wrong number"). Often the best bet is to get operator assistance or to have the operator at your hotel help put through your calls. Using phones in *telecentros* (telephone centers) or *locutorios* (telephone offices) is another good option.

## COUNTRY & AREA CODES

The country code for Argentina is 54. To call Argentina from overseas, dial the country code (54), and then the area code, omitting the first 0. The area code for Buenos Aires is 11, and all numbers in the city are preceded by 4. Other regions have different area codes, noted in individual chapters.

## DIRECTORY & OPERATOR INFORMATION

For information, dial 110. For the time, 113. For an international operator, dial 000. For information about international calls, dial 19.

## INTERNATIONAL CALLS

Be prepared for a hollow sound or even an echo of your own voice for the first minute or so of an international call. This typically goes away after the first few sentences of a conversation.

Most hotels have international direct dial, but may charge up to $3 per call for a long-distance call. International calls can also be made from telephone company offices around Buenos Aires and at telecentros.

The country code is 1 for the U.S. and Canada, 61 for Australia, 64 for New Zealand, and 44 for the U.K.

## LOCAL CALLS

Hotels charge a per minute rate that can be quite high, even for local calls. Ask the front desk ahead about calling ahead of time; the cost varies depending on whether you are calling at prime time (8 AM–8 PM) or not.

Local calls can be made from public phones with a phone cards sold at kiosks.

To call the cell phone number of a Buenos Aires resident, dial 15 before the number (unless you're also calling from a cell phone with a Buenos Aires number). Local cell phone charges are $1 per call, charged to the caller, not the recipient.

## LONG-DISTANCE CALLS

When calling from one area code to another in Argentina, add a 0 before the area code.

Many hotels charge up to $3 per call on top of the regular rate. To make a long-distance call from a public phone, look for a telecentro, which can be found throughout the city and have private telephone cabins as well as fax services. You can use your calling card to make a long-distance call from a pay phone, but you will still need to purchase a local phone card to access a line.

## LONG-DISTANCE SERVICES

AT&T, MCI, and Sprint access codes make calling long distance relatively convenient, but you may find the local access number blocked in many hotel rooms or you may be charged a fee to access the number. First ask the hotel operator to connect you. If the hotel operator balks ask for an international operator, or dial the international operator yourself. One way to improve your odds of getting connected to your long-distance carrier is to travel with more than one company's calling card (a hotel may block Sprint, for example, but not MCI). If all else fails call from a pay phone.

➤ ACCESS CODES: For local access numbers abroad, contact **AT&T** (☎ 800/874–4000). **MCI** (☎ 800/444–4444). **Sprint** (☎ 800/793–1153).

## PHONE CARDS

Phone cards are available at kiosks. One card unit buys two or three minutes of time, depending on whether you are calling at prime time (8 AM–8 PM) or otherwise.

## PUBLIC PHONES

Public phones in Argentina are reliable and are found on nearly every block. They generally operate with a telephone card, which can be purchased at any kiosk. Simply slide the card in, wait for the reading of how many minutes you have remaining, and dial the number. Some public phones are coin operated and a rare few are still operated by old phone tokens.

If you plan to use a calling card at a public phone, you'll still need a local phone card to gain access to a line. To make a long-distance call from a public phone, you're better off finding a telecentro.

## TIME

New York is one time zone behind Buenos Aires in summer (it's two in winter, as Argentina does not observe American daylight savings time), and there's only a four-hour difference between Los Angeles and Buenos Aires.

## TIPPING

In Spanish, tips are called *propinas*. Add 10%–15% in bars and restaurants (10% is enough in a casual café or if the bill runs high). Argentines round off a taxi fare, though some cabbies who frequent hotels popular with tourists seem to expect more. Hotel porters should be tipped at least $1. Also give doormen and ushers about $1. Beauty- and barbershop personnel generally get around 5%.

## TOURS & PACKAGES

On a prepackaged tour or independent vacation everything is prearranged so you'll spend less time planning—and often get it all at a good price.

## BOOKING WITH AN AGENT

Travel agents are excellent resources. But it's a good idea to collect brochures from several agencies because some agents' suggestions may be influenced by relationships with tour and package firms that reward them for volume sales. If you have a special interest **find an agent with expertise in that area**; ASTA (☞ Travel Agencies, *below*) has a database of specialists worldwide.

Make sure your travel agent knows the accommodations and other services of the place they're recommending. Ask about the hotel's location, room size, beds, and whether it has a pool, room service, or programs for children, if you care about these. Has your agent been there in person or sent others whom you can contact?

SMART TRAVEL TIPS A TO Z

Do some homework on your own, too: Local tourism boards can provide information about lesser-known and small-niche operators, some of which may sell only direct.

### BUYER BEWARE

Each year consumers are stranded or lose their money when tour operators—even large ones with excellent reputations—go out of business. So **check out the operator.** Ask several travel agents about its reputation, and try to **book with a company that has a consumer-protection program.** (Look for information in the company's brochure.) In the United States, members of the National Tour Association and United States Tour Operators Association are required to set aside funds to cover your payments and travel arrangements in case the company defaults. It's also a good idea to choose a company that participates in the American Society of Travel Agent's Tour Operator Program (TOP); ASTA will act as mediator in any disputes between you and your tour operator.

Remember that the more your package or tour includes the better you can predict the ultimate cost of your vacation. Make sure you know exactly what is covered, and **beware of hidden costs.** Are taxes, tips, and transfers included? Entertainment and excursions? These can add up.

➤ TOUR-OPERATOR RECOMMENDATIONS: **American Society of Travel Agents** (☞ Travel Agencies, *below*). **National Tour Association** (NTA, ✉ 546 E. Main St., Lexington, KY 40508, ☎ 606/226–4444 or 800/682–8886). **United States Tour Operators Association** (USTOA, ✉ 342 Madison Ave., Suite 1522, New York, NY 10173, ☎ 212/599–6599 or 800/468–7862, 🖷 212/599–6744).

### TRAIN TRAVEL

Argentina's rail system, which was built by the British, no longer plays an important role in Argentina's transportation system. Trains tend to run rather infrequently and go to few destinations and are often not as comfortable as luxury buses. The most popular routes are all from Buenos Aires to Mar de la Plata and

Bariloche. There's also a special tourist-oriented train, the Tren de los Nubes (Train of the Clouds), that goes through the Andes (☞ Chapter 7).

### FARES & SCHEDULES

Train tickets are inexpensive. Usually there are two classes. Plan to **buy your train tickets three days ahead,** two weeks in summer months, and **arrive at the station well before departure time.** Reservations must be made in person at the local train station.

### TRAVEL AGENCIES

A good travel agent puts your needs first. Look for an agency that has been in business at least five years, emphasizes customer service, and has someone on staff who specializes in your destination. In addition **make sure the agency belongs to a professional trade organization,** such as ASTA in the United States. If your travel agency is also acting as your tour operator *see* Buyer Beware *in* Tours & Packages, *above.*

➤ AGENT REFERRALS: **American Society of Travel Agents** (ASTA, ☎ 800/965–2782 24-hr hotline, 🖷 703/684–8319). **Association of British Travel Agents** (✉ 55–57 Newman St., London W1P 4AH, ☎ 0171/637–2444, 🖷 0171/637–0713). **Association of Canadian Travel Agents** (✉ 1729 Bank St., Suite 201, Ottawa, Ontario K1V 7Z5, ☎ 613/521–0474, 🖷 613/521–0805). **Australian Federation of Travel Agents** (✉ Level 3, 309 Pitt St., Sydney 2000, ☎ 02/9264–3299, 🖷 02/9264–1085). **Travel Agents' Association of New Zealand** (✉ Box 1888, Wellington 10033, ☎ 04/499–0104, 🖷 04/499–0786).

### VISITOR INFORMATION

Each province of Argentina has a tourist office in Buenos Aires that can provide you with maps and regional information (ask at your hotel or look in the phone book). The sometimes helpful Argentine Government Tourist Offices (*not* the embassy) may also be a resource for tourist information.

➤ ARGENTINA GOVERNMENT TOURIST OFFICES: **New York** (✉ 12 W. 56th

St., New York, NY 10019 US, ☎ 212/603–0443); **Los Angeles** (✉ 5055 Wilshire Blvd., Los Angeles, CA 90036 US, ☎ 213/930–0681); **Miami** (✉ 2655 Le Jeune Rd., Miami, FL 33134 US, ☎ 305/442–1366).

➤ U.S. GOVERNMENT ADVISORIES: **U.S. Department of State** (✉ Overseas Citizens Services Office, Room 4811 N.S., 2201 C St. NW, Washington, DC 20520; ☎ 202/647–5225 for interactive hot line; 301/946–4400 for computer bulletin board; FAX 202/647–3000 for interactive hot line); enclose a self-addressed, stamped, business-size envelope.

## WEB SITES

**Argentina phone book** (www.guiatelefonica.com/). **Argentina Secretary of Tourism** (www.sectur.gov.ar) **Buenos Aires Herald** (www.buenosairesherald.com/). **Embassy of Argentina** (www.embassyofargentina-usa.org/). **Tango** (www.abctango.com.ar/).

## WHEN TO GO

### CLIMATE

Because of the great variety of latitudes, altitudes, and climatic zones in Argentina, you're likely to encounter many different climates during any given month. The most important thing to remember is the most obvious—**when it's summer in the Northern Hemisphere, it's winter in Argentina, and vice versa.** Winter in Argentina stretches from July to October and summer goes from December to March.

The sea moderates temperatures in most of Argentina's cities year-round. Winter can be chilly and rainy, although average winter temperatures are usually above freezing in the coastal cities (it hasn't snowed in Buenos Aires in over 100 years).

If you can handle the heat (January–February temperatures usually range in the high 90s to low 100s 35°C–40°C), Buenos Aires can be wonderful in summer, which peaks in January. At this time, the traditional vacation period, Argentines are crowding inland resorts and Atlantic beaches, but Buenos Aires has no traffic, and there is always a seat at

shows and restaurants (though it can also feel a bit empty).

In January many businesses shut down and those that are not closed have reduced hours (this includes most banks, but not American Express). Most banks and government offices open up again in February, but it's still school vacation, so many stores remain closed.

If you have an aversion to large crowds, avoid visiting popular resort areas in January and February and in July, when they become overcrowded again due to school holidays.

Spring and fall are excellent times to visit Argentina. It's usually warm enough (over 50°F) for just a light jacket and it's right before or after the crowded, expensive tourist season.

The best time to visit Iguazú Falls is August–October, when temperatures are lower and the spring coloring is at its brightest. Rain falls all year, dropping about 205 centimeters (80 inches) annually.

Resort towns such as Bariloche and San Martín de los Andes stay open all year. Summer temperatures can get up into the high 70s (about 25°C), but most of the year, the range is from the 30s to the 60s (0°C–20°C).

The Patagonia coast is on the infamous latitude that sailors call the "Roaring Forties," with southern seas that batter Patagonia throughout the year. Thirty-mph winds are common, and 100-mph gales are not unusual. Summer daytime temperatures reach the low 80s (about 28°C), but can drop suddenly to the 50s (10°C–15°C). Winters hover near the freezing mark.

Most travelers visit Tierra del Fuego in summer, when temperatures range from the 40s to the 60s (5°C–20°C). Fragments of glaciers cave into southern lakes with a rumble throughout the thaw from October to the end of April, which is the best time to enjoy the show.

➤ FORECASTS: **Weather Channel Connection** (☎ 900/932–8437), 95¢ per minute from a Touch-Tone phone.

**SMART TRAVEL TIPS A TO Z**

The following are the average daily maximum and minimum temperatures for Buenos Aires.

| | | | | | | | | |
|---|---|---|---|---|---|---|---|---|
| **Jan.** | 85F | 29C | **May** | 64F | 18C | **Sept.** | 64F | 18C |
| | 63 | 17 | | 47 | 8 | | 46 | 8 |
| **Feb.** | 83F | 28C | **June** | 57F | 14C | **Oct.** | 69F | 21C |
| | 63 | 17 | | 41 | 5 | | 50 | 10 |
| **Mar.** | 79F | 26C | **July** | 57F | 14C | **Nov.** | 76F | 24C |
| | 60 | 16 | | 42 | 6 | | 56 | 13 |
| **Apr.** | 72F | 22C | **Aug.** | 60F | 16C | **Dec.** | 82F | 28C |
| | 53 | 12 | | 43 | 6 | | 61 | 16 |

The following are the average daily maximum and minimum temperatures for Bariloche.

| | | | | | | | | |
|---|---|---|---|---|---|---|---|---|
| **Jan.** | 70F | 21C | **May** | 50F | 10C | **Sept.** | 50F | 10C |
| | 46 | 6 | | 36 | 2 | | 34 | 1 |
| **Feb.** | 70F | 21C | **June** | 45F | 7C | **Oct.** | 52F | 11C |
| | 46 | 8 | | 34 | 1 | | 37 | 3 |
| **Mar.** | 64F | 18C | **July** | 43F | 6C | **Nov.** | 61F | 16C |
| | 43 | 6 | | 32 | 0 | | 41 | 5 |
| **Apr.** | 57F | 14C | **Aug.** | 46F | 8C | **Dec.** | 64F | 18C |
| | 39 | 4 | | 32 | 0 | | 45 | 7 |

# 1　DESTINATION: ARGENTINA

# A LAND OF SUPERLATIVES

FROM THE DENSE TROPICAL jungles in the north to the frozen landscape of Antarctica in the south, from the snowy peaks of the Andes in the West, across high plains, Las Pampas, and Patagonia to the Atlantic coast, Argentina is a land of exceptional geographic diversity. It's also a land of superlatives. The highest mountain in the western hemisphere, Aconcagua (22,834 ft), towers 4,000 ft above the crest of the Andes. Ushuaia, on the Beagle Channel in Tierra del Fuego, is the world's southernmost city. The Continental Ice Cap spreads over 8,400 sq mi in southern Patagonia, descending into glaciers that crash in gigantic chunks from 150-ft walls into the lakes and streams of the Parque Nacional los Glaciares. In the northeast, on the border with Brazil and Paraguay, the Iguazú Falls spill over a horseshoe-shape ledge into a beautiful explosion of 275 waterfalls, varying in height from 140 to 300 ft.

World-famous Argentine beef is raised in Las Pampas, the grasslands that cover hundreds of miles in the heart of the country. The topsoil of this alluvial plain is said to be six ft deep, producing grass year round that is so rich that cattle don't need to be corn fed. The Northwest and the Cuyo possess an astounding diversity of geography, from the barren multiplano to multihued mountains, deserts, deep gorges, and lush valleys with rivers and lakes. Along the south Atlantic coast on the Peninsula Valdés, countless species of marine life cavort on land and in the sea. In January, sea lions breed in rookeries, followed by killer whales, sperm whales, and elephant seals, and from September to March thousands of dignified little Magellanic penguins waddle back and forth on "penguin highways" from the sea to land in Punta Tombo.

Although Buenos Aires is now the major economic and cultural capital of Argentina, the country's history actually began in the Northwest. Five centuries before Columbus sailed to America, the Aymara people of Tiahuanaco were traveling from their capital at Lake Titicaca in Bolivia across the barren plains of La Puña down to the fertile valleys of northern Argentina. They came in search of food they could not grow on their high Andean plateau and brought back exotic fruits, feathers, and coca leaves from the subtropical lowlands.

By the mid-1400s, the Incas were following the same route from Cusco, Perú, intent upon conquering the indigenous inhabitants of northern Argentina and Chile. Although the Incas never gained complete control over the region, they did establish agricultural communities in Catamaraca, San Miguel de Tucumán, and as far south as San Juan and Mendoza. Remnants of these ancient civilizations can still be found along the Royal Road of the Incas from Bolivia southward across the Puna into San Salvador de Jujuy, Salta, Catamarca, and San Miguel de Tucumán, and over the Andes between Mendoza, San Juan, and Chile.

Argentina's first Spanish settlers landed on the banks of the Río de la Plata in 1536. But five years of attacks by the local Pehuelche convinced them to flee north to the friendlier city of Asunción in Paraguay or to sail back to Spain, leaving their horses and cattle behind to thrive on the fertile plains and ultimately become one of Argentina's great resources. At about the same time, Spanish conquerors from the Viceroyalty of Peru and Alta Peru (present-day Bolivia) were venturing south to Argentina along the now established trade route, searching for agricultural land and Indian labor to work the silver mines in Bolivia. The first permanent settlements in Argentina, beginning with Santiago de Estero in 1551, were all founded in the northwest before the end of the 16th century. Trade routes from central Chile crossed the Andes to Argentina (in order to avoid the Atacama Desert) and went north to Peru, where Spanish vessels waited in the port at Lima to carry goods between Spain and the New World. In 1620, the region of La Plata was officially incorporated into the Viceroyalty of Peru and later, in 1776, with present-day Bolivia, Paraguay, and Uruguay, was declared the Viceroyalty of La Plata.

In 1806 and 1807, the British made two unsuccessful attempts to capture Buenos Aires and the Spanish crown, and the next year, Napoleon invaded Spain and sent King Ferdinand VII to prison in France. The citizens of Argentina, emboldened, began to question Spanish leadership and its economic and military benefits. On May 25, 1810, at the *Cabildo* (Town Hall) in Buenos Aires, the Spanish viceroyalty was deposed by a revolutionary junta. Political chaos ensued, and it wasn't until July 1816 that independence was officially declared by a national congress in the city of Tucumán. Spanish Royalists persisted in attacking from their stronghold in Bolivia, and for 16 years, blood continued to spill on the battlefields of northwestern Argentina. It took General José de San Martín's brilliant and daring expedition in January, 1817, across the Andes from Mendoza to Chile with 16,000 men and 10,000 horses, to finally liberate Argentina, Chile, and Perú from Spanish rule forever. With their newly won freedom and no experience in governing, local army generals took control, and for the next 40 years, the Unitarists (those who wanted free trade with Europe, immigration, education, and a central government) fought a civil war with the Federalists (wealthy ranchers who advocated provincial government and territorial rights). The latter were represented by *caudillos* (provincial dictators)—the most infamous of them being Juan Manuel de Rosas, who ruled Argentina from 1830–1851.

Rosas was overthrown by José de Urquiza in 1852. Under Urquiza's leadership this country of warring states finally became a nation, with the signing of the constitution (modeled after that of the United States) in May, 1853. But all was not easy: Buenos Aires Province didn't accept the constitution and refused to join the federation until 1859. And the strife continued: In 1861, General Bartolome Mitre overthrew the government and was elected president the next year. Throughout this period and during the enlightened presidency of Domingo Sarmiento (1868–1874), thousands of immigrants arrived in Buenos Aires. Meanwhile, across Las Pampas and vast reaches of Patagonia, the nomadic Mapuche and tenacious Tehuelche were engaged in a battle with the National Army, led by General Julio Roca, in the infamous Conquest of the Desert

(1879–1883). The entire native population of Argentina succumbed to battle or disease, leaving a few to work on ranches or live on reservations. Europeans began moving in, fencing in the wide-open ranges, and the British built railroads to transport beef, hides, leather, wool, and wheat to Buenos Aires for export.

In the early 1900s, newly developed refrigeration made possible the export of agricultural products to Europe and the rest of the world. By the 1930s, Argentina was the eighth richest country in the world, and Buenos Aires the major South American port on the Atlantic coast. European investors and wealthy immigrants employed Europe's finest architects and city planners to design and build their city. Today, when you walk the wide avenues and narrow cobblestone streets, look up at the Art Deco, Art Nouveau, Gothic, and stately Parisian-style facades to understand why Buenos Aires is referred to as "The Paris of South America."

By 1940, however, Argentina's prosperity was not trickling down to the masses of immigrants working in the industrial sector; nor was it benefiting the rural population. Juan Perón, having grown up on an *estancia* (ranch) where his father worked, was aware of the inequalities between the wealthy upper class landowners (many of them British) and the rest of the country. Perón and his future wife, Eva, knew how to capitalize on the country's social unrest and its need for a strong, sympathetic leader. Together, they took up the cause of the disenfranchised *descamisadas* (shirtless ones) and rode to the presidency on the backs of Argentina's labor force. The adoration of the working class was rewarded by labor reform, job security, pensions, and child labor laws. When Eva Perón died of cancer in 1952, a severe drought, plummeting grain prices in Europe, and a soaring foreign trade deficit brought Argentina's economy to the brink of ruin. Perón was overthrown in 1955. Demagogue, facist, labor reformer, union leader, political genius, power-crazed, crook, dictator—Perón and "Evita" will be loved, hated, and discussed by Argentines forever.

In 1965, a repressive and fumbling government brought Perón back from exile in Spain. He was elected president, named his wife Isabel vice president, and then died in 1974, leaving her at the helm of a sinking ship. Her ineptitude got her ousted in 1976 and brought a military junta back to power. Military terrorists the likes of José Lopez Rega, General Videla, and General Galtieri launched what is known as the "Dirty War" against the perceived danger of left-wing students, nuns, priests, intellectuals, and even whole families. Thousands were jailed, tortured, raped, "disappeared," and murdered.

In 1982 General Galtieri invaded the British held *Islas Malvinas* (Falkland Islands), pitting an ill-prepared army against an enraged Great Britain. Argentina's military defeat was ultimately its victory: With it, the lies and fabrications of a ruthless military regime were finally exposed to a disbelieveing (at first) country and to the world. Galtieri was replaced by Raúl Alfonsín, who began the process of restoring democracy. Under powerful opposition from the military and a populace frustrated by catapulting inflation, Alfonsín lost in 1989 to an enigmatic governor from La Rioja Province, Carlos Menem. Although a member of the majority Peronista party, Menem began the tricky task of privatizing state-owned companies and pegging the peso to the dollar, with some success. In late 1999, however, Menem lost to Fernando de la Rua, the mayor of Buenos Aires. Although inflation is under control these days, economic and political issues continue to trouble a society that can still remember the repressive regimes of the past while rejoicing in the freedom of the present. It will be interesting to see what the future brings Argentina.

# NEW AND NOTEWORTHY

If you're traveling to Argentina from the west coast, you'll be happy to know that LAN Chile Airlines now flies from Los Angeles to Santiago, Chile, with connections to Mendoza and Cordoba. This is especially good news if you want to go skiing in both Chile and Argentina.

A current trend in Argentina is to take long weekends instead of extended vacations. So be prepared for lots of traffic and crowds on weekends, especially in summer.

In the city of Mendoza, the beautiful old Plaza Hotel, with its broad veranda, was the pride of the city until it fell into total disrepair and finally closed in 1998. Hyatt Hotels has bought it and is in the process of renovating, with an eye to reopening by 2002.

The famous Hotel Internacional, the only lodging on the Argentine side of the Iguazú Falls with a view, was taken over by Sheraton in late 1998; remodeling and modernization are in the works.

A new international airport was built in the town of Presidencia Roque Saenz Peña in Chaco Province, but it isn't yet receiving flights, even domestic ones. When it does finally open, it will make getting to this area much easier.

A Patagonian Invasion of the Rich and Famous? When CNN founder Ted Turner and his wife Jane Fonda bought the 11,000-acre *La Primavera* (Springtime) Ranch on Lago Trafúl near Bariloche, only a few local eyebrows were raised. "There isn't a more beautiful place in the world," he told a Buenos Aires newspaper. Photos of President Clinton and President Menem, smiling under a blue sky with Lago Nahuel Huapi in the background, would confirm this. Hungarian financier George Soros also succumbed to Patagonia's charms, buying the Llao Llao Hotel near Bariloche plus another million acres of Patagonian wilderness. Growing his own sweaters on the 2.2 million-acre Leleque Ranch northeast of Esquel, Luciano Benetton raises 280,000 sheep to produce wool for his Italian clothing company. French movie actor Christopher Lambert and American Sylvester Stallone have both made offers on lakefront land and ranches in the Cholila Valley. Argentines have mixed feelings about this gringo invasion and some express concern over the future ownership of what they consider their heritage.

# WHAT'S WHERE

## Buenos Aires

The gateway to all the splendors of Argentina is the sophisticated and cosmopolitan capital city of Buenos Aires, on the banks of the Río de la Plata. Here in the Capital Federal, as this sprawling metropolis is known, ten million people (one third the population of Argentina) live in the city's 46 *barrios* (neighborhoods), each with its own soccer team and its own identity. A bustling city, Buenos Aires is alive with activity, from its vast museums and Paris-like avenues to its late-night *asados* (barbecues) and tango performances.

## Las Pampas

Surrounding Buenos Aires, though worlds apart, the flat, expansive grasslands of Las Pampas radiates to the Atlantic Ocean in the east and the mountains to the west. It's home to the horses and cattle that make up the mainstay of the region's—and Argentina's—economy. Signs of active ranch life are everywhere, from the cattle grazing to the gauchos working the wide-open landscape. Alfalfa, sunflowers, wheat, and corn are also grown here. And along the coast are great beaches, which are the favorite vacation spots for Buenos Aires locals.

## Argentine Litoral

The Argentine Litoral, which encompasses the northeast region of the country, is dominated by two rivers: the Uruguay and the Paraná. Across the Río Paraná to the north lies Paraguay, and across the Río Uruguay to the east are Brazil and Uruguay. The two great rivers finally meet at the southernmost point of the region, right above Buenos Aires, where they form the famous Río de la Plata. The topography of the region varies considerably: Flat, fertile plains extend through the south; lagoons and marshlands are found near the center; dry, desolate land covers much of the west; and subtropical forest fills the northeastern corner, also home to the Cataratas del Iguazú, the impressive waterfalls that straddle Argentina and Brazil.

## The Northwest

The northwest is where Argentine history began, yet few have ventured beyond its cities—Catamarca, Jujuy, Salta, and Tucumán—to its high-mountain passes, deep red gorges, peaceful valleys, and sub-tropical jungles. In the northernmost province of Jujuy, a polychromatic palette of reds, greens, and yellows washes across the mountain slopes of the Quebrada

Humahuaca (Humahuaca Gorge) as it follows the Río Grande north. Beyond, the great high plateau of the Puna stretches along the borders with Bolivia and Chile. A mixture of pre-Columbian and Spanish culture is apparent throughout in the architecture, costumes, festivals, music, and handicrafts. In the sunny Calchaquí Valley, between Tucumán and Salta, former colonial settlements dot the landscape amidst *Torrontés* (a white-wine grape) vineyards, and in the cities, the plazas and churches recall the Spanish influence. Even pre-Inca civilizations have left their marks on ghostly menhirs.

## The Cuyo

Here you find the great wine-producing provinces of Mendoza and San Juan. North of Mendoza, the slow-paced capital city of San Juan is the birthplace of Argentina's great educator, writer, and past president, Domingo Faustino Sarmiento. It's also the gateway to the curious paleontological treasures of the Valle de la Luna (Valley of the Moon). San Luís Province is home to the giant Parque Nacional las Quijadas. The Pan-American highway passes through Mendoza, heading west over spectacular Uspallata Pass to Chile: Along the way are hot springs, Inca ruins, Los Penitentes ski area, and an incomparable view of Aconcagua. Farther south near the city of San Rafael, you can raft down the Ateul or Diamante rivers, ride horseback over the Andes, or ski at the super resort of Las Leñas near Malargüe.

## Patagonia

Argentine Patagonia extends 1,920 km (1,200 mi) along the spine of the Andes from Río Colorado in the north to Cape Horn—the southernmost land mass on the continent. On the eastern slopes of the Andes, high peaks rise above thousands of lakes, streams, glaciers, waterfalls, and ancient forests—most of them protected within five national parks in the area known as Andean Patagonia, or the Patagonian lake district. Bariloche, San Martín, and Esquel all have airports served by major airlines, and there are good bus connections to points in between. The main attraction of the southern lake district is the Parque Nacional los Glaciares near Calafate, and the Fitzroy mountains, which lie 230 km (142 mi) north. It's possible to link the two lake districts in one long adventurous drive on R40, known as "the loneliest road in the world."

# PLEASURES AND PASTIMES

## Argentine Fare

Argentina is basically a steak-and-potatoes country. The beef is so good, most Argentines see little reason to eat anything else, though pork, lamb, and chicken are tasty alternatives and *civito* (kid), when in season, is outstanding. Nothing, however, can duplicate the indescribable flavor of a lean, tender, 3-inch thick *bife de lomo* (filet mignon) or a *bife de chorizo* (like New York steak, but double the size). *Jugoso* (juicy) means medium rare, *vuelta y vuelta* (flipped back and forth) means rare, and *vivo por adentro* (alive inside) is barely warm in the middle. Argentines like their meat *bién cocido* (well cooked). *Carne asado* (roasted meat) usually means grilled *a la parrilla* (on a grill over hot coals), but it can also be baked in an oven or slowly roasted at an outdoor barbecue (*asado*). Here, the meat is attached to a metal spit (*asador*), which is stuck in the ground aslant on a bed of hot coals. A *tira de asado* (strip of rib roast), skewered on its own spit, often accompanies the asado.

A *parrillada mixta* (mixed grill) is the quintessential Argentine meal for two or more. Families gather for noon *parrilladas* (grills) in restaurants and backyards across the country. They choose from different cuts of beef, *mollejas* (sweetbreads), *chichulínes* (intestines), *salchichas* (long, thin sausages), *morcillas* (blood sausages), chicken, and *chorizos* (thick, spicy pork-and-beef sausages)—terrific on french bread slathered with *chimichurri* sauce (oil, garlic, and salt) and items such as crushed red pepper, chopped cilantro, parsley, oregano, or tomatoes. All these morsels sizzle on a portable grill delivered to your table along with french fries cooked on a hot skillet (not submerged in oil).

*Empanadas* (meat pies) are baked or fried and every province has its own version. Lamb and wild game are Patagonian specialties. Chocolate, smoked meats, and delicious jams are worth bringing home from the fruit producing areas of Andean Patagonia. In the northwest, indigenous products such as red peppers, corn, beans, and squash influence dishes such as *humitas* (steamed cornhusks) wrapped around chopped tomatoes and local cheese, empanadas, and tamales. Stews are made with beef, corn, and local vegetables.

Beyond beef, many Argentine dishes are influenced by other cultures. Pasta, pizza, and Italian specialties are on every menu in almost all restaurants. A *milanesa* (breaded veal cutlet) is a good quick snack, even better *a la neopolitana* with melted mozzarella cheese and tomato sauce. Fish has not been a favored dish in this meat-loving country, even though trout and salmon from lakes and streams yield both quality and quantity and *centolla* (giant crab) and *mejillones* (mussels) are trapped offshore in Ushuaia.

Argentines tend to ignore vegetables, except for salads, which usually include shredded carrots, tomatoes, onions, cabbage, and cucumbers. Ask for *aceite de olivo* (olive oil) or you'll get corn oil for your salad. Not to be missed, when available, is the white asparagus that grows south of Buenos Aires. Vegetables and fruits are fresh, crisp, and flavorful in their seasons—no need for hothouse assistance in this country.

A welcome sight on the dessert menu is *ensalada de fruta* (fruit salad—sometimes fresh, sometimes canned). *Dulce de leche* is a sweet caramel sauce served on pancakes, in pastries, on cookies (*alfajores*), and on ice cream.

For a chart that explains the cost of meals at the restaurants listed throughout this book, *see* Dining *in* Smart Travel Tips.

## Wine

Given the high consumption of beef rather than fish, Argentines understandably drink *vino tinto* (red wine). Malbec and Cabernet are the most popular. If you prefer *vino blanco* (white wine), try vintages from Mendoza and lesser known wineries farther north: La Rioja and Salta. Here the Torrontés grape thrives. This varietal produces a dry white with an overwhelming, unforgettable bouquet that has been a consistent prize winner in recent competitions in Germany and France. A popular summer cooler is *clericot,* a white version of sangría (also available in many restaurants), made with strawberries, peaches, oranges, or whatever fruits are in season.

## Eco-Heaven

In Argentina, where climates range from tropical to subantarctic and altitudes descend from 22,000 ft to below sea-level, every conceivable environment on earth is represented: high, low, hot, cold, temperate, dry, wet, and frozen. Because the population (about 40 million) is small relative to its land mass (roughly 2,000 mi long and 900 mi wide), a staggering variety of plants, birds, and animals thrive undisturbed in their habitats.

Along the South Atlantic coast, sea mammals mate and give birth on empty beaches and in protected bays. Guanaco, rhea, and native deer travel miles over isolated Andean trails and across windswept plains. Birds are everywhere—noisy, funny, passing above in clouds of thousands, descending on a lagoon like a blanket of feathers or rising in a flutter of pink flamingos. National parks and natural reserves cover about 9% of the country's total area.

Iguazú Falls National Park protects 2,000 species of vascular plants, thousands of butterflies and moths, more than 400 bird species, 100 mammals, and countless amphibia and insects—many of which have not been identified. Nature trails disappear into a greenhouse of intertwined lianas, creepers, epiphytes, bamboo, and hanging gardens of orchids and bromeliads. An organic carpet of decaying branches, leaves, and bushes nourish mushrooms, mosses and countless plants struggling for light under a mantle of vegetation that reaches upward to a ceiling 65 ft above. Local guides can explain the importance of every plant, spider, and insect (except, perhaps, the mosquito) and its particular eco-dependency on the millions of plants and animals, seen and unseen, around you.

In the the north central region, the Gran Chaco encompasses hundreds of miles of marshes and jungle teeming with monkeys, reptiles, land mammals, waterfowl, birds, and fish. Farther east in Corrientes Province, the Esteros de Iberá (Ibera marshlands), create agreen labyrinth of swamps, lagoons, islets, and seas of grass, where endangered species of swamp deer, maned wolves and golden alligators live with other exotic creatures of that environment: caiman, boa constrictors, anaconda, piranhas, capybara, tapir, coati, and myriad fish and fowl.

If you're looking for hot jungles, cool forests, windy plains, mountains, glaciers, swamps, or deserts, fish or fowl, birds galore, sea and land mammals, jungle beasts and bugs, exotic plants, trees, and acres of wildflowers, you can find them here in this land of unlimited bio-diversity.

## Love of the Game

River Plate, Boca Juniors, and Maradona—these names are as familiar to Argentines as the Dodgers, Yankees, and Babe Ruth are to Americans. They are the subject of fiery dispute, suicidal despair, love, hate, pride, and all the emotions that soccer arouses in this nation whose blue-and-white striped jerseys have flashed across TV screens since it won the 1978 and 1986 World Championships. Nothing can lift the spirits of an inflation-ridden, underemployed, politically and economically depressed nation like a soccer victory. (Rugby, too, attracts thousands of fans to stadiums and practice fields across the country.)

Polo, like soccer, was introduced by the British. Natural riding skills and an abundance of good horses quickly produced the world's top players, who, like soccer players, are paid enormous sums to compete for foreign teams. Argentine polo ponies, known for their quickness, intelligence, and strength, are sold the world over, as are race, show-jumping, and dressage horses. The best polo matches occur in Buenos Aires (in November), as do other equestrian events such as horse racing, show jumping, and dressage, which attract dedicated devotees both local and international.

## Outdoor Activities

Fishing in the the national parks of Patagonia's northern lake district (especially around Bariloche) is legendary. Either hire a local guide or stay a week in a rustic fishing lodge and enjoy the pristine lakes and streams jumping with trout and salmon. Opportunities, too, abound for hiking and mountain biking in Argentina's national and provincial parks, over its mountain trails, and through its forests to lakes, villages, and campgrounds. If you're a serious mountaineer, you know the challenges of Aconcagua (in Mendoza Province) and Cerro Fitzroy, Mt. Tronadór, and Lanín Volcano in Patagonia. The Club Andinos (Andean Mountaineering Clubs) in Bariloche, Mendoza, Ushuaia, and other towns organize national and international excursions.

Since Argentina's seasons are the opposite of North America's, you can ski or snowboard from June to September. Las Leñas near Mendoza (in the Cuyo), Catedral near Bariloche, and Chapelco near San Martín de los Andes (in Patagonia) are some of the best ski areas. These areas offer groomed runs, open bowls, and trails that follow the fall line to cozy inns or luxurious hotels. Smaller areas near Bariloche, Esquel, and Mendoza have good day facilities and lodgings in the towns. Tierra Mayor, a family-run nordic center near Ushuaia has such novelties as dogsled rides, snowcat trips, and wind skiing.

# FODOR'S CHOICE

## Dining

★ **1884 Restaurante Francis Mallman, Mendoza.** The young chef at this winery restaurant creates sensational Argentine haute cuisine. $$$

★ **Los Años Locos, Buenos Aires.** Come to this low-key spot along Río de la Plata for long lunches and late-night steak dinners. $$$

★ **Cabaña las Lilas, Buenos Aires.** Join presidents, movie stars, and Porteños for the best meat in the city. $$$$

★ **Cassis, Esquel.** Chef Mariana Müller de Wolf and her husband Ernesto have returned to her hometown and opened one of Argentina's finest restaurants, putting Patagonian cuisine on the map. $$$

★ **Don Jacinto, Gualeguaychú.** In this elegant restaurant, sample skillfully prepared river fish or pasta with your choice of more than 20 sauces. $$

★ **La Estancia, Comodoro Rivadavia.** For good, classic Patagonian fare head to this spot that has been made to look like a typical Argentine ranch. $$

★ **La Marmite, Bariloche.** Feel like you're in the Alps at this restaurant where the bar is cozy-chic, the service sublime, the wine list long, and the food Andean-Swiss-French. $$$

★ **Melo, Buenos Aires.** In Barrio Norte, Melo serves up traditional fare in a friendly atmosphere. $–$$

★ **Mikele's Bistro, Posadas.** The creative preparation and presentation of Mediterranean dishes earn this handsome, trendy restaurant the highest praise. $$

★ **La Rueda, Posadas.** This huge, festive restaurant is the perfect place to enjoy a parade of succulent meats. $

## Historic Sights

★ **Cementerio de La Recoleta, Buenos Aires.** This cemetery is a veritable who's who of Argentine history.

★ **San Ignacio de Miní, northeast of Posadas.** These are stunning, well-preserved remains of one of the Jesuit missions that thrived in Argentina over 200 years ago.

## Lodging

★ **Alvear Palace Hotel, Buenos Aires.** Built in 1932, the Alvear is the city's most elegant hotel. $$$$

★ **Hostería Los Notros, Glaciar Perito Moreno, El Calafate.** Eat, sleep, and wake in plain view of one of nature's most awesome spectacles while you enjoy rustic luxury. $$$$

★ **Hostería Paimún, Parque Nacional Lanín.** Not just for fishing fanatics, this simple lodge by a lake at the foot of Lanín Volcano offers the experience of being on the edge of true wilderness. $$$$

★ **Hostería Restaurant del Puerto, Colón.** The town's first hotel has colorful, two-story rooms with antique furniture and unbeatable views of the Río Uruguay. $–$$

★ **Hotel Edelweiss, Bariloche.** The best hotel in downtown Bariloche, it's big enough to offer all the amenities of a major hotel, yet small enough to be intimate. $$$$

★ **Hotel y Resort Las Hayas, Ushuaia.** At this hotel outside of town, luxurious details are the order of the day, making it among Argentina's finest. $$$$

★ **Llao Llao Hotel and Resort, Llao Llao Peninsula, Bariloche.** This world-class resort-hotel sits on a hill between two lakes surrounded by towering snowclad peaks—

an architectural jewel in one of the world's most exquisite settings.*$$$$*

⭐ **Park Hyatt, Buenos Aires.** The luxurious Park Hyatt has large rooms, great amenities, and an outstanding staff. *$$$$*

⭐ **Posada Aguapé, Colonia Carlos Pellegrini.** This small, lakeside inn is a creative approach to the traditional guest house. *$$$$*

⭐ **Sheraton Internacional Iguazú, Cataratas del Iguazú.** At this luxury hotel, have breakfast or a drink on the spacious balconies overlooking the stunning falls—and be sure to ask for a room with a view. *$$$$*

## Museums

⭐ **Calle Museo Caminito, Buenos Aires.** This pedestrians-only street has functioned as an open-air museum and art market since 1959.

⭐ **Museo de Arte Española Enrique Larreta, Buenos Aires.** Once the home of a Spanish governor, the beautiful building now houses a superb collection of Spanish colonial art.

⭐ **Museo Maritimo, Ushuaia.** Housed in the Tierra del Fuego's original penal colony, El Presidio, this museum sheds light on Patagonia's and Argentina's past.

⭐ **Museo Paleontológico Egidio Feruglio, Trelew.** This paleontology museum is a fascinating spot to learn about dinosaurs and other secrets of Patagonia's eons-old natural history.

## Natural Wonders

⭐ **Bosque Petrificado José Ormaechea, Comodoro Rivadavia.** A two-hour drive from town is this eerily lonely, wind-swept petrified forest.

⭐ **Cataratas del Iguazú, Argentine Litoral.** This set of 270 waterfalls, shaped in a horseshoe around the verdant jungle, is unquestionably one of the world's greatest wonders.

⭐ **Glaciar Moreno, Parque Nacional los Glaciares, El Calafate.** As the only advancing glacier in the world, it mystifies and delights as tons of ice peel off and crash into Lago Argentino.

⭐ **Lake Crossing from Bariloche to Chile, Patagonia.** Blue lakes, turquoise lagoons, snow-cone volcanos, waterfalls, junglelike forests, and a welcoming hotel in the middle are all part of this Andean Lake Odyssey.

⭐ **Peninsula Valdés, Patagonia.** At one of South America's best wildlife reserves, see southern right whales feeding, mating, giving birth, and nursing their offspring, and an array of other animals such as seals and penguins.

⭐ **Punto Tomba Reserve, Patagonia.** From mid-September until March, experience the largest rookery of Magellanic penguins in the world at this nature reserve.

⭐ **Saltos de Moconá, Argentine Litoral.** These picturesque waterfalls extend for nearly two miles along the Río Uruguay.

# GREAT ITINERARIES

Begin your trip to Argentina in Buenos Aires. You could spend your entire trip in the city—strolling the wide, tree-lined boulevards, visiting the numerous boutiques and cafés, touring the city's unique districts with their churches and museums, and immersing yourself in the rich nightlife. As other Argentines will tell you, however, the Porteños (as Buenos Aires locals are called) are a special breed—perhaps too pretentious for the rest of the country—and you should make an effort to visit more than the capital. Iguazú Falls are perhaps the most spectacular in the world, and the dive into nature for a few days may come as a welcome change after the crowded, noisy city. If you're searching for even greater serenity, immense Patagonia with its silent snow-capped mountains and breathtaking glaciers beckons—but you'll need at least a week to cover its great distances.

## If You Have 3–5 Days

Narrow your visit to Buenos Aires, which has more than enough to keep you happily occupied. In many ways, this is a city that comes alive at night—so be sure to enjoy the restaurant, theater, tango, and café scene.

## If You Have 6–10 Days

Spend a couple of days in Buenos Aires, and then travel to Iguazú Falls (☞ Chap ter 4), only an hour and a half flight from the capital and one of the most amazing sights on earth. You'll need at least two days to see the best waterfalls, but three or four would be better.

## If You Have More Than 10 Days

If you have time left over after visiting Buenos Aires and Iguazú Falls, Patagonia (☞ Chapter 7) has unparalleled scenery, although it can be difficult and time consuming to reach. Probably the easiest way to arrange a trip is through a tourist agency in Buenos Aires. You should plan to spend at least a week and choose to focus on either the Atlantic coast or the Andes region. Other interesting trips would be to an *estancia* (ranch) or to Mar del Plata or other beach resorts south of the capital in Las Pampas (☞ Chapter 3).

# FESTIVALS AND SEASONAL EVENTS

## SUMMER

➤ DECEMBER: Trelew celebrates the **Fiesta Provincial del Pinguino** (Provincial Festival of the Penguin).

➤ JANUARY: Cosquín is the home of the **Festival Nacional de Folklore** (National Festival of Folklore), held every January in the Plaza Próspero Molina. At the same time, the town hosts the **Festival Provincial de las Artesanias** (Provincial Festival of Artistans), during which craftspeople from all over the province come to sell their wares. During the second week in January, Viedma and Carmen de Patagones host the **Regata del Río Negro,** a race of boats from around the region.

➤ FEBRUARY: Every year during the second week of February, Camarones, in Patagonia, hosts the **Fiesta Nacional de Salmon** (National Salmon Festival), with festivities and a fishing contest.

➤ MARCH: In Viedma and Carmen de Patagones, March 7 begins the annual, weeklong **Fiesta de Soberania y la Tradicion,** during which the towns celebrate their defeat of Brazil in an 1827 incursion, with music, food, crafts, and cultural exhibits.

## WINTER

➤ JUNE: In the Northwest, **Inti Raymi** (Festival of the Sun) is celebrated on June 20, the night before winter solstice, when the sun is thanked for last year's harvest. On June 16 and 17, when the **Salta Gaucho Parade** takes place, hundreds of gauchos *Salteños* ride into Salta in full gaucho regalia: big, wide, wraparound leather chaps (for the thorny bushes that grow in the region), black boots, *bombachas* (baggy pants), knife tucked into their belts, and their signature red-and-black ponchos. The nations's best folk artists hold forth in outdoor *peñas*.

➤ JULY: The **Fiesta del Poncho** takes place in Catamarca for a week in July: Artisans from all over the province exhibit and sell their best weavings, baskets, ceramics, and wood carvings, and folk singers perform in the evening. In Tucumán, **Día de Independencia** (Independence Day) is celebrated with much fervor on July 9. In July, Bariloche hosts the **Fiesta de las Colectividades** (Party of Different Communities), a celebration of the town's diversity; dancing, music, handicrafts, and food from Europe, Scandinavia, the Middle East, Central Europe, and South America are represented.

➤ AUGUST: *Pachamama* (Mother Earth) is celebrated August 1 in Humahuaca, in Jujuy Province. On August 22, Jujuy celebrates the **Semana de Jujuy** (Jujuy Week) with a reenactment of the great 1812 exodus: Citizens dress in period costumes and ride their horses or carts through town; hotels are usually booked up during this week. The **Fiesta Nacional de la Nieve** (National Snow Festival) is a month-long winter carnival that takes place in August all over Bariloche and at the Catedrál ski area.

## SPRING

➤ SEPTEMBER: On September 24, Tucamán celebrates the **Battle of Tucamán,** commemorating Belgrano's victory over the Spanish during the War of Independence. One of Trelew's major cultural events is the **Eisteddfod de la Juventud** in early September, which celebrates the music, food, and dance of Welsh tradition. During Bariloche's **Semana Musical Llao Llao** (Llao Llao Musical Week) in September, international soloists and orchestras perform classical, jazz, and tango music at the Hotel Llao Llao.

➤ OCTOBER: **Belen de Escobar** (known as the national flower capital) holds a flower exhibition in October. The **Festival**

**Nacional de la Cerveza** (National Beer Festival, or Oktoberfest) takes place in the town of Villa General Belgrano, which was originally settled by Bavarian and Alsatian immigrants. The second half of October marks Trelew's **Eisteddfod de Chubut,** a Welsh literary and musical festival, first held in Patagonia in 1875.

➤ NOVEMBER: Each year in November, San Clemente del Tuyu hosts the festival of its patron saint, **San Clemente Romano.** The entire city comes out to see the procession, which ends in a huge asado.

# 2 BUENOS AIRES

Buenos Aires conjures up images of tango dancers, gauchos, and romantic views. But this cosmopolitan city offers so much more—great restaurants, Paris-inspired boulevards, enthralling neighborhoods, vibrant nightlife, and an intense spirit found in few other places. Whether shopping for fine clothes at its stylish boutiques, sipping café con leche at its outdoor cafés, or strolling along the Río de la Plata, it quickly becomes apparent that Buenos Aires is a place like no other.

**B**UENOS AIRES, THE NINTH LARGEST CITY in the world and the hub of the southern cone, is a sprawling megalopolis that rises from the Río de la Plata and stretches more than 200 sq km (75 sq mi) to the surrounding pampas, the fertile Argentine plains. It's the political, economic, and cultural capital of Argentina and the gateway to the rest of the country.

Revised and updated by Kristen Masick

Buenos Aires has 47 *barrios* (neighborhoods)—each with own character and its own story to tell. Most residents of Buenos Aires have lived in the same barrio for their entire lives and feel much more of an affinity to their neighborhood than to the city as a whole.

Unlike most South American cities, where the architecture principally reveals a strong Spanish colonial influence, Buenos Aires has a mix of architectural styles. Block after block of tidy high-rise apartment buildings are interspersed with 19th-century houses. Neighborhoods like Palermo, La Recoleta, and Belgrano feel more like Paris, with wide boulevards lined with palatial mansions, luxury high-rises, and spacious parks. Flowers are sold at colorful corner kiosks, the smell of freshly baked bread wafts out of well-stocked bakeries, terrace cafés can be found on every block, and pedestrians carry themselves with a fashionable reserve that is remarkably Parisian. In fact, Belgrano's vast neighborhood park is an exact replica of one in Paris and its Church of the Immaculate Conception is modeled after Rome's Pantheon. Even the Vatican Embassy on Avenida Alvear is a copy of the Jacquemart-André Museum in Paris. Other neighborhoods, such as San Telmo and La Boca, have a distinctly working-class Italian feel. Many have compared the Plaza de Mayo, principally the Avenida de Mayo, to Budapest; and the Galerías Pacífico, a shopping mall in the center of the city, was built to look like Galleria Vittorio Emanuele in Milan.

Buenos Aires locals are referred to as *Porteños* because many of them originally arrived by boat from Europe and started out in the city's port area, La Boca. Porteños are known as thinkers—they enjoy philosophical discussions and psychoanalysis (as proven by the large number of psychoanalysts per capita—in fact, the most of any city in the world). The citizens seem perpetually confused about their national identity—South American or European?—and are often concerned about how outsiders perceive them. Many are also deeply image-conscious, reflected in the lengths to which porteñas go to be beautiful. With the men's flashing stares and piquant compliments, they receive ample recognition for their efforts.

Buenos Aires has no Eiffel Tower, no internationally renowned museums, no must-see sights that clearly identify it as a world-class city. Rather, it provides a series of small interactions that have intense Latin spirit— a flirtatious glance, a heartfelt chat, a juicy steak, a beautiful tango— which combine to create a vibrant and unforgettable urban experience.

## Pleasures and Pastimes

### Dining

Dining in Buenos Aires is an art, a passion, and a pastime. Whether at home or in restaurants, meals are events. *Sobremesa* (chatting after the meal) is just as important as the meal itself, and people linger at a table long after a meal is over. The staple is beef, which is usually cooked on the *parrilla* (grill) or barbecue (*asado*). A typical meal consists of a steak accompanied by meat, french fries, salad, and red wine.

For a chart that explains the cost of meals at the restaurants listed under Dining, *below, see* Dining *in* Smart Travel Tips.

## Lodging

Buenos Aires has a mix of hotels, inns, and apart-hotels (short-term rental apartments). Although the city isn't known for its world-class facilities, it does have a few noteworthy establishments, including the Alvear Palace Hotel and the Park Hyatt. Note that in summer (January and February, in particular), when most locals are on vacation and restaurants may be empty and stores closed, Buenos Aires hotels still charge high-season rates.

For a chart that explains the cost of double room at the hotels listed under Lodging, *below, see* Lodging *in* Smart Travel Tips.

## Shopping

During the 1970s external trade was prohibited, so Argentines had to go abroad to buy quality foreign goods. Once trade was permitted again in the early 1990s, it opened up a floodgate of higher quality merchandise. This, combined with a more stable currency, has led to vastly increased selection and variety. Now it's possible to purchase not only high-quality Argentine silver and leather goods but also European fashions and clothes from national designers like Paula Cahen D'Avers. Open-air markets are the best places to buy souvenirs such as a gourd specially designed for drinking *mate* (a local tea-like beverage) or items made of silver.

# EXPLORING BUENOS AIRES

Buenos Aires is enormous and sprawling. You're best off exploring one neighborhood at a time by foot and taking public transportation—bus or *subte* (subway). Streets are basically laid out in a grid, though a few streets transverse the grid at 45-degree angles; these are helpfully called *diagonal. Avenidas* are two-way streets (at most hours of the day), while *calles* are generally one way. Each city block is exactly 100 meters long, and addresses are based on the building's measured position on the street, not by street number (for instance, 180 Calle Florida is 100 meters, or one block, from 80 Calle Florida).

## Great Itineraries

### IF YOU HAVE 3 DAYS

If you have only three days in Buenos Aires, you'll have time to appreciate the city—but at breakneck speed. Plan to spend a half day in each of the following areas: Plaza de Mayo, El Centro, La Boca, San Telmo, Palermo, and La Recoleta. If you're in town on a weekend, visit La Recoleta on Saturday and San Telmo on Sunday. If you're in town in the middle of the week, try to stick to Palermo on Monday, since its attractions are open (whereas most museums are closed on Monday). Remember to schedule time for a siesta since, with only two nights in the city, you'll want to spend one night out at a club, bar, or performance and the other enjoying an evening of tango.

### IF YOU HAVE 5 DAYS

With five days you can enjoy all of the sights described in the three-day itinerary above. You'll also have more time to explore La Recoleta or San Telmo and to explore Puerto Madero and Belgrano.

### IF YOU HAVE 7–10 DAYS

With more than a week in the Buenos Aires area, you can explore the city at a more relaxed pace, enjoying all the sights suggested in the three- and five-day itineraries above. You'll also have time to get to some areas that are more off the beaten path. On day six take a ferry trip across

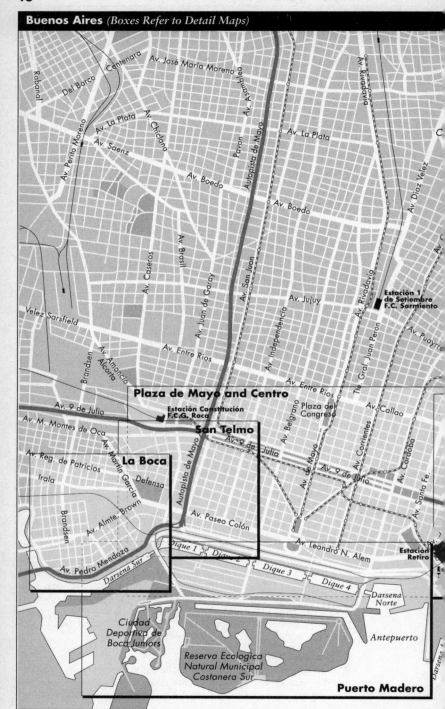

the river to picturesque Colonia, Uruguay, 50 minutes away (☞ Arriving and Departing by Hydrofoil and Ferry *in* Buenos Aires A to Z, *below*). On day seven take a trip to the suburbs and along the Río de la Plata on the Tren de la Costa, which departs from Tigre (☞ Chapter 3). With whatever time you have left, either spend it shopping and enjoying Buenos Aires, or make an excursion to the nearby towns of Luján or La Plata (☞ Chapter 3).

### When to Tour

Timing a trip to Buenos Aires involves knowing what you'll be in for in every season. The most important thing to remember is the most obvious—when it's summer in the United States, it's winter in Argentina, and vice versa. Winter in Argentina generally stretches from July to October, and summer is from December to March. Winters can be chilly and rainy, though the average temperature is always above freezing and it hasn't snowed in Buenos Aires in more than 100 years. Summer is very tropical, hot, and muggy, which is most likely to send you indoors to the air-conditioning (if you can find it) at midday but makes for wonderful, warm nights.

January is when most Porteños go on vacation—primarily to the Atlantic coast—which means that many businesses in Buenos Aires shut down and those that don't close have reduced hours (even most banks, except American Express). In February most banks and government offices open up again, but it's still school vacation, so many stores remain closed until early March. Spring (October–early December) and fall (April–early June) are the best times to visit the city. It's usually warm enough (over 50°F) to travel with just a light jacket. Theater and sports seasons are just starting up or having their grand finales; and Porteños are excited about the summer vacation they've just had or the one they're about to take, so there's an heightened energy in the air.

## San Telmo

The appealing if a bit run-down neighborhood of San Telmo, halfway between midtown Buenos Aires and the south end of the city, is comparable to New York's Greenwich Village. Its cobblestone streets are rich with early 19th-century colonial architecture and mansions, once inhabited by upper-class Spaniards. Over the years the mansions were converted into multifamily housing for the immigrant families (particularly Italians) who began moving to this neighborhood in the late 19th century. For the past 20 years these old houses have been transformed into shops, art galleries, restaurants, and bars. The neighborhood is a cradle of Buenos Aires history and culture (including the tango) and folkloric traditions. Neighborhood highlights include the Sunday flea market, the antiques shops along Calle Defensa, and the tango bars that come to life nightly.

### A Good Walk

To reach San Telmo from anywhere in the city, take Line E to the Independencia stop; from here it's an eight-block walk down Calle Estados Unidos to Calle Defensa. **Plaza Dorrego** ①, at the corner of Calles Defensa and Humberto Primo, is the focal point of San Telmo and the home of the Sunday flea market. Marking the southern edge of San Telmo are the gardens of the **Parque Lezama** ②; the Lezama home is now the **Museo Histórico Nacional** ③. Overlooking the park, visible above the trees lining Avenida Brasil, are the onion-shape domes of the **Iglesia Ortodoxa Rusa** ④. Continue north from the park along Calle Defensa, which is lined with shops and tenement apartment buildings. The street leads past many of the city's best art spaces, including the **Fundación del Rotary Club** ⑤ and the **Museo de Arte Moderno** ⑥. San

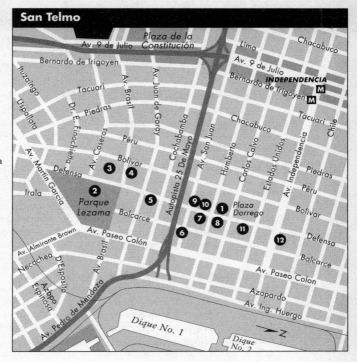

Telmo's antiques shopping district begins at the corner of Calle Defensa and Avenida San Juan. Close to the corner of the Plaza Dorrego, on Calle Humberto Primo, stands a small chapel, **Nuestra Señora del Carmen** ⑦. The adjoining cloister, which later became a hospice and then a prison for women, is now the **Museo Penitenciario Antonio Balve** ⑧. A few relics of the colonial period are still found on Calle Carlos Calvo, just off Calle Defensa, including the **Pasaje Giuffra** ⑨ along with its neighbor, the **Pasaje de la Defensa** ⑩, and **La Casa de Esteban de Luca** ⑪. Continuing along Calle Defensa, take a right on on Calle Independencia to get to the famous **Viejo Almacén** ⑫.

TIMING AND PRECAUTIONS

Plan to go to San Telmo on a Sunday, when the market on Plaza Dorrego bustles with life and there are performers singing and dancing on every corner. A few hours will give you plenty of time to see the sights, but you could easily spend a full day exploring the side streets and shops. San Telmo is one of the city's seedier districts, and you should exercise caution when walking here—especially at night. Violent crime is rare, but unemployment in San Telmo and its neighboring barrios, combined with the knowledge that foreign tourists will always hit the area for at least one tango show, has led to more instances of pickpocketing and muggings.

## Sights to See

⑪ **La Casa de Esteban de Luca** (Esteban de Luca's House). This old home, now a typical Argentine restaurant, was declared a National Historic Monument in 1941. It belonged to Esteban de Luca, a distinguished poet and soldier who wrote Argentina's first national anthem. It's a great place to stop for a bite, taking in a bit of history with your Argentine wine. ⊠ *Defensa 1000,* ☎ *11/4361–4338.*

❺ **Fundación del Rotary Club** (Rotary Club Foundation). The Rotary Club Foundation, housed in a fine postcolonial house with an enclosed courtyard, puts on monthly shows by contemporary Argentine and international artists and hosts concerts. ✉ *Defensa 1344,* ☎ *11/4361–5485.* 🎟 *Free.* ☉ *Weekdays after 4 (call for exact concert times), Sat. 8–8.*

❹ **Iglesia Ortodoxa Rusa** (Russian Orthodox Church). The church with its sky blue dome was hastily built in the late 1910s by the eclectic Danish architect Alejandro Cristophersen for the congregation of Russians who had settled in the city. The property, strangely, still belongs to Russia. ✉ *Av. Brasil 315.* ☉ *Sat. 6 PM–8:30 PM, Sun. 10 AM–12:30 PM.*

❻ **Museo de Arte Moderno** (Modern Art Museum). This old cigarette factory with a classical brick facade has been transformed into the Museum of Modern Art. It holds temporary shows by local painters and sculptors and permanent exhibits of prominent international contemporary artists. It's often possible to meet the artists here—in lectures or just hanging out at the gallery—discussing their own works and those of others. ✉ *Av. San Juan 350,* ☎ *11/4361–1121.* 🎟 *Admission; free on Wed.* ☉ *Tues.–Fri. 10–8, weekends and holidays 11–8.*

★ ❸ **Museo Histórico Nacional** (National Historical Museum). The Lezama family home, an example of a stately but decaying old mansion, is now the National Historical Museum. The focus is on the official history of Argentina from the 16th century to the beginning of the 1900s. Most prominently displayed are memorabilia relating to General José de San Martín and his campaigns in 1810 during the War of Independence against Spain. The jewel of the museum is the collection of paintings by Cándido López, a forceful precursor of contemporary primitive painting. López, who lost an arm in the Paraguayan War of the 1870s, which Paraguay fought against Argentina and Brazil, learned to paint with his left hand and produced an exciting series of war scenes on a scale that would have captivated Cecil B. DeMille. ✉ *Defensa 1600,* ☎ *11/4307–1182.* 🎟 *Free.* ☉ *Feb.–Dec., Tues.–Sun. noon–6.*

❽ **Museo Penitenciario Antonio Balve** (Antonio Balve Penitentiary Museum). This modest museum has mementos of early 20th-century prison life. Behind the museum's large courtyard is **Nuestra Señora del Carmen** (☞ *below*). Next door is an even larger church, the **Parroquia de San Pedro González Telmo** (San González Telmo Parish Church). ✉ *Humberto Primero 378.* 🎟 *Admission.* ☉ *Weekdays 10–noon and 2–5; Sun. noon–6.*

❼ **Nuestra Señora del Carmen.** This chapel behind the Museo Penitenciario Antonio Balve's (☞ *above*) large courtyard dates from the Jesuit period. Next door is the **Parroquia de San Pedro González Telmo** (San González Telmo Parish Church), which was abandoned halfway through its construction by the Jesuits in 1767, when the order was expelled from Argentina, and was not completed until 1858. The cloisters and the domed chapel to the left, designed by Father Andrés Blanqui in 1738, are the only remnants of the original structure. ✉ *Humberto Primero 378.*

❷ **Parque Lezama** (Lezama Park). Enormous magnolia, palm, cedar, and elm trees fill the sloping hillside, and winding paths lead down to the river. The land fell into the hands of an English family in the 1840s, who sold it to George Ridgely Horne, an American businessman, who in turn sold it in 1858 to Gregorio Lezama, an entrepreneur. Lezama decorated the gardens of his luxurious estate with life-size statues and enormous urns. At the end of the last century, his widow donated the property to the city, and it has since become a popular spot for family picnics on weekends. On Sunday an arts and crafts market takes place. ⊠ *Brasil and Paseo Colón.* ⊠ *Free.* ⊙ *Daily, dawn–dusk.*

**⑩ Pasaje de la Defensa** (Defense Alley).This alleyway gives you an idea of what Buenos Aires looked like 200hundred years ago. ⊠ *Off of CalleDefensa*

**❾ Pasaje Giuffra** (Giuffra Alley). A glimpse down this short alley runningtoward the river gives you a sense of what the city looked like two-centuries ago. ⊠ *Off of CalleDefensa.*

★ **❶ Plaza Dorrego** (Dorrego Square). On weekdays this square with outdoor tables shaded by stately old trees provides a peaceful haven for chess-playing pensioners. On Sunday from 10 to 5 the plaza comes alive with the bustling **San Telmo Antiques Fair.** Often you'll find a young couple dancing frenzied tangos on one corner to the music of veteran tango musicians playing violins and *bandoneons* (the local version of the accordion). The fair provides a great opportunity to buy tango memorabilia, leather goods, high-quality silver, and a wide variety of Argentine knickknacks. The buildings surrounding the plaza provide a sampling of the architectural styles—Spanish colonial, French classical, and lots of ornately decorated masonry done by Italian craftsmen—that gained a significant presence in the city in the 19th and 20th centuries.

**⑫ Viejo Almacén.** This popular nightspot for tango (☞ Nightlife and the Arts, *below,* and the Close-Up Box, The Art of Tango, *below*) is another fine example of colonial architecture. The building dates from 1798, during which time it was a general store (Almacén de Campaña). After a stint as a hospital in the 1800s, the building was purchased by Paula Kravnic, the daughter of a Russian immigrant, who transformed it into a tango bar at the turn of the century. The bar gained even greater popularity when it was purchased, in 1969, by Argentine tango sensation Eduardo Rivero. ⊠ *Av. Independencia.*

## La Boca

The vibrant working-class neighborhod of La Boca is the southern neighbor of San Telmo. The first port of Buenos Aires, La Boca has seen many waves of immigrant populations pass through its borders. The most significant and lasting group were Italian immigrants from Genoa, who arrived between 1880 and 1930. Still known as the Little Italy of Argentina, La Boca is the perfect place to find an authentic and inexpensive pizza or an impromptu tango lesson in the street.

### A Good Walk

Your entire experience in La Boca will probably center around the **Calle Museo Caminito** ⑬, an outdoor art market and museum right off Avenida Pedro de Mendoza. Once you reach the end of the Caminito, turn right on Calle Garibaldi. Four blocks down the street is the imposing **Estadio de Boca Juniors** ⑭, home to one of the most popular soccer teams in Argentina. Take a right on Calle Brandsen and another right on Calle del Valle Iberlucea to get back to the entrance to the Caminito. To your left on Avenida Pedro de Mendoza is the **Museo de Bellas Artes de La Boca de Artistas Argentinos** ⑮, a noteworthy neighborhood museum.

TIMING AND PRECAUTIONS

You could easily spend an entire day in La Boca, meandering about and taking in the sights, but you really only need 1½–2 hours to see everything. It's best to stay in the area of the Caminito, which is well patrolled by local police, and not to stray too far, as the neighborhood

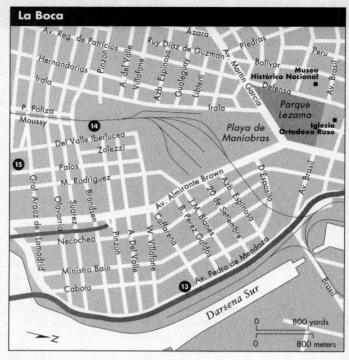

borders other barrios that aren't very safe. There are few reasons for
you to go to La Boca at night, and it would be safer not to do so. Note
that La Boca is the land of the unleashed dog: Beware where you step,
and certainly remember that while neighborhood dogs are accustomed
to people, they may not react kindly to being petted.

## Sights to See

★ ⓵⓷ **Calle Museo Caminito** (Caminito Museum Street). The Caminito is a
colorful pedestrians-only street that since 1959 has functioned as an
open-air museum and art market. It's only about a block and a half
long, but you can find numerous quality souvenirs, sculptures, and free
open-air tango demonstrations. Walking along the Caminito, notice
the distinctive, rather hastily constructed architecture, which is often
painted in vibrant colors to cover shoddy materials. ⊠ *Av. Pedro de
Mendoza and Calle Palos.* ⌚ *Free.* ☉ *Daily 10–6.*

⓵⓸ **Estadio de Boca Juniors** (Boca Juniors Stadium). The Boca Juniors are
one of Argentina's most popular soccer teams and, as such, are the proud
owners of a very distinctive stadium. If you have the chance to visit
the stadium on a game day, be prepared for crowds, pandemonium,
and street parties—and never wear red and white, the colors of River
Plate, the rival team! ⊠ *Brandsen 805.*

⓵⓹ **Museo de Bellas Artes de La Boca de Artistas Argentinos** (La Boca Fine
Arts Museum of Argentine Artists). This local fine arts museum is worth
a visit, as it provides a good overview of Argentine artistic history. It
closes in summer for renovation and to set up new exhibits, so it's wise
to call ahead to see if it's open. ⊠ *Av. Pedro de Mendoza 1835,* ☎ *11/
4301–1080.* ⌚ *Free.* ☉ *Weekdays 8–6, weekends 10–5.*

# Plaza de Mayo

In a well-known scene in the musical *Evita,* Eva Perón stands on a picturesque balcony and waves to the Argentine masses assembled on a square below. She is supposed to be here, at the Plaza de Mayo. The political and historical center of Buenos Aires, the square is home to the presidential palace and other governmental buildings. It has survived wars, floods, and political upheaval; on every corner you see evidence of its history. Its attractions are principally architectural—the cathedral, where you may catch site of visiting dignitaries (as well as Argentina's president) at Sunday services, and some well-preserved remnants of Spanish colonial architecture.

## A Good Walk

Get your bearings at the **Plaza de Mayo** ⑯. At the eastern end of the square, the Casa de Gobierno (Presidential Office Building), better known as the **Casa Rosada** ⑰, dominates the view toward the river. At the far western end of Avenida de Mayo is the tall dome that's home to Argentina's parliament, the **Congreso** ⑱. All along Avenida de Mayo, which was built in the manner of a Parisian boulevard (although more often compared to avenues in Budapest), are sidewalk cafés and interesting buildings. Across Avenida Rivadavía, adding a conservative tone to the plaza's profile, is the **Banco de la Nación Argentina** ⑲. On the next block is the **Catedral Metropolitana** ⑳, which hardly looks like a Latin-American church. Continue to the plaza's west side to see the historic town council building, the **Cabildo** ㉑. Leaving the plaza, walk one block on Diagonal Sur to reach **La Manzana de las Luces** ㉒ and the Colegio Nacional, the country's leading public school. Next to the school is Buenos Aires's oldest church, the **Parroquia de San Ignacio** ㉓. Continue east on Calle Alsina to the **Museo de la Ciudad** ㉔, which has exhibits on the history of Buenos Aires. Across Calle Defensa is the **Basilica y Convento de San Francisco** ㉕, a colonial-era church, and the smaller Capilla San Roque, to its left. Another of the city's oldest churches, **Santo Domingo** ㉖, is two blocks south on Calle Defensa. From here, you can reach Puerto Madero (☞ *below*) by walking five blocks east along Belgrano and then continuing north along the riverfront. Alternatively, you can get to Puerto Madero by walking directly east on Calle Alsina or Calle Mitre from Plaza de Mayo.

TIMING AND PRECAUTIONS

This walk will probably take about two hours, though you could easily spend a full day exploring all the sights in the area. To be safe when taking a taxi in this area, avoid hailing one in front of a bank because people will think you've just taken out money and may rob your cab; instead, hail one in front of a local coffee shop, where you're much less likely to be a potential victim of a robbery. On weekends the streets are deserted, so pay close attention to your belongings, especially when walking alone.

## Sights to See

⑲ **Banco de la Nación Argentina** (National Bank of Argentina). This imposing state bank was designed in 1940 in monumental Neoclassical style by architect Alejandro Bustillo, who designed most of the city's government buildings in the 1930s and 1940s. ⊠ *At corner of Reconquista and Rivadavía.*

㉕ **Basilica y Convento de San Francisco** (Convent and Basilica of St. Francis). Originally built in 1754, the Bavarian Baroque facade was added in 1911, and the interior was lavishly refurbished after the church was looted and burned in 1955 in the turmoil just before

# 24

# Plaza de Mayo and El Centro

Santiago del
Av. A. Alcorta
San José
SAN JOSÉ Ⓜ
Sol
Av. Brasil
Estero
Estacion
Constitución
F.C.G. Roca Ⓜ
Constitución
Autopista 25 De Mayo
Humberto
Carlos Calvo
Estados Unidos
Chile
Mexico
Venezuela
Virre
Luis Se
Salta
Lima
Plaza de la
Constitución
Lima Este
San José
Av. 9 de Julio
Santiago del Ester
B. de Irigoyen
Av. 9 de Julio
Salta
Tecuari
INDEPENDENCIA Ⓜ
Lima
Piedras
Tacuari
Bernardo de Irigoyen
SAN TELMO
Av. San Juan
Piedras
Tacuari
AV DE MA
Cochabamba
Chacabuco
Av. Independencia
Péru
Autopista 25 De Mayo
Péru
Venezuela
Av. Belgrano
Moreno
Adolfo Alsina
Museo
Histórico
Nacional ▪
Iglesia
Ortodoxo
Ruso ▪
Bolivar
Av. Julio A. Roca
Defensa
Casa de
Esteban
De Luca ▪
PLAZA
DE MAYO
Av. Martin Garcia
Parque
Lezama
Fundación
San Telmo ▪
22
Av. Almirante
Brown
Museo de Arte
Moderno ▪
Plaza
Dorrego ▪
Viejo Almacén ▪
23
21
D'Esposito
Av. Paseo Colón
Balcarce
26
24 BOLIVAR Ⓜ
Av. Brasil
Av. Paseo Colon
25
16
PLAZA DE MAYO
Pla
de
Azopardo
Av. Ing. Huergo
Plaza
P. Justo
Ⓜ
17
Av. Pedro de Mendoza
Dique 1
Plaza
P. Justo
Parque
Colón
Dique 2
Av. Eduardo Mode
Av. Brasil
Dique 3
0    800 yards
0    800 meters    N
Calabria

Perón's government fell. Inside, an archive of 20,000 books remains. ✉ *Defensa and Alsina,* ☎ *11/4331–0625.* 🎫 *Free.*

**㉑ Cabildo** (Town Council). The town council building is considered one of Argentina's national shrines. In May 1810 patriotic citizens gathered here to vote against Spanish rule. The original building dates from 1765 but has been the product of successive renovations, the latest of which was in 1948. Inside is a small museum, but the building alone is worth the trip. After visiting this monument, you can't help but notice how many places in the city are named Cabildo. ✉ *Bolívar 65,* ☎ *11/4334–1782.* 🎫 *Free.* 🕐 *Tues.–Fri. 12:30–7, Sun. 3–7; guided tours at 3 and 5.*

**⑰ Casa Rosada** (Pink House). The Casa de Gobierno (Government Palace), better known as the Casa Rosada, is the government headquarters (the president doesn't live here, though). The elite Grenadiers Regiment keeps close guard over the pale pink house. The first-floor balcony on the building's northern wing is used by the country's leaders to address the enormous crowds that gather below. This is where Evita came to rally the workers and where Madonna sang her rendition of "Don't Cry for Me Argentina" (the ugly window air-conditioning units were taken out for the movie). In back, on the basement level, the brick walls of the **Taylor Customs House**—which dates from the 1850s—have been partially uncovered after being buried for half a century, when the Plaza Colón was built. The site can be seen from the outside or as part of a visit to the adjoining **Museo de la Casa Rosada,** a museum containing presidential memorabilia. You may find it interesting that unlike a White House tour, the tour of the Casa Rosada Museum is relatively unsupervised, leading you to wonder just a little about security issues. ✉ *Hipólito Yrigoyen 211,* ☎ *11/4343–3051 or 11/4374–9841 for guided tours.* 🎫 *Free; charge for guided tours.* 🕐 *Mon.–Tues. and Thurs.–Fri. 10–6; Sun. 2–6; guided tours at 4.*

**⑳ Catedral Metropolitana** (Metropolitan Cathedral). The first building on this site was an adobe ranch house, which disappeared in 1593. Since then the land has been continually in use. But it wasn't until 1822 that the Neoclassical facade of the Metropolitan Cathedral was begun (the building itself predates the facade by a century). The remains of General José de San Martín, known as the Argentine Liberator for his role in the War of Independence against Spain, are buried here in a marble mausoleum carved by the French sculptor Carrière Belleuse. The tomb is permanently guarded by soldiers of the Grenadier Regiment, a troop created and trained by San Martín in 1811. ✉ *At Rivadavía and San Martín,* ☎ *11/4331–2845.* 🎫 *Free.* 🕐 *Guided tour weekdays 1:30, Sat. 10:30 and 11:15.*

**⑱ Congreso.** Built in 1906, the exterior was modeled after the U.S. Congress building. The building is surrounded by an attractive park, and is considered Kilometer 0 for every Argentine highway. ✉ *Plaza del Congreso.* 🕐 *Not open to the public.*

**㉒ La Manzana de las Luces** (Block of Bright Lights). This block of buildings was constructed in the early 1800s on property that originally belonged to the Jesuits, who were expelled in 1767. Home to a succession of schools, it's famous as the breeding ground for Argentina's *intelligentsía* and it houses Argentina's most famous school. The bulky Neoclassical building on the site, where the San Ignacio school once stood, is now home to the **Colegio Nacional,** the country's leading public high school. You can take a guided tour of La Manzana de las Luces and the surrounding area; though infrequent and conducted in Spanish, these tours are worthwhile (call to verify the times listed below, as tour times change frequently). Going on a tour is your only chance to view the cavernous, historic tunnels that run under La Manzana. The tours follow various routes: Circuit B brings you to the tunnels and nearby churches; Circuit C takes you to the tunnels and the old State Representatives room; Circuit D takes you through the Colegio Nacional; and Circuit E takes you to the tunnels and past historic local homes. ⊠ *Péru 272,* ☎ *11/4342–6973.* ☒ *Admission.* ☉ *Guided tours on weekends between 3 and 6:30 PM.*

**㉔ Museo de la Ciudad** (Municipal Museum). This museum houses temporary exhibitions both whimsical and probing about many aspects of domestic and public life in Buenos Aires in times past. On the ground floor, for instance, is the **Farmacia La Estrella** (Star Pharmacy), a quaint survivor from the 19th century. ⊠ *Calle Alsina 412,* ☎ *11/4331–9855 or 11/4343–2123.* ☒ *Admission.* ☉ *Weekdays 11–7, Sun. 3–7.*

**㉓ Parroquia de San Ignacio** (St. Ignatius Church). Started in 1713, this church is the only one from that era to have a Baroque facade. Behind the church, a Neoclassical facade dating from 1863 hides the old colonial building that headquartered the administrators of the Jesuits' vast land holdings in northeastern Argentina and Paraguay. In 1780 the city's first Facultad de Medicina (Medical School) was established here, and in the early 19th century was home to the Universidad de Buenos Aires (University of Buenos Aires). The tunnels underneath the building, which crisscrossed the colonial town and were used either by the military or by smugglers, depending on which version you believe, can still be visited by guided tour (☞ La Manzana de las Luces, *above*). ⊠ *Bolívar 225,* ☎ *11/4331–2458.* ☒ *Free.* ☉ *Tours on weekends at 3:30 and 5.*

★ **⑯ Plaza de Mayo** (May Square). This two-block-long square has been the stage for many important events, including the uprising against Spain on May 25, 1810, in memory of which the square was given its name. The present layout dates from 1912, when the obelisk known as the **Piramide de Mayo** was placed in the center; it was erected in 1811 to celebrate the first anniversary of the Revolution of May. A bronze equestrian statue of General Manuel Belgrano, cast in 1873, stands at the east end of the plaza. The tradition of staging celebrations and protests in this central plaza continues to this day. It's here that the Madres de la Plaza de Mayo (Mothers of Plaza de Mayo), the mothers of young *desaparecidos,* young people who were "disappeared" during the military government's reign from 1976 to 1983, still hold their Thursday-afternoon marches, which attracted international attention in the late 1970s.

**㉖ Santo Domingo.** Built in the 1750s, this convent is dedicated to Our Lady of the Rosary. On display in the chapel are four banners captured in 1806 from fleeing British troops—after their unsuccessful attempt to invade the then-Spanish colony—and two flags taken from the Spanish armies during the War of Independence. On one of the bell towers, bullet craters—testimony to the battle with British soldiers—are reminders of the conflict. The remains of General Manuel Belgrano, a hero of the War of Independence, rest in the courtyard's central mausoleum, guarded by marble angels. ⊠ *Defensa 422,* ☎ *11/4331–1668.* ☒ *Free.*

# El Centro

Your first glimpse of El Centro will most likely be en route from the airport. But be sure to return: Walking around the city center, dominated by a giant obelisk and the never-sleeping Avenida Corrientes, gives you a good feel for cosmopolitan Buenos Aires and its passionate Latin spirit. From the packed pedestrians-only Calle Florida and Calle

Lavalle to the urban calm of Plaza San Martín, this is the social and business center of Argentina.

## A Good Walk

El Centro can be reached by subte; in fact, every subway line goes through it. The most logical stop for this walk is called Estación 9 de Julio (alternately known as Estación Carlos Pelligrini), which puts you right at the obelisk as you exit the subway. The area is also accessible from Estación Plaza San Martín and Estación Lavalle.

Start your walk on **Plaza San Martín** ㉗. On one side of the park is the **Palacio San Martín** ㉘ and on another, the **Círculo Militar** ㉙. Across Calle Marcelo T. de Alvear from the Círculo, behind the sixth-floor windows of the corner apartment at No. 994 Calle Maipú, are the rooms where Jorge Luis Borges lived and wrote many of his short stories and poems. Also right here are the **Edificio Kavanagh** ㉚ and the landmark **Marriott Plaza Hotel** ㉛. The **Galería Ruth Benzacar** ㉜, with good exhibits of contemporary art, forms the entrance to Calle Florida, down a set of stairs. Take this crowded pedestrians-only shopping street south to get to one of Buenos Aires's nicest shopping centers, the **Galerías Pacífico** ㉝. Continue along Calle Florida until you reach Avenida Corrientes, the "street that never sleeps"; it's lined with theaters and cinemas and bustles with activity day and night. Turn right (west) and walk toward the giant **Obelisco** ㉞. The **Teatro Colón** ㉟ is two blocks north of the obelisk on vast Avenida 9 de Julio.

TIMING AND PRECAUTIONS

Set aside a full day to explore El Centro. It's an easy area to navigate on foot, though summer heat and crowds may leave you begging for air-conditioning. On weekdays it's packed, on Saturday it's relatively calm, and by Sunday it's nearly deserted. Many stores and most restaurants have limited hours on weekends. In January most businesses (including banks) in El Centro close, though some may have extremely limited hours. You'll notice as you meander along Calle Lavalle that, although it is a center of shopping and commerce, it's also home to many of the adult entertainment establishments in Buenos Aires. It's advised that you take proper precautions when visiting the area at night.

## Sights to See

㉙ **Círculo Militar** (Military Circle). A monument to the nobler historic pursuits of the Argentine armed forces, the Officers' Club was built by French architect Louis Sortais in 1902 in the heavily ornamental French style of the period. The **Museo Nacional de Armas** (National Arms Museum), in the basement, is packed with military memorabilia. ⊠ *Av. Santa Fe 750,* ☎ *11/4311–1071.* ☜ *Free.* ☉ *Mar.–Dec., Tues.–Fri. 2–7, Sat. 11–5, Sun. 1–6.*

㉚ **Edificio Kavanagh** (Kavanagh Building). The soaring Kavanagh apartment building was constructed in the 1930s in the then-popular Rationalist style by a displaced New Yorker. It's still one of the nicest-looking apartment buildings in the city. ⊠ *On San Martín, a few doors down from Plaza San Martín.*

㉜ **Galería Ruth Benzacar** (Ruth Benzacar Gallery). This well-designed gallery has monthly shows of significant modern Argentine artists. If you want a stimulating overview of contemporary Argentine art, ask to see the vast collection of paintings in the basement. ⊠ *Florida 1000,* ☎ *11/4313–8480.* ☜ *Free.* ☉ *Mon–Sat. 9:30–8.*

㉝ **Galerías Pacífico** (Pacífico Shopping Center). The former headquarters of the Buenos Aires–Pacific Railway, the building was designed during Buenos Aires's turn-of-the-century golden age as a copy of Milan's

Gallerie Vittorio Emanuele. In 1992 it was turned into a glossy, multilevel American-style shopping mall. In an earlier renovation a large skylighted dome was added, and five leading Argentine artists were commissioned to paint murals (☞ Shopping, *below*). ✉ *Florida 753.*

**NEED A BREAK?** On the second floor of the **Galerías Pacífico** (✉ Florida 753), above the ground-floor commotion, is a quiet oasis with comfortable couches and chairs, serving good coffee and champagne. It's right next to the information counter, where you can pick up brochures and maps.

**③①** **Marriott Plaza Hotel.** In 1908 local financier Ernesto Tornquist commissioned German architect Alfred Zucker to build the Plaza Hotel, a building that—like its namesake in New York City—still maintains its glow. ✉ *Plaza San Martín.*

**③④** **Obelisco** (Obelisk). This enormous 221½-ft-tall obelisk is one of the city's most prominent landmarks; it was built in 1936 as part of a major public-works program. If you're in Buenos Aires during an election or a major soccer match, you'll witness crowds of Porteños surrounding the obelisk, voicing their opinions about the day's events. ✉ *Av. 9 de Julio and Corrientes.*

**②⑧** **Palacio San Martín** (San Martín Palace). Once the residence of the Anchorena family, the palace has been the Ministry of Foreign Affairs since 1936. The ornate building, designed in 1909 by Alejandro Cristophersen in grandiose French Neoclassical style, is an example of the turn-of-the-century opulence of Buenos Aires. ✉ *Arenales 800.* ☉ *Not open to public.*

**OFF THE BEATEN PATH** **MUSEO DE ARTE HISPANOAMERICANO ISAAC FERNÁNDEZ BLANCO –** Built as the residence of the architect Martín Noel in the late 18th century in an eclectic post–Spanish colonial style, it's now home to the Isaac Fernández Blanco Hispanic-American Art Museum. The extensive collection of colonial silver, wood carvings, and paintings gives you a sense of the wealth and the quality of craftsmanship in colonial South America. The overgrown, almost junglelike garden provides an awesome background for the outdoor theatrical performances mounted here during the summer. ✉ Suipacha 1422, ☎ 11/4327–0228. ☞ Admission. ☉ Feb.– Dec., Tues.–Sun. 2–8.

**②⑦** **Plaza San Martín** (San Martín Square). Once a field in a muddy suburb at the northern end of the city next to the steep riverbank, Plaza San Martín gradually evolved into its present state. At one time populated by vagrants and marginal members of the rough-and-tumble colonial society, the area around the square was transformed in the late 1800s into the site of some of the most sumptuous town houses in Buenos Aires. The imposing bronze equestrian monument to General José de San Martín, created in 1862 by French artist Louis Daumas, dominates the park. French landscape architect Charles Thays designed the plaza in the 19th century, using a mix of traditional local and exotic imported trees. To get a feel for real life in Buenos Aires, plan a visit to Plaza San Martín during a weekday lunch hour and relax in the crowded park while you watch business deals being hashed out and young lovers sneaking a kiss.

**NEED A BREAK?** Wouldn't now be perfect time for a great glass of Argentine wine in a cool, hidden grotto? Then head to **Tancat** (✉ Paraguay 645, ☎ 11/4312–5442), a dark, friendly establishment where you'll most likely end up sitting at the bar as there's only one table. The menu consists of whatever the chef decides to cook that day, but the food is always good.

★ ㉟  **Teatro Colón** (Colón Theater). This opera house opened in 1908 and
has hosted the likes of Maria Callas, Arturo Toscanini, Igor Stravin-
sky, Enrico Caruso, and Luciano Pavarotti. Argentines proudly claim
that the theater has the best acoustics in the world, and few would argue.
The Italianate building with French decoration is the result of a joint
effort by several successive turn-of-the-century architects. The seven-
tier theater has a central chandelier with a sprawling diameter of 21
ft. Yet because there are only 2,500 seats, many of which are held by
season-ticket holders, the lines stretch around the block when an international celebrity is starring. A fascinating guided tour of the theater and museum provides a glimpse at the building's inner workshops,
45 ft below the street. The international season runs from April to
November. ✉ *Toscanini 1180,* ☎ *11/4382–6632.* ▢ *Admission.* ◔
*Jan.–Mar., tours hourly weekdays 10–5; fewer tours in winter.*

## Puerto Madero

The revived old port has witnessed the proliferation of offices and fine
restaurants in the past few years, making it *the* place to enjoy a coffee
or dinner and a walk along the riverfront boardwalk. The port was
originally constructed in 1890 as the European gateway to Argentina
but spent most of the 20th century abandoned due to the creation of
a new port (Puerto Nuevo). In August 1998 Puerto Madero was hon-
ored as the 47th area to be designated a barrio of Buenos Aires, a tribute to its significant transformation.

### A Good Walk

Start off from the Leandro Alem subte station and walk down Avenida
Corrientes towards the river. As you go, notice the change in architecture, from Spanish colonial buildings to modern glass high-rises and
refurbished port buildings. Continue along Avenida Corrientes, across
Calle Bouchard and past Luna Park (☞ Outdoor Activities and Sports,
*below*), where many sporting events and concerts are held. Pass Avenida
Eduardo Madero, and you are in Puerto Madero. (Note that Avenida
Eduardo Madero and Avenida Ing. Huergo are the same street but that
the name changes as you continue along the dock.) Walk one block
more to get to the main drag of Puerto Madero: Avenida Alicia M. de
Justo. Docked here is the **Buque Museo Fragata A.R.A. Presidente
Sarmiento** ㊱, an impressive Argentine battleship that is now a museum
(when it's not in use). At the end of the dock is Cine 8, one of Buenos
Aires's best cinemas; take a break here with an Argentine or Hollywood film.

TIMING AND PRECAUTIONS

You could easily spend half a day just walking Puerto Madero's 15-
block boardwalk. In the morning the dock is a nice place to sit outside and enjoy an espresso; during the day the port fills with the
commotion of business transpiring; and in the evening it attracts a fashionable crowd that comes to dine in the many restaurants. Though Puerto
Madero is well patrolled by both private security and Buenos Aires police, there are pickpockets, so you should keep an eye on your wallet
both on the dock and in restaurants.

### Sights to See

㊱  **Buque Museo Fragata A.R.A. Presidente Sarmiento** (President Sarmiento
Ship Museum). A classic warship, the *Presidente Sarmiento* was constructed in 1898 and has completed 39 around-the-world voyages. When
not being used for military training, it's docked and open to the public as a museum. ✉ *Dique 3, Puerto Madero,* ☎ *11/4334–9386.* ▢
*Admission.* ◔ *Weekdays 9 AM–8 PM, weekends 9 AM–10 PM.*

Buque Museo
Fragata A.R.A.
Presidente
Sarmiento, **36**

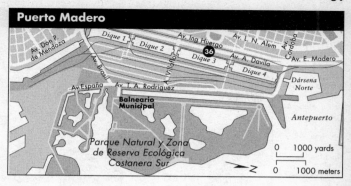

**Puerto Madero**

*Av. Don P. de Mendoza* — *Dique 1* — *Dique 2* — *Av. Ing Huergo* — *Av. L. N. Alem* — *Av. Córdoba*

*Av. Brasil* — *Av. J. Vilaflor* — *Dique 3* — **36** — *Av. A. Davila* — *Av. E. Madero*

*Av. España* — *Av. T. A. Rodríguez* — *Dique 4*

*Dársena Norte*

**Balneario Municipal**

*Antepuerto*

*Parque Natural y Zona de Reserva Ecológica Costanera Sur*

0 — 1000 yards
0 — 1000 meters

N

OFF THE
BEATEN PATH

If you find yourself feeling out of touch with nature, head to the **Reserva Ecolójica** (Ecological Reserve), just a short taxi ride from Puerto Madero. A perfect spot for bike rides and nature walks, the reserve is said to be home to more than 500 species of birds. A guided tour of the reserve called "Walking under the Full Moon" (voluntary charge) is given at 8 PM daily. The reserve is in a prime location, and many real-estate developers have their eyes on it as a site for luxury office buildings, so most Porteños don't expect the park to be here much longer. ⊠ *Av. Tristán Achával Rodríguez 1550,* ☎ *11/4315–1320.* ⊞ *Free, but voluntary donation requested for park upkeep.* ⊙ *Apr.–Dec., daily 8–6; Jan.–Mar., daily, 8–sunset.*

# La Recoleta

La Recoleta, an elegant residential and shopping district northwest of downtown, is packed with boutiques, cafés, handsome old apartment buildings, plazas, museums, and cultural centers. Once a neighborhood where nobody wanted to live, today La Recoleta is one of Buenos Aires's most sought-after districts, surpassed in trendiness only recently by Puerto Madero (☞ *above*). About 25 years ago a few brave entrepreneurs decided to take advantage of its low rents, opening some of the city's best restaurants. Upscale, European-style boutiques followed, and then members of Argentina's high society began moving here as well. Part of La Recoleta is now closed to traffic, and street-side cafés dot the area. Here people-watching is a highly developed art form, practiced predominantly by the perennially tanned and trim.

## A Good Walk

No subte route directly serves La Recoleta. The closest stop is Estación Pueyrredón, an eight-block walk south (plans, however, are in the works for a new subway line which is supposed to service the area by the year 2001).

Begin your walk on **Plazoleta Carlos Pelligrini** ㊲. On one side is the **Alzaga Unzué** ㊳. Follow Avenida Alvear, Buenos Aires's most elegant avenue, lined with some of the best in French-style architecture and boutiques and the beautiful **Alvear Palace Hotel** ㊴. Continue along Avenida Alvear to get to the **Cementerio de La Recoleta** ㊵, the final resting place for some of Argentina's most distinguished citizens. Bordering the cemetery is the **Basílica del Pilar** ㊶. Just down the block from the basilica is the **Centro Cultural La Recoleta** ㊷, where art shows and performances are held. Below the cultural center is the Design Center (☞ *Shopping, below*), a mall filled entirely with home-furnishings stores. To your right, at the bottom of the hill, is the yellow **Palais de Glace–Salas Nacionales de Cultura** ㊸, which hosts all kinds of temporary

**32**

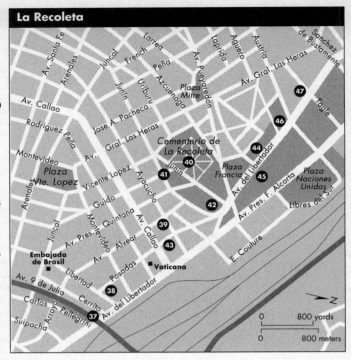

exhibits. From here walk west along Avenida del Libertador, past Plaza Francia and **Plaza Mitre** ⑷ to get to the **Museo Nacional de Bellas Artes** ㊺, the city's major art museum, the **Biblioteca Nacional** ㊻, a modern library, and the **Museo Nacional de Arte Decorativo** ㊼, a decorative arts museum in an impressive Classical building.

### TIMING AND PRECAUTIONS

Count on at least half a day to explore La Recoleta, though you could easily spend a morning or afternoon in the cemetery or art museum alone. In general, this is one of the city's safest areas and can be visited day and night.

## Sights to See

**㊷ Alvear Palace Hotel.** The city's most traditional, old-world hotel opened its doors in 1932. It remains a principal gathering place for the Porteño elite. The elegant lobby is a great spot to stop for tea or a drink (☞ Lodging, *below*). ✉ *Av. Alvear 1891,* ☎ *11/4808–2100 or 11/4804–7777.*

**㊳ Alzaga Unzué.** This French Renaissance–style house built in the late 19th century was saved from demolition by a group of local conservationists in the Perón era. Now a part of the Park Hyatt Hotel (☞ Lodging, *below*), the tower of the hotel rises from what was once the garden, and the old house is now called La Mansion. ✉ *Posadas 1086.*

**㊶ Basílica del Pilar** (Basilica of the Pillar). In 1732 Franciscan monks built this church and cloister complex, which are fine examples of early colonial Baroque. The principal altar is made of engraved silver from Peru. Today the church is a popular place for weddings, and you can sometimes see the elegantly dressed guests mingling with the craftspeople who hold a weekend fair on the slopes of the adjoining park. ✉ *Junin*

*1898, ☎ 11/4803–6793. 🖾 Free. ☉ Weekdays 7:30–1 and 4–8:30, weekends 1–6.*

**㊻ Biblioteca Nacional** (National Library). It took three decades to build the National Library, which was finally inaugurated in 1991. The eccentric modern building was the result of a design competition won by Argentine architects Clorindo Testa and Francisco Bullrich. ✉ *Aguero 2502,* ☎ *11/4806–6155.* 🖾 *Free.* ☉ *Mon.–Sat. 10–7.*

**★ ㊵ Cementerio de La Recoleta** (La Recoleta Cemetery). As you enter the tall, ominous gates of the vast, 13½-acre La Recoleta Cemetery, you can feel history around you. You may sense the wealth as well, since this is the costliest bit of land in all of Argentina, and it contains the elaborate mausoleums of a veritable who's who of Argentine history: presidents, political leaders, soldiers, authors, and other heroes. The cemetery also functions as a mini-tour of art, sculpture, and architecture. Mausoleums were built to resemble chapels, Greek temples, pyramids, and scaled-down versions of family homes. In some you need to go inside to see what's special about them; for a small tip it's often possible to get a caretaker to open one of the multifloor mausoleums for you so that you look inside. The embalmed body of Eva Duarte de Perón rests here in the Duarte family tomb. To find Evita, from the entrance walk straight to the first major crossway and turn left; walk straight until a mausoleum stands in your way; walk around it on the right and then turn right; continue three rows down and turn left (or, just follow the sea of tourists who pay tribute to her at her tomb). Look, too, for the flowers placed on the tomb and the epitaph in Spanish that reads "Don't Cry for Me." Also worth looking for is the handsome statue of Luis Angel Firpo, the world heavyweight boxing champion known as the Bull of the Pampas. There's no map of the cemetery, so be prepared to walk in circles. ✉ *Entrance on Junin.* ☉ *Daily 10–5.*

**㊷ Centro Cultural La Recoleta** (La Recoleta Cultural Center). On weekends this cultural center attracts thousands of visitors to its exhibits, concerts, and performances. It's also a resource for other arts events happening around the city. ✉ *Junin 1930,* ☎ *11/4803–1041.* 🖾 *Free.* ☉ *Tues.–Sat. after 2 (call for specific hrs), all day Sun.*

OFF THE
BEATEN PATH

**EMBAJADA DE BRASIL** – This building—now the Brazilian Embassy—has a stately Neoclassical facade. But inside is an even better treasure: A series of murals by Spanish artist José Luis Sert covers the walls and ceilings. Unfortunately, it's not open to the public. ✉ *Arroyo 1142.*

**EMBAJADA DE FRANCIA** – Now the French Embassy, this building was once the home of the Ortiz Basualdo family. The house was designed in the early 20th century by French architect Phillipe Pater; the building is of such monumental importance that the city decided to loop the continuation of Avenida 9 de Julio around the back of it rather than razing the structure. Unfortunately, it's not open to the public. ✉ *Cerrito 1339.*

**★ ㊼ Museo Nacional de Arte Decorativo** (National Museum of Decorative Art). This museum is in a magnificent French Classical landmark building (it's worth the price of admission just to enter this breathtaking structure). It houses a fascinating collection of furnishings and home decor; most was donated by Argentina's leading families. Also here is the **Museo de Arte Oriental** (Museum of Eastern Art), which has art and articles from places such as India and the Middle East. The museum café is great for a snack. ✉ *Av. del Libertador 1902,* ☎ *11/4801–8248.* 🖾 *Admission.* ☉ *Weekdays 2–8, weekends 11–7.*

**45** **Museo Nacional de Bellas Artes** (National Museum of Fine Arts). Buenos Aires's only major art museum is housed in a building that was once the city's waterworks. The museum's collection includes several major Impressionist paintings and an overview of 19th- and 20th-century Argentine art. The highlight is a room dedicated to Paraguayan War scenes painted by a soldier, Cándido López, whose work is also in the National Historical Museum (☞ San Telmo, *above*). The new wing has a selections of contemporary Argentine art and temporary exhibits. ⊠ *Av. del Libertador 1473,* ☎ *11/4803–0802 for a tour.* ☒ *Free.* ☉ *Tues.–Sun. 12:30–7:30.*

**43** **Palais de Glace–Salas Nacionales de Cultura** (Mirror Palace–National Cultural Exhibition Halls). Always worth checking out are the changing exhibits, ranging from fine art to ponchos to national foods, at this exhibition hall. The banner outside will tell you what's going on. ⊠ *Posadas 1725,* ☎ *11/4805-4354.* ☒ *Admission.* ☉ *Weekdays 1–8, weekends 3–8.*

**37** **Plazoleta Carlos Pellegrini** (Carlos Pellegrini Square). This square is surrounded by a cluster of mansions, which were once residences of the country's large landowning families and are now apartment buildings.

**44** **Plaza Mitre.** A large equestrian statue of General Bartolomé Mitre, the military hero and former president, dominates this square on Avenida del Libertador between Calle Luis Agote and Calle Aguero. The site, which was once at the edge of the river, provides a perspective on the surrounding parks.

# Palermo

Palermo, a district of parks and lakes surrounded by quiet streets and elegant mansions, offers a peaceful escape from the rush of downtown Buenos Aires. Families flock to the parks on weekends to picnic, suntan, bicycle, rollerblade, and jog. Palermo is also home to the polo field and the horse racetrack and is thus the center of horse culture in Buenos Aires. One of the city's largest barrios, Palermo has many distinct sub-neighborhoods: *Palermo Viejo* has classic Spanish-style architecture; *Las Cañitas* is a trendy place to go out at night; and *Palermo Chico* is an elegant residential area. Some of the most expensive real estate in Argentina is found along Avenida del Libertador, which cuts Palermo down the middle. But don't let Palermo's daytime tranquility fool you: At night it gives way to some of the city's best nightlife, as neighborhood bars and discos rock to Latin beats.

## A Good Walk

The Estación Plaza Italia, on Line D, takes you to the zoo and the botanical gardens in Palermo. Some of city's biggest parks are found in this neighborhood around the **Plaza Italia** 48, at the intersection of Avenida Sarmiento, Calle Santa Fe, and Calle Las Heras: the **Jardín Botánico** 49, the **Jardín Zoológico** 50, and the **Sociedad Rural Argentina** 51, the city's fairgrounds. Palermo's largest park, the **Parque Tres de Febrero** 52, is farther down Avenida Sarmiento. Essentially a part of the park, though technically freestanding, the **Paseo del Rosedal** 53 is abloom, in season, with all kinds of roses. Deeper into the park is the **Jardín Japonés** 54, a lovely Japanese garden, and the **Planetario Galileo Galilei** 55, the planetarium.

TIMING AND PRECAUTIONS

An even-paced ramble through Palermo should take no more than two hours, though you could easily spend an entire afternoon at the zoo, the Japanese Garden, and the Botanical Garden. If you're up for shopping, visit Alto Palermo (☞ Shopping, *below*), one of the city's nicer

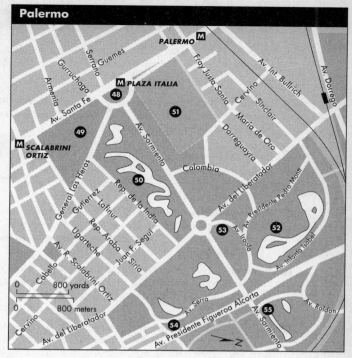

shopping centers (at the Bulnes stop on the D line), and the neighboring small boutiques along Avenida Santa Fe.

## Sights to See

**49 Jardín Botánico** (Botanical Garden). The Botanical Garden is a welcome, unexpected oasis in the city. Enclosed by large wrought-iron gates, it's hard to imagine the beauty inside until you enter. Modeled after an 18th-century French garden, the long, winding paths and hidden statues conjure up images of the gardens at Versailles. ⊠ *Av. Santa Fe 3817,* ☎ *11/4831–2951.* ⌦ *Free.* ☾ *Dawn–dusk.*

---

**NEED A BREAK?**
Near the Botanical Garden and steps away from the Palermo Polo field is **La Cátedra** (⊠ at Cerviño and Sinclair, ☎ 11/4777–4601), a perfect spot for lunch or a drink. In good weather you can eat outdoors.

---

★ **54 Jardín Japonés** (Japanese Garden). This unexpected haven, run by the Japanese Cultural Society, is a fine Japanese garden. It has streams, bridges, and fishponds (you can buy food to feed the already well-fed fish). The garden is particularly beautiful at sunset. ⊠ *Avs. Casares and Adolfo Berro,* ☎ *11/4804–4922.* ⌦ *Admission.* ☾ *Dawn–dusk.*

🖐 **50 Jardín Zoológico** (Zoological Garden). The Buenos Aires zoo, where you'll find indigenous monkeys, birds, and many other animals, is a popular weekend destination for families. The animals aren't always kept in cages according to species type, so be prepared to see some interesting and unexpected cage mates. At the entrance to the zoo you can get a horse-drawn carriage to take you through the zoo and the Botanical Garden. ⊠ *República de la India 2900,* ☎ *11/4806–7412.* ⌦ *Admission.*

🖐 **52 Parque Tres de Febrero** (February Third Park). Palermo's main park, just north of Calle Sarmiento, has 1,000 acres of woods, lakes, and walking trails. Paddle boats can be rented for use on the small lakes, and joggers, bikers, and rollerbladers all compete for the right of way on the miles of paved lanes. It's packed on weekends, with cars parked on the grass and soccer balls flying everywhere. Drinks and snacks are available at one of the park's cafés as well along Avenida del Libertador.

---

**NEED A BREAK?**　　Have a snack or coffee in the café of the **Museo Renault** (✉ Av. Figueroa Alcorta 3399, ☎ 11/4802–9626), about a 10-minute walk from the Parque Tres de Febrero.

---

★ ❸ **Paseo del Rosedal** (Rose Garden). The Rose Garden is a picturesque park full of fountains, statues of literati, and roses. On a Saturday in spring you're practically guaranteed to see a wedding here. ✉ *Av. del Libertador and Paseo de la Infanta.*

❺ **Planetario Galileo Galilei** (Galileo Galilei Planetarium). This planetarium on the western side of the Parque Tres de Febrero presents weekend-afternoon astronomy shows. ✉ *Sarmiento and Belisario Roldán,* ☎ *11/4771–6629.*

❹ **Plaza Italia.** This busy square at the intersection of Calle Santa Fe, Calle Las Heras, and Calle Sarmiento is a landmark in the area and a good place to meet. On weekends there's a crafts fair. ✉ *At Santa Fe and Thames.*

☾ ❺ **Sociedad Rural Argentina** (Rural Society of Argentina). Exhibitions relating to agriculture and cattle raising are often held at the fairgrounds here. The biggest is the annual monthlong (usually in August) **Exposición Rural** (Rural Exposition), where you can see livestock such as cows and horses, gaucho shows, and expert horse performances. ☎ *11/4774–1072.*

---

# Belgrano

Primarily a residential area, the fashionable, quiet district of Belgrano is home to beautiful mansions, luxury high-rises, and well-kept cobblestone streets leading off bustling Avenida Cabildo.

## A Good Walk

To reach Belgrano, take Line D to the last stop (at press time, Estación Virrey del Piño, though by the end of 1999 the last stop was slated to be Juramento, which is closer).

Head first to the **Museo de Arte Española Enrique Larreta** ❺⑥ for a taste of Spanish colonial art. Then cross the street to the **Museo Histórico Sarmiento** ❺⑦, which is essentially a shrine to independence from Spain. From here walk across the small **Plaza Manuel Belgrano** ❺⑧ to reach the **Parroquia de Nuestra Señora de la Inmaculada Concepción** ❺⑨. After visiting the church, take a break at one of the many cafés nearby. Two blocks along Calle Juramento from the church, across busy Avenida Cabildo, is the **Mercado** ⑥⓪, an open-air food market; it's worth the seemingly treacherous avenue crossing to experience this traditional market. Go in the other direction on Calle Juramento and take a right on Calle Tres de Febrero, a fancy residential street, to get to the **Museo Nacional del Hombre** ⑥①, an anthropology museum.

### TIMING AND PRECAUTIONS

This walk can be done in 2–3 hours, though you could easily spend more time wandering around this beautiful barrio. If you want to see all the museums, it's best to visit in the afternoon, when they're all open. The atmospheric cafés around the church are open 24 hours. Belgrano

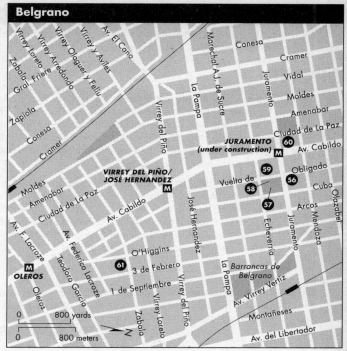

is one of the safest districts in Buenos Aires: It's patrolled around the clock by private security and city police, and there's rarely any crime, except for the occasional purse snatching.

## Sights to See

**⑥ Mercado** (Market). This open-air local market is a treasure trove of everything you'd expect to find—cheese, fresh vegetables, and local meat—as well as a few surprises. Vendors bring their wares straight from local farms, and bartering and bargaining is common. ⊠ *Juramento and Ciudad de la Paz.* ⊙ *Daily 5 PM–11 PM.*

★ **⑤⑥ Museo de Arte Española Enrique Larreta** (Enrique Larreta Museum of Spanish Art). Once the beautiful home and gardens of a Spanish governor, the building now houses one of the best collections of Spanish colonial art in Argentina. ⊠ *Juramento 2291,* ☎ *11/4783–2640.* ⊠ *Admission; Tues. free.* ⊙ *Mon.–Tues. and Fri. 2–7:45, weekends 3–7:45.*

**⑤⑦ Museo Histórico Sarmiento** (Sarmiento Historical Museum). This charming colonial-style museum gives you yet another opportunity to learn about the history of Argentina through all kinds of art and artifacts. *Cuba 2079,* ☎ *11/4783–7555.* ⊠ *Admission.* ⊙ *Tues.–Fri. and Sun. 3–8. Guided tours are available in Spanish at 4 PM Sun.*

**⑥① Museo Nacional del Hombre** (Museum of the History of Man). It won't take you long to visit this anthropology museum, where human development is explained from a Latin-American perspective. ⊠ *Tres de Febrero 1370–8,* ☎ *11/4782–7251.* ⊠ *Free.* ⊙ *Weekdays 10–6.*

**⑤⑨ Parroquia de Nuestra Señora de la Inmaculada Concepción** (Our Lady of the Immaculate Conception Church). This beautiful, brightly colored church was modeled after Rome's Pantheon. ⊠ *Vuelta de Obligado 2042,* ☎ *11/4783–8008,* ⊙ *Mon.–Sat. 7:30–noon and 4–8:30, Sun. 7:30–1:30 and 4–9:15.*

🔞 **Plaza Manuel Belgrano.** This square, named after General Belgrano, the War of Independece hero, is the site of a bustling art fair on weekends. During the week it's a simple city plaza, with a little playground filled with families and schoolchildren.

# DINING

All kinds of international fare is available in Buenos Aires, but most common are *parrillas*—restaurants serving grilled meat. These vary from upscale eateries to local spots. Different cuts of beef are available, as are chicken, sausage, and grilled cheese (*provoleta*). Meat dishes are generally accompanied by french fries and salad. Many restaurants also serve pasta (often homemade).

Cafés are a big part of Buenos Aires culture, and those in good locations are always busy, from breakfast to long after dinner. Some, called *confiterías,* have a wider selection of food—open-face sandwiches, grilled ham and cheese, "triples" (three-decker clubs filled with ham, cheese, tomatoes, olives, eggs, and onion), sandwiches made on *medias lunas* (croissants), salads, and desserts.

## Belgrano

### ITALIAN

**$$$** ✕ **La Fornarina.** This cozy basement eatery in the heart of the fash-
★   ionable Belgrano district is worth the $8 cab ride from El Centro. The homemade pastas and desserts are excellent. Traditional Argentine cuisine is also available. ✉ *Vuelta de Obligado,* ☏ *11/4783–4904. AE, DC, MC, V. Subte: Estación Juramento.*

### PAN-ASIAN

**$$–$$$** ✕ **Tao Tao.** Porteños come from all over the city for the locally influ-
★   enced Japanese and Chinese fare at Tao Tao. It's also not uncommon to see ambassadors and visiting dignitaries from Asian countries here. The surroundings are formal Chinese; the multilingual staff is excellent. As an appetizer, sample the crunchy *empanaditas* (an Argentine version of spring rolls), and for a main dish, opt for the lobster rice or the Japanese salad. ✉ *Av. Cabildo 1418,* ☏ *11/4783–5806. Reservations essential on Sat. AE, V. Closed Mon. Subte: Estación Jose Hernandez/Virrey del Piño.*

## La Boca

### ARGENTINE

**$–$$** ✕ **El Obrero.** When the rock band U2 played in Buenos Aires in 1998, they asked to be taken to the most traditional Argentine restaurant in the city—and this is where they were brought. A bustling hole-in-the-wall, it serves consistently good steaks, sweetbreads, sausages, and grilled chicken. The stark walls and cheap (even by Argentine standards) wine make it clear that you're not in a jacket-and-tie kind of place, but the food is cheap, fast, and always enjoyable. Note: Some cab drivers may not want to take you to the area around this restaurant; also you should expect a wait. ✉ *Augustín R. Caffarena 64,* ☏ *11/4363–9912. No credit cards. Closed Jan.*

## Cabalito

### SPANISH

**$$** ✕ **Los Chanchitos.** This is a typical cantina, complete with hanging hams and a noisy crowd. Dishes are abundant, often enough for two. The smoky atmosphere and flowing drinks make this a place to spend an evening. ✉ *Angel Gallardo 601,* ☏ *11/4857–3738. MC, V.*

## El Centro
ARGENTINE

**$$$** ✕ **Las Nazarenas.** Across the street from the Sheraton, in a two-story Spanish colonial–style building with wrought-iron sconces and potted ferns, this parrilla is a favorite lunch stop for business people. Meat is the order of the day, whether grilled steaks, brochettes, or *chivito* (kid). For an appetizer, order the *matambre* (a meat dish, typically served cold, made from pounded meat layered with hard-boiled egg and spices, rolled up like a log, and sliced), the grilled provolone cheese sprinkled with oregano, or the delicious empanadas. ✉ *Reconquista 1132,* ☎ *11/4312–5559. AE, DC, MC, V. Estación San Martín.*

**$$$** ✕ **Tierra de los Cocineros.** An unusual mix of Argentine fare like
★ *lomito* (a cut of beef similar to filet mignon, often served thinly sliced as a sandwich) and *ñoquis* (gnocchi) and international dishes like pad thai and curry chicken are available at this bright, modern restaurant. It's extremely popular with a business-lunch crowd, so it can take a while to get a table at midday. ✉ *Juncal 810,* ☎ *11/4393–2010. AE, DC, MC, V. Closed Sun. Subte: Estación Plaza San Martín.*

**$$$** ✕ **Tomo Uno.** In the Hotel Panamericano (☞ Lodging, *below*), this restaurant has some dishes that aren't typically found in Buenos Aires restaurants such as the tasty lamb with herbs, garnished with Spanish potatoes and spinach, and the trout with lemon sauce and roasted almonds. If you're here on Easter or Christmas Eve, this is a good place to come. ✉ *Carlos Pellegrini 525,* ☎ *11/4348–5000. Reservations essential. AE, DC, MC, V. Closed Sun. No lunch Sat. Subte: Estación 9 de Julio, Carlos Pellegrini.*

**$$** ✕ **El Palacio de la Papa Frita.** A good place for a quick meal before or after a movie, this family establishment is always packed. There's lots of good, solid food—everything from chicken salad to spaghetti to grilled steak and fries. ✉ *Lavalle 735,* ☎ *11/4393–5849 . AE, DC, MC, V . Subte: Estación Lavalle.*

**$–$$** ✕ **Melo** In Barrio Norte, a neighborhood bordering El Centro and La
★ Recoleta, Melo serves up traditional steaks, salads, and pastas. Portions are huge—usually big enough for two, and the friendly atmosphere makes up for the sparse decor. Particularly good is the brochette of meat and vegetables. ✉ *Pachero de Melo,* ☎ *11/4801–4251. No credit cards.*

**$–$$** ✕ **Pippo.** This is the place to go for *estofado* (a traditional meat sauce) and pasta as well as lomito and french fries. The food is inexpensive, the atmosphere is relaxed, and you're allowed to linger over your food as long as you like. ✉ *Paraná 356,* ☎ *11/4374–6365. No credit cards. No dinner Sun. Subte: Estación Tribunales.*

**$** ✕ **La Querencia.** This country-style restaurant serves various types of empanadas and tamales as well as rich local soups and stews such as the traditional *locro* (a stew of hard corn, cooked slowly over days). Seating is on stools, but you can also carry out. There are two locations in El Centro. ✉ *Esmeralda 1392,* ☎ *11/4822–4644. Subte: Estación San Martín;* ✉ *Junin 1304,* ☎ *11/4393–3202. Subte: Estación Facultad de Medicina. No credit cards. Closed Sun.*

CAFÉS

**$** ✕ **Florida Garden.** Sit elbow to elbow along the 20-ft bar or in the sitting room upstairs, and enjoy afternoon tea or some of the richest hot chocolate in the city. ✉ *Florida 889, near the Plaza San Martín,* ☎ *11/4312–7902. No credit cards. Subte: Estación Plaza San Martín.*

**$** ✕ **Gran Café Tortoni.** Dating from 1858, this confitería is the oldest in
★ town. Its wooden tables, original artwork, and decorated ceilings are reminiscent of a faded, glorious past. Carlos Gardel, one of Argentina's most famous tango stars, writer José Luis Borges, Argentinian presi-

# Buenos Aires Dining

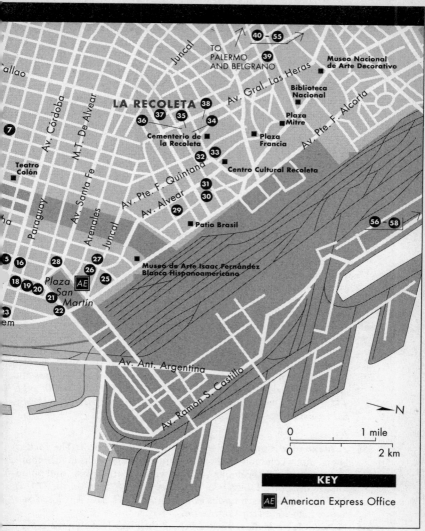

**TO PALERMO AND BELGRANO**

40 – 55
39

Juncal

Museo Nacional
de Arte Decorativo

'allao

Av. Córdoba

M.T. De Alvear

Av. Gral. Las Heras

Biblioteca
Nacional

Av. Pte. F. Alcorta

7

LA RECOLETA   38

36   37   35   34

Cementerio de
la Recoleta

Plaza
Mitre

Plaza
Francia

Av. Santa Fe

Teatro
Colón

Av. Pte. F. Quintana

32   33

Centro Cultural Recoleta

Paraguay

Arenales

Juncal

Av. Alvear

31

30

29

Patio Brasil

56 – 58

5   16

28   27

26   25

18   19   20

AE

Plaza
San
Martín

21

22

3
em

Museo de Arte Isaac Fernández
Blanco Hispanoamericano

Av. Ant. Argentina

Av. Ramon S. Castillo

N

0                    1 mile
0                    2 km

**KEY**

AE  American Express Office

dents, and many visiting dignitaries and intellectuals have had coffee here. On weekend nights there's a tango show (reservations essential). ⊠ *Near Plaza de Mayo at Av. de Mayo 829,* ☎ *11/4342–4328. AE, MC, V. Subte: Estación Avenida de Mayo.*

$   ✕ **Ideal.** Charming and a little bit tattered, this café makes you feel
★   like you've gone back in time. Not only can you come here for coffee, but you can also take beginning tango lessons and see experts perform on Tuesday and Friday nights. Some of the 1998 film *The Tango Lesson* was shot here. Unlike the Gran Café Tortoni (☞ *above*), it's fairly easy to get a table here; just beware the grouchy waiters who pretend not to understand tourists. ⊠ *Suipacha 384, near corner of Av. Corrientes,* ☎ *11/4326–0521. AE, V, MC. Subte: Estación 9 de Julio.*

$   ✕ **Petit Paris Café.** The crystal chandeliers and marble tabletops make this place feel especially like a Parisian café. A variety of coffees are served, as are tasty salads and sandwiches. ⊠ *Av. Santa Fe 774,* ☎ *11/4312–5885. AE. Subte: Estación Plaza San Martín*

### CONTINENTAL

$$$$   ✕ **La Pergola.** On the third floor of the Hotel Libertador Kempinski, this restaurant serves mouthwatering appetizers like salmon bisque and flavorful entrées, including pasta, grilled steak, and sole with shrimp, artichoke hearts, shallots, capers, asparagus, and white wine sauce. ⊠ *Maipú and Av. Córdoba,* ☎ *11/4322–8800 or 11/4322–6622. Reservations essential. Jacket and tie. AE, DC, MC, V. Subte: Estación Plaza San Martín.*

$$$$   ✕ **Plaza Hotel Grill.** Wrought-iron lamps and fans hang from the high
★   ceilings, and original Dutch delft porcelain tiles decorate the walls at this favorite spot of executives and politicians. There's an extensive wine list and a Continental menu with excellent steak, fish dishes such as salmon with basil and red wine, and quail stuffed with foie gras and grapes. ⊠ *Florida 1005, in the Plaza Hotel,* ☎ *11/4318–3000 or 11/4313–7403. Reservations essential. Jacket and tie. AE, DC, MC, V. Subte: Estación San Martín.*

### ENGLISH

$$$   ✕ **Alexander.** Come here for the food not the decor. The rack of lamb—not a common sight on Argentine menus—melts in the mouth, and the purées of vegetables such as sweet potato, squash, and pumpkin are delicious. Lunch is usually very busy. ⊠ *San Martín 774,* ☎ *11/4311–2878. Reservations essential . AE, DC, MC, V. Closed Sun. Subte: Estación Plaza San Martín.*

$$$   ✕ **Down Town Matías.** Tucked behind the Plaza Hotel on the ground floor of a modern high-rise, this restaurant serves such typical English fare as lamb stew and chicken pie in a chummy, publike atmosphere. ⊠ *San Martín 979,* ☎ *11/4312–9844. AE, DC, MC, V. No credit cards. Closed Sun. Subte: Estación Plaza San Martín.*

### FRENCH

$$$$   ✕ **Catalinas.** Superb seafood and game dishes await you at this French
★   restaurant that resembles a country inn. The lobster tail on fresh eggs, with caviar and cream, and the *pejerrey* (a small freshwater fish) stuffed with king-crab mousse are particularly savory. The dining room is packed wall to wall with businesspeople at lunch, but it draws a more varied crowd at night. Several fixed-price menus make this gourmet's delight easier on the pocket, but beware—Catalinas's wines and desserts can double the price of your meal. ⊠ *Reconquista 875,* ☎ *11/4313–0182. Reservations essential. Jacket and tie. AE, DC, MC, V. Closed Sun. Subte: Estación Florida.*

$$   ✕ **Ligure.** French cuisine adapted to Argentine tastes is the specialty here. You can get dishes like thistles *au gratin* as well as the more stan-

dard steak *au poivre* with brandy sauce. The dessert pancakes are a must. ⊠ *Juncal 855,* ☎ *11/4394–8226. AE, MC, V.*

$ ✕ **Bonpler.** If you're looking for a quick meal, come here for Argentine-style French fast food (seating is available): Salads, sandwiches, croissants, muffins, and coffee. ⊠ *Florida 481, at Lavalle,* ☎ *11/4325–9900. No credit cards. Closed Sun. Subte: Estación Florida.*

### JAPANESE

$ ✕ **Sensu.** Eat in or take out your food at this Japanese restaurant. The food is good—especially the salmon (there are also shrimp, beef, and chicken dishes, though no sushi)—and the mixed vegetables that come with every dish are a welcome change from the solitary steak plates served in most Argentine restaurants. ⊠ *Florida 528,* ☎ *11/4393–9595. No credit cards.*

### PIZZA

$$ ✕ **Filo.** Come here for the flat-bread pizza, the extensive drink list, and
★ the great party atmosphere. It's definitely not the place for a quiet, relaxing meal, as the popular bar is packed all the time. ⊠ *San Martín 975,* ☎ *11/4311–0312. AE, MC, V. Subte: Estación Plaza San Martín.*

$$ ✕ **Memorabilia.** The young and fashionable flock to this trendy restaurant-bar where the walls are painted orange and yellow, music videos are shown, and pizza is made in a purple-painted oven. Besides creative pizzas made in a brick oven, you can also get pasta, salads, and sandwiches. Often there's live music or dancing after 10 PM. ⊠ *Maipú 761,* ☎ *11/4322–7630. AE, DC, MC, V. Subte: Estación San Martín.*

### SPANISH

$$$ ✕ **Veracruz.** This old-fashioned restaurant has carefully prepared Spanish-style seafood dishes served by staid, seasoned waiters. Especially delicious is the *cazuela* (seafood stew with clams, shrimp, octopus, scallops, and lobster). ⊠ *Uruguay 538,* ☎ *11/4371–1413. MC, V. Closed Sun.*

$$ ✕ **Club Vasco Francés.** In an old racquet club, this spacious, spruced-up dining room is one of the few places in Buenos Aires where you can get frogs' legs. Seafood is flown in from Spain especially for homesick Basque diners. ⊠ *Moreno 1370,* ☎ *11/4383–5021. AE, V. Closed Sun.*

### VEGETARIAN

$ ✕ **Yin-Yang.** Yin-Yang caters to health-conscious vegetarians with a well-balanced menu of large, tasty plates of brown rice, fresh vegetables, tofu, and vegetable tarts. There are two locations: one in El Centro and one in Belgrano. ⊠ *Paraguay 858,* ☎ *11/4311–7798. No credit cards. Subte: Estación 9 de Julio;* ⊠ *Echeverría 2444,* ☎ *11/4783–1546. DC, MC, V. Closed Sun. Subte: Estación Juramento (under construction and scheduled to have opened by January 2000).*

## Costanera (Río de la Plata)

### ARGENTINE

$$$ ✕ **Los Años Locos.** Locals flock to this restaurant, along the banks of
★ the Río de la Plata, for long lunches and late-night steak dinners, served in a friendly, low-key atmosphere. It's not uncommon to be finishing up your steak at 1 AM and to see a group waiting for your table. Portions are more than generous—for most cuts of meat, order a half portion, unless you intend to share. The decor isn't noteworthy—it's basically a lot of tables, packed into a huge room that's always full, but you won't even notice after you've taken your first bite. After dinner you can cross the street to see the river at night, though it's not recommended that you stray too far from the restaurant. ⊠ *At Rafael Obligado and La Pampa,* ☎ *11/4784–8681. AE, DC, V.*

**$–$$** X **Los Platitos.** At this no-frills restaurant, jovial waiters serve up tra-
★ ditional Argentine fare like blood sausage and sweetbreads with pasta
and grilled provolone. Because it's on the Costanera (the river drive),
you'll need to take a taxi or drive. ⊠ *At Rafael Obligado and La Pampa,
on the Costanera,* ☎ *no phone. AE, DC, V.*

ITALIAN

**$$$** X **Clo-Clo.** Enjoy the view of the Río de la Plata as you feast on grilled
beef and piles of *papas fritas* (french fries). *Trucha Capri* (trout in cream
sauce with prawns) is a good way to whet your appetite. ⊠ *At Costan-
era Norte and La Pampa,* ☎ *11/4788–0487. AE, DC, MC, V.*

## Palermo

AMERICAN

**$** X **Big Momma.** Argentina's version of a deli has a little bit of every-
thing you'd expect (except pickles), such as made-to-order sandwiches,
hot pastrami, bagels and lox, and even knishes. ⊠ *At Migueletes and
Matienzo,* ☎ *11/4772–0926. AE, DC, MC, V.*

ARGENTINE

**$$$** X **Novecento.** This bistro has an American theme—New York City street
★ signs hang on the walls and the menu is in English and Spanish (in fact,
there's also a Novecento in New York City's Soho). Yet the food,
atmosphere, and crowd are all chic Porteño. The candlelit tables are
close together, which makes for intimate seating. The beef salad, a pyramid of alternating layers of green salad, steak, and french fries, is especially good. In summer there's outdoor dining. ⊠ *Báez 199,* ☎ *11/
4778–1900. V. Subte: Estación Palermo.*

**$$$** X **Río Alba.** Stacked wine bottles, hanging hams, and sports-related
memorabilia form the backdrop to such dishes as grilled tuna, salmon,
and trout; or try the juicy, lean pork with lemon slices and shoestring
potatoes. Right by the American Embassy, it's a noisy hangout for Amer-
ican expats. ⊠ *Cerviño 4499,* ☎ *11/4773–9508. AE, DC, MC, V. Subte:
Estación Palermo.*

**$$–$$$** X **Club del Vino.** With its wine cellar, wine museum, and wine bou-
tique, this is paradise if you love wine. The prix fixe wine taster's menu
includes *milanesa* (a very traditional Argentine dish of pounded meat,
breaded and fried) with sweet potatoes and flan, accompanied by mer-
lot, Malbec, and cabernet. ⊠ *Cabrera 4737,* ☎ *11/4833–0048.* ☺ *No
lunch. AE, DC, MC, V. Subte: Estación Palermo.*

**$** X **Ña Serapia.** Tasty tamales and locro and inexpensive wine make this
a perfect quick stop in Palermo. The place is small, and the atmosphere
is no-frills, but the food is consistently good. It's also one of the few
restaurants with an Argentine menu that doesn't focus specifically on
grilled meat. ⊠ *Av. Las Heras 3357,* ☎ *11/4801–5307. No credit cards.*

GREEK

**$$** X **Plaka.** Chef Lefteris Gakis prepares traditional Greek fare like
moussaka and grape leaves. Service is friendly—you're welcomed with
a glass of Greek retsina. Concerts of traditional Greek music and
dance are held on weekends. Note that the restaurant is sometimes closed
for lunch, so it's a good idea to call ahead. ⊠ *Arevalo 2725,* ☎ *11/
4777–6051. V.*

INDIAN

**$$$–$$$$** X **Katmandu.** This cozy, off-the-beaten-path spot north of Palermo has
eclectic Hindu art and two floors of Indian wares. The Indian food—
especially the curries and breads—is some of the best in Buenos Aires.
The crowd is primarily made up of expats living in Argentina and yup-
pie Porteños. ⊠ *Cordoba 3547,* ☎ *11/4963–1122. AE, DC, MC, V.
Closed Sun.*

### MEXICAN

**$–$$** ✕ **Cielito Lindo.** This Mexican cantina is a great reason to visit Palermo Viejo. The atmosphere is festive, with colorful Mexican decorations all over the walls. The food focuses on beans, rice, and spicy meats and the mixed drinks are surprisingly good for Buenos Aires (though the margaritas are definitely small by American standards). ✉ *El Salvador 4999 at Thames,* ☎ *11/4832–8054. No credit cards. Closed Sun. No lunch.*

### MIDDLE EASTERN

**$$** ✕ **Asociación Cultural Armenia.** Ex-generals and future presidents can be found enjoying extraordinary Armenian fare alongside moguls of the city's powerful Armenian community in this rather institutional-looking Palermo Viejo club. The hummus, tabbouleh, and stuffed eggplant are authentic and well prepared. ✉ *Armenia 1366,* ☎ *11/4771–0016. AE, DC, MC, V. Closed Mon. and Feb. No lunch Tues.–Sat.; no dinner Sat.*

### PIZZA

**$$** ✕ **Morelia.** In the up-and-coming neighborhood of Las Cañitas, in Palermo, is one of the best places in the city serving pizza cooked on a grill. After your meal, head across the street to one of the many trendy bars in the area. ✉ *Báez 260,* ☎ *11/4772–0329. AE, DC, MC, V. No lunch. Subte: Estación Palermo.*

**$$** ✕ **Pizza Cero.** New Age music, outdoor tables, and a dining room filled with fresh plants and flowers set the tone at this popular, upscale pizza parlor. The pizzas have crisp crusts and mozzarella cheese with an array of toppings, including eggplant, ham, and pineapple. Tasty salads and empanadas are also available. ✉ *Cerviño 3701,* ☎ *11/4803–3449. V.*

### THAI

**$$$** ✕ **Lotus neo Thai.** At this enchanting Thai restaurant, colorful flower lamps reach for the ceiling, and glowing candles bob in carefully placed bowls. Excellent dishes include red curried beef in coconut milk with pumpkin and basil leaves, fried coconut shrimp with sweet and sour tamarind sauce, and stir-fried rice vermicelli with minced shrimp, chicken, and pork. The fruit drinks are delicious but can make your bill add up. ✉ *Ortega y Gasset 1782,* ☎ *11/4771–4449. AE, MC. No lunch. Subte: Estación Palermo.*

## Plaza de Mayo

### ARGENTINE

**$$–$$$** ✕ **Calle de los Angeles.** The name of this restaurant, Street of the Angels, accurately depicts the decor (made to look like you're outside on the street) in this fun but somewhat touristy spot. Tables line both walls of the long, narrow dining room, a winding brick path runs down the middle, and tree branches hang over head, which makes you feel as if you are dining alfresco somewhere in Spain. But the food is well-prepared and artfully served Argentine parrilla. ✉ *Chile 318,* ☎ *11/4361–8822. No credit cards.*

### CONTINENTAL

**$$** ✕ **Pedemonte.** The menu is extensive and the dishes well prepared at this Continental restaurant. The three-course fixed-price menu includes such items as *pascualina de alcauciles* (artichoke pie) and pepper steak. ✉ *Av. de Mayo 676,* ☎ *11/4331–7179. Reservations essential. Jacket and tie. AE, DC, MC, V. Closed Sat. No dinner Sun. Subte: Estación Avenida de Mayo.*

### SPANISH

**$$** ✕ **Taberna Baska.** Old-world decor and efficient service are hallmarks of this busy, no-nonsense Spanish restaurant. Try such dishes such as *chiripones en su tinta* (a variety of squid in ink). ⊠ *Chile 980,* ☏ *11/ 4334–0903. AE, DC, MC, V. Closed Mon. No dinner Sun.*

## Puerto Madero

Along the banks of the Río de la Plata in Puerto Madero, a string of restaurants line the shore, where Argentines flock for late night steak dinners and slow lunches.

$$$$  ✕ **Cabaña las Lilas.** Presidents, movie stars, and Porteños come here
★     for the best meat in Buenos Aires. In fact, the restaurant has its own *estancia* (ranch) where it raises cattle for its grilled lomito and *cuadrillo* (beef cheeks). The wine cellar is well stocked with superb Argentine wines (try the Catena Zapata). Service is impeccable. If you have to wait long for a table, as you undoubtedly will, enjoy a glass of champagne in the cigar bar. ⊠ *Av. Dávila 516,* ☏ *11/4313–1336. AE, DC, V.*

## La Recoleta

La Recoleta's competition for fashionable dining is right here at the port. Quickly becoming one of the most chic places to be seen, restaurants can't open fast enough to keep up with the Saturday-evening customer demand. Take a walk along the dock (during a meal time to witness the true flavor of the area), mix with the diners, and enjoy the views of the Río de la Plata.

$$$$  ✕ **Harper's.** A fashionable lunch and dinner spot, Harper's is popular with a cross section of locals—from yuppies to businesspeople to neighborhood folks. They come here to enjoy tender steak and a hearty plate of pasta as well as a traditional favorite, *cordero del diablo* (a tangy lamb dish). Paintings by local artists hang on the walls. ⊠ *R. M. Ortíz 1763,* ☏ *11/4801–7140. AE, MC, V.*

$$    ✕ **Munich Recoleta.** This jam-packed place has been a favorite gath-
★     ering spot for almost 40 years. The basic fare consists of great steak, creamed spinach, and shoestring potatoes, all served quickly and in generous portions. The lively atmosphere attracts young and old alike. Arrive early if you don't want to wait. ⊠ *R. M. Ortíz 1879,* ☏ *11/ 4804–3981. Reservations not accepted. No credit cards.*

$     ✕ **El Sanjuanino.** Empandas and other traditional fare from the Andes are made at this long-established spot. Though you can get a quick bite here, it's primarily a takeout place. ⊠ *Posadas 1515,* ☏ *11/4804–2909. No credit cards. Closed Mon.*

$     ✕ **La Biela.** This La Recoleta café is a popular local spot for sipping espressos, gossiping, and people-watching. Although there are tables inside, where the decor is Paris-inspired, the outdoor tables are the place to be in warm weather. ⊠ *At Quintana and Junin. V.*

$$$–$$$$  ✕ **Clark's.** Deer heads hang from the dark wood panels, overlooking red-checkered tables at this Continental restaurant. Though the chefs are ambitious and innovative, they sometimes miss their mark. So stick with Clark's traditional specialties, like pasta with creamy mushroom sauce or grilled meat. The fixed-price menus, which include four courses and wine, are a good deal. ⊠ *R. M. Ortíz 1777,* ☏ *11/4801– 9502. AE, DC, MC, V.*

$$    ✕ **Mora X.** The handsome wooden bar, rich artwork, and high-windowed ceiling create an old-world, librarylike ambience. The five large paintings lining the main dining room wall represent, in order, the ma-

rina, the tango, the circus, the hunt, and the forest, and are often a point of discussion for diners. Enjoy delightful dishes such as grilled sirloin with cheddar sauce and mushrooms or sole with lemon sauce; profiteroles with raspberry sauce make a fine finish. ⊠ *Vicente López 2152,* ☎ *11/4803–0261. Reservations essential. AE, DC, MC, V.*

### FRENCH

**$$$$**
**★**
✕ **La Bourgogne.** Argentina's only truly gourmet establishment is in the Alvear Palace Hotel (☞ Lodging, *below*) and is generally considered the city's best—and one of the most expensive—restaurants in town. In the elegant dining room complete with white tablecloths and fresh roses, the sophisticated waitstaff brings you complimentary hors d'oeuvres as you peruse the menu of delicacies like foie gras, rabbit, escargots, chateaubriand, and *côte de veau* (veal steak). ⊠ *Alvear 1891,* ☎ *11/4804–4031. Reservations essential. Jacket and tie. AE, DC, MC, V.*

### ITALIAN

**$$$–$$$$**
✕ **San Babila.** This trattoria is one of the city's most popular Italian restaurants. *Pappardelle al pesto* (butterfly pasta in a pesto sauce) and *tortelloni di zucca* (oversize tortellini with pumpkin filling) are good bets, and the fixed-price menus give you more options. ⊠ *R. M. Ortíz 1815,* ☎ *11/4802–8981. AE, DC, MC, V.*

### JAPANESE

**$$$$**
✕ **Midori.** This Japanese restaurant and sushi bar in the Caesar Park Hotel (☞ Lodging, *below*) is brightly lighted, modern, and clean. Try the *teppanyaki* dishes—prime cuts of meat, fish, and seafood grilled right at your table. ⊠ *Posadas 1232,* ☎ *11/4819–1100. Reservations essential. AE, DC, MC, V. No lunch. Closed Mon.*

### MIDDLE EASTERN

**$$$**
✕ **Syrian Club.** The breathtaking second-floor restaurant at the Syrian Club has a curved double staircase leading up to the third floor and a welcoming lobby bar on the entrance level. Come here for a superb Middle Eastern buffet with such items as hummus, stuffed grape leaves, and lamb. Belly dancers entertain and coffee-ground readers predict fortunes. ⊠ *At Ayacucho and Melo. AE, V.*

## San Isidro

### ARGENTINE

**$$$$**
**★**
✕ **Rosa Negra.** Across from the San Isidro racetrack in the loft of a former horse stable, Rosa Negra serves Argentine parrilla and Italian cuisine to a sophisticated crowd. Try the traditionally prepared meats such as the lomito or the seafood ravioli. Be prepared to wait for a table—over an hour on Saturday—there's free champagne and plenty of people-watching to make it entertaining. ⊠ *Dardo Rocha 1918,* ☎ *11/4717–2685 . AE, V.*

# LODGING

Buenos Aires has a variety of fine hotels. Some of the more expensive ones were built for the 1978 World Cup, while others opened at the turn of the century or even before. It's important to remember, however, that you're not in the United States (or Canada or England) and that where you stay is part of the adventure. So while some things may be hard to understand or tolerate (why aren't there screens on the windows, for instance?), try to stay flexible. With the exception of the top luxury hotels, most establishments have a small, family-run feel, with all the charming quirks that that entails.

Most rooms have a bidet, but not every room has a television. In many of the smaller hotels, it's not possible to make a direct-dial long-

# Buenos Aires Lodging

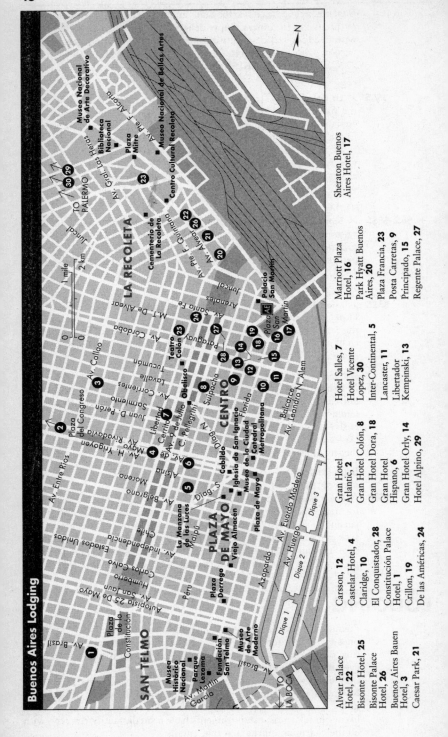

Alvear Palace Hotel, **22**
Bisonte Hotel, **25**
Bisonte Palace Hotel, **26**
Buenos Aires Bauen Hotel, **3**
Caesar Park, **21**

Carsson, **12**
Castelar Hotel, **4**
Claridge, **10**
El Conquistador, **28**
Constitución Palace Hotel, **1**
De las Américas, **24**

Gran Hotel Atlantic, **2**
Gran Hotel Colón, **8**
Gran Hotel Dora, **18**
Gran Hotel Hispano, **6**
Gran Hotel Orly, **14**
Hotel Alpino, **29**

Hotel Salles, **7**
Hotel Vicente Lopez, **30**
Inter-Continental, **5**
Lancaster, **11**
Libertador Kempinski, **13**

Marriott Plaza Hotel, **16**
Park Hyatt Buenos Aires, **20**
Plaza Francia, **23**
Posta Carretas, **9**
Principado, **15**
Regente Palace, **27**

Sheraton Buenos Aires Hotel, **17**

distance call from your room—you must either use a phone in the lobby or call the front desk to ask for a long-distance line. Don't expect to see such amenities as ice makers or vending machines.

In addition to the prices quoted, a 21% tax is generally added. Check-in time is usually after 3 PM, and check-out time is usually before noon, though these times are more flexible in smaller hotels.

## El Centro

**$$$$** ▦ **Claridge.** The public rooms of this styish hotel, with their wood paneling and high ceiling, have a distinctly British feel. There's an Anglo-Argentine clientele to match. Rooms are done in shades of blue, with dark wood furnishings with bronze fittings. The health club and pool are nice pluses. ⊠ *Tucumán 535, 1049,* ☎ *11/4314–7700, 800/223–5652 in the U.S.,* FAX *11/4314–8022. 155 rooms, 6 suites. Restaurant, bar, room service, pool, health club, concierge, business services, meeting rooms. AE, DC, MC, V.*

**$$$$** ▦ **El Conquistador.** This hotel, near Plaza San Martín, is popular with businesspeople. The wood paneling in the public rooms and the small art gallery in the lobby lend a cozy touch, and the cheerful restaurant serves breakfast and snacks. Large windows, flowered bedspreads, and light pink carpets brighten rooms. ⊠ *Suipacha 948, 1008,* ☎ *11/4328–3012,* FAX *11/4328–3252. 130 rooms, 14 suites. Restaurant, piano bar, massage, sauna, exercise room. AE, DC, MC, V. Subte: Estación San Martín.*

**$$$$** ▦ **Crillon.** Right across from Plaza San Martín, the Crillon was built in classic French style in 1948 and remodeled in 1995. Front rooms have beautiful views and are large and luminous. The lobby is stately and sedate, which may explain why this establishment appeals to provincial governors and the well-to-do from the interior. ⊠ *Av. Santa Fe 796, 1059,* ☎ *11/4310–2000, 0800/84448,* FAX *11/4310–2020. 84 rooms, 12 suites. Restaurant, bar, in-room safes, room service, concierge, business services, meeting room. AE, DC, MC, V. Subte: Estación Plaza San Martín.*

**$$$$** ▦ **Inter-Continental.** One of Buenos Aires's newest luxury hotels, the Inter-Continental was designed with Argentina of the 1930s in mind. The elegant lobby, with marble, leather, bronze, and wood, leads to an outdoor terrace with a fountain. Rooms are adorned with large black armoires, marble-top nightstands, sleeper chairs, and black-and-white photos of Buenos Aires. The hotel's location in Monserrat, just above El Centro, is a mixed blessing—the neighborhood is quiet, but there's not much to do nearby. ⊠ *Moreno 809, 1091,* ☎ *11/4340–7100,* FAX *11/4340–7119. 315 rooms and suites. Restaurant, 2 bars, room service, indoor pool, health club, concierge, business services, meeting rooms, parking. AE, DC, MC, V.*

**$$$$** ▦ **Libertador Kempinski.** This European-style hotel near the banking district serves as the base for many visiting businesspeople. The lobby, with its marble floor, has a bar and is a good spot to rendezvous. Standard rooms are classic but petite; the pastel-shaded deluxe rooms have walk-in closets, marble baths, and mahogany furnishings. ⊠ *Av. Córdoba 690, 1054,* ☎ *11/4322–8800,* FAX *11/4322–9703. 197 rooms, 6 suites. Restaurant, bar, coffee shop, room service, indoor-outdoor pool, health club, concierge, meeting rooms, travel services. AE, DC, MC, V.*

**$$$$** ▦ **Marriott Plaza Hotel.** One of the city's grandest hotels is across from
★ Plaza San Martín. Marriott has poured millions into the hotel since it was purchased in 1994. Crystal chandeliers and Persian carpets decorate the public rooms—the president of Argentina likes to entertain visiting dignitaries here. Some rooms have great bay windows overlooking the park; all are spacious and elegatly appointed. ⊠ *Florida*

1005, 1005, ☎ 11/4318–3000, 800/228–9290 *in the U.S.*, FAX *11/4318–3008. 274 rooms, 38 suites. 2 restaurants, bar, café, in-room safes, room service, pool, health club, concierge, business services, meeting rooms. AE, DC, MC, V. Subte: Estación San Martín.*

**$$$$** ▦ **Sheraton Buenos Aires Hotel.** The headquarters of Sheraton's South American division, this huge hotel at the bottom of Plaza San Martín has a broad range of facilities. The standard-looking rooms have views of either the Río de la Plata or the British Clock Tower and park at Retiro. It's especially popular with American businesspeople and tour groups. In late 1996 the separate Park Tower, part of Sheraton's Luxury Group, was built next door with spacious, expensive rooms that have cellular phones, entertainment centers, and 24-hour butler service. ✉ *San Martín 1225, 1104,* ☎ *11/4318–9000, 800/325–3535 in the U.S.,* FAX *11/4318–9353. 603 rooms, 29 suites. 4 restaurants, bar, coffee shop, pool, 2 tennis courts, health club, concierge, business services, meeting rooms, car rental, parking (fee). AE, DC, MC, V. Subte: Estación Retiro.*

**$$$** ▦ **Bisonte Hotel.** This hotel, on a popular shopping street, has a small, marble-floor lobby and an upstairs coffee shop overlooking a tree-lined square. Rooms are small, and the decor is on the stiff side, however. Breakfast is included in the rates. ✉ *Paraguay 1207, 1057,* ☎ *11/4816–5770,* FAX *11/4816–5775. 87 rooms. Coffee shop, business services. AE, DC, MC, V. Subte: Estación 9 de Julio.*

**$$$** ▦ **Bisonte Palace Hotel.** This brightly lighted version of its sister establishment, the Bisonte Hotel (☞ *above*), is centrally located and popular with business travelers. Decor is standard—modern and comfortable—and you're well taken care of, though the atmosphere is a bit cold and formal. Because it's on a busy corner, rooms higher up are better bets for peace and quiet. Breakfast is included in the rate. ✉ *M. T. de Alvear 902, 1058,* ☎ *11/4328–4751,* FAX *11/4328–6476. 62 rooms. Coffee shop, room service. AE, DC, MC, V. Subte: Estación San Martín.*

**$$$** ▦ **Buenos Aires Bauen Hotel.** With its theater, auditorium, tango shows, and city tours, the Bauen is a beehive of activity. It's near the intersection of two noisy avenues lined with lively restaurants, cafés, movie houses, and theaters, so avoid the lower floors if you think you'll be bothered by the noise. ✉ *Av. Callao 360, 1022,* ☎ *11/4370–1600, 800/448–8355 in the U.S.,* FAX *11/4372–0315. 226 rooms, 28 suites. Restaurant, bar, coffee shop, refrigerators, room service, pool, barbershop, beauty salon, convention center. AE, DC, MC, V. Subte: Estación Callao.*

**$$$** ▦ **Carsson.** A long, mirrored corridor leads to the lobby, far from the sound of downtown traffic. An English atmosphere pervades—rooms have staid stripes of green and deep red and Louis XIV–style furniture and are larger than the average Buenos Aires hotel room; ask for one off the busy street. Service is first rate. ✉ *Viamonte 650, 1053,* ☎ *11/4322–3551,* FAX *11/4322–0158. 108 rooms, 9 suites. Bar, coffee shop, in-room safes, room service, nursery, laundry service, business services, meeting rooms, parking (fee). AE, DC, MC, V. Subte: Estación Lavalle.*

**$$$** ▦ **De las Américas.** In this modern residential hotel just off the shopping stretch of Avenida Santa Fe, the sunken lobby is drearily decorated. But rooms are comfortable and larger than you'd expect. The clientele consists mainly of South American tour groups and visitors from the provinces. ✉ *Libertad 1020, 1012,* ☎ *11/4816–3432,* FAX *11/4816–0418. 150 rooms, 15 suites. Coffee shop, room service. AE, DC, MC, V. Subte: Estación Tribunales (close, but probably not close enough if you're carrying bags).*

**$$$** ▦ **Gran Hotel Colón.** Near the Obelisk, off busy Avenida 9 de Julio, the shiny, modern Colón has suites with private patios; standard rooms, however, are shoe-box size. Airport buses leave from out front. ✉ *Av.*

*Carlos Pellegrini 507, 1009,* ☎ *11/4320–3500, 800/448–8355 in the U.S.,* FAX *11/4320–3507. 183 rooms, 23 suites. Restaurant, bar, room service, pool. AE, DC, MC, V. Subte: Estación 9 de Julio.*

$$$ 🏨 **Posta Carretas.** This modern and very comfortable property has the atmosphere of a mountain inn. Wood paneling abounds, creating a coziness that contrasts with the bustle outside. Some of the brightly decorated rooms have hot tubs. ✉ *Esmeralda 726, 1007,* ☎ *11/4322–8534,* FAX *11/4326–2277. 40 rooms, 11 suites. Bar, room service, pool, exercise room, sauna, business services. AE, DC, MC, V. Subte: Estación San Martín.*

$$$ 🏨 **Principado.** Built for the World Cup in 1978, this hotel has reception areas with large windows and lots of light and a two-tier Spanish colonial–style lobby with leather couches. The highlight is the friendly coffee shop. Rooms are modern and comfortable. ✉ *Paraguay 481, 1057,* ☎ *11/4313–3022,* FAX *11/4313–3952. 88 rooms. Coffee shop. AE, DC, MC, V. Subte: Estación San Martín.*

$$$ 🏨 **Regente Palace.** The winding brass staircase, numerous mirrors, and neon lights in the lobby make you feel like you've entered a '70s casino or a Burt Reynolds movie. Yet rooms are pleasant if small and are decorated with black wood furniture and bedspreads and curtains in beige and rose. It's near Plaza San Martín on a block with several cafés and trendy shops. ✉ *Suipacha 964, 1008,* ☎ *11/4328–6800,* FAX *11/4328–7460. 150 rooms, 6 suites. Restaurant, snack bar. AE, DC, MC, V. Subte: Estación San Martín.*

$$ 🏨 **Castelar Hotel.** Rooms have that rather institutional style associated with a business hotel; yet they're comfortable, and the lobby is small and inviting. The hotel spa has a Turkish-style bath—a rarity in Buenos Aires. It's an ideal place if you plan to focus on the Plaza de Mayo area. Breakfast is included in the rates. ✉ *Av. de Mayo 1152, 1085,* ☎ *11/4383–5000,* FAX *11/4383–8388. 50 rooms. Bar, snack bar, spa, exercise room, laundry service, dry cleaning, meeting rooms. AE, MC, V. Subte: Estación Avenida de Mayo.*

$$ 🏨 **Gran Hotel Dora.** A cozy lobby with a small bar greets you at this old-fashioned hotel. Rooms are comfortable, elegant, and decorated in Louis XVI style. It caters primarily to Europeans and Argentines who want a Continental atmosphere. ✉ *Maipú 963, 1006,* ☎ *11/4312–7391,* FAX *11/4313–8134. 96 rooms. Bar, snack bar, meeting rooms. AE, DC, MC, V. Subte: Estación San Martín.*

$$ 🏨 **Hotel Salles.** This quiet, central establishment is one of the few family-oriented hotels in the heart of the theater district. Rooms are adequate, the decor businesslike and institutional; personal service is a focus. ✉ *Cerrito 208, 1010,* ☎ *11/4382–3962,* FAX *11/4382–0754. 80 rooms, 5 suites. Coffee shop. AE, DC, MC, V. Subte: Estación 9 de Julio.*

$$ 🏨 **Lancaster.** The countess who decorated this traditional and central
★ hotel made good use of her family heirlooms—old family portraits, marble pillars, and a 200-year-old clock grace the lobby. All rooms have antique mahogany furniture, and some have views of the port of Buenos Aires. ✉ *Av. Córdoba 405, 1054,* ☎ *11/4312–4061,* FAX *11/4311–3021. 88 rooms, 16 suites. Restaurant, bar, room service, meeting rooms. AE, DC, MC, V. Subte: Estación Leandro N. Alem.*

$ 🏨 **Gran Hotel Atlantic.** If you're looking for inexpensive if basic rooms and friendly (though not very quick) service, this is the place for you. ✉ *Castelli 45, 1031,* ☎ *11/4951–0081,* FAX *11/4951–0081. Bar, room service, parking. AE, DC, MC, V. Subte: Estación Plaza de Miserre.*

$ 🏨 **Gran Hotel Hispano.** The Spanish colonial architecture and small but charming rooms with flower motifs give this hotel a traditional yet friendly feel. Guests are primarily from neighboring Latin American countries. ✉ *Av. de Mayo 861, 1084,* ☎ *11/4345–2020,* FAX *11/4345–*

*5266. 60 rooms. Bar, breakfast room, ice cream parlor, laundry. AE, DC, MC, V. Subte: Estación Piedras.*

**$** 🏨 **Gran Hotel Orly.** Off Calle Florida, the Orly draws Brazilian tourists and visitors from the interior. Although the entrance is impressive, rooms are plain and small and have noisy air-conditioners. The old-timer reception staff seems to be frozen in the previous century. But you can't beat it if you're looking for a clean, basic, inexpensive place to sleep. ⊠ *Paraguay 474, 1057,* ☎ *11/4312–5344,* 𝔽𝔸𝕏 *11/4312–5344. 168 rooms, 8 suites. Bar, coffee shop. AE, DC, MC, V. Subte: Estación Facultad de Medicina.*

## Palermo

**$$** 🏨 **Hotel Alpino.** This hotel has functional if uninteresting rooms. The Parque Zoológico and the Jardín Botánico are within easy walking distance. Breakfast is included in the rates. ⊠ *Cabello 3318, 1425,* ☎ *11/4802–5151,* 𝔽𝔸𝕏 *11/4802–5151. 35 rooms. Bar, in-room safes, parking. AE, DC, MC, V. Subte: Estación Plaza Italia.*

## La Recoleta

**$$$$** 🏨 **Alvear Palace Hotel.** Built in 1932 as a luxury apartment building,
★ the Alvear has since become the city's most elegant hotel and is often the site of receptions for visiting diplomats and dignitaries. Rooms are done in French Empire–style, in regal burgundy and deep blue, and have large windows, silk drapes, and feather beds. The hotel is convenient to many museums and good restaurants. ⊠ *Av. Alvear 1891, 1129,* ☎ *11/4808–2100 or 11/4804–7777, 800/448–8355 in the U.S.,* 𝔽𝔸𝕏 *11/ 4804–0034. 100 rooms, 100 suites. Restaurant, coffee shop, lobby lounge, piano bar, tea shop, indoor pool, health club, concierge, business services, meeting rooms. AE, DC, MC, V.*

**$$$$** 🏨 **Caesar Park.** Opposite Patio Bullrich, this Westin-operated hotel is near La Recoleta and Plaza San Martín. The lavish, spacious rooms have tasteful fabrics, period furniture, marble bathrooms, and good light, though they're a bit generic when compared with other historic hotels. Upper floors have a panoramic view of the river. If you're staying at the hotel, you have access (for a fee) to a nearby 18-hole golf course. ⊠ *Posadas 1232, 1011,* ☎ *11/4819–1100, 800/228–3000 in the U.S.,* 𝔽𝔸𝕏 *11/4819–1120. 172 rooms, 20 suites. 3 restaurants, bar, in-room modem lines, room service, indoor pool, beauty salon, health club, business services, meeting rooms. AE, DC, MC, V.*

**$$$$** 🏨 **Park Hyatt Buenos Aires.** On the edge of La Recoleta, the luxuri-
★ ous Park Hyatt has a 13-floor marble tower and an adjacent turn-of-the-century mansion, with private butler service for its handsome suites. This is where Madonna stayed for two months during the filming of *Evita.* In addition to its million-dollar art collection, the hotel houses a beautiful Roman-style pool, health club, and landscaped garden. Guest rooms are the largest of any Buenos Aires hotel, and outstanding service ensures many repeat visitors (when you check in, the hotel staff sits down with you to determine your needs). ⊠ *Posadas 1086, 1011,* ☎ *11/4326–1234, 800/233–1234 in the U.S.,* 𝔽𝔸𝕏 *11/ 4326–3736. 116 rooms, 50 suites. Restaurant, bar, coffee shop, room service, pool, health club, concierge, business services, meeting rooms. AE, DC, MC, V.*

**$$$–$$$$** 🏨 **Plaza Francia.** The best-situated small hotel in town, the Plaza Francia overlooks the park of the same name. Rooms are large and have a French feel, with overstuffed pillows, head rolls, and crisp white curtains. Ask for one with a park view, though if traffic noise bothers you, get an inside room. ⊠ *Pasaje E. Schiaffino 2189, 1129,* ☎ 𝔽𝔸𝕏 *11/4804–9631. 36 rooms, 14 suites. Room service. AE, DC, MC, V.*

### San Telmo

$$ 🏨 **Constitución Palace Hotel.** This hotel is near La Boca and San Telmo in the neighborhood of Constitución (you need to use caution in this area at night). Rooms are stark but you can't beat the price; breakfast is included in the rates. If you're planning any trips out of town, this hotel is right next to one of the city's main train stations, Constitución. ⊠ *Lima 1697, 1138,* ☎ *11/4305–9010,* FAX *11/4305–9015. 150 rooms. Bar, room service, in-room modem lines, laundry, meeting rooms. AE, DC, MC, V. Subte: Estación Constitución.*

### Vicente Lopez

$–$$ **Hotel Vicente Lopez.** In the charming and fashionable suburb of Vicente Lopez, this quiet hotel is close to the river and steps from the commuter train, which can bring you to downtown in 15 minutes. Embassies in the suburbs often house visiting guests here. Rooms are clean if minimal. ⊠ *Libertador 902, 1001,* ☎ *11/4797–3773. 30 rooms. Parking, breakfast room. AE, DC, MC, V. Subte: Estación Vicente Lopez.*

# NIGHTLIFE AND THE ARTS

Listings of events can be found daily in the English-language *Buenos Aires Herald* as well as in the more comprehensive Friday edition. If you read Spanish, check out the more complete weekend section in the Friday edition of *La Nación.*

## The Arts

Except for some international short-run performances, tickets to most events are surprisingly easy to get. Tickets can be purchased at the box office of the venue or at various ticket outlets. **Ticketmaster** (☎ 11/4326–9903) sells tickets for events at the Colón, Luna Park, Teatro Globo, and the Teatro Municipal San Martín, and accepts MasterCard and Visa for phone purchases. **Ticketron** (☎ 11/4321–9700) has tickets to the same venues as Ticketmaster as well as to local theaters and music halls. **Musimundo,** a record store with several branches throughout the city (there's one in every mall) sell tickets for concerts. Note that, like most other businesses in Argentina, theaters take a summer vacation (January–February). To see theater productions in January and February, you may have to drive to the beach! Men usually wear jackets and ties to theater performances, and women also dress accordingly.

### Classical Music and Opera

By any standard, the **Teatro Colón** (⊠ Ticket office: Tucumán 1111, ☎ 11/4382–4784) is one of the world's finest opera houses. Tiered like a wedding cake, the gilt and red-velvet auditorium has unsurpassed acoustics. Pavarotti has said that the Colón has only one thing wrong with it: the acoustics are so good, every mistake can be heard. An ever-changing stream of imported talent bolsters the well-regarded local company. The opera season runs from April to November. The **National Symphony,** is also headquartered in the Colón Theater and also runs from April to November.

### Dance

When you think dance in Buenos Aires, you think of the tango—and this is the capital of that most passionate of dances (☞ The Art of Tango, *above*). But dance is not only about the tango: Porteños also gather in droves on weekends to dance to the pulsating beats of samba and salsa. **Salsón** (⊠ Av. Alvarez Thomas 1166, ☎ 11/4637–6970), which is *the* place for salsa in Buenos Aires, has salsa lessons on Wednesday and Friday nights at 9 PM. If you want to learn Brazilian dance, head to

# THE ART OF TANGO

A MIXTURE OF PASSION, sensuality, nostalgia, and melancholy, the tango is the dance of Argentina and Buenos Aires is its capital. Every child learns it, every couple knows it. You can experience the culture of tango everywhere in Buenos Aires: at a show at the world-famous Casablanca, in a spontaneous outburst on Calle Florida, at a glitzy nightclub, or at a neighborhood spot in San Telmo. Opening days and times of tango halls regularly change, so call to verify before you arrive. If you'd prefer to bask in the history of the dance, retrace the footsteps of Carlos Gardel, the tango's great hero (he died in a plane crash in 1935 at the age of 40), in the Mercado del Abasto neighborhood and then visit his grave at the Chacarita Cemetery.

You'll see advertisements for tango performances everywhere. The best performances are at **Casa Blanca** (⊠ Balcarce 668, ☎ 11/4331–4621) in San Telmo. **Michelangelo** (⊠ Balcarce 433, ☎ 11/4331–9659) combines folk, tango, and international music in a dinner show at its striking, remodeled old warehouse location. A very traditional show takes place at San Telmo's **El Viejo Almacén** (⊠ Balcarce and Independencia, ☎ 11/4307–6689). More authentic and considerably less expensive tango shows are staged at 10 PM weeknights at the **Gran Café Tortoni** (⊠ Av. de Mayo 829, ☎ 11/4342–4328).

**Akarense** (⊠ Donado 1355 at Av. Los Incas, ☎ 11/4651–2121) draws the best dancers to its beautiful hall. You can dance tango Tuesday, Friday, Saturday, and Sunday nights at **Club Almagro** (⊠ Medrano 522, ☎ 11/4774–7454) with porteños of all ages who come to enjoy their national dance. **La Galería del Tango Argentino** (⊠ Av. Boedo 722) has competitions and shows; tango *fantasía*, a version that allows dancers to show off their abilities, is very popular here. **Ideal** (⊠ Suipacha 384, ☎ 11/4601–8234) is less intimidating; people of all ages come here to practice, while teachers offer informal instruction. **Regine's** (⊠ Av. Río Bamba 416) is a small place reminiscent of Fellini's *Satyricon*. The very special **Sin Rumbo** (⊠ Tamborini 6157, ☎ 11/4571–9577) attracts old *milonga* (a sambalike dance that predates the tango) dancers. The very large **Social Rivadavia** (⊠ Av. Rivadavía 6465, ☎ 11/4632–8064) has two dance floors and music mainly from the '40s. **Viejo Correó** (⊠ Av. Diaz Velez 4820, ☎ 11/4958–0364) has a more sophisticated atmosphere than most of the other tango spots.

Another place to become one with tango is through a private lesson at the **Estudio Guillermo Alio** (⊠ Magalanes 859, ☎ 11/4303–1276); Mr. Alio's daughter, who works in the studio, speaks fluent English. Another place for a lesson is the **Academia Nacional de Tango** (⊠ Av. de Mayo 833, ☎ 11/4345–6967) on Monday, Wednesday, and Friday nights at 7:30; don't worry about bringing a partner—they will pair you up if needed.

**Sudaca** (✉ Sarmiento 1752, ☏ 11/4371–0802) for a quick samba lesson. **La Trastienda** (✉ at Balcarce and Belgrano, ☏ 11/4434–2760) is a large dance hall hosting salsa classes and energetic crowds; it also occasionally doubles as a performance space for tango shows.

The **National Ballet Company** is headquartered at the Colón (☞ Classical Music and Opera, *above*) but gives open-air performances in Palermo in summer. World-class contemporary dance is performed several times a year at the **Teatro San Martín** (✉ Av. Corrientes 1530, ☏ 11/4374–8611 or 11/4331–7553).

## Film

First-run Hollywood movies, Argentine films, and Italian comedies are shown at the more than 50 theaters in the downtown area alone. Most of these are along two parallel streets, Avenida Corrientes and Calle Lavalle. The *Herald* has daily listings. The names of the films are generally given in Spanish, but English-language films are shown undubbed, with Spanish subtitles. Seats are assigned at movie theaters: When purchasing tickets, you can choose your seat. Ushers, who expect a one-peso tip, show you to your seats if a movie has already begun or if the theater is particularly crowded. Tickets are usually around $7.50, but the first show of the day is half price, and all cinemas are half price all day Wednesday. The following theaters show Argentine and Hollywood films: **Belgrano Multiplex** (✉ at Obligado and Mendoza, ☏ 11/4781–8183); **Paseo Alcorta** (✉ at F. Alcorta and Salguero, ☏ 11/4806–5665); and **Puerto Madero** (✉ Av. M. de Justo 1960, ☏ 11/4315–3008).

## Theater

Buenos Aires has some 40 theaters, ranging from those presenting Argentine dramatic works to those showing foreign plays in translation, musicals, and *revistas* (revues) with comedians and dancers known for the brevity of their costumes. **La Plaza** (✉ Av. Corrientes 1660, ☏ 11/4382–4177) is an open-air shopping center with a small outdoor amphitheater and two theaters, along with shops and small restaurants. Publicly supported theater, mime, puppet shows, and dance are performed on the three stages of the municipal theater complex, **Teatro San Martín** (✉ Av. Corrientes 1530, ☏ 11/4374–8611 or 11/4331–7553).

# Nightlife

It's good to begin with a basic understanding of the Argentine idea of nightlife: A date at 7 PM is considered an afternoon coffee break; theater performances start at 9 PM or 9:30 PM; the last movie begins after midnight; and nightclubs don't begin filling up until 2 AM. Tango, too, gets going after midnight and never seems to stop (☞ The Art of Tango, *above*). Porteños never go early to discos—they wouldn't want to be seen before 2 AM. In fact, even you wanted to go early, you might not be allowed in: "early evening" hours (meaning before midnight) are often reserved for teenagers, and no one over 18 may be permitted to enter until after that time. For the most part, Buenos Aires's dance clubs attract young crowds (in the 18–30 age range). The best places to go out are in La Recoleta, Palermo, and Costanera Norte. Note that the subte closes at 10 PM, so if you go out late, either count on taking a taxi home or waiting until 5 AM for the subte to start running again.

## Bars and Clubs

BELGRANO

**New York City** (✉ Av. Alvarez Thomas 1391, ☏ 11/4555–5559), decorated to look like a spot in downtown Manhattan, is primarily filled with people in their teens and early twenties. **Tobaggo Cigar and Arts**

**Café** (⊠ Alvarez Thomas 138, ☎ 11/4553–5530) is all about cigar culture (and hosts events).

**Ave Porco** (⊠ Av. Corrientes 1980, ☎ 11/4953–7129), in the theater district, has a little bit of everything—a techno dance room, an upstairs lounge, and a back patio. **La Cigale** (⊠ 25 de Mayo 722, ☎ 11/4813–8275) has a large bar to lean up to and good music. For a little Irish-bar atmosphere and some Guinness, check out **Druid In** (⊠ Reconquista 1040, ☎ 11/4312–3688). **Dunn** (⊠ San Martín 986) is a small bar where electronic music is the soundtrack of choice. At **Morocco** (⊠ Hipólito Yrigoyen 851, ☎ 11/4342–6046) you never know when you'll see an impromptu drag show. An older, more refined crowd goes for drinks and cigars to the Marriott's elegant **Plaza Bar** (⊠ Florida 1005, ☎ 11/4318–3000). For a quick tango lesson and a beer, head to **Sedon** (⊠ at 25 de Mayo and Córdoba, ☎ 11/4361–0141). **Shamrock** (⊠ Rodríguez Peña 1220, ☎ 11/4812–3584) is an Irish-style bar where an English-speaking expat crowd is often found; happy hour is from 6–9PM.

**Open Plaza Junior** (⊠ Av. F. Alcorta, ☎ 11/4782–7204), which caters to a very fashionable crowd, has a sprawling bar, pool tables, a disco, a restaurant, and a shark tank. **Tequila** (⊠ Costanera Norte and La Pampa, ☎ 11/4788–0438) is one of the most happening bars in the city; expect a line out the door.

**Buenos Aires News** (⊠ Infanta Isabel, ☎ 11/4778–1500) is one of the city's trendiest nightspots—you might even see a model or rock star. **El Living** (⊠ Marcelo T. de Alvear 1540, ☎ 11/4811–4730) is a trendy disco and bar with lounge chairs and great drinks. **Gallery** (⊠ Azcuénaga 1771, ☎ 11/4807–1652) draws a young crowd with live salsa bands and frozen margaritas; the restaurant, which opens at 8:30, serves rather bland Tex-Mex dishes. The city's most popular disco is **La Morocha** (⊠ Av. Dorrego 3307, ☎ 11/4778–0050); January–March this location is closed, and a branch of it opens at the beach in Uruguay. **Mundo Bizarro** (⊠ Guatemala 4802, ☎ 11/4773–1967) is a cool bar with a hip crowd. **Nero** (⊠ Marcelo T. de Alvear 538, ☎ 11/4313–3458) has a minimalist appeal.

**El Divino** (⊠ Cecilia Grierson 225, ☎ 11/4315–2791), in a space that was built to resemble the Sydney Opera House, appeals to an affluent, fashionable set.

Like so many capitals around the world, Buenos Aires has its own **Hard Rock Café** (⊠ in La Recoleta Design Center, Av. Pueyrredón 2501, ☎ 11/4807–7625), serving typical American drinks and snacks; on weekends an irritatingly high cover is charged. **The Spot** (⊠ Ayacucho 1261, ☎ 11/4811–8955) is a cocktail bar with a daily happy hour.

One of Buenos Aires's most traditional bars, **Dorrego** (⊠ Defensa 1098, ☎ 11/4361–0141) was once a general store; it's now the place (best in the afternoon) to down Quilmes beers and peanuts.

## Gay and Lesbian Bars and Clubs

Right in El Centro, **Angels** (⊠ Viamonte 2168) has several dance floors and attracts a primarily gay and transvestite clientele. **Bunker** (⊠ Anchorena 1170), an old standard, draws a gay and mixed crowd.

**Confusión** (⊠ Av. Scalabrini Ortíz 1721), in El Centro, hosts techno dance parties until dawn for a gay, lesbian, and transvestite crowd. **Teleny** (⊠ Juncal 2479) has good drinks and live drag shows.

## Jazz Clubs

Buenos Aires has serious jazz musicians and enthusiastic audiences. **Café Tortoni** (⊠ Av. de Mayo 825, ☎ 11/4342–4328) has jazz on weekends. **Gazelle Jazz Club** (⊠ Estados Unidos 465, ☎ 11/4361–4685), in San Telmo, is the place to see local and foreign groups. **The Jazz Club** (⊠ La Plaza Complex, Av. Corrientes 1660) often has jazz concerts in the evening and serves good drinks and snacks. **Notorious** (⊠ Av. Callao 966, ☎ 11/4813–6888) has jazz shows several times per week, and when there isn't live music, you can play music on your table's CD player. **Patio Bullrich** (⊠ Av. del Libertador 750) frequently has evening jazz performances. At **Salo** (⊠ Arroyo 1167) jazz and blues are played in a dark, Paris-like setting.

# OUTDOOR ACTIVITIES AND SPORTS

## Participant Sports

### Athletic Clubs

Athletic clubs in Buenos Aires are not only gyms with weightlifting equipment, aerobics classes, and pools, but the're also places to participate in organized sports. **Club de Amigos** (⊠ Av. Alcorta, ☎ 11/4801–1213) has pickup soccer games and tennis lessons as well as a gym and a pool. **Coconor** (⊠ Rafael Obligado and Salguero, ☎ 11/4788–5995) is the closest that Buenos Aires comes to a beach club: For $25 per day you can mix and mingle at this sports club with a pool operated by Club Med. **Punta Carrasco** (⊠ Costanera Norte and Sarmiento, ☎ 11/4807–1010) is a sports complex with a swimming pool, tennis courts, organized sports, and lots of people-watching.

### Bicycling and Running

It's unusual to see people running on the streets; jogging and biking are usually confined to parks like the Parque Tres de Febrero in Palermo (there's usually a stand in the park where you can rent bikes) and the Reserva Ecológica (Ecological Reserve; ☞ Off the Beaten Path *in* Puerto Madero, *above*). For an enclosed, bikers-only atmosphere at a nominal admission charge, head to the **Velodromo** (⊠ Av. Tornquist).

### Chess

Pursuing a hobby, especially one with such a universal language as chess, is a good way to meet Argentines. It's played at the **Gran Café Tortoni** (⊠ Av. de Mayo 829, ☎ 11/4342–4328); upstairs at the **Confitería Ideal** (⊠ Suipacha 384, ☎ 11/4326–0521); in the mansion wing of the **Park Hyatt Buenos Aires** (☞ Lodging, *above*); and in the basement lounge of the **Richmond** (⊠ Florida 468, ☎ 11/4322–1341).

### Golf

**Cancha Municipal de Golf** (⊠ Tornquist and Olleros, ☎ 11/4772–7261 or 11/4772–7576) is a public golf course that's 10 minutes from downtown in Palermo. **Costa Salguero** (⊠ Rafael Obligado and Salguero, ☎ 11/4804–2444) is a complete sports and health complex, with a focus on golf. For more information call the **Asociación Argentina de Golf** (Argentine Golf Association, ⊠ Av. Corrientes 538, 11th and 12th floors, ☎ 11/4394–2743). The plush **Miraflores Country Club** (⊠ Ruta Panamericana, Km 35½, ☎ 3327/454–800), in the suburb of Garín (follow signs on the highway to the town of Pilar), is open to nonmembers on Tuesday, Saturday, and Sunday, for a $30 greens fee.

## Paddle Tennis

Paddle tennis, a typical Argentine game that is sort of a cross between tennis and squash, is popular with all ages. The city has hundreds of courts. **Circuito KDT** (⊠ Salguero 3450, ☎ 11/4802–2619) has excellent courts available by reservation. **Recoleta Squash** (⊠ Ayacucho 1669, ☎ 11/4801–3848) is open to nonmembers, but you must reserve in advance.

## Spa

Buenos Aires' **Colmegña Spa** (⊠ Sarmiento 839, ☎ 11/4326–1257) is as relaxing as it gets. For $99 you can have a full day at the spa, including a Turkish bath, body peel, massage, hair, and lunch. An appointment is essential; it's open Tuesday–Saturday 11–8.

## Squash

A good place to play is at the central **Olimpia Cancilería** (⊠ Esmeralda 1042, ☎ 11/4313–7375), which also has racquetball courts. Another possibility is **Recoleta Squash** (⊠ Ayacucho 1669, ☎ 11/4801–3848).

## Tennis

Many of the athletic clubs (☞ *above*) have tennis courts that you can use for a fee. There are public tennis courts at the **Buenos Aires Lawn Tennis Club** (⊠ Av. Olleros 1510, ☎ 11/4772–9227). Arrangements can be made through the executive offices at the **Sheraton** (⊠ San Martín 1225, ☎ 11/4318–9309) to play on the hotel's courts for $15 per hour.

# Spectator Sports

## Boxing and Wrestling

Boxing and wrestling matches are held in **Luna Park** (⊠ Bouchard 465, ☎ 11/4311–1990 or 11/4312–2538), an indoor arena. Check the *Herald* for details.

## Cricket

Cricket is played at the suburban **Hurlingham Club** (⊠ Av. J. A. Roca 1411, ☎ 11/4665–0401) and other Anglo-Argentine enclaves. Check the *Herald* for information.

## Horse Racing

Historians consider the strong Thoroughbreds from Argentina one of the factors that favored the British in the South African Boer War. Argentines on spending binges brought, and occasionally still bring, the best stock in the world home to breed, and swift Argentine horses are prized throughout the world. Although the past 40 years of rough economic times have handicapped the Thoroughbred industry, Argentine horses still win their share of races in North America and Europe. There are two main tracks in Buenos Aires; check the *Buenos Aires Herald* for schedules. Generally, races take place on Wednesday and Saturday at **Hipódromo de San Isidro** (⊠ Av. Márquez 504, ☎ 11/4743–4010), in the historic suburb of San Isidro. Closer to downtown, in Palermo, is the dirt track at the traditional **Hipódromo Argentino** (⊠ Av. del Libertador 4000, ☎ 11/4777–9009).

## Polo

Argentine polo has been compared to a performance of the Bolshoi Ballet in its heyday—a strenuous display of stunning athletic showmanship. At the **Canchas Nacionales** (National Fields), on Avenida Dorrego in the barrio of Palermo in Buenos Aires, sold-out crowds cheer on national heroes. There are two seasons: March–May and September–December. Tickets can be purchased in advance through ticket agencies (☞ Nightlife and the Arts, *above*) or on the day of the event; general admission is about $7. The best teams compete in the Argentine Open Championships in November. For match information contact the **Asociación Argentina de Polo** (✉ H. Yrigoyen 636, 1st floor, Apt. A, ☎ 11/4331–4646).

## Soccer

In a 1998 survey conducted by the *Clarín,* the most widely circulated paper in Argentina, thousands of Argentines were asked, "What brings you joy?" Twenty percent responded that it was their families; 13 percent said money; and 50 percent responded soccer—proof that soccer is a huge part of Porteño life. Soccer matches are held year-round. To see another side of Argentine passion, go to a game. Sitting among tens of thousands of roaring fans can be a disconcerting experience, especially if you get swept off your perch in the bleachers as a human wave slides five rows back and forth to cheer a goal. For this reason, it's recommended that you pay for a seat (around $40–$60) rather than opting for the often chaotic and frequently dangerous (but cheaper) standing-room section. Passions run especially high when La Boca's Boca Juniors take on their arch-rivals, River Plate, from the upper-crust district of Belgrano. (The rivalry has a deeper political and socioeconomic significance: Supporters of Boca are drawn from Buenos Aires's working class, while River Plate is traditionally the team of the city's more urbane middle and upper classes.) Major games are played at the **Estadio Boca Juniors** (✉ Brandsen 805). Tickets can be purchased at the stadium before the game.

## Tennis

Guillermo Vilas, José Luis Clerc, and Gabriela Sabatini are all products of local clubs. Most professional tennis matches are played at the **Buenos Aires Lawn Tennis Club** (✉ Av. Olleros 1510, ☎ 11/4772–9227).

# SHOPPING

There was a time not so long ago when Argentine families went to Miami to purchase quality goods. But the situation has changed with the lifting of trade bans and items are becoming much more widely available. Unfortunately, clothing made in Argentina is generally not that well constructed, though this is improving as well.

When shopping in Buenos Aires as a foreigner, keep your receipts: The 21% VAT tax, added to almost every purchase you'll make, is entirely refundable for purchases of more than $200. When you depart, plan enough time to visit the return desk at the airport to obtain your refund.

## Shopping by Area

### Avenida Santa Fe

Downtown Avenida Santa Fe is great for browsing: lining it are hundreds of little boutiques and bustling cafés. It's a good place to find fashionable, reasonably priced clothes.

### Calle Florida

Crowded, pedestrians-only Calle Florida, the main downtown shopping street, is lined with McDonald's (there are four and counting along this 10-block street), persistent vendors, and stores of all kinds. It's a good place to go first to establish a quality and price standard, as well as for last-minute souvenirs and food especially packaged for plane trips. The street is also home to the city's best bookstores. Keep in mind that the closer you get to Plaza San Martín, the better the offerings.

### La Recoleta

With its designer boutiques and expensive stores, concentrated on Avenida Alvear, and Calle Quintana, La Recoleta is the finest area to shop in the city.

### San Telmo

San Telmo is the antiques shopping district. Many old homes have been converted into shops, like those in the Pasaje de la Defensa (Defense Alley). One of these is an elaborate Italianate house built in the 1850s that once belonged to the Ezeiza family (namesake of the town where your plane will land, if you fly into Argentina). At the turn of the century it was transformed into a tenement for immigrants and now houses several dozen antiques vendors.

## Shopping Malls

**Abasto** (⊠ Av. Corrientes 3200) is a shopping mall, with the usual clothing stores and restaurants, in a renovated old marketplace, which is modernized inside but has the original facade.

**Alto Palermo** (⊠ Corner of Av. Santa Fe and Av. Colonel Diaz, subte: Line D to Estación Bulnes) has three floors of clothes shops, cafés, and toy and book stores right on the bustling Avenida Santa Fe.

**Galerías Pacífico** (Pacífico Shopping Center; ⊠ Florida 753, at Av. Córdoba) is in the former headquarters of the Buenos Aires–Pacific Railway, a building designed during Buenos Aires's turn-of-the-century golden age in the style of Milan's Gallerie Vittorio Emanuele. In 1992 it was transformed into a glossy, multilevel California-style shopping center (in an earlier renovation a large skylighted dome was added, and five leading Argentine artists were commissioned to paint murals). Currently managed by a consortium owned by George Soros, the Galerías Pacífico stands out as one of the finer places to shop as well as to have a quick lunch on busy Calle Florida.

**Paseo Alcorta** (⊠ at Av. Alcorta and Salguero), in Palermo, has chic Argentine clothing stores for men and women, as well as internationally known stores like Christian Dior and Yves St. Laurent, a four-screen movie theater, and a food court.

**Patio Bullrich** (⊠ Av. del Libertador 740), near the Park Hyatt, has some of the finest and priciest shops in town as well as a six-screen movie theater. This multilevel mall was once the headquarters for the Bullrich family's auction house, Buenos Aires's most renowned auctioneers. The basement held hundreds of head of cattle during auctions, and the upper floors were dedicated to selling paintings, furniture, and antiques, including portraits of the livestock and their owners. If you look carefully at the walls on the upper level, you can still see stucco heads of steers emerging in relief. The auction house now functions next door under the name of Posadas (☞ Art and Antiques, *below*).

**Solar de la Abadia** (⊠ Marie Luis Campos and Arcos) is a great place to pick up souvenirs, buy trendy clothes, or have a snack. As it's on the border of Belgrano and the Cañitas section of Palermo, it's also a good place to begin or end a walk around the area. It's about a 10-minue walk from the Museo Nacional del Hombre, and about 20 minutes from Plaza Belgrano.

## Specialty Shops

### Art and Antiques

Most antiques shops are grouped together in San Telmo (☞ Shopping by Area, *above*). The city's largest auction house, **Posadas** (⊠ Posadas

1227, ☎ 11/4327–025 or 11/4815–3573) has furnishings and artwork from many local estates.

## Bookstores

Numerous bookstores can be found along Calle Florida. **El Atheneo** (⊠ Florida 340, ☎ 11/4340–4325) is perhaps the most famous, and sells a wide selection of works by Argentine authors, and classics and best-sellers in English, as well as beautiful souvenir coffee table books depicting the tango and scenes from Argentina.

## Clothing

European designer shops are mostly concentrated along Avenida Alvear and Calle Quintana. Chain stores selling trendy (and often very skimpy) clothing are found all over Buenos Aires. Most of these stores are in malls (☞ Shopping Malls, *above*) as well as along Avenida Santa Fe 800–1500 in the Plaza San Martín area and along Avenida Cabildo 1600–2200 in Belgrano. **Chocolate** has good quality women's clothes that appeal to a twenty-something crowd. **Ona Saez** sells both men's and women's casual and trendy nightclub clothing. **Paula Cahan D'Anvers** sells more conservative, though very small, women's clothing for casual occasions and work. **Via Vai** is a great place for separates, like that sundress or sweater you may have forgotten to pack. **Vitamina** is aimed at younger.

## Fur

Quality fur coats—made of stub-tailed nutria, red fox from Tierra del Fuego, and gray Magellanic fox—can be found in Buenos Aires for half the the price that you would pay in the United States. **Charles Calfun** (⊠ Florida 918, ☎ 11/4311–1147) has an excellent selection. **Dennis Furs** (⊠ Florida 925, ☎ 11/4311–2154 or 11/4312–1630) is one of the city's leading fur coat dealers.

## Handicrafts

**Mercado de las Luces** (⊠ Peru and Alsina, subte: Line E to Estación Bolívar) is a small store selling all kinds of handmade souvenirs; note that many are overpriced (the same items can sometimes be purchased for less in the outdoor markets in Belgrano and San Telmo). **Patio del Cabildo** (⊠ Av. de Mayo and Bolívar), a crafts store in the Cabildo Museum, sells traditional souvenirs and artwork; it's only open Thursday and Friday 11–8.

## Jewelry

The gold district in Buenos Aires is concentrated in and around **Calle Libertad,** between Avenidas Corrientes and Rivadavía: Here you can find inexpensive gold jewelry (mostly 18K). Bargaining is expected and you should watch out for fake stones. An honest jeweler will usually divulge the preciousness of a stone if asked, but if you don't ask, they won't tell. Emeralds from Brazil can be a bargain. One semiprecious stone, *rodocrosita,* known as the "rose of the Inca," is native only to Argentina; these range from pink to ruby red.

**Antonio Belgiorno** (⊠ Av. Santa Fe 1347, ☎ 11/4811–1117) is a top silversmith who creates beautiful, quality silver pieces. Decorated sculptures of birds in flight from **Cousino** (⊠ Paraguay 631, 3rd floor, Suite A, ☎ 11/4312–2336; ⊠ in Sheraton Hotel) are exhibited in the National Museum of Decorative Arts. **Guthman** (⊠ Viamonte 597, ☎ 11/4312–2471) has an acclaimed selection of jewelry. Internationally renowned **H. Stern** (⊠ in Sheraton, Plaza, Hyatt, Inter-Continental, and Alvear Palace hotels; ☞ Lodging, *above*) is a good place for fine Argentine jewelry.

## Leather

Argentina's reputation for fine leather goods is occasionally well deserved. The leather is very high quality, but sometimes craftsmanship is lacking. You can find items made of cowhide, kidskin, pigskin, sheepskin, lizard, snake, and porcupine in an array of colors. Clothing styles range from conservative to hip—everything from bikinis to evening gowns made of leather. Prices for leather goods are generally better than abroad, but be sure to check the quality and stitching before you buy. **Casa López** (⊠ M. T. de Alvear 640, ☎ 11/4311–3044) carries jackets and bags. Polo equipment and saddles can be found at **H. Merlo** (⊠ Juncal 743). **La Martina** (⊠ Paraguay 661, ☎ 11/4311–5963) carries furnishings for the discriminating equestrian. **Murillo 666** (⊠ Murillo 666, ☎ 11/4855–2024 has a wide selection of women's bags and jackets at good prices. For briefcases and other leather bags, try **Pullman** (⊠ In the Galerías Pacífico, ☎ 11/4325–4111). **Rossi y Caruso** (⊠ Av. Santa Fe 1601, ☎ 11/4811–1538) has the best in riding equipment as well as handbags, clothing, shoes, and boots; King Juan Carlos of Spain and many other celebrities are customers here.

## Sheepskin and Wool

Argentina has traditionally been the world's largest exporter of wool. Several big-name Italian designers such as Benetton get their wool from here. **IKS** (⊠ Alisa Moro de Justo 2040, 1st floor, ☎ 11/4311–4747) is a factory outlet for sweaters. **Silvia y Mario** (⊠ M. T. de Alvear 550), another downtown outlet, stocks a huge selection of cashmere and very elegant two-piece knit dresses. Sheepskin jackets at **Ciudad de Cuero** (⊠ Florida 940) would make the Marlboro man leap off his mount to purchase a winter's supply.

## Shoes

For men's loafers, **Guido** (⊠ Florida 704) is Argentina's favorite. For men's and women's shoes that look great and last forever, try **López Taibo** (⊠ Av. Corrientes 350, ☎ 11/4328–2132). Shoes and boots can be found at **Rossi y Caruso** (⊠ Av. Santa Fe 1601, ☎ 11/4811–1538).

# Markets

Open-air markets can be one of the best shopping experiences in Buenos Aires (and can be good places to find souvenirs). The markets listed below are open all day Saturday and Sunday, though none really gets going until the early afternoon. Feel free to try to bargain: often it works, and if it doesn't, you can be assured of finding a similar item at another stall. The markets all carry basically the same types of goods, but if there's one not to miss, it's the San Telmo Market: ongoing entertainment, such as tango dancing, keeps the atmosphere particularly energetic.

**Belgrano Square** (⊠ Juramento and Vuelta de Obligado, subte: Line D to end). **Recoleta Feria** (⊠ Av. Libertador and Av. Pueyrredón). **San Telmo** (⊠ Plaza Dorrego). **Vuelta de Rocha handicraft market** (⊠ Av. Pedro de Mendoza and Caminito Palos).

# BUENOS AIRES A TO Z

## Arriving and Departing

### By Airplane

Most international flights land at **Ezeiza Airport** (☎ 11/4480–0217), 34 km (21 mi) and 45 minutes from downtown Buenos Aires. Ezeiza is served by a variety of foreign airlines, as well as domestic airlines with international routes (☞ Airplane Travel *in* Smart Travel Tips A to Z for more information). If your airline doesn't fly directly to Buenos Aires, it may be possible to fly into Brazil and take a 2–3 hour flight on **Aerolineas Argentinas** (☎ 11/4961–9361) to Ezeiza.

Domestic flights within Argentina generally depart from the **Aeroparque Jorge Newbury** (☎ 11/4773–9805), in Belgrano. A taxi ride from the Aeroparque to the center of Buenos Aires should cost less than $10 and, without much traffic, should take about 15–25 minutes.

BETWEEN THE AIRPORT AND DOWNTOWN

At Ezeiza Airport, *remises* (taxis in which the price for a ride is pre-arranged) tickets can be purchased from the well-marked transportation counter in the airport. Regular taxi service from the airport to downtown costs at least $35. Taxis are the most common means of transportation between Ezeiza and downtown, as there is no train service. It is possible to take a city bus ($2), which operates on a regular schedule, but the ride will take close to two hours, and there is a baggage limit of two bags.

**Manuel Tienda León** (✉ Santa Fe 790, ☎ 11/4383–4454) provides 24-hour airport bus service ($15) to all downtown hotels. These vans and minibuses depart from the airport at scheduled intervals throughout the day. For the return trip, Tienda León provides frequent van service to the airport from its office in front of the Obelisk, as well as other locations throughout the city. It's a reliable service and is nearly as fast as a taxi, but costs about half the price.

## By Bus

Most long-distance and international buses arrive at and depart from the **Estación Terminal de Omnibus** (✉ Av. Ramos Mejía 1680, ☎ 11/4310–0700). There are more than 60 individual bus companies housed inside the terminal, which can be confusing—but there is a logic to the chaos. Bus companies are arranged in order of destinations served, not by name. In general, a few different companies serving the same destination will be clumped together, which makes it easy to compare times and prices. For more information, *see* Bus Travel *in* Smart Travel Tips.

## By Car

Avenida General Paz completely encircles Buenos Aires. If you're driving into the city from the exterior, you'll know you're in Buenos Aires proper once you've crossed this road. If you're entering the city from the north, chances are you will be on the Ruta Panamericana, one of the country's newest and nicest highways. Autopista 25 de Mayo leads out of the city center toward the airport. R2, which is often under construction, goes between Buenos Aires and the beach resorts in and around Mar del Plata.

## By Hydrofoil and Ferry

Hydrofoils and ferries cross the Río de la Plata between Buenos Aires and Uruguay several times a day. Boats often sell out quickly, particularly on summer weekends, so it's important to book tickets at least a few days in advance. This can be done by going to the dock or ticket sales office, or by reserving tickets with a credit card via phone. The most popular company, with the most frequent service, is **Buquebus** (✉ Av. Córdoba and Av. Madero; ✉ in Patio Bullrich shopping mall, ☎ 11/4317–1001). Buquebus provides service for passengers and their vehicles between Buenos Aires and Colonia, Montevideo, Piriápolis, and Punta del Este Uruguay. The 2½-hour ride between Buenos Aires and Montevideo costs about $110 (round-trip) for tourist class and $140 for first class. There's also a cheaper and slower (and less environmentally sound) ferry between Buenos Aires and Colonia, which costs about $55 round-trip. **Ferry Lineas Argentina** (✉ Florida 780,

☎ 11/4314–5100) also serves the Buenos Aires–Uruguay route on a smaller scale with fewer boats per day.

# Getting Around

## By Bus

*Colectivos* (local buses) run all over the city. Routes are marked on blue signs at bus stops, and the fare is required in exact change. Fares are based on destination—the minimum fare is 65¢, and the typical ride through the city is about 70¢. There is also a more comfortable and expensive bus called the *diferencial* (stated on a sign on the front of the bus), which is climate controlled and on which you are assured a seat; it costs about $2 for an average city ride and runs less frequently.

As you board the bus, tell the driver your destination, and he will advise you of the fare that you should drop into the machine next to the driver. The machine will print a ticket, which you must keep throughout your journey on the bus as (theoretically) it can be collected any time. Drivers are usually nice enough to tell you where to get off. If they happen to forget, you can be sure that the locals on the bus will remind you, since foreigners are often an object of gentle curiosity on city buses. City buses run all night, but with far less frequency (sometimes only once every hour) after midnight.

## By Car

Porteños drive with verve and independence—and with a general disdain for traffic rules. A more convenient and comfortable option is to have your travel agent or hotel arrange for a car with a driver (known as a *remise*), especially for a day's tour of the suburbs or nearby pampas. This service costs about $20–$25 per hour, sometimes with a three-hour minimum and an additional charge per kilometer if you drive outside the city limits. Remises usually end up being quite a bit cheaper than cabs for long rides and are at least marginally cheaper for rides within the city.

The following companies arrange remise service: **Mitre Remises** (✉ General Roca 1510, Vincente Lopez, ☎ 11/4796–2829 or 11/4794–7228); **Movicar** (☎ 11/4815–1585; **Remises Plaza de Mayo** (✉ Azopardo 523, ☎ 11/4331–4705); **Remise Rioja** (✉ Olivos 2286, ☎ 11/4794–4677 or 11/4794–7228); and **Remises Universal** (✉ 25 de Mayo 611, 4th floor, ☎ 11/4315–6555).

If you prefer to try your hand at dealing with Buenos Aires road rage by being your own driver, you can rent a car at tourist-friendly **Annie Millet** (✉ Paraguay 1122, ☎ 11/4816–8001, FAX 11/4815–6899). **Avis** (✉ Ezeiza Airport, ☎ 11/4480–9387; ✉ Jorge Newberry Airport, ☎ 11/4776–3003; ✉ Cerrito 1527, ☎ 11/4326–5542; ☎ 800/4445–6284). **Budget** (✉ Av. Santa Fe 11527, ☎ 11/4311–9870). **Primer Mundo** (✉ Av. Libertador 6553, ☎ 11/4787–2140) is smaller than Annie Millet but offers excellent service and better prices. **Thrifty** (✉ Leandro N. Alem 699, ☎ 11/4315–0777). For more car-rental agencies, *see* Car Rental *in* Smart Travel Tips.

### PARKING

Parking has been privatized in Buenos Aires, so ticket-happy entrepreneurs are busy putting yellow-metal boots on the front wheels of cars that stand too long at a meter and towing violators off to nearby parking lots. Fines start at $75. There are a few public underground parking garages and numerous private garages. They start at $2–$3 for the first hour and are typically $1.50 per hour thereafter. Most shopping malls have parking garages, which are usually free or give you a reduced rate with a purchase.

## By Commuter Train

The city is served by six private commuter rail lines, which provide extensive service throughout the city proper and the suburbs. The trains run on a surprisingly consistent schedule: every 5–10 minutes during rush hour, with far fewer trains off-peak. You can get train schedules at stations.

Tickets must be purchased before boarding the train. They can be bought from an attendant or, at some stations, through an automatic machine. Fares are based on the point of departure and the destination. In general, fares range from 40¢ for a journey of a few stops to $2 for a trip to the end of the line; the fare for an *ida y vuelta* (round-trip) ticket to Tigre on the Delta is only $1.60.

On some lines there is a more expensive train called the *diferencial*, which is temperature controlled and on which you are assured a seat. These are usually about four times the cost of the regular trains and run far more infrequently; nonetheless, it may be worth the money and the wait on brutally hot days in January.

Hold onto your ticket: Once on board, a uniformed ticket collector may ask you to show your ticket. If you do not have your ticket, you will be asked to pay an on-the-spot fine of $3.50–$6.50. Although the price of the fine may be relatively insignificant, the time it takes to pay the fine could cause you to miss your stop.

Following are the six commuter train lines and the stations from which they arrive and depart in Buenos Aires. **Línea Belgrano** (✉ Estación Retiro, Av. Ramos Mejía 1430, ☎ 11/4317–4407). **Línea Mitre** (✉ Estación Retiro, Av. Ramos Mejía 1398, across from Sheraton Hotel, ☎ 11/4317–4445). **Línea Roca** (✉ Estación Constitución, Av. Brasil 1138, ☎ 11/4304–0038). **Línea San Martín** (✉ Estación Retiro, Av. Ramos Mejía 1552, ☎ 11/4317–4445). **Línea Sarmiento** (✉ Estación Once, Bartolomé Mitre 2815, ☎ 11/4861–0043). **Línea Urquiza** (✉ Estación Lacroze, Av. Federico Lacroze 4181, ☎ 11/4553–0044).

## By Subway

Buenos Aires's subway system, known as the *subte,* is excellent. It's the oldest in South America, dating from 1913, and many of the stations are decorated with historic scenes of the city or murals by contemporary artists. The subte serves only a small part of the city and does not go anywhere near the suburbs. It was constructed at a time when Buenos Aires consisted of El Centro and La Boca. At that time, Belgrano was a suburb, and anything beyond that was countryside. However, in the last 70 years, Buenos Aires has spread significantly, eating up suburbs and incorporating them into the city far faster than the subway can keep up. But the subway is expanding.

The subte system consists of five lines, which all basically start service in El Centro and then fan out in different directions. Line A, the oldest and most historic line, runs from Plaza de Mayo to Primera Junta. It's worth a trip on Line A, even if you don't need to travel anywhere, just to see the old wooden subway cars. Line B goes from Línea Alem, which is in the financial district of El Centro, near Puerto Madero, to Federico Lacroze. Line C connects the two major train stations, Retiro and Constitución, making stops along the way in El Centro. Line D runs from Catedral on Plaza de Mayo to Jose Hernández, in Belgrano (a new stop is under construction, and as of January 1, 2000, the final stop on Line D was due to be Juramento, also in Belgrano). Line E goes from Bolívar, a few blocks from Plaza de Mayo, to Plaza de los Virreyes. A new line, to be called Line H, which would wrap around the city, is currently in the planning stage and should be in place by 2002.

At press time, tokens cost about 50¢, but discussions are underway to raise the price. One token is valid for any length trip on the subway. The subway is closed between 10 PM and 5 AM.

## By Taxi

Taxis are everywhere in Buenos Aires, so you should never have a problem getting one on the street. Cabs are generally independently owned and operated, and as such, their owners are always on the lookout for business. They are usually safe, but keep in mind that robberies of taxis do occur, especially in areas known to have banks, so be aware. If you don't like the look of a cab, or don't feel comfortable with the driver, do not get in the car. Another cab will be along in a matter of seconds.

Note that hailing a cab involves holding your arm out in a perpendicular fashion, as if you were pointing to something across the street. The traditional New York manner of hailing a cab, with the hand raised up in the air, will flag down a bus in Buenos Aires.

Meters start at $1.20 and increase in small increments per ¼ kilometer. In the central downtown area, fares are about $2–$4; out to Recoleta will cost you $5–$6; San Telmo $4–$6; and Belgrano $8. **City Taxi** (☎ 11/4585–5544) are yellow-roofed, metered cabs.

# Contacts and Resource

## Banks and Currency Exchange

U.S. dollars are frequently accepted throughout Buenos Aires by cab drivers and at restaurants, hotels, and shops. Establishments that accept U.S. dollars often post signs stating that fact. It's always handy to have pesos with you for the occasions when dollars are not accepted. The amount of pesos you require can usually be obtained by making a purchase with a large U.S. dollar bill and requesting the change in pesos (as pesos and dollars are often used interchangeably, you can request your change in either currency).

There is a currency exchange desk at the Ezeiza Airport, right near the exit to the parking lot. Currency can also be exchanged at any of the locations listed below. Most banks are open weekdays 10–3. **America** (⊠ Sarmiento 501, ☎ 11/4393–0054; **Baires** (⊠ San Martín 215, ☎ 11/4325–8547). **Banco Piano** (⊠ San Martín 347, ☎ 11/4394–2463). **Chase Manhattan Bank** (⊠ Arenales 707, 5th floor, ☎ 11/4319–2400. **Citibank** (⊠ Bartolome Mitre 502, ☎ 11/4329–1000. **Forex Cambio** (⊠ Marcelo T. de Alvear 540, ☎ 11/4312–7729). **Republic National Bank of New York** (⊠ Bartolome Mitre 343, ☎ 11/4349–1600. **Western Union** (⊠ Av. Cordoba 917, ☎ 11/4322–7774).

## Churches and Synagogues

**Comunidad Bet El** (⊠ Sucre 3338. **Holy Cross** (⊠ Estados Unidos 3150. **St. Andrew's** (⊠ Av. Belgrano 589).

## Embassies and Consulates

Besides providing assistance, each of the following embassies also hosts a Thursday evening cocktail party (call any embassy to find out the location of the next event).

**Australia** (⊠ Villanueva 1400, ☎ 11/4777–6580). **Canada** (⊠ Tagle 2828, ☎ 11/4805–3032). **Ireland** (⊠ Suipacha 1280, 2nd floor, ☎ 11/4325–8588). **South Africa** (⊠ Marcelo T. de Alvear 590, ☎ 11/4317–2900). **United Kingdom** (⊠ Luis Agote 2412, ☎ 11/4803–6021). **United States** (⊠ Colombia 4300, ☎ 11/4777–4533).

## Emergencies
**Ambulance** (☎ 107). **Fire** (☎ 1100). **Hospital** (British Hospital, ✉ Perdriel 74, ☎ 11/4304–1081). **Police** (☎ 101 or 11/4383–1111).

There's a **pharmacy** (*farmacia*) on nearly every block in Buenos Aires. Your hotel will be able to guide you to the nearest one. Local pharmacies take turns staying open 24 hours; so at any time of day, you can go to pharmacy nearest your hotel, and if it's closed, there will be a sign indicating what pharmacy is open.

## English-Language Media
The best source of information in English is the *Buenos Aires Herald*. It can be purchased at any kiosk throughout the city, for $1 on weekdays and for $1.50 on Sunday. Kioskos on Calle Florida and in front of the Alvear Hotel sell international newspapers, including the *International Herald Tribune*, the *New York Times*, the *Financial Times*, and the *Wall Street Journal*. However, these newspapers are always supplied three days after press date and are always expensive (the Sunday edition of the *New York Times*, for instance, is available on Tuesday). Most bookstores sell an overpriced and very limited selection of English-language material.

## Health and Safety
Buenos Aires is generally a safe city. Violent crime is rare and at any time of night, you'll see young children and old ladies strolling about, apparently unconcerned about the hour or the darkness. Police consistently patrol areas where tourists are likely to be. That said, keep in mind that Buenos Aires is a big city and take precautions: Pickpocketing and robberies are not uncommon. Go out at night in pairs or, better yet, in groups.

Most fresh foods are well washed with city water, which is potable.

## Telephones, Internet, and Mail
### TELEPHONES
Public phones are found on nearly every block and usually operate with a telephone card, which can be purchased at any kiosk. Simply slide the card in, wait for the reading of how many minutes you have remaining, and dial the number. Some public phones are coin operated, and a rare few are still operated by an old phone token. To make a long-distance call from a pay phone, go to a Telecentro, which are found throughout the city and have private booths and fax services. (Note that you still need a local phone card to make a long-distance call, even if you have your own calling card.)

If you need to call the cellular phone number of a resident of Buenos Aires, dial 15 before the number: This is the access code to reach a cellular phone from a noncellular phone (you don't need to dial this number if you're calling from another cellular phone with a Buenos Aires number). Local cellular phone charges are $1 per call, charged to the caller.

### MAIL
Post offices are found every six or seven blocks or so throughout the city and are typically open weekdays from 9 to 6. Most are also open on Saturday until 1, but often, even if the office is closed, a pleading smile will let you in to mail a letter. Stamps are available at kiosks, but most people go directly to the post office and stand in line to mail a letter, which seems to drastically reduce lost mail.

International Express services take 3–5 days to reach the United States from Argentina. Services available include: **DHL** (✉ Moreno 631, ☎

11/4347–0600; **Federal Express** (⊠ Maipu 753, ☎ 11/4630–0300; and **UPS** (⊠ Bernardo de Yrigoyen 974, ☎ 11/4307–2174.

INTERNET

The Internet is available in Buenos Aires. Your hotel may have access, or you can try a Telefonica or Telecom phone office. Internet cafés are not common; occasionally some new ones open, but they don't seem to have much luck. Two to try are **Cyber Express** (⊠ Florida 482, ☎ 11/4325–0935); and **Dos H's Bar** (⊠ Viamonte 636, ☎ 11/4326–0878).

## Tour Operators and Travel Agents

BUS TOURS

**Buenos Aires Tours** (⊠ Lavalle 1444, ☎ 11/4371–2304 or 11/4371–2390) organizes extensive bus tours of the city and can help you plan travel all over the country. **Cauces Tours** (⊠ Maipu 995, ☎ 11/4314–9001) arranges bus tours of the city and neighboring suburbs and also arranges travel throughout Argentina.

WALKING TOURS

If you understand Spanish, you can take advantage of the free guided walking tours offered by the **Municipalidad** (⊠ City Hall; Sarmiento 1551, 5th floor, ☎ 11/4372–3612). The schedule varies each month (in summer it's closed); details are available from the tourist office (☞ Visitor Information, *below*).

## Visitor Information

Information kiosks run by the city along Calle Florida, have English-speaking personnel and city maps, but few brochures. A great place to get friendly tourist advice and tons of brochures, maps, and even vacation-planning tips is at the information counter on the second floor of the Galerías Pacífico shopping center (☞ Shopping, *above*).

You can get information over the phone, on weekdays, 9–5, from the **Dirección de Turismo del Gobierno de la Ciudad de Buenos Aires** (Tourist Department of the City of Buenos Aires; ☎ 15/4763612). The **Secretaria de Turismo de la Nación** (⊠ Av. Santa Fe 883, ☎ 11/4312–2232 or 11/4312–5550), the national tourism office, runs a telephone information service, which is toll free from any point in Argentina, 24 hours a day.

# 3 LAS PAMPAS

The grassy flatlands of Las Pampas are the home of the gaucho, the Argentine cowboy. Here the game of Pato was born, horse training is the order of the day, and polo abounds. Experience this traditional world of the gauchos by staying for a day or two on a ranch. Or enjoy the beautiful coastline while relaxing at one of the beach towns along the Atlantic.

By Kristen
Masick

**L**AS PAMPAS ARE AN UNENDING SEA OF GRASS, occasionally interrupted by the welcome sight of low,
rolling hills. The region is made up of the provinces
of Buenos Aires, La Pampa, Córdoba, and Santa Fe, and occupies nearly
one-quarter of Argentina. Named for the native Quéchua word for flatlands, Las Pampas's famous fertile grasslands are home to the horses
and cattle that make up the mainstay of the region's—and Argentina's—
economy. All over are signs of active ranch life, from the cattle grazing to the gauchos working the wide-open spaces. The region is also
noted for its crops; throughout are extensive farms dotted with alfalfa,
sunflowers, wheat, and corn. Another gem is its coastline, with its great
Atlantic beaches that are good for surfing.

## Pleasures and Pastimes

### Beaches

All along the region's coastline are *balnearios* (small beach clubs)
where you can rent tents and umbrellas and find casual meals. The
beaches are all connected by the Ruta Interbalneario (Interbeach
Route), which can sometimes be treacherous due to potholes, hairpin
turns, and Indy 500–style drivers. But it's also a beautiful drive. The
season begins in December, but really springs to life in January and
February. (Note that beaches are windy year-round.) Some towns,
such as Mar del Plata and Pinamar, are known for their nightlife,
party attitude, and sophisticated crowds. Others, such as Necochea,
are more low key. All are popular vacation spots.

### Dining

Cuisine in Las Pampas, not surprisingly, centers on beef. A typical meal
consists of grilled meat accompanied by tossed salad and lots of red
wine. Larger towns like Mar del Plata and Córdoba have some spots
serving international fare, and most towns have a pasta restaurant or
two. Note that you may have to ask for silverware: The gauchos are
accustomed to using a knife both for cutting and eating.

For a chart that explains the cost of meals at the restaurants listed throughout this chapter, *see* Dining Price Categories *in* Smart Travel Tips.

### Estancias

Occasionally, along the never-ending horizon, you encounter an oasis
that brings you back in time. Here maté is sipped at high tea, when
the estancia owner sits down with his *peóns* (ranch hands) in a gesture of communion. It's here that the gaucho throws the famous
*boleadora*, three stones tied together, which are used to tangle up the
legs of a cow and immobilize it. The estancias are truly working
ranches. The rounding up and branding of cattle is a daily event as are
horse breaking and training. And in the evening there's the traditional
*asado* (barbecue). You can observe or even participate in estancia activities. A day at an estancia is typically spent enjoying an asado, accompanied by empanadas and Argentine red wine, while watching a
traditional demonstration of gaucho skill and dexterity. To get a more
complete feel of gaucho life, you'll want to spend more than just one
day at an estancia.

### Lodging

Most hotels in Las Pampas, especially during tourist season (December–January), require a credit card number to secure a reservation. Some
even require partial payment prior to check-in. Check-out time is generally 11 AM, though small-town hotels may be more flexible. Most
hotels have a small room where breakfast—typically coffee, juice,

bread, and *medias lunas* (croissants)—is served. Except for the very rare case (for example, the Sheraton in Mar del Plata or in Córdoba), don't expect the same amenities that you find in hotels in the United States or Europe (for instance, in smaller towns, rooms may not have a lock on the door). Note, too, that it's often equired that you leave your key at the front desk when when departing the hotel for the day. One of the most exciting options in the area is stay at a working *estancia* (ranch).

For a chart that explains the cost of a double room at the hotels listed throughout this chapter, *see* Lodging Price Categories *in* Smart Travel Tips.

# Exploring Las Pampas

It's best to explore Las Pampas by car, as there are countless small villages and deserted beaches that are difficult or impossible to get to otherwise. Many beach towns are connected by public bus, though service is sporatic in June–September.

## Great Itineraries

### IF YOU HAVE 3 DAYS

From Buenos Aires, travel to the town of ⊞ **Luján** ⑪, a place of pilgrimage for worshippers of the Virgin of Luján. Later that day, continue on to the beach town of ⊞ **Mar del Plata** ⑤. Stay here for two more days while you explore some of the surrounding towns.

### IF YOU HAVE 7 DAYS

If you have seven days, begin by following the three-day itinerary above. From ⊞ **Mar del Plata** ⑤, continue down to the lovely beach town of ⊞ **Necochea** ⑦ and spend a couple of days here. For your last two days, head to ⊞ **Bahía Blanca,** a major port town that provides a good idea of urban life outside of Buenos Aires. Alternatively, from Buenos Aires, head to the ⊞ **Córdoba** ⑭ region for three days. On the fourth day, go to the mountain resort town of ⊞ **Villa Carlos Paz** ⑮, using it as a base to explore the area for the next three days.

### IF YOU HAVE 10 DAYS

From Buenos Aires, head down to ⊞ **Necochea** ⑦; either spend the night here or go on to ⊞ **Mar del Plata** ⑤. From Mar del Plata, follow the interbeach highway, stopping at ⊞ **Villa Gesell** ④ and ⊞ **Pinamar** ③; spend two days in the town of your choice. Continuing along the highway, you begin to approach Buenos Aires again (this 10-day itinerary has you making two big loops around Las Pampas). Before you reach Buenos Aires, stop in one of the nearby towns, such as **La Plata** ①, **Luján** ⑪, or ⊞ **Tigre** ⑩. Spend the night in Tigre or even in Buenos Aires. The next morning, head into Las Pampas *secas* (dry); drive for about five hours through seemingly endless fields and cattle ranches until you reach ⊞ **Rosario** ⑬. After a night here, continue on to ⊞ **Córdoba** ⑭, spending one or two nights in the provincial capital and the others in one of the surrounding mountain resort towns.

## When to Tour

Peak season is summer (January–March). During this time it can be difficult to get a table at a restaurant or a room in a hotel, so be sure to make reservations well in advance. Winter (June–September) has a different feel: The beaches get cold and windy and sometimes even those who consider themselves permanent residents have moved to their Buenos Aires apartments. Some restaurants close up for the winter, and you can't count on a hotel necesarily being open (call ahead). Nonetheless, some of the larger resort towns like Mar del Plata and Córdoba

## Las Pampas

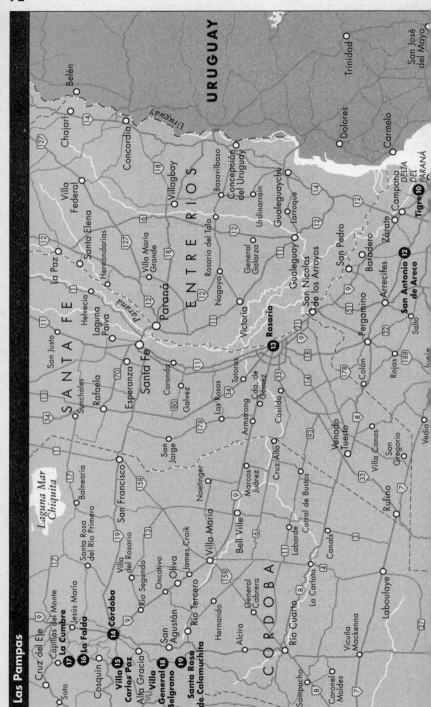

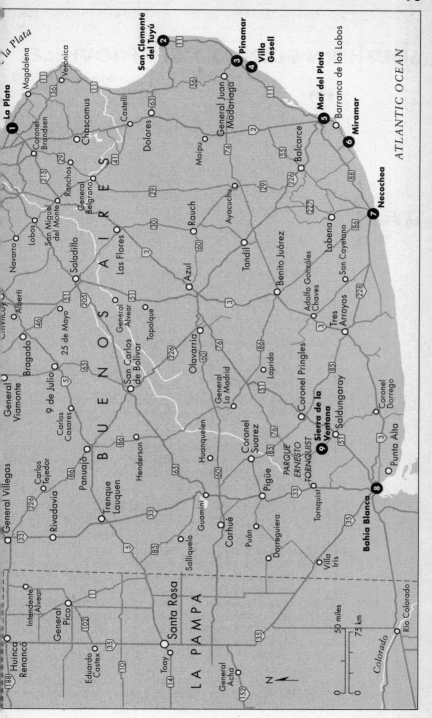

have year-round facilities and a very relaxed atmosphere in winter. Most hotels described below are open year-round unless otherwise noted.

# SOUTHERN BUENOS AIRES PROVINCE

Southern Buenos Aires Province is synonymous with one thing—*la playa* (the beach). Every summer Argentines flock to the resort towns along the coast, many of which were originally large estates converted along the same lines: with a *rambla* (a pedestrians-only street in the center of town) and a central plaza with a church. It can be difficult to find accomodations along the coast because the few places available (most people have vacation homes) fill up quickly. It's easy to get to this string of small beach towns from Buenos Aires; markers along the highway show kilometers traveled from the center of Buenos Aires, designated at the Plaza del Congreso (the Congreso is at Kilometer 0).

## La Plata

**❶** *50 km (31 mi) southwest of Buenos Aires via R1 and R14.*

La Plata's *Piedra Fundacional* (Founding Stone), in the town's main park, the Plaza Moreno, was laid in 1882, when it was decided that the Province of Buenos Aires needed a capital. The city was almost entirely planned, with a street layout that loosely resembles Washington, DC. Today it's famous for its university, political connections, and docile urbanity.

The **Universidad Nacional de La Plata** (La Plata National University) is one of the most famous universities in Argentina and one of the few with a campus in the style of a North American or European school. ✉ *776 Av. 7,* ☎ *221/4833349.*

At the **Museo de Ciencias Naturales** (Natural Science Museum) you can see one of the largest paleontological collections in South America. ✉ *Paseo del Bosque 1900,* ☎ *221/4839125.* ▦ *Admission.* ☉ *Daily 10–6.*

The Eva Perón–founded **Ciudad de los Niños** (Children's City) is part amusement park and part museum containing miniature replicas of historic Argentine buildings that children can walk through. ✉ *Ruta General Belgrano.*

The **Parque Zoológico y Botánico** (Zoo and Botanical Garden) is a beautiful place to spend an afternoon. ✉ *Entrance at corner of Av. Iraola and Av. 52.* ▦ *Admission.* ☉ *Tues.–Fri. 9–5:30, weekends 9–6.*

### Dining and Lodging

$     ✕ **Modelo.** This place, which has been around longer than anyone can remember, is a great place for a quick snack or a full meal of grillled meat and french fries. ✉ *Calle 5 and Calle 54. AE, MC, V.*

$$$$  ✕▥ **Estancia Juan Gerónomo.** In the tiny village of Magdalena, south of La Plata, is this picturesque little estancia, which is perfect for a weekend away from the city. An early 1920s ranch on 400 acres that have been set aside as a World Natural Biosphere Reserve, it's owned and operated by the Munis Barreto family. All meals are included and are served in the Tudor-style main house. Daily activities include hiking, birding, fishing, and horseback riding. Day visits can be arranged. ✉ *In Magdalena, near village of Chascomus (map provided upon reservation),* ☎ *11/49374326,* ℻ *11/43270105. 11 rooms. Restaurant, hiking, horseback riding, fishing, laundry service.*

$$    ▥ **Hotel del Rey.** This hotel is near the main sights in La Plata. Reservations are accepted without a credit card, but you must check in by 7 PM to keep your room. ✉ *Plaza Paso 180,* ☎ *221/4270177,* ℻ *221/*

4251604. 90 rooms. Restaurant, bar, in-room safes, room service, laundry service, meeting rooms, parking. AE, MC, V.

## Nightlife and the Arts

Because it's so close to Buenos Aires, most La Plata residents head there for a cultural fix. Nightlife in La Plata generally revolves around quiet nights at a coffee shop or the movies. Try: **Cine 8** (⊠ Calle 8 between calles 51 and 53, ☎ 221/4834001); **Opera** (⊠ Calle 58 770, ☎ 221/4226502); and **San Martín** (⊠ Av. 7 923, ☎ 221/4839947).

## Outdoor Activities and Sports

The parks surrounding the museum and the university are filled on weekends with bicyclists, joggers, and picnickers. You can go fishing at the **Club de Pesca** (⊠ Calle 45 912, ☎ 221/4838974).

# San Clemente del Tuyú

❷ 308 km (192 mi) southeast of Buenos Aires via R2 and R11; 258 km (160 mi) southeast of La Plata.

Founded in 1935 as a summer resort, San Clemente del Tuyú is the starting point of the string of beach towns that extends down the Atlantic coast. Though it's not quite as beautiful as its neighbors farther south, it's less expensive and has a more down-to-earth feel. Its proximity to Buenos Aires (less than four hours) makes it especially popular with Porteño families who are traveling on public transportation. Like most beach towns, San Clemente del Tuyú has a promenade where you can take in the warm summer breezes. There's also a pier that stretches 150 ft over the ocean.

Ⓒ The pride and joy of the town is **Mundo Marino** (Marine World). Sea animal shows, featuring whales and dolphins, are the main attractions. There are also rides and games for children and laser shows at night. ⊠ Av. Décima 157, ☎ 2252/30300, FAX 2252/421501. ☞ Admission. ☺ Jan.–Feb., daily 10–10; Mar.–Dec., hours vary, call for info.

The small **Museo Histórico y de Ciencias Naturales** (Museum of History and Natural Sciences) has exhibits that display reptile, insect, and fossil remains. ⊠ Calle 3 between Calle 1 and Costanera. ☞ Free. ☺ Daily 6 PM–10 PM.

Just outside town is the **Reserva de Vida Silvestre Campos del Tuyú,** a 3,000-acre nature reserve established in 1979 to help protect the native deer. The park is filled with hiking trails; it's a good idea to pack a picnic.

## Shopping

Every weekend at the **Paseo Artesenal** (⊠ Plaza Sarmiento), in the heart of the town, local artisans display their arts and crafts.

# Pinamar

❸ 320 km (198 mi) southeast of Buenos Aires via R2, 120 km (74 mi) north of Mar del Plata via R11.

The chic resort town of Pinamar attracts the Argentinian jet set, including film and television stars, models, and politicians (those who haven't gone to the even snootier Punta del Este in Uruguay). It's an idyllic little beach town with lush trees and family-run shops lining the main avenue. In 1997 Pinamar made the news when a photographer from the prestigious Argentine newspaper La Nación was found murdered here. His photos of famous politicians in questionable circumstances apparently led to his murder (which for months was deemed a suicide). In the same period, a teenage visitor plunged to his death from a Pinamar hotel balcony, leaving many unanswered questions.

### Dining and Lodging

As with most beach towns, Pinamar's restaurants tend to fade in and out of quality (and business) with the season. Generally, any spot on busy Avenida Bunges is a good bet.

**$$$**   🏨 **Los Pasajeros.** At Los Pasajeros, accommodations are more like apartments than rooms: You get a duplex with one or two bedrooms and a kitchenette and dining area on the ground floor. The look is Argentine country, with exposed brick walls and heavy wooden furniture. ✉ *Del Tuyú 919,* ☎ *2254/490618,* 🖷 *2254/490625. 30 units Restaurant, bar, kitchenettes, pool, exercise room. V.*

**$$–$$$**   🏨 **Soleado Hotel.** The modern Soleado, constructed in 1998, is just a few feet from the beach; some rooms have ocean views (ask for one of these). The decor is tasteful if reminiscent of a nice hotel chain in the United States. ✉ *Sarmiento and Nuestros Malvinas,* ☎ *2254/ 490340,* 🖷 *2254/490201. 52 rooms. Restaurant, bar, room service, parking. V.*

### Nightlife

Most of Pinamar's nightlife centers on the cafes and ice-cream parlors on Avenida Bunge and the blocks branching off of it. At the **Casino del Bosque** (✉ Av. Júpiter and Av. Bunge) you can try your luck with roulette, blackjack, and other games; entrance is free 6 PM–10 PM, but there's a cover charge after that. As in other beach towns, going to the movies is an immensely popular nighttime activity; buy your tickets early in the day so that you can be assured of a seat. Usually there's one Hollywood movie playing: **Cine Bahia** (✉ Bunge and Burriquetas, ☎ 0254/481012); **Cine Pinamar** (✉ Bunge and Burriquetas, ☎ 0254/ 482747); and **Cine Teatro Oasis** (✉ Shaw and del Lenguado, ☎ 0254/ 483334).

## Villa Gesell

➍  *360 km (223 mi) southeast of Buenos Aires: take R2 to R56 in Conesa, then pick up R74 to Villa Gesell.*

Villa Gesell was settled in 1931 by Argentine naturalist Don Carlos Idaho Gesell, who promised to create a summer paradise full of pine trees and lush forest. Although he accomplished this task, he instead used the wood to manufacture baby furniture. By 1940 his company, Casa Gesell, was doing very well, and he sold it to investors who decided to transform Villa Gesell into a nature preserve and vacation spot. The first tourists arrived in 1942, and Villa Gesell has been a destination ever since, catering primarily to affluent Argentine families who are attracted to the tranquillity, the beaches with dunes, and the alpine architecture. The town particularly prides itself on the preservation of its dunes, so vehicles are not allowed on the beach.

At the **Casa de la Cultura** (Culture House) you can see displays of local crafts. It's also the site of yearly arts festivals, including the Villa Gesell song festival in February. ✉ *Av. 3 between Paseos 108 and 109.* ☎ *Free.* ☉ *Mon.–Sat. 10–6.*

Picturesque **Faro Querandi** (Querandi Lighthouse), about 15 km (9 mi) south of Villa Gesell, is surrounded by lush forest and rolling sand dunes and is an idea spot for a sunset stroll. The only way to get to the lighthouse is via a beach-access road for which a four-wheel-drive vehicle is necessary. In summer you may be able to catch a bus here from Villa Gesell; ask your hotel for the schedule.

Just a few miles down the Ruta Interbalnearia from Villa Gesell is the town of **Mar de las Pampas,** which makes a great day trip. It has quiet, sometimes deserted beaches, a beach club where you can rent chairs and have a drink, and small tea shops where you can get a snack.

## Dining and Lodging

Villa Gesell is primarily residential: Most vacationers here rent or own houses, villas, or apartments, which means that there aren't many accommodations in town.

**$$** ✕ **Ariturito.** At this family-run restaurant, enjoy homemade pastas and sauces and traditional grilled meats. ⊠ *Av. 3 and Paseo 126,* ☎ *2255/463037. AE, DC, MC, V.*

**$$–$$$** ⊡ **Hotel Atlantico.** The charmingly decorated ocean-view rooms vary in price depending on their location in the hotel (ground floor is cheaper than second floor, corner rooms are more expensive than hall rooms). ⊠ *Av. 1 and Paseo 105,* ☎ *2255/462253 or 11/4833–0489 for reservations (in Buenos Aires),* FAX *2255/462561. 35 rooms. Restaurant, bar, laundry service, parking. AE, DC, MC, V.*

## Nightlife and the Arts

In summer, music and theater productions take place at the **Anfiteatro Natural** (⊠ Paseo 102 and Av. 10). Nightlife centers around **Avenida 3,** which from January to February is made into a pedestrian walkway. Going to the movies is another popular nighttime activity: **Atlantic** (⊠ Paseo 105 between calles 2 and 3); **Atlas** (⊠ Paseo 108 between calles 3 and 4); and **San Martín 1 and 2** (⊠ Paseo 105 between calles 2 and 3).

## Shopping

The **Feria Artesanal y Regional** (⊠ Av. 3 between calles 112 and 115), the local crafts market, is a good place to pick up some inexpensive silver jewelry and leather goods.

# Mar del Plata

**⑤** *400 km (248 mi) south of Buenos Aires via R2 (under construction at press time); to reach Mar del Plata from La Plata, take R215 and pick up R2 in Cruce de Echeverry.*

Mar del Plata, known as Mardel, is the most popular beach resort in Argentina. Founded in 1581, it became a Jesuit village in 1747, inhabited by missionaries trying to convert the local population. Some fine examples of colonial Spanish architecture still exist. Accompanying them today are high-rise hotels and tourist-oriented shops along the beach and extending into town. The rest of Mardel consists mainly of summer houses. Life here centers around the beach, day and night. When not enjoying the beach—there are 47 km (29 mi) of picturesque coastline—people stroll along it or spend hours sitting at the outdoor cafés along the ever-crowded Playa Popular. In summer (December–February), Mardel gets very crowded, which is part of its appeal for many people. Although prices are high and the beaches are packed, everyone wants to be in Mardel for the scene (even though only a few miles away there are equally beautiful but uncrowded beaches). Most hotels and restaurants stay open throughout the year, or at least well into fall (March–May), which is a more tranquil time to visit.

One spot of note is the **Iglesia Stella Maris** (Stella Maris Church). Inside is a marble altar dedicated to Mary, who is appropriately the patron saint of fishermen and fishing, which plays a big role in the town's economy.

More of a sea-themed amusement park than a true aquarium, the **Mar del Plata Aquarium** has performing dolphins and sea lions, water-skiing shows, and a 3-D movie. If you want to escape from the entertainment, the aquarium also has a beach with beach chairs, umbrellas, and a bar. ✉ *5600 Av. Martínez de Hoz,* ☎ *223/4670700,* ℻ *223/4670705.* ▣ *Admission.* ◷ *Jan.–Feb., daily 10 AM–10:30 PM; Mar.–Dec., hours vary, call for schedule.*

For an incredibly panoramic view of the area, head south to **Barranca de los Lobos.** At 148 ft, it's a great place to watch the breakwaters and the yellow fishing boats heading back to the coast at sunset.

### Dining and Lodging

$$    ✕ **Castilla y Leon.** Spanish-influenced Arabic food is served in a lively atmosphere. At night there are often flamenco and other kinds of dance performances. ✉ *H. Yrigoyen 2067,* ☎ *223/4930040. V.*

$$    ✕ **El Ciervo Rojo.** This traditional restaurant has a buffet of *parrilla* (grilled meats), pastas, and salads. On Saturday night there's a show with dinner. ✉ *Santa Fe 1844. V.*

### Nightlife and the Arts

Mar del Plata has a lively party scene, and the venues seem to change nightly (anyone on the beach can tell you where to go dancing that particular night). For a night of salsa (with lessons), head to **Azucar Salsoteca** (✉ Constitución 4478, ☎ 223/4957938). Tango shows are held at **Malena Club de Tango** (✉ Rivadavia 2312, ☎ 223/4958533); make reservations for the 11 PM show, which always fills up. The **Centro Cultural General Pueyrredon** (✉ Catamarca and 25 de Mayo) is the place for theater, especially in summer. Going to the movies is another way to spend the evening; Mar del Plata cinemas generally have the same Hollywood films that are playing in Buenos Aires: **Casino** (✉ Punto Mogotes Puán 1744, ☎ 223/4851121); **Olimpia** (✉ Rivadavia and Santa Fe); and **Santa Fe** (✉ Santa Fe 1854, ☎ 223/4919728).

### Outdoor Activities and Sports

**Banquina Pescadores** (✉ At the puerto, ☎ 223/4891612) organizes boat tours of the coast departing from the port every 40 minutes 10–6; Bus 551 goes to the wharf.

### Shopping

**Paseo Diagonal** (✉ Diagonal Pueyrredon 3050), which was built for rainy days, is part shopping mall and part entertainment complex: Inside are stores, cinemas, restaurants, a bank, and an arcade. It's open daily 7:30 AM–2 AM.

## Miramar

❻    *45 km (28 mi) south of Mar del Plata via R11.*

With a year-round population of just under 20,000, Miramar is one of the biggest and most residential of the coastal towns. A quiet town where getting around by bike is common, Miramar is particularly popular with families. Corn, sunflowers, and wheat are also grown here. Entering the city, you first see the **Arco General San Martín** (General San Martín Arch), erected in honor of the liberator of Argentina. The town's central park, the 6-acre **Parque los Patricios,** has a beautiful little lake. Miramar likes to promote itself as the "*ciudad de los niños* (city of children)," and on weekends the park is packed with families and kids.

### Nightlife and the Arts

Nightlife in this quiet town centers on **Calle 9 de Julio,** a *peatonal* (pedestrians-only walkway). The **Casino** (✉ 9 de Julio between 26 and 28) is a popular place to stop and try your luck on the stroll down Calle 9 de Julio. Like many coastal towns, Miramar has its share of movie theaters: **Cine Astral** (⊠ Calle 21 between calles 30 and 32, ☎ 2291/430376 ); **Cine Atlántico** (⊠ Calle 21 between calles 30 and 32, ☎ 2291/420167); and **Cine y Teatro Gran Rex** (⊠ Calle 21 between calles 18 and 20, ☎ 2291/420370).

## Outdoor Activities and Sports

Miramar's perfect waves make it ideal for surfing and body-boarding. **El Pomol** beach is supposed to have the best waves in Argentina. **Club Náutico** (⊠ R11, at 4 Km), just north of the city, rents jet skis and organizes waterskiing. Miramar is also known as a **bicycling** town and as a result, bikes can be rented on almost every street corner. It's possible, too, to rent all-terrain vehicles on the beach, but some establishments require that you have an international driver's license. The **Golf Club Miramar** (⊠ Ruta 11, at 4 Km, ☎ 2291/420833), 1½ km (1 mi) from the city center, is an 18-hole course with views of the ocean.

## Shopping

**Shoping Down Town** (⊠ calles 22 and 23), really spelled this way, is a typical small-town shopping mall, good for necessities. A main shopping area is around the **Plaza San Marco** (⊠ Calle 21 between calles 18 and 20).

# Necochea

**❼** *60 km (37 mi) southwest of Mar del Plata; 500 km (310 mi) southwest of Buenos Aires.*

A calm, picturesque seaside town, Necochea is close to Mar del Plata but light-years away in attitude. While Mar del Plata is devoted to vacationers and summer fun, Necochea, when not focusing on tourist spillover and the beach, is a low-key town devoted to the cultivation of sunflowers, which bloom in the surrounding fields in late summer. As an alternative to the beach, there's the **Parque de Diversiones** (Amusement Park), with its rather rickety selection of attractions, like a roller coaster and bumper cars, right across from the bus station.

## Nightlife and the Arts

The **Cine Teatro Paris** (⊠ 2874 Calle 59) generally shows two international movies at any given time. The town has a **casino,** but it's much less popular than the one in Mar del Plata and its hours of operation vary considerably with the seasons.

## Outdoor Activities and Sports

Most equipment, from beach chairs to boats, can be rented right on the beach.

## Shopping

The local mall, the **Shopping Toledo** (⊠ Av. 58 and Av. 75) has your basic shops and is good if you forgot to pack something.

# Bahía Blanca

**❽** *653 km (405 mi) southwest of Buenos Aires via R3 (about 9 hrs).*

Bahía Blanca is at the very edge of Buenos Aires Province and has more in common with neighboring Patagonia in character and attitude. It was founded in 1828, primarily as a fishing center, though other industries also grew rapidly. Its name, which means "white bay," comes from the town's salt mines. Though there isn't much to do here, visiting Bahía Blanca can give you a good idea of Argentine life in a large town outside Buenos Aires. A massive urban renewal project over the past few years has made the town much more attractive. Its two principal avenues are Avenida Alem and Avenida Colón, which transect the city and the central square, the Plaza Rivadavía. In the town's fine arts museum, the **Museo de Bellas Artes** (⊠ Plaza Rivadavía), is primarily a collection of works by artists focusing on gauchos.

### Lodging

$$   🏨 **Argos.** This hotel has comfortable, simply decorated rooms and is close to the heart of the city. ⊠ *España 149,* ☎ FAX *291/4550404. 144 rooms. Restaurant, bar, breakfast room, room service, meeting rooms, parking. AE, DC, MC, V.*

$$   🏨 **Austral.** Near the center of town, this fairly large hotel has clean but plain rooms. ⊠ *Av. Colón 159,* ☎ *291/4561700,* FAX *291/4553737. 230 rooms. Restaurant, breakfast room, room service, parking. MC, V.*

$   🏨 **Automovil Club Argentino.** This standby is a budget favorite of families and backpackers. Rooms are clean but sparsely furnished. Note that some rooms open directly onto the parking lot, so you'll want to avoid these. ⊠ *Av. Sesquicentenario between Rutas 3 and 35,* ☎ *291/ 4540151. 40 rooms.*

## Sierra de la Ventana

❾ *120 km (74 mi) north of Bahía Blanca, 602 km (373 mi) southwest of Buenos Aires.*

The Sierras de la Ventana, together with the Sierras de Tandil, are the oldest geological strata in South America. In these hills rests the sleepy village of the same name, Sierra de la Ventana (without the *s*), which makes a good base for hiking and other mountain sports. It also has many fine examples of well-preserved local architecture, such as homes with the same wrought-iron gates they had a century ago.

The **Parque Ernesto Tornquist** is a nature reserve on land that was donated to the province by the wealthy Argentine Tornquist family almost 60 years ago. The park has the best hiking in the area, especially on the mountain known as the **Cerro de la Ventana** (The Window). The 3,280-ft climb takes about two hours and can be steep in places; the trail is well marked and popular—on weekends in summer, count on sharing the trail with many other hikers, particularly if it's not a great beach day. From the top is an excellent view of the surrounding pampas.

# NORTH TO CÓRDOBA

The province of Córdoba and its capital city of the same name have had an important role in Argentine history. Before Buenos Aires became the country's major hub, Córdoba served as a an essential linking point between the Spanish in Peru and Spain. Gradually, Buenos Aires became the center of things and left the province to its rolling hills and quiet lakes.

Córdoba marks the center of the region; from here the hills spill out, dotted with charming mountain towns. Some are tiny and others are big resorts with everything you would expect. A meandering drive through these mountain towns is a lovely way to spend a day or two— or even an entire summer.

Food in Córdoba's mountain towns is traditional and meat based. Not only is Córdoba famous for its beef, but it's also known for its barbecued kid. Another specialty is *alfajores* (*dulce de leche* sandwiched between two cookies). Although each town may not have a full-scale restaurant, there's usually an inn or a coffee shop.

# Tigre and the Paraná Delta

⑩ *30 km (19 mi) northwest of Buenos Aires on the Ruta Panamericana or 35 km (22 mi) northwest of Buenos Aires on Avenida Libertador.*

A drive through the shady riverside suburbs of Buenos Aires takes you to the river port town of Tigre, the embarkation point for boats that ply the Delta del Paraná. The delta is a vast maze of canals, tributaries, and river expanding out from the Paraná like the veins of a leaf. A boat trip from Tigre through the delta makes a nice day trip from Buenos Aires, especially when the weather is nice. For an especially memorable ride, take an afternoon sunset cruise. Along the way you'll travel past colorfully painted houses built on stilts to protect them against floods. The most comfortable way to travel the delta's waterways is aboard a large catamaran. As you walk around town, different proprietors will offer to arrange a trip on their boat or catamaran. If they aren't offering you what you want in terms of tour length or price, ask for a reference, and you'll probably be sent a few blocks down the pier to someone who fits your needs. In addition, the small motor launches that deliver groceries and mail and take children to school and people to work can drop you off at the delta island of your choice for a nominal fee. **Tigre River Delta** (⊠ Lavalle and R. Fernandez,, ☎ 0800/TIGRE) gives out maps and advice on traveling in this area.

🐚 Aside from the river, the main attraction is the **Tren de la Costa** (Train of the Coast), originally built in 1895 as a passenger train and refurbished in 1990. Along its way from Buenos Aires to Tigre, the train meanders through some of Buenos Aires's most fashionable northern suburbs, giving you a glimpse of exclusive areas that you wouldn't otherwise see. It stops at 11 stations along the way. The train fare depends on the number of stops you make, but isn't much more than $4 one way.

🐚 At the end of the Tren de la Costa is the **Parque de la Costa** (Park of the Coast), Argentina's largest, most modern amusement park. If you want to combine a trip here with sightseeing, take the ferry-boat trip on a half-hour ride on the river delta. It also has an IMAX theater and restaurants with surprisingly good Argentine fare. ⊠ *At the last stop on the Tren de la Costa.* 🎟 *Admission.* ☉ *Park hours vary by day and month, so call for schedule.*

## Outdoor Activities and Sports
**Club Náutico ACA Delta** (⊠ take Ruta Panamericana to Tigre and pick up R27 at Náutico exit) is a club on 36 acres of delta area. Although there are bungalows and a campground, it's primarily a day resort for families. Activities include fishing, boating, swimming in three pools, tennis, and go-carting (for kids under eight). It also has two restaurants, a barbecue, and an ice cream stand, so you won't go hungry.

## Shopping
The **Mercado de Frutos** (Fruit Market) in Tigre is a good place to find handcrafted items for good prices (often less than in La Recoleta or San Telmo markets in Buenos Aires), though curiously there's no fruit for sale. It's also a bit of a junk sale.

# Luján

⑪ *60 km (40 mi) west of Buenos Aires via R7.*

The main reason that people come here is to visit the imposing **Basilica de la Virgen de Luján** (Virgin of Luján Basilica), dedicated to the

Virgin of Luján, the patron saint of the Argentine people. In 1630 a mule train, originating in Portugal, made its way out of Buenos Aires. Among the items being carried were two terra-cotta statues of the Virgin. After the caravan stopped for a break along the banks of the Río Luján, one of the oxen pulling the statues refused to budge. Finally, it was realized that one of the statues of the Virgin had fallen out and was blocking the way. Taking this as a sign that this is where the Virgin wanted to stay, the basilica was constructed on the spot where the caravan stopped. Every year at least 4 million people make the pilgrimage to Luján to pray to the Virgin. The local **Museo Histórico** (History Museum) provides a good description of the history of the Virgin as well as the gauchos and the native peoples of the area.

### Dining and Lodging

$$$$ ✕🏨 **Estancia Villa Maria.** This incredible ranch is on the outskirts of Luján, about 20 minutes from the airport. It was built in the 1890s by Argentine architect Alejandro Bustillo and is surrounded by breathtaking gardens landscaped by Charles Thays. All meals, served in traditional Argentine family style, are included, and the staff speaks English and French. Be prepared to be pampered—the service is excellent. ⊠ *Pereda, in village of Máximo Paz (Km 47 on R205),* ☎ *11/ 4964–2710,* ℻ *11/4964–2710. 15 rooms. Restaurant, pool, tennis court, biking, horseback riding, laundry service. No credit cards.*

## San Antonio de Areco

⓬   *110 km (68 mi) west of Buenos Aires.*

In the early 1700s, when Buenos Aires was still a part of the viceroyalty of Peru and San Antonio de Areco was the last Spanish-populated settlement on the border of the native inhabitants' territory, the town was a regular stop on the route to Peru. The town has come to represent gaucho life, most notably at the **Museo Gauchesco Ricardo Guiraldes** (Gaucho Museum), where traditional estancia buildings and a *pulpería,* the tavern where the gauchos gathered, have been recreated.

### Dining and Lodging

$$$$ ✕🏨 **Estancia El Ombu de Areco.** This fantastic 1890s house on acres of lush land was built by General Richieri. A stay here, complete with gaucho and folkloric shows, participation in daily ranch activities, horseback rides, and tours of the nearby town, provides a great respite from Buenos Aires (you can also do all this for just $65 per day). Meals consist of a small breakfast and a full asado lunch and dinner. ⊠ *Call for directions,* ☎ *11/4836–0600 weekdays, 326/492080 weekends. 9 rooms. Restaurant, pool, laundry service, parking. V.*

$$$ ✕🏨 **Estancia La Bamba.** The main house here dates from around 1832 and is done in traditional style with beautiful, roofed verandas, and an inside courtyard with a well. The setting provides lovely views of the surrounding plains and all kinds of ranch activities. Prices are for two people and include all meals. Some of the staff speaks English. ⊠ *Reservations in Buenos Aires: Cerrito 1574, 6th floor,* ☎ *11/4815–7201,* ℻ *11/4815–7201. 7 rooms. Restaurant, laundry service, parking.*

## Rosario

⓭   *320 km (198 mi) northwest of Buenos Aires.*

Though its size is impressive for Argentina, Rosario has little in the way of sights. It's really an academic town, famous for its university, its poets, and its writers, which enjoys a reputation as a smaller, friendlier version of Buenos Aires. Founded in 1730 by families fleeing attacks by the indigenous population in Santa Fe, Rosario has great cultural and historical significance for Argentina. It was here in 1812 that General Belgrano created the Argentine flag. The impressive **Monumento a la Bandera** (Flag Monument) commemorates the event.

You could easily spend a very pleasant day in Rosario, visiting its small museums and galleries. The **Centro Cultural Parque de España** (⊠ Sarmiento and Río) often has exhibits on historical figures and shows by Argentine artists. The **Casa del Artista Plástico** (House of Visual Arts; ⊠ Av. Belgrano and Sgto. Cabral) has permanent displays of works by Argentine artists and hosts lectures. The **Biblioteca Argentina Doctor Juan Álvarez** (Dr. Juan Alvarez Argentine Library; ⊠ 1550 Pasaje Dr. Juan Alvarez) is a cultural center and library dedicated primarily to Rosario.

### Lodging

$$$  🏨 **Hotel Libertador.** This place is like an American chain hotel, which means that you get comfortable, modern rooms and a buffet breakfast. ⊠ *Corrientes 752,* ☎ *341/4241005,* ℻ *341/4241005. Bar, breakfast room, laundry service, parking. AE, DC, MC, V.*

$$$  🏨 **Hotel Presidente.** A slightly more expensive option than the Libertador is this hotel right down the street. Most of the tasteful rooms have a small sitting area and cable TV that gets foreign channels. The pool is small but well kept and secluded from the street. ⊠ *Corrientes 919,* ☎ *341/4242789,* ℻ *341/4242789. Restaurant, bar, pool, laundry service, parking. AE, DC, MC, V.*

$$  🏨 **Hotel Garden.** This hotel is convenient to the bus and train stations. Most rooms have views of the garden surrounding the hotel. ⊠ *Callao 45,* ☎ *341/4370025,* ℻ *341/4371413. Restaurant, bar, laundry service, meeting room, parking. AE, DC, MC, V.*

### Nightlife

Rosario is a university town with a population that is open-minded for Argentina. Though most bars are not specifically gay-and-lesbian, some are noted for their gay-friendly staff and crowd: **Del Mar** (⊠ Tucumán and Balcarce); **Inicios** (⊠ Av. Mitre 1880); and **Kiss** (⊠ Córdoba 1630).

---

# Córdoba

⓮  *710 km (426 mi) northwest of Buenos Aires.*

Córdoba is the capital city of the province of the same name. The southern plains of the Córdoba Province form the northern part of Las Pampas. The town itself was founded in 1573, before Buenos Aires was even an idea. Today Córdoba is the second-largest city in Argentina. But it's still struggling between the modernization that it has so resisted and the traditional lifestyle that has been holding it back from prosperity. This contrast is apparent: Beautiful parks and historic 17th-century buildings like the cabildo, rest side by side with industrial buildings (the city is a manufacturing hub, principally for the auto industry). Also notable is the abundance of churches in Córdoba, a testament to the city's intensely Catholic past. The city is known, too, for its university, giving the city its nickname, La Docta. The **Parque Sarmiento** (Sarmiento Park), designed by French architect Carlos Thays, is a nice place to take a break; it's especially crowded on weekends. A good day trip out of Córdoba is to nearby mountain towns such as **Villa Carlos Paz** (☞ *below*); most are centered around lake activity or mountain climbing (and often both).

### Lodging

$$$–$$$$  🏨 **Ducal Suites Hotel.** Rooms are simple and tasteful and include a kitchenette (hence all rooms are designated "suites"). Rates include tax and breakfast. ⊠ *Corrientes 207,* ☎ *351/4268888,* ℻ *351/4268840. 82*

suites. *Bar, kitchenettes, room service, pool, exercise room, sauna, laundry service, parking. AE, DC, MC, V.*

**$$$–$$$$** 🏨 **Sheraton Córdoba Hotel.** The modern glass facade sticks out in Córdoba, but the Sheraton is a welcome retreat if you're looking for a level of service and amenities that's closer to that available back home. The hotel prides itself on hospitality—you're treated to a welcome drink upon arrival—and facilities include such progressive (for Argentina) things as no-smoking rooms. ⊠ *Duarte Quiróz 1300,* ☎ *351/4889000,* FAX *351/4889150. 188 rooms. Restaurant, bar, no-smoking rooms, room service, tennis courts, beauty salon, sauna, exercise room, business services, parking. AE, DC, MC, V.*

**$$** 🏨 **Dallas Hotel Córdoba.** Downtown and close to the train station, it's certainly not luxurious, but this hotel is comfortable and has its own charms. Room rates include tax and breakfast, making this an even better bargain. An added bonus: You can use the hotel's E-mail. ⊠ *San Jeronimo 339,* ☎ *351/4216091,* FAX *351/4218024. Bar, laundry service, parking. AE, DC, MC, V.*

**$$** 🏨 **Hotel Mediterraneo.** This hotel is just off the popular walkway L. Cañada, near the center of town. Rooms are soundproofed and tastefully decorated, and the hotel offers airport transfers. ⊠ *Marcelo T. de Alvear 10,* ☎ *351/4240086,* FAX *351/4240111. Bar, breakfast room, pool, laundry service, parking. AE, DC, MC, V.*

# Villa Carlos Paz

**⑮** *36 km (22 mi) west of Córdoba.*

Rapidly expanding, hilltop Villa Carlos Paz is one of the province's major cities after Córdoba. It's a popular summer destination for Argentines, who come to swim in the Lago San Roque (Lake San Roque) and go hiking, mountain biking, horseback riding, and fishing. A walk around town gives you a sense of why it's so charming. The town's central pedestrian walkway is lined with shops and cafés, filled both day and night. Contact the **Secretaria de Turismo** (⊠ Av. San Martín 400, ☎ 3541/421624) for information about tour companies organizing horseback riding, mountain biking, hiking, fishing, and other kind of trips. **Trencito** (⊠ Belgrano and San Martín, Villa Carlos Paz, ☎ 3541/421521) arranges tours of Villa Carlos Paz and the surrounding areas.

## Dining and Lodging

**$$$** ✕ **Coyote.** Come here for Argentine fare in a funky, Santa Fe (New Mexico)–type setting. ⊠ *Av. Atlántica 629,* ☎ *3541/434666.*

**$$$** ✕ **Il Gatto.** Modeled after the restaurant of the same name in Buenos Aires, Il Gatto stands out here for its crowd and good meat and pasta dishes. ⊠ *Libertad and Belgrano,* ☎ *3541/422361.*

**$$** ✕ **El Rancho Porá.** This traditional Argentine restaurant is a popular *parrilla* (grills) with families. ⊠ *Uruguay 472,* ☎ *3541/425592.*

**$$$** 🏨 **Portal del Lago Hotel and Resort.** In a woodsy, natural setting on Lago San Miguel, this hotel is ideal for longer stays. You have a choice of a room in the main house or a little cabin. Prices include tax and breakfast. ⊠ *Lago San Miguel,* ☎ *3541/424931,* FAX *3541/424932. Restaurant, pool, tennis courts, laundry service, meeting rooms, parking. CP. AE, DC, MC, V.*

**$$** 🏨 **Gran Lourdes Hotel.** Rooms at this town center hotel are surprisingly modern. Like most places in the area, it's oriented toward enjoying the outdoors, with a woodsy garden and access to the lake beaches (about 325 ft). Internet and modem access are available, and room rates include tax and breakfast. ⊠ *Cassaffousth 63,* ☎ *3541/423347,* FAX *3541/423347. Restaurant, bar, room service, pool, laundry service, meeting rooms, parking. CP. AE, DC, MC, V.*

**$** 🖥 **Hotel Jalisco.** Because it's in a residential area, this pleasant hotel is less expensive. Yet nothing is really that far away. Rooms are comfortable. Internet access is available. ⊠ *San Roque 463,* ☎ *3541/427200,* FAX *3541/424561. Restaurant, bar, pool, laundry service, parking. MC, V.*

## Nightlife

The **casino** (⊠ Av. Uruguay and Liniers, ☎ 3541/425515) is a popular nighttime attraction. The **Chez Ami Disco** (⊠ L. N. Alem and Hernandez, ☎ 3541/424598); **Keops,** in an unmistakable pyramid outside of town; and the **Khalama Discoteca** (⊠ Av. Estrada 113, ☎ 3541/422494) are frequented by a young crowd.

## Outdoor Activities and Sports

The activities listed below are available in most of the mountain towns around Córdoba, but equipment and information are far easier to come by in Villa Carlos Paz.

### FISHING

Trout fishing season is from November to March. The waters around Villa Carlos Paz are generally packed with the fish, which were originally stocked in the lakes years ago to satisfy the needs of British tourists. Most people fish on their own, but the tourist office (☞ *above*) can put you in touch with fishermen who will pick you up at your hotel, rent you equipment, and bring you out for a day on their boats.

### HIKING

Hiking trips, lasting anywhere from one day to a week, are gaining popularity in the area. Hikers typically focus on climbing the **Cerro Champaquí,** traveling along the **Sierras Grandes,** or visiting the **Volcanes de Pocho.**

### MOUNTAIN BIKING

The most common mountain-bike adventure in the area is the tour of **Los Grandes Lagos.** Another good spot to go mountain biking is in the nearby village of **La Cumbrecita.**

# La Falda

🌀 *66 km (41 mi) northwest of Córdoba.*

Like most resort towns, the primary activities in La Falda are relaxing and strolling the streets. Avenida Diagonal San Martín, Avenida Santa Fe, Avenida Córdoba Sud, and Avenida Eden are the town's central streets. Another good spot for walking is the Plaza Villa Eden, the park between Diagonal Santa Fe, Libertad, and Independencia.But the town's pride and joy and the reason it was founded in the first place is the famous **Hotel Eden.** The man responsible for the construction of the hotel, at the turn of the last century, was German colonel Robert Bahlke, who had become enamored of the region. The once-luxurious 100-room structure was originally frequented by socialites, old-money-eyed elite, and luminaries such as Albert Einstein (in 1925). But its ignominious claim to fame came during World War II, when it was supposedly used as a hideout for Nazi soldiers (townspeople will often tell you that their parents or grandparents saw Hitler here, although there's no proof he was ever in La Falda). And in 1945 the Argentine government sequestered Japanese diplomats and their families here before deporting them. The hotel closed its doors to guests in 1965, but it's still La Falda's most recognizable landmark. Presently, funding is awaited in order to reopen it as a casino or a casino-hotel.

The **Iglesia del Santísimo Sacremento** is another one of La Falda's landmarks. At 3,082 ft above sea level (the highest point in the city), its neo-Romantic architecture is visible from most points in town. If you're a geology buff, head to the **Museo del Viejo Minero** (Mineral Museum), which has one of the country's most representative collections of natural minerals.

## La Cumbre

**⑰** *50 km (31 mi) north of Villa Carlos Paz.*

Originally constructed by British railway workers in the late 1800s, La Cumbre has a distinctively Victorian look. That, combined with its elevation of 1,400 ft and its now predominantly Swiss population, makes the town seem as if it's in the Alps.

## Villa General Belgrano

**⑱** *88 km (54½ mi) south of Córdoba, 12 km (7 mi) north of Santa Rosa de la Calamuchita.*

Between two picturesque little lakes, Embalse del Río Tercero and Embalse de los Molino, Villa General Belgrano is a perfect place to relax and enjoy a slightly less Latin version of Argentina. Reminiscent of southern Germany, it stands to reason that it was Bavarians and Alsatians who originally settled this Calamuchita Valley town. Today it strives to retain its German heritage, with an Oktoberfest, the Festival Nacional de la Cerveza, the Viennese Cookie Festival, and an Alpine Chocolate Festival.

## Santa Rosa de Calamuchita

**⑲** *12 km (7 mi) south of Villa General Belgrano.*

In the Calamuchita Valley, Santa Rosa de Calamuchita is one of the most picturesque areas in Córdoba Province and home to Los Grandes Lagos (The Great Lakes: Embalse del Río Tercero and Embalse de los Molinos). The main activity in Santa Rosa is strolling along the Río Santa Rosa and going to its lakeside beaches, including La Choza, La Olla, and Puchuquí, all equipped with chairs and umbrellas.

# LAS PAMPAS A TO Z

## Arriving and Departing

### By Airplane

The city of Córdoba is served by **Ingeniero Aeronáutico Ambrosio Taravella International Airport.** Although it's technically an international airport, it primarily provides connecting flights to major airlines in Buenos Aires as well as domestic flights. **Aerolineas Argentinas** (☎ 11/4961–9361 in Buenos Aires) flies out of Córdoba and can provide a transfer on its own planes out of Buenos Aires to major hubs in the United States and Europe. **Varig** (☎ 11/4342–4420 in Buenos Aires), the airline of Brazil, also serves the airport and can provide connections to Europe and the United States via its hubs in Sao Paulo and Rio. The **Aeropuerto Internacional de Rosario** (✉ R9, ☎ 341/4512997) is an international airport that's similar to Córdoba's. Daily flights depart from here going to Buenos Aires and Rio on **Aerolineas Argentinas** (☞ *above*) and **Varig** (☞ *above*). The **Aeropuerto Provincial de Villa Gesell** is primarily a summer airport. Two companies provide service between Buenos Aires and Villa Gesell: **Aerolineas Argentinas** (☎ 11/4961–9361 in Buenos Aires) and **LAPA** (☎ 11/4912–1008 in Buenos Aires). The **Aeropuerto de Mar del Plata** (✉ on R2, about 5 mins outside the city) is the beach region's main airport. There are frequent flights year-round from here to Buenos Aires on **Aerolineas Argentinas** and LAPA (☞ *above*). Note that this is a coveted ticket in summer, so make reservations early.

### By Boat
Boats are a good way to get around in the Tigre River Delta.

### By Bus
Going to the beach from Buenos Aires by bus is very common. Every beach town has at least a bus stop, and many have a bus station or a bus ticket office in the center of town. The bus from Buenos Aires to La Plata costs about $5 one-way and takes 1½ hours. Buenos Aires to Mar del Plata takes about five hours and costs about $30. Each of the beach towns is connected in some way by a local bus system. For Rosario and Córdoba, take the bus at the Retiro station in Buenos Aires. From Córdoba, local bus companies can connect you with nearly every mountain town in the region. Most towns, however small, have some sort of bus stop or even a bus station. Remember that when traveling to some of the smaller towns, buses may only go or depart from there once a day.

### By Car
Driving is the best and most convenient option for getting to towns in the region, but beware of the windy, curvy, and often single-lane mountain roads. You can hire a car and drivers from most hotels for a generally very reasonable rate (the driver's services often cost less than the car rental itself).

## Getting Around

### By Boat
Fishermen may be willing to take you between coastal towns on their boats; arrangements can be made right at the pier, or your hotel can probably point you in the right direction.

### By Bus
All the beach and mountain towns are connected in some way by a local bus system (☞ Arriving and Deparing By Bus, *above*).

### By Car
The most common and convenient way to get around Las Pampas is to rent a car. Many roads leading to the beaches are new, though not all have been completed. Gas stations aren't very common, but when you do find them, they're generally modern and clean. In an emergency contact the Automovil Club Argentino, the Argentine equivalent of AAA: **ACA** (☎ 91/550076 in Bahia Blanca; 323/24003 in Lujan; 23/950031 in Mar del Plata; 254/82743 in Pinamar; and 21/929040 in La Plata).

*Remises* (hired cars with drivers) can be rented in nearly every beach town and can take you from one town to the next at generally reasonable rates. Remises in the smaller towns are usually individually owned and run, so you'll need to ask at your hotel where to call for one. Rates are arranged with the driver or company prior to departure. Typically, trips originating in smaller towns are cheaper than those originating in cities. For instance, the ride from Mar del Plata to Necochea costs about $80, but in the reverse direction it's $55.

### By Taxi
Ask the hotel or restaurant to call a remise (a car service) for you; it's generally far less expensive in this area than in Buenos Aires.

# Contacts and Resources

### Banks and Currency Exchange

Local banks in Córdoba and Rosario have 24-hour ATMs; most banks are on either the NYCE or Cirrus systems. In La Plata: **Banco Francés** (⌧ Calle 47 641, ☎ 21/255414); **Bank of Boston** (⌧ Av. 51 652, ☎ 21/223022); **Citibank** (⌧ Av. 47 673, ☎ 21/254444). In Miramar: **Banco Provincia** (⌧ Calle 21 1209, ☎ 2291/420829); **Casa Fortuna** (⌧ Calle 21 between calles 24 and 26).

### Emergencies

Emergency phone numbers are nationwide (☞ Emergencies *in* Smart Travel Tips). Miramar's **Hospital Municipal** (⌧ Diagonal José Maria Dupuy 1150, ☎ 2291/420837) has some English-speaking doctors.

### Health and Safety

When hiking, stay on marked trails. There are rescue services, but they are not nearly as comprehensive as those in other countries. On beaches you should be careful of the unexpected: There's a good chance you'll be sharing the seemingly quiet beaches with off-road vehicles, roaring fires, and the occasional wild horse or stray cow.

### Telephones and Mail

For long-distance calls, look for *telecentros* (telephone centers) in the larger towns. Local calls can be made from public phones using a phone card purchased in coffee shops and at kiosks. Miramar: **Posteo** (⌧ Corner of Calle 32 and Calle 17, ☎ 2291/420661. Cell phones can be rented in La Plata from **Movicom** (⌧ Calle 47 between calles 7 and 8) for very reasonable daily rates.

### Visitor Information

In most of the beach towns, hotels are the best places to get information. Even if you're not a guest, almost every hotel will give you a map and point you in the right direction. Some of the towns have their own tourist information desks, which typically keep bankers' hours, so they may not be around when you need them. Many tour agencies in Buenos Aires can help you make arrangements.

# 4 ARGENTINE LITORAL

After hiking through the lush jungle in sweltering heat, there's nothing quite like bathing under the cool spray of the spectacular Iguazú Falls. Keep your bathing suit and sandals on as you explore remote marshlands filled with wildlife or relax on soft sandy beaches on the banks of the Uruguay and Paraguay rivers. And be sure to include a trip to the fascinating Jesuit mission ruins.

By Brad Weiss

**I**N THE NORTHEAST PART OF THE COUNTRY, nestled between Brazil, Uruguay, and Paraguay, is the Argentine Litoral. El Litoral, meaning "the coastal area," consists in part of the provinces of Entre Ríos, Corrientes, and Misiones—collectively known as Mesopotamia—which are framed by the Paraná and Uruguay rivers. These two enormous rivers start in Brazil and converge near Buenos Aires in the Río de la Plata, which empties into the Atlantic Ocean. The fourth province of the Argentine Litoral, El Chaco, extends to the west, a part of the fertile river basin that gives way to the barrenness that blankets vast portions of the region.

The four provinces of the Argentine Litoral have little in common: Entre Ríos is a region of flat green plains with beaches along the banks of the Paraná and Uruguay rivers; Corrientes is dominated by lagoons and marshland; Misiones has several minor mountain chains and is covered by subtropical jungle; and Chaco is marked by flatlands often so dry that human existence is infeasible. This is a rural region with no large cities and with very small provincial towns—most of which seem abandoned during the lengthy siesta period that starts around noon and lasts until 4 or 5. The real attraction is in the natural surroundings—in the numerous kinds of plants and animals and the abundance of waterfalls, especially in Misiones. The most famous are the Cataratas del Iguazú, the breathtaking set of 270 falls that plummet more than 200 ft.

Sights of historical significance include the former home and the numerous monuments to General Justo José Urquiza, the first constitutional president of Argentina, in Entre Ríos. Also scattered throughout the region are the ruins of Jesuit missions, which are remnants of the remarkable society that thrived from 1610 until 1767. San Ignacio Miní, the most frequently visited Jesuit site, is fairly well conserved and has been partially reconstructed; other missions, however, have not been repaired and aren't as easily visited since getting around this region can be difficult. But this means if you do get to these out-of-the-way sights, you'll most likely have them all to yourself.

## Pleasures and Pastimes

### Dining

It seems as if every menu in the region has been photocopied from the same source—only the prices differ. Almost every restaurant serves *pastas caseras* (homemade pastas), typical Argentine *asados* (barbecued meats), and grilled river fish, most notably *surubí* (a regional fish) and *merluza* (hake). In this region of famously long siestas, lengthy, leisurely lunches are eaten around noon or 1. Dinner is eaten quite late, often not until 11 or even midnight. Reservations are rarely necessary.

For a chart that explains the cost of meals at the restaurants listed throughout this chapter, *see* Dining Price Categories *in* Smart Travel Tips.

### Fishing

On nearly every town's *costanera* (riverside walkway) you find people stationed with fishing poles in hand and fresh catches by their feet. The region's rivers, primarily the Paraná and Uruguay, offer some of the country's most challenging and fruitful fishing. The *manguruyú* (another type of regional fish) caught here can weigh well over 200 pounds and the surubí as much as 125 pounds. The real prize, however, is the famously feisty *dorado* (golden fish). This fish is the subject of a national fishing competition that takes place every August in the town of Paso de la Patria in Corriente; here you'll find several inns that organize fishing tours. In general, the best time for fishing is between September and March.

## Lodging

Lodging tends to be expensive in relation to the quality of service and facilities provided, and there's a lack of decent midprice accommodations. Unless otherwise specified, all hotels listed have rooms with private bathrooms, telephones, and color television with cable, as well as complimentary breakfasts.

For a chart that explains the cost of a double room at the hotels listed throughout this chapter, *see* Lodging Price Categories *in* Smart Travel Tips.

## Yerba Maté

This herbal infusion has long been an integral component of not only the region's diet but also its culture. It was first cultivated by the Guaraní, who later introduced it to the Jesuit missionaries. Yerba maté here is much like tea in England, in that it often serves as the basis of social interaction: People drink it at almost any hour of the day, and it's often extended to strangers as a welcoming gesture. Typically, ground-up yerba maté leaves are placed in a carved-out gourd covered with cow leather. Then hot water from a thermos is added, sometimes accompanied by a spoonful of sugar. The infusion is sipped through a metal tube with a filter at the bottom. When finished, the gourd is refilled with hot water and is passed to the next person in line. In the provinces of Corrientes and Misiones, which are the nation's largest yerba maté–producing regions, it's not uncommon in public places to find an enormous kettle containing hot water with which to fill your thermos to make the drink.

# Exploring the Argentine Litoral

One problem in exploring this region is that the notable sights are generally far apart, often with very little of interest in between them. This is especially true to the west, in the provinces of Corrientes and Chaco. If time is an important factor, it would be better to explore the province of Misiones, which has a greater concentration of noteworthy destinations. The most common form of transport in the region is buses, which run regularly and are very comfortable. Some destinations have airports, but flights can be inconsistent. If you're just going to Misiones, it's easiest to take one of the regular flights between Buenos Aires and Posadas or Cataratas del Igauzú.

## Great Itineraries

### IF YOU HAVE 5 DAYS

Make the ⊡ **Cataratas del Iguazú** ⑲, the spectacular falls on the border of Argentina and Brazil, your main focus. Allow at least three days to see the falls from both the Argentine and Brazilian sides, taking advantage of such activities as boat rides past the falls and hikes through the surrounding jungle. You can stay near the falls or in the close-by town of ⊡ **Puerto Iguazú** ⑱. On the fourth day take the three-hour bus ride or drive south to ⊡ **Posadas** ⑩. Spend a day and night here, using it as a base to explore the ruins of the Jesuit missions **San Ignacio Miní** ⑫, **Nuestra Señora de Loreto** ⑬, and **Santa Ana** ⑭. On day five return to the Cataratas del Iguazú.

### IF YOU HAVE 7 DAYS

Spend three days at the ⊡ **Cataratas del Iguazú** ⑲, staying near the falls or in ⊡ **Puerto Iguazú** ⑱. On day four drive or take the bus two hours to see the main Jesuit ruin, **San Ignacio Miní** ⑫. Later that day,

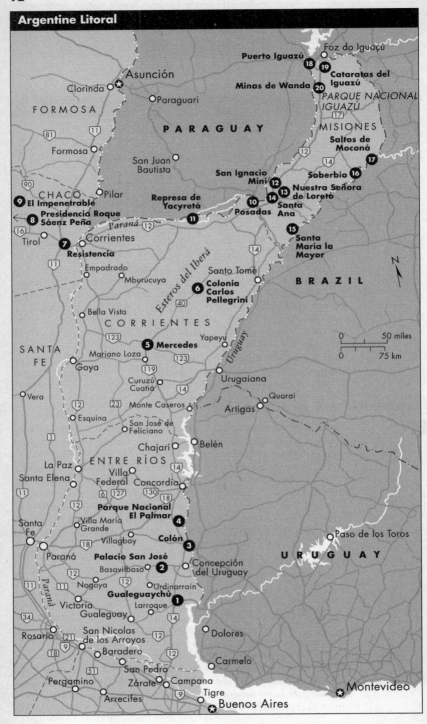

## Argentine Litoral

take a bus or drive to **Posadas** ⑩; you can arrange to be picked up by one of the *posadas* (inns) in ⊡ **Esteros del Iberá** (most of the inns are in ⊡ **Colonia Carlos Pellegrini** ⑥). Your options are many: Take a boat trip through the wildlife-rich marshlands or scuba dive in the crystal-clear waters. On day seven head back to the Cataratas del Iguazú.

IF YOU HAVE 10 DAYS

Go to the ⊡ **Cataratas del Iguazú** ⑲ for three days, staying near the falls or in ⊡ **Puerto Iguazú** ⑱. On the morning of day four, take the somewhat long bus or car ride to the tiny town of ⊡ **Soberbio** ⑯. Spend a day and a night in the charming posada here while you arrange your journey by land or sea to the spectacular **Saltos de Moconá** ⑰. Be sure to find out the waterfalls' condition before you go—when the water level is high, the falls disappear completely. On the morning of day six, take the bus or drive to ⊡ **Posadas** ⑩. Here you can arrange (through your posada) to be taken to the **Esteros del Iberá** (most of the inns are in ⊡ **Colonia Carlos Pellegrini** ⑥). On the ninth day head back to Posadas. On the morning of day ten, head back to Cataratas de Iguazú, stopping for a few hours on the way at **San Ignacio Miní** ⑫.

## When to Tour

If you don't like the heat, don't go to Chaco, Corrientes, or Misiones in the summer (December–March). Entre Ríos, however, is most popular in January and February, when Carnaval takes place, and it's the best time for the beach. Esteros del Iberá is best June–September when more wildlife is visible, though most species can be seen year-round. The waterfalls of Saltos de Moconá are generally more spectacular December–July, though they could disappear at any time, depending on the weather. The Cataratas de Iguazú are always breathtaking, you can save considerably by not coming in high season (November, December, July, and Easter). During this time, reservations are recommended all over the region, often up to a month in advance.

# ENTRE RÍOS

Straddled by the Río Paraná (Paraná River) to the west and the Uruguay River to the east, this province has been fairly isolated from the exterior. The lack of significant contact with the rest of the country is apparent in the reserved disposition of the province's population, most of whom are descendants of French, German, Spanish, and Italian immigrants. The province's isolation, however, did not prevent many Entrerrianos, as its inhabitants are known, from playing decisive roles in the country's fight for liberation from the Spanish in the early 1800s. In fact, native Entrerriano General Justo José de Urquiza (1801–1870) became Argentina's first constitutional president in 1853; you'll see monuments to him all over the province.

With the construction in the 1970s of several bridges connecting Entre Ríos to Uruguay and the building of South America's only river tunnel, which connected the region to the province of Santa Fé, the area's physical isolation ended. And with the advent of MERCOSUR (a free-trade agreement signed between Argentina, Brazil, Uruguay, and Paraguay in 1991), Entre Ríos became an important trade crossroads for products going to and coming from Uruguay and Brazil. It also significantly boosted its own exports—most notably beef, poultry, citrus fruits, rice, and lumber. Tourism is also another source of income: In summer (December–March), many Porteños and other Argentines come to these tranquil towns to spend the weekend on the riverfront beaches and to attend one of the celebrated carnivals.

# Gualeguaychú

❶ *220 km (132 mi) north of Buenos Aires.*

Meaning "river of the large jaguar" in native Guaraní, Gualeguaychú was founded in 1783 by the Spanish. It's Entre Ríos's most popular summer vacation destination, in part because it's so close to Buenos Aires. It's also the southernmost and the largest of the *Corredor del Uruguay,* the chain of riverside towns running along the eastern border of the province. Most of the town's action is centered on the costanera, the street running along the narrow Río Gualeguaychú. Like a boardwalk, the costanera is lined with restaurants, bars, arcades, clothing shops, and artisan stands. It's particularly lively on summer weekends, when the benches are filled with young and old sipping yerba matés and watching the world go by.

The big draw on weekends from the end of January to the end of February is carnaval. Though not in the same league as the large Brazilian carnivals, Gualeguaychú's is considered Argentina's best. Twice a weekend, revelers flock to the enormous *corsodromo* (a long strip of pavement with bleachers on both sides; ⊠ Av. Rocamora and Av. Parque Cándido Irazusta) for celebratory performances. The impressive productions, with large casts, music, garish costumes, and elaborate floats, all conform to that year's carnival theme.

| NEED A BREAK? | Stop in at **Bahillo** (⊠ Costanera 154, ☎ 3446/426240), an out-of-this-world ice cream parlor. |
|---|---|

The town's central square, the Plaza San Martín, is dominated by the large, concrete **Catedral San José,** with its two imposing towers. The cathedral's construction in 1863 was sponsored by General Urquiza, who was at that time the governor of the province. Despite some signs of decay, its ornate interior is still an impressive sight; one of its most noteworthy features is an organ made of 2,200 pipes. ⊠ *Plaza San Martín.* 🎫 *Free.* ☉ *Daily 9:30 AM–11 AM and 6 PM–11 PM.*

In 1898 the **Instituto Magnasco** (Magnasco Institute) became the country's first library to be founded by women. Aside from the thousands of old and rare books, it also contains 16th-century Jesuit statuary, antique furniture, a collection of weapons from World War I, and temporary exhibits by the region's most prominent artists. ⊠ *Camila Nieves 78,* ☎ *3446/427287.* 🎫 *Free.* ☉ *Weekdays 10–noon and 4–8; Sat. 10–noon.*

## Dining and Lodging

To handle the large crowds that descend on the town on summer weekends, there are ample lodging options, including hotels, campgrounds, bungalows, and cabanas. You can also go to the tourist office and find families who will put you up in their homes for around $15 per night.

$$ ★ **X Don Jacinto.** This elegant and colorful restaurant has full-length windows through which you can see all of the activity on the costanera. Seafood and homemade pastas are the specialties. Vegetarians beware: The *canelone de verduras* (cannelloni with green vegetables), typically meatless, contains small quantities of cow brains for flavoring; it is, however, quite tasty. ⊠ *Urquiza 52,* ☎ *3446/429222. AE, DC, MC, V. Closed Tues.*

$ **X Pizzeria Piamonte.** On the Costanera, this popular spot serves delicious pan pizza with a thick crust and lots of cheese. Dining outdoors on the softly lighted patio with a fountain in the middle is quite pleasant. ⊠ *San Lorenzo 282,* ☎ *3446/428462. MC, V.*

**$$** 🏠 **Hotel Puerto Sol.** To go with the name, Hotel Sun Port, this place
**★** is done entirely in yellow and blue. Right off the Costanera, it has com-
fortable, attractively decorated rooms, many with river views. The hotel
is small, so make reservations up to a month in advance, especially dur-
ing Carnaval weekends. ⊠ *San Lorenzo 477, 2820,* ☎ FAX *3446/*
*434017. 12 rooms. Bar, air-conditioning, in-room safes. AE, DC, MC.*

**$$** 🏠 **Hotel Embajador.** This hotel near Plaza San Martín is considered
the city's most luxurious. Though it has fairly large rooms with all the
standard amenities, it's slightly aged and has little character. Note that
weekend and holiday rates are considerably higher. ⊠ *San Martín and*
*3 de Febrero, 2820,* ☎ *3446/424414,* FAX *3446/426051. 80 rooms, 1*
*suite. Bar, air-conditioning, minibars, room service, casino. AE, DC,*
*MC, V.*

**$** 🏠 **Hotel Alemán.** Resembling a Bavarian chalet (at least from the out-
side), this hotel, built more than 50 years ago, is one of the city's oldest. It's right near the bus station in the center of town. Rooms, while
simple, are clean and comfortable, and many are centered on a nice,
plant-filled patio. ⊠ *Bolivar 535, 2820,* ☎ *3446/426153,* FAX *no fax.*
*24 rooms. Fans. No credit cards.*

## Nightlife and the Arts

Most bars and clubs—whose popularity changes with the season—are
along the costanera. **Parada 1** (⊠ San Lorenzo and Concordia, ☎ no
phone) is generally a happening spot in the evenings. One common post-
carnival destination is the dance club **Quintana** (⊠ San Lorenzo and
Gervasio Mendés, ☎ no phone). Another option for a night on the town
is the **Hotel Embajador Casino** (⊠ San Martín and 3 de Febrero, ☎
3446/426259). The few theater productions and classical music concerts in town are usually held at the **Teatro Gualeguaychú** (⊠ Urquiza
283, ☎ 3446/431757).

## Outdoor Activities and Sports

The town has a number of *balnearios* (riverfront beaches) within
walking distance of town, most with a thin strip of sand. The beaches
get very crowded on summer weekends and holidays. On the Río
Gualeguaychú (Gualeguaychú River) are two notable and very similar balnearios: **Costa Azul,** on the northern end of town, and **Solar del
Este,** slightly farther north. Both have camping facilities, food stands,
and all kinds of sports facilities. The largest, most popular, and most
developed balneario is Ñandubaysal, 15 km (9 mi) east of town on the
Río Uruguay (you'll need to take a bus from the bus station or a $10
taxi ride). Here you'll find a campground, horseback riding, a wide
variety of water sports, bars, and a supermarket; to organize activities
or rent tents, go to the information desk in the main complex. Jet skis
can be rented for about $15 per 10 minutes at **Costa Azul** (⊠ On the
beach, ☎ 0446/431130) or at **Solar del Este** (⊠ On the beach, ☎ 3446/
433303). **Cabaña de Carlitos** (⊠ at Ñandubaysal balneario) has jet skis
and sailboats for about $10 per hour. **Nautica** (⊠ Playa Nautica, on
the south end of Ñandubaysal, ☎ 3446/425858) has paddleboats,
kayaks, and canoes. Motorboats for fishing and a guide cost about $40
per person per day at the **Playa Nautica** (☎ 3446/430244).

## Shopping

Along the costanera are a number of artisan and souvenir shops carrying baskets, leather goods, tapestries, and yerba maté gourds. On summer weekends craftspeople often sell their wares on Plaza Colón, at
the southern end of the costanera. The widest selection of crafts is found
at **El Gaucho** (⊠ San Lorenzo 346, ☎ 3446/15635657).

# Palacio San José

❷ *70 km (42 mi) southwest of Colón, 35 km (22 mi) west of Concepción del Uruguay.*

This stately residence was once the home of General Urquiza and is now one of the most significant historical monuments for Argentines, much like Mount Vernon for Americans. The enormous pink palace was constructed between 1848 and 1857 in a mix of colonial and Italian Renaissance styles. It has 31 rooms, a chapel, elaborate courtyards, and extensive gardens. It was here that Urquiza was supposedly assassinated by his political enemies in 1870, although no one was ever arrested or charged for the murder. Unfortunately most of the valuable coins and silverware were stolen and were never recovered. The entrance fee includes an hour-long guided tour; the guides don't speak English, but there are explanatory signs in English. ✉ *Off R39,* ☎ *3442/432620.* ⌦ *Admission.* ⊘ *Daily 9–12:45 and 2–8.*

# Colón

❸ *44 km (26 mi) north of Concepción del Uruguay, 320 km (198 mi) north of Buenos Aires.*

Along this riverside corridor of quaint little towns, Colón outdoes them all. With its pretty beaches a few blocks from the town center, thermal baths, and fully equipped spa, it's one of the best places in the region to spend a few days relaxing. It's also close to the Parque Nacional El Palmar (☞ *below*) and the former residence of General Urquiza, the Palacio San José (☞ *above*). The friendly, easy-going residents—most of whom are descendants of Swiss, French, and Italian immigrants who were offered land for agrarian pursuits—also make the town pleasant.

Founded in 1863, the town served as a port from which farmers could ship products such as rice, oranges, and poultry to the rest of Argentina and other countries. During World War II the town experienced great prosperity as it became a major exporter of grain and meat to Europe. After the war, as demand declined, the economic situation declined, and many residents flocked to Buenos Aires.

Colón's **Aguas Termales** (Thermal Baths) have several pools, an excellent view of the river, and a snack bar. The water, which surges from nearly a mile below the surface, is said to contain many proven health-enhancing elements; at 93°F, it's warm but not extremely hot. ✉ *La Valle and Savatier,* ☎ *no phone.* ⌦ *Admission.* ⊘ *Daily 8–midnight.*

## Dining and Lodging

Dining is not one of Colón's highlights and its restaurants' menus differ little from one another; the majority are found on Urquiza between the central plaza and the river. Hotels in Colón, however, are rather impressive in terms of quality: Though there aren't many to choose from, three are highly recommended (make reservations well in advance for summer weekends). Besides hotels, there are campgrounds, cabanas, and bungalows, which are good for families and groups.

$ ✕ **La Costera.** It's not pretty—it hardly even looks like a restaurant—but according to locals, owner Alberto Passadore is the undisputed grill master of Colón. From your seat in the backyard, you can watch him at work in his enormous grilling pit. Don't bother asking for the menu; it's just meat and it's cheap. ✉ *Moreno and Brown,* ☎ *076025498. No credit cards.*

$ ✕ **La Plaza.** This elegantly rundown house, one of the town's oldest,
★ once belonged to Colonel Lezcano, General Urquiza's accountant. These days it's a restaurant, which is ideal for lunch or dinner. Opt for

# In case you want to see the world.

**At American Express, we're here to make your journey a smooth one. So we have over 1,700 travel service locations in over 130 countries ready to help. What else would you expect from the world's largest travel agency?**

do more

**Travel**

# In case you want to be welcomed there.

We're here to see that you're always welcomed at establishments everywhere. That's why millions of people carry the American Express® Card – for peace of mind, confidence, and security, around the world or just around the corner.

do more

Cards

# In case you're running low.

We're here to help with more than 190,000 Express Cash locations around the world. In order to enroll, just call American Express at 1 800 CASH-NOW before you start your vacation.

do more **AMERICAN EXPRESS**

**Express Cash**

# And in case you'd rather be safe than sorry.

We're here with American Express® Travelers Cheques. They're the safe way to carry money on your vacation, because if they're ever lost or stolen you can get a refund, practically anywhere or anytime. To find the nearest place to buy Travelers Cheques, call 1 800 495-1153. Another way we help you do more.

do more AMERICAN EXPRESS

**Travelers Cheques**

one of the tables on the shady sidewalk, overlooking Plaza San Martín. The special "tourist menu" includes an appetizer, entree, and dessert for about $8. Or you might try the succulent *pollo cristobal* (chicken in orange sauce served with rice). ⊠ *12 de Abril and Alejo Peyret,* ☎ *3447/424037. AE, DC, MC, V.*

$ ✕ **Viejo Almacen.** There's nothing fancy about this restaurant, though it's nicer than the name "Old Warehouse" suggests. Come here for a good sampling of river fish, pasta, and steak. ⊠ *Urquiza and Paso,* ☎ *3447/422216. AE, DC, MC, V.*

$$$ ⌷ **Hotel Internacional Quirinale.** This enormous, luxury, riverside hotel
★ offers a level of comfort and number of facilities unparalleled along the rest of the Corredor del Uruguay. Many of the large, modern rooms have spectacular views of the river. The decor is far from daring, but no expense was spared in providing the highest quality furnishings. You must pay to use the hotel's spa, but the pool, gym, and tennis court are free. ⊠ *Av. Costanera and Noailles, 3280,* ☎ *3447/ 421133,* ☎ ﬁﬁ *3447/421978. 168 rooms, 14 suites. Restaurant, 2 bars, air-conditioning, minibars, room service, pool, beauty salon, massage, sauna, spa, tennis court, health club, laundry, meeting room. AE, DC, MC, V.*

$$ ⌷ **Hotel Palmar.** At this hotel several blocks from the river, you may be reminded of a scene from an old western when you walk into the lobby, replete with a shiny saloon, deer heads on the walls, dark wood paneling, and classic iron-railed stairs. Rooms have three classifications: "modern," each of which has a large bathroom but is a bit dark; "special modern," which is the biggest, most luxurious, and most expensive; and "colonial," with a more classical style. Take a look at all three types to decide which suits you best. ⊠ *Blvd. Ferrari 295, 3280,* ☎ *3447/421952,* ☎ ﬁﬁ *3447/421948. 37 rooms. Restaurant, 2 bars, air-conditioning, room service, laundry. AE, MC, V.*

$–$$ ⌷ **Hostería Restaurant del Puerto.** Completely restored in 1998, this
★ was the town's first hotel and later became the restaurant from which its name comes. The old-fashioned furnishings and vibrant colors of the colonial patio and lobby define charming. All rooms consist of two floors and easily fit five people. Instead of air-conditioning and television, they have antique wooden fans and memorable views of the river. Rooms are 20% off from Sunday to Thursday, making this an even better bargain. Bicycles are available for free rental. ⊠ *Alejo Peyret 158, 3280,* ☎ *3447/422698,* ﬁﬁ *3447/421398. 10 rooms. Restaurant, bar, fans, bicycles, laundry. No credit cards.*

## Nightlife

Nightlife in Colón is very limited. **Café del Teatro** (⊠ 12 de Abril 338) is a old standby for coffee or drinks. The only true dance club is **Mediterraneo** (⊠ Peyret and Alberdi, ☎ 3447/421926); on weekends the impressive white structure fills with a younger crowd. **Moment's Music Bar** (⊠ 12 de Abril 167, ☎ 3447/422932) is a popular watering hole with a more modern ambience. You can always pursue your fortunes at the **casino** (⊠ Urquiza and Alem, ☎ 3447/421535).

## Outdoor Activities and Sports

Along the banks of the Río Uruguay are five *playas* (beaches). The beaches' yellow-tinted sand isn't as soft and abundant as ocean sand, but it does provide a comfortable spot to lie down and bury your feet. All the beaches have jet skiing, kayaking, and windsurfing. The largest, **Playa Norte,** is at the north end of town; it has a campground and is the only one with restaurants; on summer weekends it gets very crowded. Closest to the center, on the south side of town, is **Balneario Piedras Colorados,** named for its reddish-colored stones; it also has a camping area. Farther south are three smaller beaches: **Balneario**

Inkier, **Playa Nueva** (the prettiest), and **Playa Honda.** All are either within walking distance or a short taxi ride away.

The Uruguay River is best appreciated by boat: **Ita i Cora** (⊠ a stand near entrance to Hotel Quirinale at Costanera and Noailles, ☎ 3447/ 423360) organizes two different boat trips: One (1½ hours, $15) goes to an interesting sand-bank formation; the second trip (3½ hours, $35) also includes a stop at a deserted island, on which you take a short hike through the vegetation. Ita i Cora also arranges land safaris by jeep: The three-hour trip ($20) includes visits to an old mill, a semi-precious-stonecutting workshop, and sand dunes. An English-speaking guide is available.

**Golf Club Colón** (⊠ Camino Costera Norte, ☎ 3447/421858), next to the thermal baths, has nine holes and a nice view of the river. Unlimited play costs $10, and clubs are available to rent.

### Shopping
Alpaca sweaters, baskets, wood statues, semiprecious stone jewelry, ceramics, and other crafts by more than 70 local artisans are found in the **Centro Artesanal La Casona** (⊠ 12 de Abril 106), an old colonial building in front of Plaza San Martín. It's open weekdays 7 PM–11 PM and weekends 9–1 and 7–11.

## Parque Nacional El Palmar

❹ *50 km (30 mi) north of Colón.*

This 21,000-acre national park was created in 1966, primarily to protect the extraordinary Syagrus Yatay palms, which grow up to 50 ft and have been known to live for up to 800 years. At the turn of the century, these palms covered vast portions of the province as well as Brazil and Uruguay, but agriculture, cattle raising, and forestry in the 20th century rendered them nearly extinct. The visitor center has a small museum detailing the park's flora and fauna. Ask the park ranger for a map of the two short trail walks. One starts at the visitor center and ends at the beach, passing ruins of a house built in 1780. The other, a circular path about 1 km (½ mi) long, starts at the campground, which is just down the hill from the visitor center, cuts through the subtropical forest, and passes by Arroyo Los Loros, a tranquil stream along which you are likely to see *vizcachas* (similar to chinchillas) and iguanas. You may also spot foxes, deer, and capybaras, the world's largest rodent (though they're a less common sight). In the morning and at sunset, a wide variety of birds such as *ñandus* (rheas), egrets, and herons abound. You could easily spend a few hours in the park. Next to the visitor center are a restaurant and campground (reservations aren't necessary). ⊠ *Off R14.*

# CORRIENTES AND CHACO

The provinces of Corrientes and Chaco have more differences than similarities. Corrientes is dominated by marshy wetlands; Chaco by lands so dry it can hardly support human life. The neighboring capitals—Corrientes and Resistencia—separated only by the Río Paraná, have markedly distinct cultures, best reflected in the people. The notoriously proud Correntinos, many of whom are descendents of the first Spanish settlers, are said to have more allegiance to their province than to Argentina. Correntinos also tend to be fiercely political: Party colors are worn daily and even painted on tombstones, making for colorful cemeteries. Chaqueños, on the other hand, tend to be more laid-back and unassuming. The province has a large indigenous community, largely consisting of the Wichi, and most of the province's inhabitants are of mixed European and indigenous heritage. As in most of the region, the provincial capitals and major towns are not very interesting on their own; they're only places you'll need to pass through on your way elsewhere. The true gems are the utterly remote areas that serve as sanctuaries for an abundance of plants and wildlife.

## Mercedes

**❺** *350 km (210 mi) northwest of Colón.*

Apart from a pleasant square in the center, this tiny town offers nothing in the way of beauty or tourist attractions. You have to pass through here, however, on the trip between Esteros del Iberá and destinations to the north. There are no recommendable hotels, so plan on stopping here for as short a time as possible.

## Colonia Carlos Pellegrini and the Esteros del Iberá

**❻** *192 km (120 mi) northeast of Mercedes, 870 km (522 mi) northeast of Buenos Aires.*

The 3-million-acre Esteros del Iberá marshland covers nearly 20% of Corrientes Province. It's made up of more than 60 *lagunas* (lagoons), some of which are crystal clear, thus the name Esteros del Iberá (Brilliant Waters in native Guaraní). The lagoons are interconnected in a labyrinthlike formation, which some consider to be one enormous lake because the lagoons are separated only by masses of floating vegetation. It's in this vegetation that the true beauty of the Esteros del Iberá is found: A spectacular mix of water lilies, hyacinths, red ferns, and irises makes a colorful home for many forms of wildlife and birds. The 368 species of birds that live here include storks, flamingos, blue and purple herons, red cardinals, and several varieties of eagles. On a typical two- or three-hour boat trip (arranged through a posada in Colonia Carlos Pellegrini), you'll also see capybara, alligators, and *ciervo del los pantanos* (marsh deer) and, perhaps, though less likely, *aguará guazú* (maned wolf), *lobito de rio* (neotropical otter), and *venado de las pampas* (pampas deer), which are in danger of extinction because they were heavily hunted for their pelts over the years. In order to protect the wildlife and the fragile ecosystem, the provincial government declared this a natural reserve in 1983.

The capital of the Esteros del Iberá is the tiny village of Colonia Carlos Pellegrini. Here you'll find the park's **information center** (there's no phone or address, but there's a park ranger here 24 hours a day). The small museum in the information center has displays on the marshland and its animal and plant life. A short path leads from behind the center into the forest, where you may run across a family of friendly and curious howler monkeys.

### Dining and Lodging

You have four possible accommodation options in the area, three of which are in Colonia Carlos Pellegrini and have very similar facilities and services and cost about the same. Most hotels listed here charge a room rate that includes a boat trip on the lake, a hike, and all meals. Note that there's nowhere to eat other than at the various inns and lodges, which serve a mix of local and international cuisine. You must pay extra for English-speaking guides (generally about $50 per day), horseback riding ($8 per hour per person), fishing trips ($50 per four hours), and ground transportation to the towns of Mercedes or Posadas (round-trip $150 and $300, respectively). To preserve the rustic atmosphere, none of the hotels have televisions.

**$$$$** ✕⛺ **Estancia Rincón del Diablo.** This extensive cattle ranch is on the edge of Laguna Itatí. Guest quarters are reasonably large and comfortable but blandly decorated. The real draw is the natural surroundings: The crystal-clear lake provides perfect conditions for scuba diving (equipment is provided), sport fishing, and kayaking. You can also go horseback riding or hiking. The room rate includes all of these activities (except scuba diving and more extensive fishing trips), all meals, and transportation to and from Mercedes, 60 km (36 mi) south. ✉ *Av. Atanacio Aguirre, Km 1, Mercedes 3470,* ☎ *3773/420103,* 🖷 *3773/420247. 5 rooms. Restaurant, fans, horseback riding, dock, scuba diving, boating, fishing. AE, DC, MC, V.*

**$$$$** ✕⛺ **Posada Aguapé.** This handsome inn in Colonia Carlos Pellegrini
★ is on picturesque grounds next to Laguna Iberá. The two guest houses are built in typical Corrientes style—long one-story buildings with white-plaster walls and metal roofs supported by large wooden posts—with unique touches of eucalyptus branches, palm trunks, and rustic antiques. The original guest house has four medium-size rooms with a direct view of the lake. The eight rooms in the newer guest house are larger and more elaborately furnished. The inn also has a small pool, a reading/recreation room, and a pleasant open-air restaurant. Meals, featuring delicious and plentiful combinations of local and international favorites, are included in the price. *For information write to:* ✉ *Coronel Obarrio 1038 (San Isidro), Buenos Aires 1642,* ☎ 🖷 *11/4742–3015. 12 rooms. Restaurant, fans, pool, horseback riding, dock, video room, gift shop, boating. FAP. No credit cards.*

**$$$$** ✕⛺ **Posada de la Laguna.** This inn is nearly identical to Posada Aguapé (☞ *above*), and it's practically next door, also with direct access to Laguna Iberá. The lovely grounds contain a pool, an indoor restaurant (serving international cuisine), and one guest house built in typical Corrientes style. The comfortable guest rooms are fashionably rustic. Owner Elsa Guiraldes lives on the premises to ensure guests' total satisfaction. Several package deals facilitate transportation between Buenos Aires and Posadas. ✉ *Colonia Carlos Pellegrini, 3471,* ☎ *3773/5629827 or 3773/5629532,* 🖷 *3773/422044. 6 rooms. Restaurant, fans, pool, horseback riding, dock, boating. FAP. MC, V.*

**$$$** ✕⛺ **Hostería Ñandereta.** This large stone-and-log house in Colonia Carlos Pellegrini resembles an Alpine ski lodge. In the cozy lobby, animal hooves hang from the wooden walls. Rooms are very comfortable, with simple wooden interiors and checkered curtains and bedspreads. The friendly, helpful staff speaks English. Note that the hotel doesn't have direct access to the lagoon, but its private dock is only a short drive away. There is a full meal plan. *For information, write:* ✉ *Box 290, New York, NY 10185–0290,* ☎ *3773/421741 in Mercedes,* 🖷 *3773/420155 in Mercedes. 6 rooms. Restaurant, fans, horseback riding, snorkeling, dock. FAP. MC, V.*

# Resistencia

❼ *1,019 km (632 mi) north of Buenos Aires.*

The capital of Chaco Province, with 300,000 inhabitants, is deservedly nicknamed "*la ciudad de las esculturas*" ("the city of sculptures"). Throughout the city—on street corners, in parks, on medians, and on lawns—are sculptures ranging from Neoclassic busts to postmodern abstract figures. Every year for two weeks in late July and early August, the city hosts an international sculpting competition. It's fascinating to watch as the internationally renowned artists transform raw material (the medium changes every year) into fine sculptures. All work is performed in the enormous Plaza 25 de Mayo, which contains a beautiful fountain, towering palm trees, and, of course, many statues. If you're passing through Resistencia on your way to Presidencia Roque Sáenz Peña during this period, it may be worth spending a day and watching the artists at work. If not, there's little in this town to warrant an overnight stay.

# Presidencia Roque Sáenz Peña

**8** *565 km (339 mi) northwest of Colonia Carlos Pellegrini, 168 km (104 mi) west of Resistencia.*

Natural cotton balls litter the roads surrounding this small town in the heart of Chaco, so it's no wonder that it's nicknamed the "*capital nacional de algodón*" ("national capital of cotton"). The town was originally called "Km 173," which is its location on the railway. But in 1912, when it was officially founded, it was named after Argentina's at the time, Presidencia Roque Sáenz Peña, who was a proponent of the region. Life in this town of 68,000, where rush-hour traffic consists mostly of bikes and scooters, is very tranquil, especially in summer when temperatures often exceed 100°F. In the hopes of attracting more visitors to the town, an international airport was built in 1998, but it hasn't even taken any national flights yet. It's not clear if or when these will even start, as negotiations have stalled between the airline companies and local officials.

The town's top attraction (6 km [4 mi] southeast of town) is the 370-acre **Complejo Ecológico Municipal** (Municipal Ecological Complex), one of Argentina's primary centers for the recuperation and reproduction of endangered animals. The enormous on-site zoo contains more than 2,000 animals and more than 208 species. The majority of these animals—including jaguars, monkeys, alligators, pumas, flamingos, and condors—come from the Parque Nacional Chaco (Chaco National Park), 150 km (90 mi) northeast (the park itself isn't that interesting). Animals, such as tigers, lions, a hippopotamus, and baboons, have also been brought here through an exchange program with many of the world's best zoos. The complex is very popular on weekends because it also has soccer fields, playgrounds, and cookout facilities by the lake. To get to the zoo, either take a taxi (about $5) or catch Linea 1, which passes through the central plaza on Calle 10. ✉ *R95, Km 1,111 (1,000 ft from R16),* ☎ *3732/424284.* 🎫 *Admission.* ☉ *Daily 7 AM–8 PM.*

Health-seeking foreigners and Argentines come to town specifically for the **Complejo Termal** (Thermal Bath Complex). The bath's chemical composition, made up in part of sodium, potassium, calcium, and magnesium, makes it especially effective in relieving stress and symptoms of arthritis. Twenty-four private baths tap into the 105°F water that surges from 480 ft below the surface. Also here are saunas, Turkish baths, and skilled masseuses; prices are very reasonable. ✉ *Calle 23 554,* ☎ *3732/421587.* 🎫 *Admission.* ☉ *Daily 6–12:30 and 2:30–9.*

The **Museo Histórico de la Ciudad** (City History Museum) has a variety of displays, including two extraordinary fossils. The first is a 200,000-year-old, 4-ft fossil of a glyptodon, a predecessor of the armadillo, which became extinct 10,000 years ago; the second is a 10,000-year-old fossil of a 5-ft tortoise shell. Another noteworthy item is a small meteorite from Campos Cielo, a sight in southwest Chaco where an enormous meteorite shower fell 6,000 years ago. ✉ *Calle 12 and Calle 1,* ☎ *3732/420654.* 🎫 *Admission.* ☉ *Weekdays 1:30–8.*

## Dining and Lodging

**$** ✕ **Chilis Plaza.** Two blocks from the central plaza, this trendy yet casual restaurant is easily recognizable from the huge red awning and gigantic speakers in front. You can eat outside on the patio or inside, where golden stars hang from the high ceiling. The menu includes a variety of regional dishes: One tasty specialty is the *supremo pollo chili plaza* (chicken stuffed with cheese, ham, hearts of palm, and carrots, served in a cream sauce). ⊠ *Calle 14 and 9 de Julio,* ☎ *3732/426776. No credit cards. No lunch Sun.*

$ ✕ **La Estancia.** Everyone sits facing the television because it's the most interesting thing to look at in this simple restaurant. Nevertheless, the menu is varied, the food is quite good, and the prices are very reasonable. You might try the brochette *mixto* (grilled beef, chicken, pork, onions, peppers, and tomatoes on a skewer). ⊠ *Calle 17 586,* ☎ *3732/423937. No credit cards.*

$ ✕ **Hotel Gualok Restaurant.** This is the most elegant and expensive restaurant in town—but it's not really very elegant or expensive. The handsome yet slightly worn decor has not changed since the restaurant opened in 1979. Specialties include *pollo Singapur* (sweet-and-sour chicken) and *pollo ajillo* (chicken with garlic sauce). ⊠ *Calle 12 1198,* ☎ *3732/420521. AE, MC, V.*

$$ ▥ **Hotel Gualok.** Constructed in 1979 by the state lottery association, this hotel was once considered the epitome of luxury. Today, with insufficient funds for even rudimentary maintenance, the large structure is in a clear state of decay. Many rooms have shoddy rugs, chipped tables, peeling paint, and exposed wires. Yet it's one of the few lodging options in town. On the positive side, it has a nice pool, a decent restaurant, a casino, and thermal baths next door. Request rooms on the fourth and fifth floors—they were less effected by water damage. Note that you can access the Internet at the hotel for the charge of a local telephone call. ⊠ *Calle 12 1198, 3700,* ☎ ☏ *3732/420521. 106 rooms, 2 suites. Restaurant, bar, air-conditioning, minibars, pool, casino, laundry, meeting room. AE, DC, MC, V.*

$ ▥ **Hotel Presidente.** Built in 1996, this hotel next to the tourism of-
★ fice is an excellent bargain. Rooms are cozy and clean. Included in the rate is an impressive breakfast and free laundry. Make reservations a week in advance since this small hotel is very popular, especially with business travelers. ⊠ *Calle 17 464, 3700,* ☎ ☏ *3732/424498. 26 rooms, 1 suite. Restaurant, air-conditioning, minibars, meeting room, laundry. No credit cards.*

### Nightlife and the Arts

**Password** (⊠ Calle 3 between calles 10 and 12, ☎ 3732/425229), open only on weekends, is a dance club popular with a younger crowd. **Saravá** (⊠ At calles 12 and 11, ☎ 3732/424266) is an elegant, dimly lighted bar near the main plaza. Sporadic cultural events are held at the **Teatro Septiembre** (⊠ Calle 1 between calles 8 and 10, ☎ 3732/421587).

### Shopping

Most of the town's shops are on Calle 12. **Mercado Artesanal** (⊠ calles 12 and 1), next to the history museum, sells local crafts; it's open daily 8–noon and 4–8.

## El Impenetrable

❾ *180 km (108 mi) northwest of Presidencia Roque Sáenz Peña.*

A desolate wilderness, El Impenetrable (The Impenetrable), in the northwest part of Chaco Province, covers nearly a third of the province, as well as much of the province of Formosa and part of Paraguay. It was named by Spanish explorers who couldn't traverse the area because of the scarcity of water. Indeed, the extremely arid climate and temperatures that commonly exceed 110°F make this a very unforgiving land. Even today it's sparsely populated, with just a few scattered villages, mostly inhabited by members of the indigenous Wichi. In fact, it's possible to drive for hours through the eerie-looking landscape without seeing any signs of other people: no telephone or electrical wires, no signs, no cars, and no houses. Then, out of nowhere a boy will appear on a bicycle, trudging through the red sandlike soil to an unimaginable destination.

Although life is barely sustainable for humans, many forms of wildlife thrive here. The landscape is marked by several types of cacti, specially adapted palm trees, thorny shrubs, and the famous *quebracho,* a strange, often gigantic tree that has an enormously convex trunk and is hollow inside. Its name, which means "axe breaker," is attributed to the toughness of its wood, once used as railroad ties. This is also the last frontier for some nearly extinct species, including wolves, anteaters, armadillos, jaguars, pumas, and eagles, and many birds. An especially impressive sight is the thousands of small blue, bright yellow, and mint green butterflies fluttering about.

Getting to the area is difficult. With even the slightest bit of rain, the dirt roads become impassable to all but specially equipped jeeps and trucks. Presently, jeep trips are only organized by one company, **Quiyoc** (☞ Tour Operators and Travel Agencies *in* Argentine Litoral A to Z, *below*). Depending on the length of the trip, a tour may also include stops at Nueva Pompeya, an old Jesuit mission, and Villa Río Bermejito, a small village with a white-sand riverside beach; canoe rides on the river and hikes are also possible. With a group of at least three, the trip costs about $100 per person per day. Because of the current lack of accommodations, tents are the only option. You probably won't feel a need to spend more than two or three days in the region. You could even take a day trip from Presidencia Roque Sáenz Peña (for $65 per person), but you'll miss a lot if you're only there for such a short time.

# MISIONES

The small, banana-shaped province of Misiones juts out from the Argentine mass, surrounded by Paraguay to the east and Brazil to the west. Nowhere else in Argentina is there such a gorgeous subtropical landscape: The lush, green vegetation stunningly contrasts with the rich red tones of the soil, and its three minor mountain chains give picturesque texture to the forest. The region also has an abundance of waterfalls—the most famous are the Cataratas de Iguazú, but the lesser-known ones such as the Saltos de Moconá are almost as spectacular.

Though nature is the main attraction, the area is also known for its Jesuit mission ruins. The Jesuits, who came here in the early 17th century, were the first in a long line of foreigners to make their home in this province. After Misiones split off from Corrientes in the 1880s, the provincial government, in order to promote agricultural production, offered very cheap land to those wanting to immigrate here. The result was that people came in large numbers from all over—Switzerland, Germany, Poland, Lithuania, France, Italy, Spain, and even Japan—giving the province the ethnic diversity that it has today.

## Posadas

**❿** *518 km (311 mi) east of Presidencia Roque Sáenz Peña, 1,060 km (636 mi) northeast of Buenos Aires, 310 km (192 mi) east of Corrientes.*

The capital of the Misiones Province, Posadas is on the southern bank of the Río Paraná. It's here that one of the first Jesuit missions in the area, Reduccín Nuestra Señora de la Encarnación de Itapúa, was established in 1615. The mission later moved across the Río Paraná to present-day Encarnación, Paraguay. The area that is now Posadas was later occupied by Paraguayan troops, who used it as a base for doing commerce with Brazil. During the Guerra de la Triple Alianza (War of the Triple Alliance, 1865–70), Argentina took possession of the land and the valuable stockpile of Brazilian products and christened the town Posadas. Of the wave of immigrants who came to the area in the late 19th century, many settled in Posadas. Today many descendants of these immigrants still live here, giving the town of nearly 250,000 a more cosmopolitan feel than other provincial capitals in the region. The tree-lined streets, plazas, and costanera make the town very pleasant, though there's actually little to do. It's primarily a base for exploring other sights in the area, most notably the Jesuit mission ruins.

Before you visit the Jesuit mission ruins, it helps to get some background at the **Museo Arqueológico Andres Guacurari** (Andres Guacurari Archaeology Museum). You can learn about the unique society created by the missionaries and see objects found at the missions, such as ceramic tiles, a printing press, clothing, a Bible translated into Guaraní, and wooden statues of Jesus. ⊠ *General Páz 1865,* ☎ *3752/435845.* ⊡ *Admission.* ☉ *Daily 8–11 and 3–6.*

## Dining and Lodging

$$ ✕ **Mikele Bistró.** Dining in the antique house with glass ceilings and
★ mustard-color walls is pure pleasure. The imaginative menu has a delightful sampling of beautifully presented Mediterranean cuisine. The saltimbocca, a succulent steak marinated in red wine sauce, is excellent, as are the seafood dishes like *surubí a la crema de limón* (a regional fish in a lemon cream sauce). The passion fruit mousse is a must for dessert. ⊠ *Córdoba 474,* ☎ *3752/423110. AE, DC, MC, V. Closed Mon.*

$ ✕ **El Oriental.** Depending on how long you've been in the region, you may be desperate for a change of cuisine: This is as exotic as it gets. The Chinese food here won't knock you off your feet, but it's generally tasty and quite inexpensive. Beware: In this carnivorous country, even the spring rolls have meat. The decor is quasi-Chinese, with fitting wall paintings and music. It's a bit outside the city, so you may want to take a (short) taxi ride here. ⊠ *Cabred 2470,* ☎ *3752/430586. AE, DC, MC, V.*

$ ✕ **La Rueda.** There's no better place in town for a "running spit" and
★ a "free fork." Less literally translated, *espeto corrido* and *tenedor libre* mean all-you-can-eat meat and salad. The enormous 30-year-old restaurant is a true town establishment. As suggested by the name, there's a wheel motif that pervades everything from the shape of the ceiling to the chairs. Although the restaurant is a bit outside town, the excellent quality of the meat and the very reasonable prices make it a good dining option. ⊠ *Juan Manuel de Rosas 6380,* ☎ *3752/454111. AE, DC, MC, V. No dinner Sun.*

$$–$$$ ▥ **Julio César.** Though it's considered to be the most luxurious accommodation in town, the hotel is clearly not what it used to be. The location is ideal, and the hotel's facilities are excellent, yet rooms have shoddy rugs and peeling paint. Note that the superior rooms cost $15 more than standard rooms and are only slightly nicer. Internet and E-mail access are available. ⊠ *Bolivar 1879, 3300,* ☎ *3752/440990,* ℻ *3752/435302. 100 rooms, 5 suites. Restaurant, bar, air-conditioning, minibars, room service, exercise room, laundry, meeting room. AE, DC, MC, V.*

$$ ▥ **La Aventura.** It has the feel of a far-away weekend resort, yet it's
★ only 15 minutes from town. Thirty small cabanas are on stunning grounds. There's a fantastic view of the Río Paraná, just below. You can sunbathe on the small strip of beach or by the large pool. Other

recreational facilities include two tennis courts, two paddleball courts, and a volleyball court. The cabanas are clean, modern, and have everything you might want: air-conditioning, television, and a fully functioning kitchenette. ☒ *Av. Urquiza and Av. Zapiola, 3300 (take Av. A. Guacurarí from the north end of town due west to Av. Urquiza),* ☎ FAX *3572/465555. 30 cabanas. Restaurant, 2 bars, air-conditioning, kitchenettes, room service, pool, 2 tennis courts, volleyball, beach, fishing, laundry. AE, DC, MC, V.*

$ ⊞ **Le Petit Hotel.** This small hotel, really more of a house, six blocks from the town center, is the best bargain in town. Picasso reprints hang in the lobby and halls and the modest-size guest rooms, with wood paneling, are cozy and well maintained. ☒ *Santiago del Estero 1630, 3300,* ☎ *3752/436031. 10 rooms. Air-conditioning. No credit cards.*

### Nightlife

You can dance to the best of the '60s, '70s, and '80s at **Años 60** (☒ Entre Ríos 1951, ☎ 3752/427930), in the Hotel Julio Cesár. At the **Casino Club** (☒ San Lorenzo 1950, ☎ 3752/428686) gamble the night away. **Glass** (☒ Bolivar 1887, ☎ 3752/429619) is a classy, upscale bar with outdoor seating in front of the central plaza. **Menterato** (☒ San Lorenzo 1971, ☎ 3752/428380) is a hip bar with live music every Saturday night and Internet access.

### Shopping

For crafts, head to the **Mercado de Artesanias** (☒ Sarmiento 319, ☎ 3752/425427); it's open Monday–Saturday 8–noon and 4–8. Everything from clothes to electronics comes over from cheaper Paraguay and can be found daily at the **Mercado de las Villenas** (☒ Av. Roque Sáenz Peña between Sarmiento and Santa Fe).

## Represa de Yacyretá

⓫ *90 km (54 mi) southwest of Posadas.*

Though it's not especially beautiful, the enormous, modern Represa de Yacyretá (Yacyretá Dam)—one of the world's largest—on the Río Paraná is an impressive sight. The dam stretches 1½ km (1 mi) across the river and measures 67 km (40 mi) in total extension. If the containing wall were to break, it would flood Buenos Aires, roughly 1,100 km (660 mi) away, to the equivalent of eight stories high. It has 20 gigantic turbines, each 46 ft in diameter, through which 52,500 cubic ft of water pass per second. Presently it's only working at 50% efficiency, but when it reaches 100%, set to have happened by 2000, it will supply 40% of Argentina's power. The project has also been a study in corruption and inefficiency: Construction started in 1983, and projected costs were $1.5 billion; today it's still not completed and has already cost more than $11 billion. Free guided tours, which last about an hour, are provided four times daily. Some guides speak English. From Posadas you must take an hour-long bus ride to Ituzaingo, where a taxi can take you to the nearby *relaciones publicas* (public relations) building. Inside are models, posters, and a 10-minute video. Here you meet the guide and catch the minivan to the dam. Tours leave at 9, 11, 3:15, and 4:30 from Monday through Saturday, and at 9 and 11 on Sunday. ☎ *3786/420050 for information.*

## San Ignacio Mini

⓬ *59 km (36 mi) northeast of Posadas.*

San Ignacio Miní is the best preserved and most frequently visited of the Jesuit missions ruins (for more on the missions, *see* Close-Up Box, The Jesuits: God's Warriors, *below*). The mission was originally established in 1610 in Guayrá, a region of present-day Brazil. In 1632, seeking refuge from Portuguese slave traders who were raiding the mission, capturing the native populations living there, and selling them in Brazil, the mission relocated to a spot near the Río Paraná. In 1695 it moved again, 3½ km (2 mi) away, to where its ruins are today. At the mission's height in 1733, the mission had over 3,300 Guaraní inhabitants; there were never more than three Jesuits at any one time.

The mission's layout was typical of others in the region—it had a school, a cemetery, a church, a school, and living quarters surrounding a central green. Where it stood out was in the development of music and the arts. It was one of the first music conservatories in the region, and the precision with which instruments were constructed and played here gained the mission fame throughout the New World and Europe. An excellent example of the stellar artwork created here remains on the facade of the church—the Hellenic columns and traditional Guaraní images sculpted by both the Jesuits and Guaranís into the red sandstone.

Shortly after the expulsion of the Jesuits in 1767, the mission was abandoned and left to the jungle. In the 1940s, however, the National Commission of Historic Monuments began restoring the mission: What you see today is a mixture of the original buildings and new construction. One aspect that cannot be reproduced is the surrounding environment: The jungle was gradually cut down as the town of San Ignacio sprang up, and now ugly brick buildings peek behind the ruins and a mess of restaurants and artisan shops line the outside walls. It's most likely that you'll just stop in San Ignacio for a few hours. Hour-long guided tours (note that few guides speak English) are available throughout the day for $10, in addition to the admission fee. The small museum contains a model of the mission, original tiles, and various metal objects unearthed during the restoration. ⊠ *In town of San Ignacio,* ☎ *3752/ 470186 for information.* ⊘ *Daily 7–7.*

### Lodging

**$** 🏨 **Hotel San Ignacio.** The only option for an overnight stay is this inexpensive hotel four blocks from the ruins. The majority of people who stay here are young backpackers, and the facilities cater to this crowd: a bar, paddleball court, and recreation room with two pool tables and old arcade games. The four simple, clean cabanas all have two rooms and can sleep four to five people. The hotel usually fills up by late afternoon so it's a good idea to make a reservation. The only phone is the public one in the lobby. ⊠ *San Martín 823, San Ignacio 3322,* ☎ *3752/470047,* 🖷 *3752/470422. 4 cabanas. Bar, air-conditioning, recreation room. No credit cards.*

## Nuestra Señora de Loreto

**⓭** *9 km (5 mi) south of San Ignacio Miní, 50 km (30 mi) northeast of Posadas.*

The history of this Jesuit mission is very much intertwined with that of San Ignacio Miní (☞ *above*). They were founded near each other in the same year by the same Jesuits, and they migrated together in 1632 from what is now Brazil to the Río Paraná area. The mission moved around several more times before ultimately arriving at its final location in 1686. Because of its great economic productivity, Nuestra Señora de Loreto was one of the most important missions in the region. It was a major supplier of yerba maté and cloth to other parts of the Spanish colony and had extensive cattle ranch land. When demand for yerba maté declined after 1750, the mission successfully

# THE JESUIT MISSIONARIES

**O**VER A SPAN OF MORE THAN 150 years, Spanish Jesuit missionaries established 30 missions in the area that now encompasses parts of present-day Argentina, Paraguay, and Brazil. They created an extraordinary society that is still a subject of great interest to scholars, social theorists, and even Hollywood (their tory is told in the 1986 film *The Mission*, starring Robert De Niro and Jeremy Irons).

In 1534 a Catholic priest named San Ignacio de Loyola founded the Jesuits, who were officially approved by Pope Paul III in 1540. With the objective of "seeking the greater glory of God and salvation of souls," they concentrated their efforts on spreading Catholicism throughout the world. In the mid-16th century the first Jesuits arrived in South America, in what is today Peru and Brazil. In 1607 the Jesuit Diego Torres went to Asunción and established the Jesuit province of Paraguay.

The first missions were created in 1610 in the region of Guayrá in present-day Brazil. The Franciscans had previously entered these territories but failed to convert the indigenous Guaraní. The Jesuits were almost immediately successful. Their tactic was to send in a few Jesuits, who bestowed presents on the tribal chiefs and befriended them and then unobtrusively lived among the community, learning the culture and language before spreading their teachings and establishing the missions. The Guaraní, quickly won over, helped construct the missions alongside the Jesuit missionaries. At their apogee, the largest missions had more than 4,000 Guaraní living there, generally along with two or three missionaries.

The greatest problem the missions faced at their outset was the constant raiding by Portuguese slave traders, who found the concentrations of Guaraní to be easy targets. For this reason, the missions of the Guayrá region relocated in 1631 to the banks of the Paraná and Uruguay rivers. Nevertheless, the attacks continued. In 1640 the royal crown of Spain granted the missions the right to use firearms and to raise armies in self-defense. In the following year Jesuits and Guaranís fought side by side and defeated the slave traders in the Battle of Mbororé.

With the defeat of the slave traders, the missions could now concentrate more on their own development. They became economically self-sufficient through cattle ranching and the cultivation of crops such as corn, manioc, sugar, tobacco, rice, and yerba maté. They also produced honey and made highly detailed metal works, leather goods, and cloth. The missions had an effective communication system, which allowed for the sharing of information and the promotion of uniformity among the different missions in the area. For instance, nearly all had the same physical layout, with an enormous central plaza, surrounded by living quarters, a church, a school, workshops, and a cemetery.

Culturally, too, the missions were quite advanced. Musical instruments were crafted at missions, which had their own choruses and orchestras. Some missions had astronomical observatories. At Nuestra Señora de Loreto, a printing press was built on which works such as the Bible were printed in Guaraní and Spanish (both languages were taught in the mission schools). And an architectural and artistic style, Baroque-Guaraní, developed in the buildings and sculptures at the missions.

But in 1767, when the missions were at their economic and cultural peak, King Carlos III of Spain expelled the Jesuits. The prevailing theory as to why this sudden decision was made is that the king feared that the missions had gained too much power and that they provided too much competition for the region's many influential plantation owners. After the Jesuits departed, the communities they left behind rapidly fell apart. Governmental mismanagement led to large-scale migration of the Guaraní to the large cities or back to the jungle. And most who remained behind at the old missions were killed by Paraguayan troops fighting for territorial expansion.

turned much of its efforts toward rice farming. The mission also obtained widespread fame around 1700 for its printing press, one of the first in the New World: This enabled them to publish numerous books, especially the Bible, in the native Guaraní language.

In 1731 the mission reached its maximum number of inhabitants: close to 7,000 Guaranís. However, most left in the years following the Jesuits' expulsion in 1767. Those who remained were forced to move away in 1817 by the Paraguayans, who were trying to seize large parts of the Misiones Province. After evacuating the inhabitants, the Paraguayans set fire to the entire mission, and for this reason little of it exists today. The jungle engulfed the remains and only within the last 10 years have they been uncovered. No restoration or reconstruction has yet taken place. Nonetheless, a visit to the ruins gives you an idea of the Jesuit missions' original environment. There's also a visitor center with a small museum displaying ceramics and metal objects found during excavations. Guides are available only during high season (November, December, July, and Easter), but they don't speak English. ⊠ *3 km (2 mi) off R12 (look for the sign)*, ☎ *3752/470190.* 🖾 *Admission.* ⊘ *Daily 7–7.*

## Santa Ana

🔟 *6 km (4 mi) south of Loreto, 45 km (27 mi) northeast of Posadas.*

The Santa Ana mission was founded in 1633 in the region of Tapé, in southern Brazil. In 1660, to escape invading Portuguese slave traders intent on capturing the native population, the two Jesuit leaders and 2,000 Guaranís relocated to the present location. The mission, which once covered about 1,000 acres, was one of the largest in the region and its church, the Iglesia de Santa Ana, was considered one of the most beautiful. It also had highly advanced metal workshops in which iron and copper were used to make a wide range of products, including knives, swords, spears, and arrows. Not surprisingly, the mission was the most important center for defense in the region.

When the Jesuits were expelled by King Carlos III of Spain in 1767, the mission was at its apogee, with 4,300 Guaraní inhabitants. Soon after, disease, land conflicts, and poor administration caused a significant reduction in the Guaraní population. By 1784 only 1,800 remained at the mission. In 1821 the Paraguayans, who were looking to seize the land on which the missions sat, sacked and burned the missions. All who did not flee into the forest were killed. The few remains of the mission were taken over by the jungle, and before excavations commenced in 1993, the red-sandstone blocks were covered with moss, split apart by huge roots, and engulfed by mighty trees. In 1997 the visitor center was built with its small museum displaying old ceramics, metal products, and photos from the excavation process. Guides are available year-round, but they don't speak English. ⊠ *Just off R12 (follow signs).* ⊘ *Daily 7–7.*

## Santa María la Mayor

🔟 *108 km (65 mi) southeast of Posadas.*

Santa María la Mayor is the least visited of the missions, largely due to its inaccessibility. But it's worth trying to get to since the walls of the artisan workshop, school, and church are still almost entirely intact. The mission was founded in 1636 near the sight of the Mbororé War, during which the Jesuits and Guaranís defeated the Portuguese slave traders who had been raiding the missions and capturing the Guaranís to sell as slaves. In 1637 the mission moved to its present-day spot. The mission has a distinct layout: Instead of just one central plaza, it has a whole sequence of plazas throughout. It never reached the size or importance of many of the other missions, but construction of a new and grander church was just beginning when the Jesuits were expelled in 1767. There's an information center on the premises, and guided tours are available in Spanish only. ⊠ *Off R2 west.* ☉ *Daily 7–7.*

## Soberbio

**16** *283 km (170 mi) northeast of Posadas.*

This tiny town is the closest to Saltos de Moconá (☞ *below*) and thus the logical base for a trip there, even though the road connecting the town to the falls is horrendous. The town itself has nothing to offer and only one nice hotel. Across the Río Uruguay, which runs alongside Soberbio, you can see the pretty green hills of Brazil. In fact, the only television station that the town gets is Brazilian, so it's no wonder that nearly everyone speaks Portuguese, while few in the Brazilian town across the river speak Spanish.

### Dining and Lodging

$$ ✕🔟 **Hostería Puesta del Sol.** From its spot close to the top of a hill,
★ this charming inn offers a panoramic view of the town below and the rugged Brazilian countryside just across the Río Uruguay. A lush landscape of banana trees and purple flowers covers the 40-acre grounds, with a lovely pool, an open-air restaurant, four bungalows, and a main guest house. All guest quarters are simply but nicely decorated and quite comfortable. Rooms in the main guest house sleep up to three and the bungalows up to six. Trips to Saltos de Moconá are run by the inn: With a group of at least three, a trip costs roughly $60 per person for either a land or boat excursion. In high season (November, December, July, and Easter), you must make a reservation in advance and give a deposit for one night (which is a slight risk since the falls could suddenly disappear in a day or two). The restaurant serves simple but tasty local favorites. ⊠ *Calle Suipacha Soberbio; for information write to* ⊠ *San José 124, Buenos Aires 1076,* ☎ FAX *3755/495161. 7 rooms, 4 bungalows. Restaurant, fans, room service, pool, volleyball, laundry. No credit cards.*

## Saltos de Moconá

**17** *86 km (52 mi) northeast of Soberbio.*

The Saltos de Moconá (Moconá Falls) are a set of waterfalls that run for 3 km (2 mi) along a geological fault that's filled by the Río Uruguay. It also marks the border of Brazil and Argentina. The falls are fed by the Pepirí, Guazú, and Yabotí rivers, which come from the Argentine side and plunge into the Río Uruguay below. The name Moconá means "that which sucks all" in Guaraní, a reference to the powerful whirlpools created by the falling water. The heights of the falls vary considerably according to the water level—they average 33 ft high and can reach up to 56 ft, but they can disappear altogether with heavy rains. It's very difficult to predict when this will occur, and when it does, it can happen in the span of just a few days. December through July are generally the best months to see the falls, though there are no guarantees that they will be there when you are.

The best way to explore the falls is by motorboat, though you can also explore them by land. Traveling alongside the falls on the Río Uruguay is the best way to get an idea of their amazing length. Most excursions leave from Soberbio (☞ *above*) and take about 4½ hours round-trip. When traveling by land, a jeep or specially equipped truck is necessary because of the horrible road conditions; without having any flat tires or other mechanical problems, which are common, the trip by land takes about three hours each way. The best views are on the Brazilian side (make sure to bring your passport), but note that the border is closed on weekends.

If you really want an adventure, explore the falls on the Argentine side: As long as the water level is not too high, you can walk through the river that feeds into the falls. No climbing is necessary since the upper level of the waterfall is on the Argentine side. Nevertheless, slippery rocks, often a few feet under the surface, make walking treacherous at times, but the reward is an exhilarating view at the precipice of the falls. The best place to ford the river is in the **Parque Provincial Moconá** (Moconá Provincial Park), just beyond the ranger's station. The approximately 2,500-acre park was created in 1988 in order to protect this natural wonder. For now, the difficult accessibility of the falls keeps the number of visitors low. ⊠ ☎ *3755/441001 for information about the condition of the falls.*

## Puerto Iguazú

**⑱**   *308 km (185 mi) northeast of Posadas, 17 km (10 mi) southeast of the Cataratas del Iguazú.*

This small town of 25,000 is the best base for visiting the stunning Cataratas del Iguazú (☞ *below*). The town originated as a port for shipping wood from the region. It was in the early 20th century that Victoria Aguirre, a high-society Porteña, funded the building of a road that extends to Cataratas de Iguazú to make it easier for people to visit the falls. You may find Puerto Iguazú preferable than its Brazilian neighbor, Foz de Iguaçú, because it's considerably more tranquil and safe (when you go to the Brazilian side, leave your valuables in the hotel and be on the alert; crime is more frequent there). But there's isn't much to do here, as the main attraction in the area are the falls.

### Dining and Lodging

Besides staying in town, you can also stay in the Parque Nacional Iguazú at the Sheraton Internacional Iguazú (☞ *below*); the Garganta del Diablo, one of the best restaurants in the area, is in the hotel. Competition from hotels in Brazil, which are cheaper, forces hotels in Puerto Iguazú to keep rates down and during low season (late September–early November and February–May, excluding Easter), rooms are discounted up to 50%. The town's restaurants are far from spectacular; generally, the best eating is found in the nicer hotels.

$  ✕ **El Charo.** This restaurant is in a shabby old house that looks like it
★  could easily be blown down with a huff and a puff: All the paintings are tilted, the roof is sinking, and the cowhide on the seats is faded. Nevertheless, this is one of town's most popular restaurants because of its consistently delicious and inexpensive *parilladas* (a sampling of grilled meat), as well as its pasta and grilled fish. Note that napkins come only by request. ⊠ *Av. Córdoba 106,* ☎ *3757/421529. No credit cards.*

$  ✕ **Jardín Iguazú.** Close to the bus terminal, this restaurant serves a wide variety of tasty food and is open 24 hours a day. At lunch and at odd hours, when everything else is closed, there's a good fixed-price menu, which for about $4 provides an empanada, a salad, a main dish with pasta and meat, and a beverage. The place is all rather shiny, with highly polished stones on the floor and a stage (used for live music in the evenings) speckled with silver chips. ⊠ *Av. Misiones and Córdoba,* ☎ *3757/423200. AE, MC, V.*

$$$
★

✕🖭 **Hotel Cataratas.** Though this redbrick hotel with green window sills and white awnings isn't especially attractive from the outside, inside is a different story. The classy lobby and ample guest rooms are tastefully decorated with the finest materials and furnishings. Ask for a master double, which is the same price but slightly nicer than the standard double. The hotel also has beautiful grounds and excellent facilities, including an enormous pool, sauna, exercise room, and courts for tennis, paddleball, and volleyball. The high-quality restaurant, serving international cuisine, has an à la carte menu and a fixed-price buffet (dinner only). ⊠ *R12, Km 4 3370*, ☎ *3757/421100*, 𝔽𝔸𝕏 *3757/ 421090. 80 rooms, 2 suites. Restaurant, bar, air-conditioning, in-room safes, minibars, room service, pool, sauna, massage, tennis court, exercise room, volleyball. AE, DC, MC, V.*

$$–$$$

🖭 **Hotel Esturion.** This slightly aged hotel has gardens behind and sweeping views of the river. It also has a very helpful staff. Rooms show some signs of wear and tear, though they are spacious and have all the modern amenities you would expect at a luxury hotel; many have balconies with nice views of the river. The restaurant is sometimes the subject of complaints, especially from those whose package deal provides only a few choices at meals. ⊠ *Av. Fronteras 650, 3370*, ☎ *3757/420020 or 3757/420161, 800/338–2288 in the U.S.*, 𝔽𝔸𝕏 *3757/420414. 114 rooms, 4 suites, 4 apartments. Restaurant, coffee shop, air-conditioning, in-room safes, minibars, pool, 2 tennis courts, massage, sauna, exercise room, dance club. AE, DC, MC, V.*

$

🖭 **Los Helechos.** It's such a great bargain that this hotel doesn't need to discount its rooms during the off-season. It's also convenient to the center of town and two blocks from the bus terminal. Rooms are simple but clean and comfortable; half have air-conditioning and television (these cost $10 more). ⊠ *Paulino Amarante 76, 3370*, ☎ 𝔽𝔸𝕏 *3757/ 420338. 54 rooms. Restaurant, bar, pool, laundry. AE, DC, MC, V.*

## Nightlife

Puerto Iguazú is very quiet at night—more happens on the Brazilian side. But on weekends Puerto Iguazú's **Blanco Paraiso** (⊠ Aguirre 262, ☎ 3757/422534) has live music. At **Lautaro Play's** (⊠ Av. Brasil 49, ☎ 3757/423386), you can have a drink, go dancing, or play pool. Another option is to try your luck at the fancy, European-style casino in the **Iguazú Grand Hotel Resort & Casino** (⊠ R12, Km 1,640, ☎ 3757/ 498050).

## Shopping

Numerous souvenir shops line the main strip, **Avenida Aguirre,** and the surrounding blocks. All carry similar items, such as yerba maté gourds, semiprecious stones, baskets, and weavings.

# Cataratas del Iguazú

⑲  *297 km (178 mi) northeast of Posadas, 238 km (143 mi) northeast of San Ignacio, 1,357 km (814 mi) northeast of Buenos Aires.*

The Cataratas del Iguazú (Iguazú Falls) are one of the wildest wonders of the world, with nature on the rampage in a unique show of sound and fury. The grandeur of this Cinemascopic sheet of white water cascading in constant cymbal-banging cacophony makes Niagara Falls and Victoria Falls seem sedate. At a bend in the Río Iguazú (Iguazú River), on the border with Brazil, the falls extend for almost 3 km (1½ mi) in a 270-degree arch. Iguazú is made up of some 275 separate waterfalls—in the rainy season there are as many as 350—that send their white cascades plunging more than 200 ft onto the rocks below. Dense, lush jungle surrounds the falls: Here the tropical sun and the omnipresent moisture make the jungle grow at a pace that produces a towering pine tree in two decades instead of the seven it takes in, say, Scandinavia. By the falls and along the roadside, rainbows and butterflies are set off against vast walls of red earth, which is so ubiquitous that eventually even peso bills long in circulation in the area turn red from exposure to the stuff.

Allow at least two full days to see this magnificent sight, and be sure to see it from both the Argentine and Brazilian sides. The Brazilians are blessed with the best panoramic view, an awesome vantage point that suffers only from the sound of the gnatlike helicopters that erupt out of the lawn of the Hotel das Cataratas (☞ Dining and Lodging, *below*) right in front of the falls. (Unfortunately, most indigenous macaws and toucans have abandoned the area to escape the whine of the helicopters' engines.) The Argentine side offers the better close-up experience of the falls, with excellent hiking paths, catwalks that approach the falls, a sandy beach to relax on, and places to bathe in the froth of the Río Iguazú. Local travel agencies and tour operators offer trips that will take you to both sides. If you want to set your own pace, you can tour the Argentine side and then take a taxi or one of the regularly scheduled buses across the International Bridge, officially called the Ponte Presidente Tancredo Neves, to Brazil. Note that if you're a Canadian, U.K., or U.S. citizen crossing into Brazil from Argentina or Paraguay, you don't need a visa for a short visit to the falls. You must, however, pay an entry fee and have your passport stamped. Always keep your passport handy as immigration authorities keep the region under close watch.

The best way to immerse yourself in the falls is to wander the many access paths, which are a combination of bridges, ramps, stone staircases, and wooden catwalks set in a forest of ferns, begonias, orchids, and tropical trees. The catwalks over the water put you right in the middle of the action, so be ready to get doused by the rising spray. (Be sure to bring rain gear—or buy it from vendors along the trails on the Brazilian side.) If tropical heat and humidity hamper your style, plan to visit between April and October, though the falls are thrilling year-round. Be aware, however, that the river can get so high in April and May that access to certain catwalks is impossible.

The falls on the Argentine side are in the **Parque Nacional Iguazú** (Iguazú National Park), which was founded in 1934 and declared a World Heritage Site in 1984. The park's **Centro de Informes** (Information Center, ☎ 3757/420180), in what was the park's original hotel, makes a good first stop. Useful maps are posted on the walls, and friendly, multilingual rangers are happy to help you understand the layout of the park. The rangers also preside over a small observation point and museum that have local fauna and exhibits related to the area's history. In an adjoining room are slide shows on Argentina's national park program. On the nights of a full moon, rangers lead groups from the visitor center for a free night walk through the upper trails. The sensation of walking through the subtropical forest at night is eerie and exciting and shouldn't be missed. The roar of the falls drowns out the sounds of the jungle and what was all bright green, red, and blue in the daytime takes on luminous hues of phosphorescent whites. Check at the visitor center for details about tours. The snack bar in the visitor center has tables on the lawn, and the restaurant, **El Fortín**—across from the parking lot—has an all-you-can-eat barbecue and sandwiches.

The **Circuito Inferior** (Lower Circuit), on the Argentine side, is an approximately 1-km-long (½-mi-long) looped trail that consists of a metal catwalk with protected promontories that offer some of the best views of the falls. On this route you cross the small, peripheral **Salto Alvar**

Núñez, falls named for the Spanish conquistador Alvar Núñez Cabeza de Vaca, who accidentally stumbled onto the spectacle in the 16th century; the **Peñon de Bella Vista** (Rock of the Beautiful View); and the **Salto Lanusse** (Lanusse Falls), those farthest from the Garganta del Diablo (Devil's Throat), the tallest cataract (☞ *below*). These preliminaries get you warmed up for the main event. In the distance on the right are the impressive **Salto Dos and Salto Tres Mosqueteros** (Two and Three Musketeers Falls). Halfway along this circuit you get a panoramic peek at what is to come. Through the foliage you can see the gigantic curtain of water in the distance. The trail leads along the lower side of the **Brazo San Martín**, a branch of the river that makes a wide loop to the south. This tributary pushes to get back to the river's main course, opening up dozens of minor and a few major waterfalls along a face of rock that measures almost a mile. On the back side of the circuit—that is, where the trail loops around and starts heading back to your starting point—the **Salto Ramírez** (Ramírez Falls); the **Salto Chico** (Small Falls); and the **Salto Dos Hermanos** (Two Brothers Falls) appear directly before you, opposite the bridge. This section of your circuit, about 1 km (½ mi) long, offers the most exciting panoramic view of the Garganta del Diablo, the **Salto Bossetti** (Bossetti Falls), and the Salto Dos Hermanos. Allow about two hours to walk this circuit. There's no way to get lost on the catwalk, but English-speaking guides, found at the visitor center, can be hired to provide detailed explanations of the falls.

At the vantage point opposite the Salto Bossetti, a trail leads along the edge of the river to a small pier, where sturdy little boats take you across a branch of the river to **Isla San Martín** (San Martín Island). This free boat service operates all day, except when the river is too high. On the island a steep climb up a rustic 160-step stairway leads to a circular trail opening onto three spectacular panoramas of the **Salto San Martín** (San Martín Falls), the **Garganta del Diablo**, and the **Salto Ventana** (Window Falls). If you want to just sit and watch 1,300 cubic yards of water splash below you every second, this is the place to do it. From the southernmost point you see **Salto Escondido** (Hidden Falls), and from the easternmost point, a breathtaking panorama of the falls on the Brazilian side: **Salto Santa María, Salto Floriano,** and **Salto Deodoro.** Few people make the effort to cross the river to Isla San Martín and do this climb, so you can often enjoy the show in solitary splendor. The island has a small beach near the point where the boats land; you can stretch out on the sand to dry out from the mist and warm up after traipsing under the thick tropical greenery. Allow about an hour for the trip to Isla San Martín from the vantage point opposite the Salto Bossetti. Unless you climb up the stairway on Isla San Martín, you'll probably find the hike very easy, and no special footwear is necessary.

The **Circuito Superior** (Upper Circuit)—not a circuit at all but a path about 3,000 ft long—borders the ridge on the south side of the river, along the top of the falls. The trail leads across the rapid waters of the **Brazo San Martín**, a branch of the river, providing great views of **Dos Hermanos, Bossetti, Chico,** and **Ramírez.** The most powerful waterfall rising in front of you at the end is **San Martín**, the park's widest. From the catwalk you look out upon a seemingly endless stretch of waterfalls whose white foams of fury don't subside until they're well down river. You can also see Isla San Martín and the Brazilian side, with the pink walls of the Hotel das Cataratas peeking through the foliage. Count on about an hour and a half to walk this fairly easy circuit; arrows on the path point you in the right direction (or you can just follow the crowds).

The tallest and most renowned waterfall, evocatively named the **Garganta del Diablo** (Devil's Throat), is a breathtaking spectacle as it furiously spills over the precipice and plummets over 230 ft. The force of the water is so great that rising mist prevents you from seeing the bottom; as you stand and watch the river fall off into space, the awesome roar below is your only confirmation that the water has reached its destination. Expect to get wet. The best viewing point is from the 1,000-ft-long catwalk that crosses over the river and leads right up to the gorge. To get to the catwalk, you need to take a boat from **Puerto Canoas,** a settlement 4 km (2½ mi) up the river from the visitor center. The five-minute boat trip runs several times each hour and costs $4 round-trip. Puerto Canoas has a basic campground with no facilities, 1 km (½ mi) farther on the banks of the Río Nandú (Nandú River), along with a restaurant and bar open for lunch only. The hourly bus from Puerto Iguazú to the national park ends its route at Puerto Canoas, and taxis are available at the visitor center ($10 round-trip with a wait). The whole excursion takes about two hours.

Add to your outings to the different panoramic points overlooking the falls with a hike in the jungle. The **Sendero Macuco** (Macuco Trail), which extends 4 km (2½ mi) into the jungle, ending at the **Salto Arrechea** (Arrechea Falls) farther downriver from the main falls, is maintained by the **Centro de Investigaciones Ecológicas Subtropicales** (Center for Subtropical Ecological Investigation, ☎ 3757/420180). The trail is very carefully marked, and descriptive signs in Spanish explain the jungle's flora and fauna. The closest you'll get to a wild animal is likely to be a paw print in the dirt, though you may be lucky enough to glimpse a monkey. The foliage is dense, so the most common surprises are the jungle sounds that seem to emerge out of nowhere. You can turn back at any point, or continue on to the refreshing view of the river and the Salto Arrechea. The best time to hear animal calls and to avoid the heat is either early in the morning or just before sunset. The battalions of butterflies, also best seen in the early morning or late afternoon, can be marvelous, and the intricate glistening cobwebs crisscrossing the trail are a treat in the dawn light. Plan on spending about three hours for the whole trip.

On the Brazilian side, the falls, known in Portuguese as the Foz do Iguaçu, can be seen from the **Parque Nacional Foz do Iguaçu,** Brazil's national park. The park is 25 km (16 mi) along a paved highway southwest of downtown Foz do Iguaçu, the nearest town to the falls on the Brazilian side. The **park entrance** (⊠ Km 17, Rodovia das Cataratas, ☎ 045/5238383) is the best place to get information; it's open daily 7 AM–6 PM, and the entrance fee is roughly $3. Much of the park's 457,000 acres is protected rain forest—off limits to visitors and home to the last viable populations of panthers as well as rare flora such as bromeliads and orchids. The falls are 11 km (7 mi) from the park entrance. The luxurious, historic Hotel das Cataratas (☞ Dining and Lodging, *below*) is near the trailhead. Public parking is allowed on the highway shoulder and in a small lot near the hotel. The path to the falls is 2 km (1 mi) long, and its walkways, bridges, and stone staircases lead through the rain forest to concrete and wooden catwalks that take you to the falls. Highlights of the Brazilian side of the falls include first the **Salto Santa Maria,** from which catwalks branch off to the **Salto Deodoro** and **Salto Floriano,** where you'll be doused by the spray. The end of the catwalk puts you right in the heart of the spectacle at **Garganta do Diabo** (Devil's Throat in Portuguese), from a different perspective than the Argentine side. The tallest and most popular falls extend for 3 km (1½ mi) in a 270-degree arch, and the water thunders down 180 ft. Back on the last section of the main trail, there's a building with facilities, including a panoramic elevator; it's open daily 8:30–6, and there's a very small fee. A balcony brings you close to the far left of **Salto Deodoro**. The trail ends at the road some 35 ft above.

## Dining and Lodging

**$$$** ✕ **Garganta del Diablo.** This restaurant in the Sheraton Internacional Iguazú (☞ *below*) is one of the area's finest. As the harpist plucks away, you can savor the expertly prepared dishes from the international menu. The trout in pastry and the surubí in banana leaves are especially exquisite. The restaurant only serves dinner (after the last bus has left for Puerto Iguazú, which means an expensive taxi ride if you're not a guest at the hotel). ⊠ *Parque Nacional Iguazú,* ☎ *3757/491800. AE, DC, MC, V.*

**$$$** ✕ **Zaragoza.** In a quiet neighborhood on a tree-lined street in Brazil's Foz do Iguaçu, this cozy restaurant is owned by Paquito, a Spanish immigrant. The fare includes a great paella, the house specialty, as well as several delicious fish options. The surubí, definitely merits a try. ⊠ *Rua Quintino Bocaiúva 882, Foz do Iguaçu, Brazil,* ☎ *045/5743084. AE, V.*

**$$$$** ✕🏨 **Hotel das Cataratas.** Not only is this stately hotel on the Brazil-
★ ian side in the national park (with wonderful views of the falls), but it also provides the more traditional comforts—large rooms, terraces, hammocks—of a colonial-style establishment. This pink building is surrounded by galleries and gardens; its main section has been declared a Brazilian national heritage sight. The restaurant serves traditional Brazilian fare. ⊠ *Km 25, Rodovia das Cataratas 85850–970, Brazil,* ☎ *045/ 5232266 or 0800/452266,* 𝔽𝔸𝕏 *045/5741688. 200 rooms. 2 restaurants, bar, coffee shop, pool, 2 tennis courts, shops. AE, DC, MC, V.*

**$$$$** 🏨 **Sheraton Internacional Iguazú.** Half the rooms in this luxury hotel
★ have direct views of the falls, so be sure to reserve one well in advance (they are about 30% more expensive). Floor-to-ceiling windows reveal the inspiring scene to the lobby, restaurants, bars, and even the pool. The spacious balconies are ideal for breakfast or a drink. Rooms are large and comfortable, though they have the same furnishings as when the hotel opened in 1979. But major changes are expected for the near future because the hotel has recently come under Sheraton management. ⊠ *Parque Nacional Iguazú 3372,* ☎ *3757/491800,* 𝔽𝔸𝕏 *3757/ 421600. 180 rooms, 4 suites. 2 restaurants, 2 bars, air-conditioning, minibars, room service, pool, 3 tennis courts, sauna, biking, laundry, meeting rooms. AE, DC, MC, V.*

# Minas de Wanda

**㉔** *43 km (26 mi) south of Puerto Iguazú.*

The Minas de Wanda (Mines of Wanda) are two of the largest sites for semiprecious stone in Argentina. Volcanic activity 120 million years ago created the deposits of amethyst, crystal, quartz, topaz, and agate. The two adjacent and nearly identical mines, the **Compañía Minera Wanda** (☎ 076971350) and the **Tierra Colorada** (☎ 07027401) are both about a mile off R12, where the bus lets you off and where you'll be greeted by representatives from both mines trying to steer you to their establishments. From the bus stop you can walk or take one of the taxis normally waiting there to the mines. On the tours (free) of the mines and workshops, guides (some speak English) explain how the stones are extracted, cut, and treated. Of course, the tours end in the gift shop, where semiprecious stone clocks, paperweights, jewelry, mobiles, ashtrays, and other items are sold; don't count on any great bargains.

# ARGENTINE LITORAL A TO Z

## Arriving and Departing

### By Bus

Traveling to the Argentine Litoral from Buenos Aires is relatively easy.

COLÓN

Buses leave regularly from Buenos Aires to Colón, passing through Gualeguaychú and other towns on the Corredor del Uruguay. These include **Jovibus** (☎ 3446/434875) and **Nuevo Expreso/Flechabus** (☎ 3446/423822). The trip from Buenos Aires takes close to five hours, but from Colón, only two. **Tata** (☎ 3447/422996) is the only company with a direct route between Colón and Presidencia Roque Sáenz Peña. The **Colón Terminal de Omnibus** (✉ Paysandú and Sourigues, ☎ 3447/421716) is about 10 blocks northwest of the town center.

GUALEGUAYCHÚ

Buses between Buenos Aires and Gualeguaychú take about three hours, cost about $20, and run regularly. The two bus companies that travel this route most frequently are: **Nuevo Expreso/Flechabus** (☎ 3446/423822) and **Tata** (☎ 3446/424349). Nuevo Expreso and **Jovibus** (☎ 3446/434875) have regular service between Gualeguaychú and Colón; the trip takes two hours. The **Gualeguaychú Terminal de Omnibus** (✉ Bolívar and Mons. Chalup, ☎ 3446/427987) is in the city center.

MERCEDES

From Mercedes to Presidencia Roque Sáenz Peña, there's only one direct bus—it's generally easier to go through Resistencia. The trip takes four hours to Resistencia from Mercedes and three more to Presidencia Roque Sáenz Peña. **Aguila Dorado** (☎ 3773/422209) goes once daily from Mercedes to Presidencia Roque Sáenz Peña and Resistencia. **Flechabus** (☎ 3773/422209) and **La Nueva Estrella** (☎ 3773/420165) each go from Mercedes to Resistencia twice daily. The **Mercedes Terminal de Omnibus** (✉ San Martín and J. Alfredo Ferreyre, ☎ 3773/420165) is in the town center.

POSADAS

The **Posadas Terminal de Omnibus** (✉ R12 and Av. Santa Catalina) is 6 km (4 mi) southwest of the town center (a $4 taxi ride). **La Estrella** (☎ 3752/455177) and **Cruzero del Norte** (☎ 3752/455515) have several daily buses to Buenos Aires. Buses to Puerto Iguazú leave nearly every hour, and the trip takes around five hours: **Aguila Dorado** (☎ 3752/456600) and **Martignoni** (☎ 3752/457353) have the most frequent service. All of these buses pass by the three Jesuit ruins on R12, and some actually enter the town of San Ignacio, making an even more convenient trip. To get to Yacyretá Dam, you must take the bus to Ituzaingo; the trip is made nearly every hour, most frequently by **Ciudad de Posadas** (☎ 3752/425545). To Soberbio, take Aguila Dorado or **Capital del Monte** (☎ 3752/452160), which each goes twice daily.

PRESIDENCIA ROQUE SÁENZ PEÑA

The **Presidencia Roque Sáenz Peña Terminal de Omnibus** (✉ Calle 15, ☎ 3732/420280) is a few blocks and a $2 taxi ride from the center of town. Four companies each have one daily bus to Posadas, which takes about eight hours: **La Estrella** (☎ 3732/425414); **Nueva Estrella** (☎ 3732/429881); **Ta-La Estrella** (☎ 3732/423450); and **Vosa** (☎ 3732/427676). If no times are convenient, you can go through Resistencia, where buses regularly leave for Posadas.

PUERTO IGUAZÚ

Organized tours to Puerto Iguazú and the Cataratas de Iguazú by bus can be arranged through most Buenos Aires travel agencies. **Via Bariloche** (☎ 3757/421917) has the quickest and most comfortable service between Puerto Iguazú and Buenos Aires; the trip takes 16 hours, costs about $70, and includes meals. **Expreso Singer** (✉ Perito Moreno 150, ☎ 3757/422891) takes 21 hours and costs $40. The **Puerto Iguazú Terminal de Omnibus** (✉ Av. Cordoba and Misiones, ☎ 3757/423006) is in the center of town.

RESISTENCIA

Between Resistencia and Buenos Aires, there are five buses daily on **Flechabus** (☎ 3772/460685) and **La Internacional** (☎ 3772/460902). **La Termal** (☎ 3722/460907) travels from Resistencia to Presidencia Roque Sáenz Peña six times a day and **Estrella** (☎ 3722/460905) five times a day. The **Resistencia Terminal de Omnibus** (✉ Malvinas and Av. MacLean, ☎ 3722/461098) is 4 km (2 mi) west of the town center.

## By Car

To get from Buenos Aires to Gualeguaychú by car, take R9 north to R14 north; the trip usually takes takes 2–3½ hours. R14 continues along the entire Corredor del Uruguay. The trip from Gualeguaychú to Colón along R14 takes about two hours. To get to Mercedes from Colón, take R14 north to R119 north; the trip takes about four hours. To get from Mercedes to Colonia Carlos Pellegrini, take R40 northeast; the trip is about three and a half hours. From Mercedes to Presidencia Roque Sáenz Peña, take R123 north to Corrientes; cross over to Resistencia on R11 and then head northwest on R16; expect to spend between five and six hours on the road. To get from Presidencia Roque Sáenz Peña to Posadas, head to Corrientes and then go east on R12. To reach San Ignacio Miní, Santa Ana, and Nuestra Señora de Loreto (3 km [2 mi] off R12) from Posadas, take R12 northeast. Continue on R12 to reach Puerto Iguazú. To get to Santa María la Mayor from Posadas, take R12 northeast to R4 and then southeast to R2 west. From Posadas to Soberbio, take R12 northeast to R7 and then east to R14 east to R212 southeast. Puerto Iguazú is a two-day, 1,363-km (818-mi) drive from Buenos Aires on R12 and R14 (it's quickest to take R14 to Posadas, then R12 to the Cataratas). The roads are paved and rarely crowded.

## By Plane

GUALEGUAYCHÚ

**Oreon** (☎ 11/4772–6458 in Buenos Aires for information) has inconsistent summer flights between Buenos Aires and Gualeguaychú in small, 20-seat commuter planes. Gualeguaychú's tiny airport, the **Aerodromo** (✉ Urquiza and R14, ☎ 3446/493029), is 12 km (7 mi) west of town; the 15-minute taxi ride to town costs around $5.

IGUAZÚ

Argentina and Brazil each has an airport at Iguazú. The Argentine airport is 20 km (12 mi) southeast of Puerto Iguazú, Argentina; the Brazilian airport is 11 km (7 mi) from Foz do Iguaçú and 17 km (10½ mi) from the national park. **Austral** (✉ Av. Victoria Aguirre 295, Puerto Iguazú, ☎ 3757/420849 or 3757/420168) flies three times daily between Buenos Aires and the Argentine airport near Iguazú; the trip takes an hour and a half. **LAPA** (☎ 3757/420390) also flies to and from Buenos Aires and is usually cheaper. Normal rates are $200 each way, but promotional rates, called *banderas negativas,* are sometimes available if you reserve ahead. The Brazilian airlines—**Transbrasil** (☎ 0455/742029), **Varig** (☎ 0455/741424), and **Vasp** (☎ 0455/742999)— have offices in Foz do Iguaçú and offer connecting flights all over Brazil.**Airport Transfer:** The **Colectivo Aeropuerto** (☎ 3757/420298) shuttle has service to hotels in Puerto Iguazú for $3. To get from the hotel to the airport, call two hours before your departure, and the shuttle will pick you up. Taxis to Puerto Iguazú cost $18.

POSADAS

Posadas's airport, the **Aeropuerto Libertador General San Martín** (⊠ Off R12, ☎ 3752/451903) is 10 km (6 mi) southwest of the town center; flights only go to and from Buenos Aires. **Austral** (☎ 3752/433340) and **Lapa** (☎ 3752/440300) each has two daily flights to and from Buenos Aires; the trip takes about an hour and a half.

**Airport Transfer:** A taxi from the airport into Posadas costs $10–$15 and takes a half hour. You could also take the take Becivega Bus 28 from the airport to Calle Junin in front of Plaza San Martín.

## Getting Around

### By Bus
Traveling by bus is the principal means of transportation in the region (☞ Arriving and Departing by Bus, *above*). If there's no public transportation to an out-of-town sight, you need to make other arrangements, such as a taxi or tour. Buses to Puerto Iguazú leave from Posadas almost every hour; the trip takes around three hours; **Aguila Dorado** (☎ 3752/456600) and **Martignoni** (☎ 3752/457353) have the most frequent service. Most buses that go between Posadas and Puerto Iguazú pass by the three Jesuit ruins on R12, and some actually enter the town of San Ignacio, making an even more convenient trip. To get to Yacyretá Dam, you must take a bus to Ituzaingo. The trip is made nearly every hour, most frequently by **Ciudad de Posadas** (☎ 3752/425545). From Posadas to Soberbio, Aguila Dorado and **Capital del Monte** (☎ 3752/452160) each goes twice daily. From Puerto Iguazú to the falls, take **El Practico** (☎ 3757/422722) from the terminal; buses leave every hour 7–7 and cost $4 round-trip. To get to the Minas de Wanda from Puerto Iguazú, you can take any bus going to Posadas. These buses leave nearly every hour and take about 45 minutes. For information call **Pasajes Noerja** (☎ 3757/422722), at the bus terminal.

### By Car
*See* Arriving and Departing By Car, *above*.

CAR RENTALS

There aren't many places to rent cars in the region; you're better off renting a car in Buenos Aires and driving from there. In Posadas, **Dollar Rent a Car** (⊠ Colón 1909, ☎ 3752/430901) has cars for about $90 per day. In Puerto Iguazú cars are available from **Leader Rent a Car** (⊠ Eppens 30, ☎ 3757/423220).

### By Taxi
Taxis (*remises*) are generally inexpensive; the fare is based on the number of blocks traveled. Taxis can be hailed, but it's generally easier to call one. In Colón: **Remis–Palmar** (☎ 3447/421278). A trip to and from El Palmar, with a wait, should cost around $35; to the Palacio San José is slightly more. In Gualeguaychú: **Remís Gualeguaychú** (☎ 3446/422612). In Posadas: **Remises Nivel** (☎ 3752/428500). In San Ignacio, independently owned taxis can often be found on Avenida San Martín near the ruins. A good way to explore the other ruins is to have a taxi take you from San Ignacio to Nuestra Señora de Loreta, wait, and then drop you off at Santa Ana. From there you can return to Posadas by catching a bus on the highway, a short walk from the ruins. It should cost about $15 and take about two hours. If you want the taxi driver to wait at Santa Ana with you and then drop you off on the highway, it will probably cost an additional $10. In Presidencia Roque Sáenz

Peña: **Remis Sáenz Peña** (☏ 3732/425041). In Puerto Iguazú: One of the biggest taxi companies is **Remisse Union** (☏ 3757/421328); taxis are available for short rides and longer day trips. With a group of three or four, you may find this a more economical and certainly more convenient way to get around.

## Contacts and Resources

### Banks and Currency Exchange

ATMs linked to the Cirrus system are found throughout the region. In Colón there's nowhere to exchange money, but there are ATMs. In Gualeguaychú you can exchange money at **COFIBAL** (✉ Urquiza 834, ☏ 3446/426106), open weekdays 8–noon. A reliable bank in Gualeguaychú is **Bank Boston** (✉ 25 de Mayo and Churuaruin, ☏ 3446/434319), open weekdays 7–1. In Posadas, **Cambio Mazza** (✉ Bolívar 1932, ☏ 3752/440505) only changes traveler's checks; it's open weekdays 8–noon and 4–8. For other banking needs in Posadas, go to **Bank Boston** (✉ Colón 1630, ☏ 3752/420113); it has ATMs and is open weekdays 8–1. Dollars and pesos are used interchangeably in Puerto Iguazú; to exchange other currencies, but not traveler's checks, go to **Argecâm** (✉ Av. Victoria Aguirre 562, ☏ 3757/420273), open Monday–Saturday 8–7. For other banking needs in Puerto Iguazú, try **Banco Misiones** (✉ Av. Victoria Aguirre, ☏ 3757/420212), open weekdays 7–1; it has ATMs. There's nowhere to exchange foreign currency in Presidencia Roque Sáenz Peña, but for other banking needs, including ATM transactions, go to **Banco Nación** (✉ Calle 12 7, ☏ 3732/420300), open weekdays 7–11:30.

### Emergencies

#### AMBULANCES AND HOSPITALS

For ambulances call the hospitals directly. **Colón**: Sanatorio Médico Quirúrgico (✉ Artigas 211, ☏ 3447/421212). **Gualeguaychú**: Centro Médico San Luis (✉ Urquiza 513, ☏ 3446/423743). **Posadas** (☏ 107); Hospital Dr. Ramón Madariasa (✉ Av. Lopez Tones and Cabral, ☏ 3752/447000). **Presidencia Roque Sáenz Peña**: Hospital 4 de Junio (✉ Malvinas Argentinas 1350, ☏ 3732/420667). **Puerto Iguazú**: Hospital Samic (✉ Av. Victoria Aguirre 131, ☏ 3757/420626).

#### FIRE

**Colón** (☏ 3447/421415). **Gualeguaychú** (☏ 3446/423333). **Posadas** (☏ 100). **Presidencia Roque Sáenz Peña** (☏ 3732/421661). **Puerto Iguazú** (☏ 3757/420885).

#### PHARMACIES

**Colón**: Farmacia Francia (✉ San Martín 1050, ☏ 3447/422008), open 24 hours. **Gualeguaychú**: Farmacia Modelo (✉ Urquiza 1788, ☏ 3446/423219); this and other pharmacies have rotating 24-hour shifts. In Posadas, **Marconi** (✉ Bolívar and San Lorenzo, ☏ 3752/424909) is open 24 hours. **Presidencia Roque Sáenz Peña**: Farmacia Tranchet (✉ Calle 12 and Calle 3, ☏ 3732/420537) is on a rotating 24-hour shift with other pharmacies in town. **Puerto Iguazú**: Farmacia Bravo (✉ Av. Victoria Aguirre 423, ☏ 3757/420479), open 24 hours.

#### POLICE

**Colón** (☏ 3447/421111). **Gualeguaychú** (☏ 3446/422222). **Posadas** (☏ 101). **Presidencia Roque Sáenz Peña** (☏ 3732/420710). **Puerto Iguazú** (☏ 3757/421224).

### Consulate

In Puerto Iguazú, the **Brazilian consulate** (✉ Av. Guaraní 70, ☏ 3757/421348) is open weekdays 8–11:30. A tourist visa is necessary to enter

Brazil from Argentina and it may take a couple of days, so do it ahead of time.

## Telephones, the Internet, and Mail

Card-operated public phones are easy to find. Telephone cards can be purchased in many shops and kiosks. For long-distance calls and to send faxes, find the nearest *telecentro* (telephone center); to send mail, look for the *correo* (post office).

### COLÓN
**Correo** (✉ 12 de Abril 431, ☎ 3447/421631); open weekdays 8–12:30 and 4:30–8, Saturday 8–12:30. **Telecentro** (✉ 12 de Abril 338, ☎ 3447/421479); open daily 8 AM–11 PM.

### GUALEGUAYCHÚ
**Correo** (✉ Urquiza and Angel Elias, ☎ 3446/426387); open weekdays 7–1 and 4–8. **Telecentro** (✉ Luis N. Palma and Fray Mocho, ☎ 3446/427531); it's open daily 7–1. **Visionet** (✉ San Martín and Maipú, ☎ 3446/432200) has Internet connections; it's open weekdays 7–noon and 4–7.

### POSADAS
**Correo** (✉ Bolivar 193, ☎ 3752/424411); open weekdays 8–noon and 4–8 and Saturday 8–noon. **Telecentro Plaza San Martín** (✉ Ayacucho 2025, ☎ 3752/449719) has long-distance calling as well as fax services and Internet access; it's open daily 6 AM–midnight.

### PRESIDENCIA ROQUE SÁENZ PEÑA
**Correo** (✉ Calle 10 602, ☎ 3732/420501); open weekdays 7–noon and 4–8 and Saturday 7–noon. **Telecentro Chaco** (✉ Calle 12 1020, ☎ 3732/426630); you can also send faxes and access the Internet; it's open Monday–Saturday 7 AM–midnight and Sunday 8:30 AM–midnight.

### PUERTO IGUAZÚ
**Correo and Telecentro** (✉ Av. Victoria Aguirre 254, ☎ 3757/422454); open daily 7 AM–midnight). **Intercom Iguazú** (✉ Av. Victoria Aguirre 240, ☎ 3757/423180), open Monday–Saturday 8–1 and 4–10, has Internet access.

## Tour Operators and Travel Agencies

### COLÓN
**LHL** (✉ 12 de Abril 162, ☎ 3447/422222) organizes half-day trips to El Palmar and Palacio San José for $15 per person when in a group.

### GUALEGUAYCHÚ
A reliable travel agency for booking flights and tours is **Local Tur** (✉ Paraguay 95, ☎ 3446/432221). **Lancha Ciudad de Gualeguaychú** (✉ Plaza Colón, ☎ 3446/423248) has a 40-person boat that goes for short trips along the Río Gualeguaychú four times per day for about $5 per person. **Siroco** (☎ 3446/440273) has a 20-person sailboat that travels along the Río Uruguay three times a day for $15 per person.

### POSADAS
The only tour operator in Posadas is the reliable **Abra** (✉ Entre Ríos 1896, ☎ 3752/423282), which arranges trips of varying length and price (they tend to be on the expensive side); the most popular are to the Jesuit mission ruins, Yacyretá Dam, Saltos de Moconá, and the Cataratas del Iguazú. English-speaking guides are available.

### PRESIDENCIA ROQUE SÁENZ PEÑA
**Tobas** (✉ Calle 17 480, ☎ 3732/423105) is a reliable travel agency. At **Quiyoc** (☎ 3732/420721), owner Nestor Medina arranges personalized trips to El Impenetrable, Esteros del Iberá, and Campos de

Cielo (a field where a meteorite shower fell 6,000 years ago), as well as fishing trips to several spots in Chaco and Corrientes.

PUERTO IGUAZÚ

All tour operators in Puerto Iguazú arrange basically the same trips: to Itaipu Dam, the San Ignacio ruins, a helicopter ride on the Brazilian side, and a circuit of falls on both sides. Two of the most reliable agencies are: **Aguas Grandes** (⊠ Mariano Moreno 58, ☎ 3757/421240) and **IGR** (⊠ Bompland 110, ☎ 3757/420239). **Iguazú Explorer** (⊠ In Sheraton Internacional Iguazú Hotel, ☎ 3757/421600) has four trips to the jungle and falls. The best is the Gran Aventura, which includes a truck ride through the forest and a boat ride to San Martín, Bossetti, and the Salto Tres Mosqueteros (be ready to get soaked). Another tour takes you to Garganta del Diablo. Park ranger Daniel Somay organizes personalized Jeep tours through his **Explorador Expediciones** (☎ 3757/421632) in Puerto Iguazú. Bring binoculars to see the birds.

## Visitor Information

**Cataratas de Iguazú** (⊠ Visitor center at park entrance, ☎ 3757/420180), open daily 7 AM–8 PM. **Colón** (⊠ Av. Costanera and E. Gouchón, ☎ 3447/421233), open daily 7 AM–10 PM. **Gualeguaychú** (⊠ On costanera at intersection of Tiscornia and Goldaracena, ☎ 3446/423–668), open 8–8 in winter and 8 AM–10 PM in summer. **Presidencia Roque Sáenz Peña** (⊠ Calle 17, between calles 10 and 12), open Mon.–Sat. 7:30AM–1 AM. **Puerto Iguazú** (⊠ Av. Victoria Aguirre 311, ☎ 3757/420800), open daily 7–1 and 2–8. **Secretaría de Turismo de la Provincia de Misiones** (⊠ Colón 1985, Posadas, ☎ 3752/447540 or toll-free 0800/50297) is the tourism authority for the province; it's open weekdays 7 AM–8 PM and weekends 8–noon and 4:30–8.

# 5 THE NORTHWEST

Vibrantly colored mountains form a backdrop to whitewashed adobe hamlets, which remain frozen in their colonial past. From the fertile green valleys to the high deserts dotted with giant cacti, pre-Hispanic cultures carry on in music, crafts, and festivals. Across the high, lonely stretches of La Puña, indigenous people still herd their llamas, goats, and burros on the paths their Inca ancestors used 500 years ago. The major cities of Catamarca, San Miguel de Tucumán, Salta, and San Salvador de Jujuy have a past to be proud of—for here, Argentina's great heroes first settled the country, fought for its independence, and developed its bountiful resources.

**T**HE HISTORY OF ARGENTINA BEGAN in the Northwest, in the provinces of Jujuy, Salta, and Tucumán, along the ancient road of the Incas. In the late 1400s, the Incas traveled southward from Peru along this route to conquer the tribes of northern Argentina and Chile. Half a century later the Spaniards traveled the same route in search of gold and silver. By 1535 the Royal Road of the Inca had become a well-established trade route between the mines in the north and the agricultural riches of Argentina to the south. Examples of the pre-Hispanic and colonial cultures remain in the architecture, music, language, dress, and craftsmanship found in small villages throughout the region. Churches built by the Jesuits in the 17th century in all sizes, shapes, and colors dot the landscape; Inca ruins lie half-buried in remote valleys and high plateaus; and pre-Inca mummies continue to be discovered in the highest peaks of the Andes near Salta.

By Eddy Ancinas

The landscape, too, is incredibly varied: From the 22,000-ft-high Andean peaks to the high, barren plateau known as La Puña, subtropical jungles, deserts with multicolor mountains, and narrow sandstone gorges cut by raging brown rivers. Much of it is desert, cut and eroded by rivers that wash away everything in sight during winter rains, leaving deep red-rock canyons (*quebradas*) with strange rock formations and polychromatic mountainsides, resembling parts of the American Southwest. Snow-capped peaks, some over 18,000 ft, in the Aconquija range in Tucumán form a startling backdrop to the lush green subtropical jungle that climbs the slopes of the pre-cordilleras (foothills).

## Pleasures and Pastimes

### Dining

The unique cuisine of the Northwest is influenced by its Indian heritage: Corn and potatoes are common ingredients in many of the region's dishes. Some of the fare: *Locro,* a soup of corn, beans, and red peppers, which becomes a stew when meat is added; *tamales,* ground corn baked with potatoes and meat and tied up in a corn husk; *humitas,* also cooked in a corn husk, combine corn and goat cheese in a soufflé. Not to be missed is baked or grilled *cabrita* (goat), a specialty of the region. A strange concoction of green-squash marmalade called *cayote* is often served for dessert with nuts.

For a chart that explains the cost of meals at the restaurants listed under Dining, *below, see* Dining *in* Smart Travel Tips.

### Folklore and Festivals

Argentina's rich history is celebrated at a variety of local festivals in the Northwest's high mountain villages and colonial cities. Two-thousand-year-old Inca rituals, Catholic beliefs, political history, gaucho tradition, agricultural practices, local handicrafts, and regional food are all represented in parades, performances, costumes, music, and dancing. *Inti Raymi* (Festival of the Sun), celebrated since Inca times on June 21 (winter solstice), marks the end of one year's planting and the beginning of the next. The Indian population, many of them dressed in traditional costumes handed down through generations, come from nearby villages to sing, dance, play music, and pay tribute to *Pacha Mama* (Mother Earth), and to pray to *Inti,* the Sun, for a good harvest. Festivities begin the night before in Huacalera on the Tropic of Capricorn (106 km/65 mi north of San Salvador de Jujuy in the Humahuaca Valley). The *Virgen de la Candelaria* (Patron Saint of Humahuaca) is celebrated on February 2 in Humahuaca, Jujuy. During the event, groups of *sikuris* (bands of young men playing Andean flutes) parade through the cobblestone streets accompanied by dancers and musicians. Spanish custom is represented by a bull, which is let loose so that festival participants can try to remove the strings of coins wrapped around his horns. There's also a rodeo. The *Fiesta del Poncho* (Gaucho Parade), held on June 17 in Salta, is an impressive display of the power of the legendary gauchos and their fine horses. Argentina's leading folk music groups entertain throughout the city. *Carnaval* (Mardi Gras) is celebrated in towns and villages throughout the Northwest. In the city of Salta, a parade of floats depicting historic events is accompanied by dancing characters wearing feathered and mirrored masks—some of them caricaturing local dignataries. Beware of *bombas de agua* (water balloons) dropping from balconies. *El Exodo Jujueño* (Jujuy Exodus), also known as the *Semana de Jujuy* (Week of Jujuy), is an historic festival held August 23–24 to commemorate General Belgrano's successful evacuation of the city in August, 1812, before the Spanish troops arrived. Hotels fill far in advance for this event. In Tucumán, Independence Day is celebrated on July 9, and the battle of Tucumán on September 24.

## Lodging

Hotels in the Northwest's major cities tend to be modern and comfortable. Many *estancias* (ranches) in the foothills accept guests and are listed with local tourist offices. *ACA* (Automobile Club Argentina) maintains good campgrounds with many amenities (☞ Auto Clubs *in* Car Travel *in* Smart Travel Tips). Note that as you travel farther north into smaller towns, English is rarely spoken.

For a chart that explains the cost of double room at the hotels listed under Lodging, *below, see* Lodging *in* Smart Travel Tips.

# Exploring the Northwest

To fully appreciate the historical significance and the scenic and cultural diversity of the Andean Northwest, you must visit not only the major cities of San Salvador de Jujuy, Salta, and San Miguel de Tucumán, but also the high plateaus, deep canyons, and colonial villages wherein lie the stories of pre-Hispanic civilizations, conquering Spaniards, and the determining forces of nature.

The high altitude desert (*áltiplano*), known as La Puña, covers an area 90,000 sq km (55,900 sq mi) from Catamarca north, across the Andes into Bolivia, Peru, and Chile. The snow-covered peaks look down upon this arid plateau. Alpaca, guanaco, llama, and *vicuña* (a kind of camel) are the only animals you see; dry grasses and thorny shrubs with deep roots searching for moisture, the only plants. The wind is relentless. Who would live here? Just as you've asked yourself this question, the colorful red poncho of a *coya* (native woman of this region) momentarily brightens the barren landscape, as she appears out of nowhere, herding her llamas into an unseen ravine. Most people can't breathe at this altitude, let alone walk or sleep: Luckily, ordinary mortals can experience a taste of La Puña from *El Tren a los Nubes* (The Train to the Clouds) in Salta, or by car driving north from Humahuaca to La Quiaca on the Bolivian border.

Down in the valleys, the colonial villages of Cafayate and Cachi bask in the warm sunny Calchaquíes Valley on the border of Tucumán and Salta. The soaring cliffs of the Talampaya Canyon in La Rioja, the Quebrada de Las Conchas between Salta and Cafayate, and the Quebrada de Humahuaca in San Salvador de Jujuy all impress with their peculiar rock formations.

## Great Itineraries

### IF YOU HAVE 5 DAYS

If you have less than a week, begin your stay in ⊞ **Salta** ⑥ with a city tour. From Salta take an all-day or overnight excursion southwest to ⊞ **Cafayate** ⑦, in the Calchaquíes Valley. On day two (or three), drive north on La Cornisa Road (R9) to the provincial capital of ⊞ **San Salvador de Jujuy** ①. After a tour of the city and its historic landmarks, spend the night in town or farther north at the Hotel Termas de Reyes. Early the next morning head for Purmamarca, a small village, behind which the Cerro de los Siete Colores (Hill of the Seven Colors) rises in a polychromatic wall. Follow the Río Grande up the colorful gorge to **Humahuaca** ③, a typical Indian village at 9,000 ft. On your last day in the area, head north of Humahuaca or explore one of the branches of the gorge.

### IF YOU HAVE 7 DAYS

Begin your trip in ⊞ **San Miguel de Tucumán** ⑧. On day two head to ⊞ **Tafí del Valle** ⑨ and spend the night there. The next day travel over the mountains into the Calchaquíes Valley and on to ⊞ **Cafayate** ⑦. On day four continue north to ⊞ **Salta** ⑥; spend two days here so that you have time to take the Tren a los Nubes. From Salta follow the excursion to ⊞ **San Salvador de Jujuy** ①, detailed in the five-day itinerary above, adding on a trip farther north to **La Quiaca** ④ on the Bolivian border. Another option is to explore along R40, which passes through colonial villages from Cafayate to Cachi.

### IF YOU HAVE 10 DAYS

Spend two nights in ⊞ **San Miguel de Tucumán** ⑧ and the third in ⊞ **Tafí del Valle** ⑨. On days four and five make ⊞ **Cafayate** ⑦ your base, using one day to follow R40 to Cachi and one to visit the bodegas Etchart and Michel Torino. Head to ⊞ **Salta** ⑥ on day six; allow one full day to take the Tren a los Nubes and one to explore the city. On the eighth day a leisurely drive on the Cornisa Road takes you north to ⊞ **San Salvador de Jujuy** ①. Spend your last two days visiting the town and the Quebrada de Humahuaca, an impressive gorge.

## When to Tour

Summer (January–March) is hot and rainy, and winter (June–September) is cold, so the best times to go are in the spring (October–December) and the fall (April–May). Rooms in better hotels may fill up in peak season and during Easter weekend and fiestas, so advance reservations are advised.

# San Salvador de Jujuy

❶ *1,643 km (1,020 mi) northwest of Buenos Aires, 97 km (60 mi) north of Salta, and 459 km (285 mi) north of Tucumán.*

San Salvador de Jujuy (San Salvador to those who live there, Jujuy to those who don't) is the capital of the province of Jujuy. Founded by Spaniards in 1593, it was the northernmost town on the military and trade route between the Spanish garrisons in Peru and the northern cities of Argentina. A good place to start any visit in a Spanish colonial town is the **Plaza General Belgrano.** On one side is the cathedral, which was built in 1764 and has an ornately carved, gold-plated pulpit, said to be the finest in South America. On the second floor of the **Casa de Gobierno** (Government House), which faces the plaza on San Martín, is the **Salón de la Bandera,** where there's an original Argentine flag donated by General Belgrano in 1813 after the great Battle of Salta during the War of Independence. ⊠ *San Martín 450.* ⊡ *Free.* ☉ *Weekdays 8–12 and 4–8; other times ask guard permission to enter.*

**The Northwest**

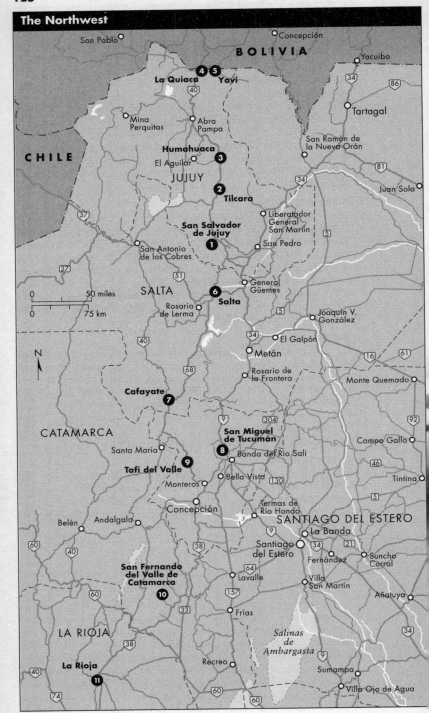

In the **Iglesia de San Francisco** (Church of San Francisco), two blocks west of the plaza, is a wooden pulpit carved by local Indians. ⊠ *Belgrano and Lavalle.*

Continuing on Belgrano three blocks, turn left on Lamadrid and walk one block to see the oldest church in Jujuy, the **Capilla de Santa Barbara** (Chapel of Santa Barbara), built in 1777. ⊠ *San Martín and Lamadrid.*

The **Museo Arqueologico Provincial** (Provincial Archaeology Museum) contains archaeological treasures, such as a 2,600-year-old ceramic goddess and a mummy of a two-year-old child dating back 1,000 years. Ceramic pots painted with geometric designs from Yavi and Humuhuaca are constantly being added to the collection, and a diorama shows what life was like here 9,000 years ago. ⊠ *Lavalle 434,* ☏ *388/4221343.* ☑ *Admission.* ⊙ *Daily 9–noon and 3–9.*

Arms, trophies, and memorabilia from military campaigns collected from the 25 years of fighting for independence are on display at the **Museo Histórico Provincial Juan Lavalle** (Juan Lavalle Provincial History Museum). The adobe building was once the home of General Juan Lavalle, a hero of the wars of independence and an enemy of the dictator Juan Manuel de Rosas. A replica of the door through which Lavalle was shot in 1746 is part of the exhibit. ⊠ *Lavalle 252,* ☏ *388/4221355.* ☑ *Small contribution.* ⊙ *Weekdays 9–1 and 4–8; Sat. 9–noon and 4–8.*

The **Museo Histórico en Maquetas y Miniaturas** (Historical Museum in Miniatures and Maquettes), created in 1975, is an unusual way of displaying Argentine and world history—through the use of tin and lead miniatures and models depicting events such as the English invasion, battles in the War for Independence, and the exodus from Jujuy. ⊠ *Gordaliza 1511,* ☏ *388/4224243.* ⊙ *Weekdays 8–12:30 and 4–10; weekends and holidays 9–noon and 3–8.*

For more information about the town and the surrounding area and to arrange tours and accomodations, visit the **Dirección Provincial de Turismo** (⊠ Belgrano 690, ☏ 388/4221326, 🖷 388/4221325), on Jujuy's main street. The English-speaking staff is enthusiastic.

From town R9 follows the Río Grande north between two high (9,850 ft) ridges forming the **Quebrada de Humahuaca** (Humahuaca Gorge). In summer and fall torrential rains mixed with mud and melting snow from the high mountains rush down the mountainsides, carving deep ravines and pouring into the chalky gray Río Grande. Often this flow of water washes out the road, leaving it in need of constant repair. Variegated tones of pink, red, and gray color the canyon walls like giant swaths of paint. As the gorge deepens and narrows, the colors become more vibrant and mustard and green are added to the already-polychromatic hues. Bright green stands of alamo trees surround whitewashed villages, contrasting with the deep red tones in the background.

## Dining and Lodging

$$ ✕ **Alto la Viña.** High on a hill overlooking the city, this simple country-style restaurant has flowery curtains and red-checkered tablecloths. The fare is the usual pastas, meat, fish, and fowl served with fresh vegetables—hearty and healthy. ⊠ *R56, Km 4,* ☏ *388/4262626. AE, DC, MC, V.*

$ ✕ **Confitería Carena.** The most comfortable spot in Jujuy is right in the middle of town at this *confitería* (which is like a cafeteria). *Licguados* (fruit milkshakes), sandwiches, hamburgers, alcoholic drinks, tea, and cakes are all served in a huge room with soft, upholstered chairs. ✉ *Belgrano and Balcarce*, ☎ *388/4222529*.

**$**  ✗ **Manos de Jujuy.** Ponchos on the walls, old paintings, and native artifacts give this small restaurant, whose name in English is the Hands of Jujuy, an authentic atmosphere. A guitar by the fireplace is put to use on weekends when local musicians play. The food is typical and inexpensive: empanadas, *humitas* (sweet corn, cheese, and red pepper tamales), tamales, and pasta, each for less than $5. ✉ *Senador Perez 222,* ☎ *388/4222368. DC, MC, V. No lunch Sun. No dinner Mon.*

**$**  ✗ **La Posta de Lozano.** This small inn, 19 km (12 mi) north of Jujuy on R9, is the perfect spot to stop for lunch if you're driving from Salta— or even if you're just driving from Jujuy. It's in a parklike setting with swings and a creek. Delicious humitas are prepared by Mama in the kitchen. ✉ *Off R9,* ☎ *388/4980050.*

**$$$**  ▥ **Jujuy Palace Hotel.** Large rooms with balconies overlooking the street, a rooftop gym, and a fine second-floor dining room with first-class service add to the comforts of this exceptional hotel. ✉ *Belgrano 1060, 4600,* ☎ FAX *388/4230433. 55 rooms, 5 suites. Restaurant, bar, exercise room, sauna, meeting rooms, parking. AE, DC, MC, V.*

**$$**  ✗▥ **Hotel Termas de Reyes.** Although it's a good place to cure your aches, pains, and travel stress in the thermal baths, baths, that's not its only plus: It also makes a good jumping-off point for exploring the Quebrada (☞ *above*). It's also above the fog that frequently shrouds the city, and it has cheerful rooms and an experienced staff. Excursions all over the area can be arranged. ✉ *R4, Km 19, Quebrada de Reyes 4600 (19 km [12 mi] from town),* ☎ FAX *388/4922522.* ✉ *Reservations: Sen. Perez 154,* ☎ FAX *388/4223938. 50 rooms. Restaurant, café, pool, massage, travel services. MC, V.*

**$$**  ▥ **Semana Wasi.** Up a flight of stairs from the street, this clean, tasteful small hotel is ideal for groups or families, as the rooms, dining rooms, and living spaces resemble a private home. Some rooms are on street level and open onto a common patio, a nice, private space for family or friends to gather. ✉ *Balcarce 354, 4600,* ☎ FAX *388/4221191. 16 rooms, 1 apartment. Bar, café. MC, V.*

## Outdoor Activities and Sports

With its incredible canyons, painted mountains, wild rivers, and high Puña, hiking and horseback riding are great in the area around Jujuy. The most interesting places are separated by miles of wild open terrain, making driving to them a necessity. The tourist office (☞ *above*) can help you organize trips. Another solution is to stay at **Autocamping El Rufio** (✉ *R9, Km 14, Yala,* ☎ FAX *388/4909344*), 15 km (9 mi) from town on the Río Yala; it has cabins and campsites and organizes hikes and horseback rides.

## Shopping

Jujuy is a one-street shopping town—**Calle Belgrano,** which has rather mundane choices. The exception is **La Hilandería** (✉ Av. Bolivia 1501 ☎ 388/4235121), about 15 minutes from downtown by taxi, where 100% pure white lamb's wool and llama hair are woven into blankets, ponchos, and pillow covers; cotton adds to the variety of textural designs. The factory is open for tours on weekdays.

*En Route*   Continuing along R9 for 65 km (40 mi), a 3-km (2-mi) detour west on R52 leads you to the **Cerro de Siete Colores** (Mountain of Seven Colors) rising up behind the village of **Purmamarca.** This road, once an ancient route of the Incas, continues across a great salt plain and then climbs up over the Andes to the Atacama Desert of Chile.

# Tilcara

**②** *83 km (51 mi) north of San Salvador de Jujuy via R9.*

The town of Tilcara, founded in 1600, is on the eastern side of the Río Grande at its confluence with the Río Huasamayo. Many battles during the War of Independence were fought in and around Tilcara, as indicated on a monolith by the gas station. Two museums on the town's main Plaza Alvarez Prado are worth visiting.

At the **Museo Arqueologico** (Archaeology Museum), run by the University of Buenos Aires, you can see pre-Hispanic tools and artifacts found in the nearby *pucará* (an Indian fort). ⊠ *Belgrano 445.* ☉ *Daily 9–6.*

At the **Museo Regional de Pintura José Antonio Terry** (Jose Antonio Terry Regional Museum of Painting), in an 1880 house, works by painter José Antonio Terry, who primarily focused on the scenery, people, and events in Tilcara, are on display. ⊠ *Rivadavía 459,* ☉ *Tues.–Sat. 9–7, Sun. 9–noon and 2–6.*

On a hill above the left bank of the Río Grande, about a mile from town, are the remains of the **Pucará de Tilcara** (Tilcara Fort). This fortified, pre-Inca settlement was part of a chain throughout the Quebrada.

Seven km (4 mi) west of town is **La Garganta del Diablo** (The Devil's Throat), a narrow red-rock gorge with many waterfalls that you can walk to. The tourist office in San Salvador de Jujuy (☞ *above*) can recommend guides and excursions to this area.

*En Route*   About 15 km (9 mi) farther north before reaching **Huacalera**, R9 crosses the Tropic of Capricorn (23 degrees, 27 minutes south of the equator). If you happen to be there at noon, December 21, check to see if the monolith casts a shadow.

# Humahuaca

**③** *126 km (78 mi) north of San Salvador de Jujuy.*

The narrow stone streets of the village of Humahuaca, enclosed by solid whitewashed walls, hark back to pre-Hispanic civilizations, when the first aboriginal tribes fought the Incas who came marauding from the north. Their struggle for survival continued into the 16th century, when the Spanish arrived and Jesuit missionaries built unpretentious little churches in villages throughout the valley. At 9,000 ft, Humahuaca is at the threshold of La Puña.

# La Quiaca

**④** *163 km (101 mi) north of Humahuaca, 289 km (179 mi) north of San Salvador de Jujuy.*

On the Bolivian border, the frontier and former railroad town of La Quiaca, at 11,300 ft, is cold, windy, and not on most people's itinerary. The town, however, is the base for exploring the **Laguna de los Pozuelos,** the largest body of water in La Puña and a home to more than 50,000 birds, mostly Andean flamingos.

# Yavi

**⑤** *15 km (9 mi) east of La Quiaca.*

Beginning in 1667, Yavi was occupied by noble Spanish families and was the seat of the Marquis de Campero, a feudal lord with considerable property. The train tracks running along the side of the river once connected Argentina with Bolivia and Peru: Those who remember this route (including Paul Theroux in the *The Old Patagonian Express*) would like to see it rebuilt. Walk into the town chapel to see the slabs of alabaster used in the windows casting a golden light on the gilded carvings of the altar and pulpit.

# Salta

**6**  *2 hrs from Buenos Aires by plane; 311 km (193 mi) north of Tucumán on R9 or 420 km (261 mi) north of Tucumán on R68 via Tafí del Valle; 186 km (116 mi) northeast of Cafayate on R68; 92 km (57 mi) south of San Salvador de Jujuy on R9 or 311 km (193 mi) south of San Salvador de Jujuy on R34 (La Cornisa Rd.).*

Salta is the best base for a thorough exploration of the Northwest, from La Puña to the subtropical jungle, red-rock canyons, colonial villages, and fertile valleys. With its single-story houses, wooden balconies, and narrow streets, Salta, founded in 1582, is Argentina's finest colonial city. (For tour agencies offering extensive city tours, ☞ Tour Operators *in* The Northwest A to Z, *below*.)

Begin your tour of the city at the **Plaza 9 de Julio.** The cathedral on the square is known as the most beautiful colonial church in Argentina. Across the plaza is the **Cabildo** (Town Hall), first constructed in 1582 and reconstructed many times since. The **Museo Histórico del Norte** (Historical Museum of the North) occupies two floors of the Cabildo with exhibits about the pre-Hispanic, colonial, and religious history of Salta and the Northwest. ✉ *Caseros 549,* ☎ *387/4215340.* ☺ *Tues.–Fri. 9:30–1:30 and 3:30–8:30, weekends 9:30–1:30 and 5–7:30.*

The **Museo Histórico José Evaristo Uriburu** (José Evaristo Uriburu Historical Museum) is in a simple adobe building that was the Uriburu home in 1810 (Uriburu was twice president of the republic). The entrance from the street into an interior courtyard, thick adobe walls, and a reed-and-tile roof are fine examples of colonial architecture. Furniture, costumes, paintings, and family documents are displayed in six rooms. ✉ *Caseros 417,* ☎ *387/4215340,* ☺ *Tues.–Sun. 9:30–1:30 and 3:30–8:30.*

Continuing along Calle Caseros to Calle Córdoba, you encounter the bright terra-cotta facade of Salta's landmark, **Iglesia San Francisco** (St. Francis Church), with its many white pillars and 173-ft-high belfry. The first temple and convent were built in 1625; the second, erected in 1674, was destroyed by fire; the present church was completed in 1759. The belfry houses the *Campaña de la Patria* (Bell of the Fatherland), made from the bronze cannons used in the War of Independence's Battle of Salta. A museum of religious art and furniture of the period is in the sacristy. ✉ *Caseros and Córdoba.*

The **Convento de San Bernardo** (San Bernardo Convent), three blocks from the Iglesia San Francisco, is the oldest religious building in Salta. The wooden door was hand-carved by indigenous craftsmen in 1762. ✉ *Córdoba.*

The **Tren a los Nubes** (Train to the Clouds) leaves Salta at 7 AM for the 14-hour roundtrip excursion from Salta to the high desolate Puña and back. The trip begins at 4,336 ft, as the train climbs out of the Lerma Valley into the mountains. As the train rattles over steel bridges that span wild rivers, it winds ever upward through many turns and tunnels, and passes over the 2,000-ft-high **Viaducto La Polvorilla**, until it reaches the top at 13,770 ft, just beyond **San Antonio de los Cobres.** At this point you can disembark to test the thin air and visit a train-side market set up by locals. When the train returns the short distance to San Antonio de Los Cobres, it makes a second stop, and the market reappears. The only town of its size in La Puña, San Antonio de Los Cobres is an important customs and trucking stop on the road (R40) to Chile. Zinc, copper, and silver are still mined in this area. The trip up is a fascinating experience, not only for the scenery and the engineering marvel that is the train and the viaducts, but especially to experience La Puña—a place few people ever see except from an airplane. The trip down, however, although alleviated by music, movies, and naps, can be excruciatingly long. Trips run every Friday, April–June and October–mid-December. July–September, trains run Friday and Saturday and an extra day in July–August. For $95 you get a guide, a post office, lunch in the dining car, a first-aid car equipped with oxygen for altitude sickness, and the experience of a lifetime. Reservations are essential. *In Salta:* ⊠ *Caseros 431,* ☎ *387/4314984,* FAX *387/4316174. In Buenos Aires:* ⊠ *Esmeralda 1008,* ☎ FAX *11/4311–4282.*

## Dining and Lodging

$$$  ✕ **El Solar del Convento.** Once a Jesuit convent, and still owned by the
★    Jesuits, The Sun Room of The Convent is in a spacious room under a thatch roof supported by poles of native wood. The original tile floors and walls washed with ochre paint are decorated with animal masks. An enormous *tapero* (a patchwork of handwoven saddle blankets) dominates the room. Tasty appetizers, such as grilled red peppers with melted mozzarella and little cheese muffins with chimichurri sauce, begin a meal of innovative adaptations of local foods. Naturally, a giant grill at the entrance is sizzling with meat at lunch and dinner. ⊠ *Caseros 444,* ☎ *387/4245124. AE, DC, MC, V.*

$$  ✕ **La Posta.** Red, gold, and green—the colors of the mountains—and funny gaucho pictures on the walls give a nice local ambience to this downtown eatery. Start with the appetizer/salad bar and then move on to pork *adobado* (cooked in clay) or *cabrito al asador* (barbecued goat), when it's in season. ⊠ *456 España,* ☎ *387/3247094. DC, MC, V.*

$$$$  🏨 **Hotel Salta.** Built in 1890 in the heart of the city, this hotel in a handsome neocolonial building has wooden balconies, blue-and-white tiling, sitting rooms on every floor, and a poolside bar-restaurant with an area set aside for barbecues. Antique furniture and a view of the plaza, the church steeple, and the surrounding mountains make every room attractive. Frescoes in the dining room were painted by local master Ernesto Scotti. The staff speaks English. ⊠ *Buenos Aires 1, 4400,* ☎ FAX *387/ 4310740. 97 rooms. Restaurant, bar, tea room, pool, laundry service and dry-cleaning. AE, DC, MC, V.*

$$$  🏨 **Hotel Provincial.** Walk into the modern lobby, with polished pink-and-gray-marble floors, and you immediately feel the hospitality. The shop in the lobby sells clothing and accessories designed locally. The ninth-floor roof terrace has a gym, a swimming pool, and a bar-grill. Rooms are tasteful and large—almost suites—and have tables and chairs. ⊠ *Caseros 786, 4400,* ☎ FAX *387/4322000. 81 rooms, 5 suites. Restaurant, bar, minibars, no-smoking rooms, pool, exercise room. AE, DC, MC, V.*

$$  🏨 **Hotel Victoria Plaza.** This basic, businesslike hotel is right on the plaza and close to everything in town. It has a street-side café open 24 hours and a large second-floor breakfast room. Rooms are modest but well maintained. Airport transfers can be arranged. ⊠ *Zuviría 16, 4400,* ☎ *387/4318500 or 0800/48883135,* FAX *387/310634. 86 rooms, 1 suite. Restaurant, bar, café, minibars, meeting rooms. AE, DC, MC, V.*

## Nightlife and the Arts

One hot spot is the **Casino de los Nubes** in the Hotel Provincial (☞ Dining and Lodging, *above*). **El Rastro Peña** (⊠ Av. San Martín 2555, ☎ 387/4342987) is a big auditoriumlike dining hall—that is until the lights dim and the beat of a drum, the whine of *quenas* (bamboo pipes), and the strumming of a guitar begin. National folk groups appear regularly. Reservations are advised and shows begin at 10:30 PM.

## Outdoor Activities

**Turismo de Estancia** (Farm Tourism or Agro-Tourism) provides the opportunity to stay on a working farm or ranch where you can you ride horses, hike, and get to know the countryside. At some estancias in the Calchaquíes and Lerma valleys, you can also participate in wine- and cheese making. The tourist office in Salta (☞ Visitor Information *in* The Northwest A to Z, *below*) has a list of farms and ranches.

## Shopping

At the **Mercado Artesanal** (✉ Av. San Martín 2555, ☎ 387/432808) you could spend hours inside the 1882 Jesuit monastery that houses the market, and at the open stalls across the street. You can find all kinds of items, including red-and-black Salteño ponchos, alpaca knitwear and weavings, leather goods, wood masks of animals, and fine silver. It's open daily 9–9.

*En Route*   Driving south toward Cafayate on R68 through the **Quebrada de Las Conchas** (Canyon of the Shells), notice the red-sandstone cliffs, sculpted by eons of wind and water into strange yet recognizable rock formations with imaginative names such as Los Castillos (The Castles), El Anfiteatro (The Amphitheater), and the Garganta del Diablo (Devil's Throat). A much longer route to Cayafate (180 km [112 mi]), on a narrow, gravel road, follows the **Calchaquíes Valley** along its river through colonial hamlets, untouched and little changed over the years. **Cachi**, 175 km (108 mi) north of Cafayate, is the most interesting town, with its old church, archaeological museum, and 20,800-ft mountain on the horizon.

## Cafayate

 *185 km (115 mi) southwest of Salta via R68, 340 km (211 mi) southwest of Salta via R40, 230 km (143 mi) northwest of San Miguel de Tucumán.*

Basking in the sunny Calchaquíes Valley, Cafayate deserves much more than a day to absorb its colonial charm, see its fine museums, shop for authentic handicrafts, and visit some of its surrounding vineyards, for which it's known. Street-side cafés, shaded by flowering quebracho trees, face the plaza, where a burro is likely to be tied up next to a car. Look for the five naves of the yellow-painted cathedral on the plaza.

For 66 years, Rodolfo Bravo collected and catalogued funerary and religious objects from local excavations. These objects, made out of clay, ceramic, metal, and textiles, are on display at the **Museo Regional y Arqueologico Rodolfo Bravo** (Rudolfo Bravo Regional and Archaeological Museum). Artifacts from the Incas (15th century) and Diaguitas of the Cahchaquí Valley are also part of the collection. ✉ *Colón 191,* ☎ *3868/421054.* ☉ *Upon request.*

Learn about winemaking at the **Museo de la Vid y el Vino** (Museum of Grapevines and Wine), which was created in 1981 in a building dating back to 1881. Machinery, agricultural implements, and old photographs tell the history of winemaking in this area. ✉ *R40, Av. Güemes,* ☎ *3868/421125.* ☉ *Daily 8–8.*

For a sample of Cafayate's Torrontés white wine, head to one of two well-known vineyards near town: **Etchart Bodega** (✉ Finca La Florida), south of town on R40 and within walking distance; and **Michel Torino Bodega** (⊠ Finca La Rosa).

## Dining and Lodging

$ ✕ **La Casona de Don Luís.** This restaurant with an interior, vine-covered patio is especially pleasant on a sunny afternoon. Come here to feast on humitas and locro and drink local Torrontés wine while listening to a guitarist playing gaucho laments. ⊠ *Salta and Almagro,* ☎ *3868/421249. No credit cards.*

$ ✕ **Juanita.** Everything is freshly made, on the spot, and served in the front room of this family house—it's the closest thing to home cooking in town. ⊠ *Camino Quintana de Niño 60. No credit cards.*

$$ ☷ **Gran Real.** The swimming pool, patio, barbecue spot, and quiet rooms with basic furnishings more than make up for the torn plastic furniture in the lobby. ⊠ *Av. General Güsemes 128, 4427,* ☎ *3868/421231,* FAX *3868/421016. 34 rooms. Bar, café, pool. MC, V.*

$ ☷ **Hotel Tikunaku.** This small *residencial* (pension) with carpeted rooms is clean and comfortable and has an attentive staff. Note that there's a 10% discount if you pay with cash. ⊠ *D. de Almagro 12, 4427,* ☎ FAX *3868/421148. 7 rooms. Café, parking. V.*

## Outdoor Activities and Sports

The town is flat, so bicycles are a common means of transportation. The tourist office on the plaza can suggest nearby destinations for hiking or biking. If you're ambitious, take a long ride along the Río Calchaquí on R40 (Argentina's longest highway and its almost longest river); along the way you'll pass through quiet colonial hamlets and ever-changing scenery. Bicycles and camping and fishing equipment can be rented at **Rudy** (⊠ Av. Güemes 175). Horses are available from **La Florida** (⊠ at the Etchart Bodega), 2 km (1 mi) south of town.

## Shopping

Shops around the plaza are filled with good-quality *artesanías* (handicrafts).

# San Miguel de Tucumán

**❽** *1,310 km (814 mi) northwest of Buenos Aires, 597 km (370 mi) north of Córdoba, 243 km (151 mi) north of Catamarca, and 311 km (193 mi) south of Salta.*

Although Tucumán Province is the smallest in Argentina, it's one of the richest in industry, commerce, culture, and history. Once an international trade route between the mineral riches of the north and the agricultural riches of the south, it's now a major producer of sugar cane, tobacco, livestock, and citrus fruits—in fact, Tucumán is the largest producer of lemons in the world. The high and dry plains in the eastern portion of the province contrast with lush green forests and jungle in the pre-cordillera, which rises to the snow-packed 8,000-ft Aconquija mountain range. Copious amounts of rainfall and the variety of climates has earned Tucumán the title Garden of the Nation.

The capital city of Tucumán (as locals call it) is beloved by all Argentines as the cradle of their independence. On July 9, 1816, congressmen from all over the country gathered in what is now called the **Casa Histórica de la Independencia** (Historical House of Independence) to draft Argentina's Declaration of Independence from Spain. A nightly sound-and-light show reenacts the arrival of these representatives and the historic signing; it's quite moving if you understand Spanish. ⊠ *Congreso 151.* ☷ *Admission.* ☉ *Wed.–Mon. 9–1 and 3:30–7:30.*

In the center of town is the **Plaza Independencia** (Independence Square). On one side is the monumental government house and across the street is the cheery, bright yellow **Iglesia de San Francisco** (St. Francis Church) and the more somber cathedral. Behind the government house and the church are two pedestrian-only shopping streets.

Tucumán is home to the **Universidad Nacional de San Miguel de Tucumán** (National University of San Miguel de Tucumán). The students, combined with the constant flow of commercial activity, make the streets crowded and traffic intense.

An escape to the **Parque 9 de Julio** (July 9th Park), with its artificial lake for boating, its tennis courts, and its lovely gardens, provides a peaceful interlude. ⊠ *Av. Soldati Paseo de los Próceres (6 blocks east of the plaza).*

## Dining and Lodging

$$
**✕ Floreal.** Grilled trout with shrimp and artichokes, hare cooked with
★ prunes, meringue with chocolate sauce, and many more delectable items are beautifully prepared and presented in a romantic setting of walls washed in sunset tones. ⊠ *25 de Mayo 568,* ☎ *381/4212806. AE, DC, MC, V. Closed Sun.*

$$
**✕ Restaurant Paquito.** If you're longing for good grilled beef, chicken, french fries, and fresh salad, this is the place. Pastas, pizzas, and regional specialties round out the menu. ⊠ *Av. San Martín 1165,* ☎ *381/4222898. AE, DC, MC, V.*

$
**✕ Tia Tota.** Come to this really basic regional restaurant with wood-burning ovens for the ultimate empanada. And be sure to take a peek in the kitchen. ⊠ *Laprida 585. No credit cards.*

$$$
**✕🏨 Gran Hotel del Tucumán.** This huge, modern, luxury hotel is the choice spot for presidential visits, large groups, and conventions. Six blocks from downtown, it looks out on the Parque 9 de Julio—a good spot for a stroll after a bountiful buffet lunch or gourmet dinner in the international restaurant. You may find the hotel's low ceilings, polished wood floors, and nice, chain-hotel furnishings attractive and comfortable—or you may find them impersonal. ⊠ *Av. Soldatti 380, 4000,* ☎ *381/4502250,* ℻ *381/450222. 143 rooms, 7 suites. Restaurant, bar, piano bar, minibars, pool, exercise room, salon, sauna, baby-sitting, meeting rooms, business services. AE, DC, MC, V.*

$$
**✕🏨 Hotel Carlos V.** Just steps off Tucumán's busiest street and close to restaurants, shops, telephone offices, and banks is this hotel with a mature, well-maintained feel. It has a bustling lobby and street-side café set back under an arched brick facade, and a restaurant in a quiet salon where you can enjoy a prodigious lunch buffet or an elegantly served dinner. Cream-colored walls, dark wood, and carpeted rooms also provide an escape. There's an internet connection in the business center. ⊠ *25 de Mayo 330, 4000,* ☎ *381/4311666,* ℻ *381/4311566. 70 rooms. Restaurant, bar, café, business services, meeting rooms, parking. AE, DC, MC, V.*

$$$
**🏨 Hotel Del Sol.** Most of the rooms and the spacious, second-floor bar and buffet restaurant of this modern hotel look out on a leafy canopy of trees covering the main plaza. Polished granite floors, little nooks, and wood-paneled walls lend a distinctive air. A gallery lines the first-floor corridors, with displays by local artists. ⊠ *Laprida 35, 4000,* ☎ *381/4311755,* ℻ *381/4312010. 88 rooms, 12 suites. Restaurant, bar, pool, meeting rooms. AE, MC, V.*

$$$
**🏨 Hotel Metropol.** The comfort-conscious Swiss owners have decreased the quantity of rooms and increased the quality by making them bigger. The English-speaking personnel and the hearty breakfasts add to the appeal of this hotel a block from the plaza. ⊠ *24 de Septiem-*

*bre 524, 4000,* ☎ *381/4311180,* ℻ *381/4310379. 73 rooms, 10 suites. Piano bar, snack bar, room service, pool, meeting rooms, rental car, travel services. AE, DC, MC, V.*

## Nightlife and the Arts

With so many students and businesspeople in town, there's plenty of nightlife—mostly in the form of late-night cafés, bars, and discos. *Peñas* (folk-music and dancing show) are held at the Gran Hotel del Tucumán (☞ Dining and Lodging, *above*). Concerts and recitals are performed in historic buildings and outdoor facilities. For up-to-date information, ask at your hotel or at the tourist office (☞ The Northwest A to Z, *below*).

## Outdoor Activities and Sports

The jungle and the glorious high hills make for great mountain-biking terrain. Horseback riding and hiking are also good in this area. The tourist office can provide suggestions and information on maps, guides, and equipment rental. Swimming, waterskiing, rowing, sailing, and fishing are possible on Lago Cadillal, an artificial lake 29 km (18 mi) from town; buses for the lake leave frequently from town, and campsites are available. If you're interested in playing golf, head about 30 minutes up a windy road into the green hills southwest of town to Villa Nougues, a summer resort town with a golf course.

## Shopping

**Mendoza** and **Muñecas** (which becomes Buenos Aires) are two *peatonales* (pedestrians-only streets) that intersect one block west and one block north of the plaza and are good for shopping. The **Gran Via** (✉ Entrance on Av. San Martín at Muñeca) shopping center is an immense, air-conditioned labyrinth of shops and restaurants. The clothing shops are much like those in Buenos Aires—lots of items for sports and stylish menswear, and women's clothing oriented mainly toward super-skinny teenagers. **El Cardon** (✉ Crístomo Alvarez 427) has the best selection of regional articles from all over Argentina.

# Tafí del Valle

**❾** *143 km (89 mi) southwest of Tucumán via R38 and R307.*

This ancient valley was inhabited by the Daguita people around 400 BC, later visited by the Incas, and settled by Jesuits in 1700 (until they were expelled in 1760). It remained isolated from the rest of the country until 1943, when a road was built from the town of Tucumán. The Sierra de Aconquija to the west and the Cumbres de Calchaquíes to the north enclose the high (6,600-ft) oval-shape valley and its artificial lake, Lago Angostura. The size of this often fog-shrouded valley can best be appreciated from El Pinar de los Ciervos (The Pinegrove of the Deer), just above the actual town of Tafí del Valle. Cerro Pelado (Bald Mountain) rises from the side of the lake to 8,844 ft.

Of primary interest is the **Parque de los Menhires** (Menhirs Park). The entrance to the park is about 5 km (3 mi) from the road into the village of **El Mollar** (a popular spot for vacation homes). Scattered about the landscape are stone monoliths said to be more than 2,000 years old. It's a good walk to the top of the hill, where you can see the reservoir from whose depths many menhirs were rescued and relocated when the dam was built. These ancient dolmens can still be found in the surrounding country, although many were brought to the park in recent years. Some are 6 ft tall and are carved with primitive cat or human motifs. The drive out of the valley toward the Calchaquíes Valley over a 10,000-ft pass gives you a glimpse of stone Indian ruins, isolated menahirs, and then nothing but cactus as you leave the huge sweep of green valley and enter the desert landscape of La Puña.

### Dining and Lodging

The main street, **Calle Golero,** has a variety of simple restaurants.

$   ✕ **El Portal del Tafí.** This café-restaurant serves sandwiches and local specialties such as locro, humitas, and tamales, as well as fish from the region. ⊠ *Av. Diego de Rojas,* ☎ *no phone. No credit cards.*

$$   ☷ **Hotel Mirador del Tafí.** Large urns filled with native plants, stone, and wood adorn this hotel overlooking the lake and valley. Rooms, done in soft desert pastels, with tile floors and wrought-iron lamps, open out onto a garden and a view of the valley. In winter, fireplaces in the lobby and the open-beam dining room keep out the cold. A string of horses for rent are tied to a hitching post at the entrance. ⊠ *Off R307, Km 61, 4137,* ☎ FAX *3867/421219. 32 rooms. Restaurant, café, horseback riding. AE, MC, V.*

### Outdoor Activities and Sports

You can fish for trout or *pejerrey,* sail, windsurf, water ski, or row on **Lago Angostura.** Rentals, guided tours, and campground information is available in El Mollar (☞ *above*). Horses can be rented December–March from **Otto Paz** (contact the tourist office, your hotel, or call ☎ 3867/421272 for information).

### Shopping

This region is famous for its cheeses, hand-loomed ponchos, blankets, and leather, all sold in the shops around the plaza.

---

## San Fernando del Valle de Catamarca

**❿** *1,150 km (714 mi) northwest of Buenos Aires, 440 km (273 mi) north-west of Córdoba, 243 km (151 mi) south of Tucumán via R38.*

San Fernando del Valle de Catamarca is the capital of Catamarca Province, which has the most dramatic changes of altitude of any region in the country. The barren north has miles of *salinas grandes* (salt flats) at 1,300 ft. In the west, the Aconcija Range has some of the highest mountains in the Andes, including the world's highest volcano, Ojos del Salado, at 22,869 ft. Fortified towns occupied first by the Daquita and later by the Incas are visible in the foothills.

Known by locals as Catamarca, the town was founded by the governor of Tucumán in 1683 (the fertile valley in which it sits used to be part of Tucumán Province). The valley has a mild climate year-round and the agreeable colonial city has a nice unhurried feel. The pride of the town is the central **Plaza 25 de Mayo** on which sits the bright, terra-cotta-color cathedral.

The **Museo Archeológico Adán Quiroga** (Adán Quiroga Archaeology Museum), three blocks north of the plaza, has exhibits ranging from 10,000-year-old stone objects found in the nearby mountains to items from the Spanish conquest. Stone and ceramic ceremonial pipes and offerings from the tombs of ancient cultures dating to the 3rd century are also part of the collection. ⊠ *Sarmiento 450,* ☎ *3833/437413.* ☉ *Weekdays 8–12:30 and 2:30–8:30; weekends 8:30–12:30 and 3:30–5:30.*

### Dining and Lodging

$$   ✕ **Valmont.** In an old building on the plaza, conservative pink and gray suggest the gentility of an old club, which this is. The food is truly international: French, Russian, Swiss, and Italian. At lunch time, you may

only have room for the appetizer buffet. ⊠ *Sarmiento 683,* ☎ *3833/ 450494. DC, MC, V.*

**$$** ✗ **Viejo Bueno.** The bare floor and the soccer on TV make this a local favorite. The grilled meats and chicken come in half and quarter portions. ⊠ *Esquiu 480,* ☎ *3833/424224. DC, MC, V.*

**$$** ⊞ **Ancasta.** This sleek, ultramodern hotel was designed by the owner's architect son. Good taste and attention to detail prevail throughout: on the sandstone walls covered with fine art (for sale), in the carpeted lobby, and in the custom-designed furniture. Rooms are sleek and spacious, with mostly built-in furniture. ⊠ *Sarmiento 520, 4700,* ☎ *3833/431464,* ⅢX *3833/435951. 85 rooms, 5 suites. Restaurant, bar, room service, exercise room, sauna, meeting room. AE, DC, MC, V.*

**$$** ⊞ **Hotel Leo III.** The regal crest of Leo III can be seen at the top of the brick-colored tower of this modern hotel from almost every corner in Catamarca. The entrance is in a shopping arcade, which has a communications office with telephone, fax, and Internet service. From each of the nine floors, and the roof garden, you can see the Aconquija mountains. ⊠ *Sarmiento 727, 4700,* ☎ ⅢX *3833/432080. 37 rooms. Restaurant, bar, café, pool, meeting room. AE, DC, MC, V.*

## Outdoor Activities and Sports

Catamarca is just recently awakening to its potential for recreational tourism. The sparsely populated foothills and mountains west of town are ideal for mountain climbing, hiking, and horseback riding, and decent fishing can be found in the Calacaste and Punilla rivers to the northwest. For information, maps, and guides, contact the tourism office (☞ Visitor Information *in* The Northwest A to Z, *below*).

## Shopping

Shops in town sell jewelry and other items made from local, semiprecious rose quartz as well as carvings out of cardon wood, ponchos, carpets, textiles, and blankets woven from alpaca, wool, and vicuña.

# La Rioja

⑪ *1,167 km (725 mi) northwest of Buenos Aires, 460 km (286 mi) northwest of Cordoba, 388 km (241 mi) south of Tucumán via R38, 155 km (96 mi) southwest of Catamarca.*

In this province of red earth, deep canyons, and Argentina's former President Carlos Menem is the eponymous provincial capital of La Rioja. The town was founded in 1591 by Juan Ramirez de Velasco, a Spanish conqueror of noble lineage who named the city after his birthplace in Spain. Surrounding the town are high red mountains with many interesting shapes eroded into form by wind and water, and green valleys of vineyards and olive trees. The central **Plaza 25 de Mayo** is named for the date the town was established. An earthquake in 1894 destroyed most of the town's colonial buildings, save the **Covento de Santo Domingo** church, which is the oldest building in Argentina (it's one block from the plaza).

The main attraction in the region is the 220-million-year-old **Parque Nacional Talampaya** (Talampaya National Park), which is 460 km (285 mi) round-trip from La Rioja. The gorge here is one of Argentina's most spectacular natural wonders; in one place it narrows to 262 ft between a wall of solid rock 480 ft high. Pictographs and petroglyphs by pre-Hispanic natives are preserved on canyon walls. Wind and erosion have produced strange columns and formations, providing nesting spots for condors. Tours by four-wheel-drive vehicles to the park can be arranged in La Rioja at the **Dirección General de Turismo** (⊠ Av. Perón y Urquiza,

☎ 3822/428839). The nearest town with accommodations is Villa Unión, 55 km (34 mi) away from the park.

### Dining and Lodging

$   ✕ **Il Gatto.** Part of a chain based in Córdoba, this trattoria-style restaurant across the street from the plaza makes good pastas and fancy salads. ⊠ *Pelagio B. Luna,* ☎ *3822/421899. MC, V.*

$   ✕ **La Vieja Casona.** This big old house with wooden floors and a frontier atmosphere is a good place to try regional specialties. ⊠ *Rivadavía 427,* ☎ *3822/425996. DC, MC, V.*

$$$   🏨 **Plaza Hotel.** On Saturday nights, the whole town seems to circle the plaza—by foot, motorcycle, bicycle, or car. The hotel's café, which faces the square, is the perfect spot to watch this Riojano ritual. Inside, everything looks new and polished, and rooms are carpeted, quiet, and simply furnished. Drinks and snacks (excellent olives!) are served in the reception area, the small bar, and the restaurant-café. ⊠ *San Nicolás de Bari and 9 de Julio, 5300,* ☎ *3822/425218,* FAX *3822/422127. 60 rooms, 3 suites. Restaurant, bar, café, pool. AE, DC, MC, V.*

### Outdoor Activities

Hiking, camping, and guides in the Talampaya National Park can be arranged through the tourist office (☞ *above*).

### Shopping

The locally produced olives (*aceitunas aimugasta*) are outstanding, as are the dates and the date liquer; these can be purchased in shops around the main plaza. **Regionales El Changuito** (⊠ B. Mitre 315), on the plaza, sells antique spurs, knives, leather belts, old coins, maté gourds, and *bombillas* (the straw you drink matethrough). A **craft market** (⊠ Pelagio B. Luna 790) takes place Tuesday–Friday 9–noon and 3–8, and weekends 9–noon.

# THE NORTHWEST A TO Z

## Arriving and Departing

### By Airplane

**Aerolíneas Argentinas** has flights from Buenos Aires to Catamarca (☎ 3833/424450), La Rioja (☎ 3822/426307), Salta (☎ 387/4310862), San Salvador de Jujuy (☎ 3833/4225414), and Tucumán (☎ 381/4311030). The only connecting flight is between La Rioja and Catamarca. **Southern Winds** (☎ 351/47750808, FAX 351/4211841), based in Córdoba, flies to Salta (☎ 387/42108081) and Tucumán (☎ 381/4225554). **Lapa** (⊠ Av. Santa Fe 1970, 2nd floor, Buenos Aires, ☎ 11/48196200) flies from Buenos Aires to Catamarca (☎ 3833/434772), San Salvador de Jujuy (☎ 388/4230839), La Rioja (☎ 3822/4235197), Salta (☎ 387/4317080), and Tucumán (☎ 381/4302630).

### By Bus

Buses from all the major cities in Argentina have service to cities in the Northwest. Buses will even pick you up along the road when prearranged. All terminals are a short taxi ride from downtown (☞ Getting Around by Bus, *below*).

### By Car

A long monotonous drive across central Argentina to Córdoba or Santiago del Estero brings you within striking range of the Northwest. You then have to decide what route you want to go from here. North on R9, the ancient road of the Incas, takes you to Tucumán, Salta, San Salvador de Jujuy, and on to Bolivia. Southwest on R64 lie Catamarca, La Rioja, and El Cuyo (wine country). Another optioin is to fly to a major city in the Northwest (for instance, Salta) and then rent a car. The roads in the region are good and not very crowded. Before you set out, it's a good idea to visit an ACA (Automobile Club Argentina) office for maps and road information (☞ Car Travel *in* Smart Travel Tips A to Z).

### By Train

**El Tucumano** (in Buenos Aires: ✉ El Retiro, Hall Central, ☎ 11/4313–8060; in Tucumán: ✉ Corrientes 1075, ☎ 381/4307100), the train operated by Tufesa (Tucumán Ferrocarriles S.A.), travels from Buenos Aires to Tucumán on weekdays, and returns to Buenos Aires on Thursday and Sunday (it's the only train into the Northwest). Train have air-conditioning, first-class seating (ask for these when you book), a bar, a restaurant, and sleeper cars.

## Getting Around

### By Bus

Buses in the Northwest are frequent, dependable, convenient, and by far the best way to get around. When you decide what time you want to travel, you can choose a company accordingly. Local tourist offices can advise which companies go where or look up "Transportes" in the yellow pages. It's a good idea to buy tickets a day or two in advance; most bus companies have offices at town bus terminals.

CATAMARCA

**Terminal de Omnibus** (✉ Güemes 850, ☎ 3883/423415). **Andesmar** (☎ 3833/42377) and **La Estrella** (☎ 3833/423455) go from Catamarca to Tucumán and San Salvador de Jujuy.

LA RIOJA

The **Terminal de Omnibus** (✉ Artigas and España, ☎ 3822/425453) is rather seedy. **Andesmar** (☎ 3822/422430) and **La Estrella** (☎ 3822/426306) go to Catamarca, San Salvador de Jujuy, and Tucumán.

SALTA

**Terminal de Omnibus** (✉ Av. Hipólito, ☎ 387/4214716). **Atahualpa** (☎ 387/4214795) travels north to San Salvador de Jujuy and La Quiaca. **El Indio** (☎ 387/4219519) goes to Cafayate.

SAN SALVADOR DE JUJUY

**Terminal de Omnibus** (✉ Dorrego and Iguazú, ☎ 388/426229). **Andesmar** (☎ 388/4233293) goes south to Salta, Tucumán, Catamarca, La Rioja, and Mendoza (20 hrs). **Panamericano** (☎ 388/427281) goes to Salta and north to Humahuaca and La Quiaca.

TUCUMÁN

The **Terminal de Omnibus** (✉ Brígido Terán 350) could be an airport: It has a shopping center, post office, telephone and communications offices, car rental services, tourist office, bank, and restaurants. **Empresa Aconquija** (✉ Lavalle 395, ☎ 381/4330205 in town; 381/4227620 at the terminal) goes to Tafí del Valle and on to Cafayate (☎ 3867/420251); to continue on to Salta from Cafayate, you must change to El Indio. **Panamericano** (☎ 381/4310544) and **El Tucumano** (☎ 381/4226442) go to Salta and San Salvador de Jujuy by a more direct route.

### By Car

Traveling outside of the Northwest's cities is easier by car, as many villages, canyons, parks, and archeological sites are neither on a bus route nor included in tours. For some short trips, like going from Tucumán to Tafí del Valle or Salta to Cafayate, it might be worth it to split the *remis* (taxi) fare with a companion. Most downtown hotels have enclosed garages, which is where you should leave your car.

Renting a car can be expensive, especially since agencies generally charge additional for miles, drop-off fees, and tax. But when you've come so far, the investment is probably worthwhile. The following agencies rent cars: **aiAnsa International** (✉ Caseros 374, Salta, ☎ 387/4217533; **Avis** (✉ Belgrano 715, San Salvador de Jujuy, ☎ 388/4225880); **Localiza** (☎ central reservations 0800/9992999; ✉ Esquiú 789 and at the airport, Catamarca ☎ 3833/435838; ✉ Salta, ☎ 387/4314045; ✉ San Juan 935, Tucumán, ☎ 381/4215334).

## By Taxi
*Remises* (taxis) can be found at airports, bus stations, and usually on the corner of the main plaza—or your hotel can call one for you.

# Contacts and Resources

## Banks and Currency Exchange
Dollars and pesos are not as interchangeable in this region as in Buenos Aires. Fees for changing traveler's checks vary. For ATMs, look for the sign BANELCO. Banks are generally open 7–1 and 4–8.

### CATAMARCA
An ATM can be found at **Banco de Galicia** (✉ Rivadavía 554) and at **Banco de la Nación** (✉ San Martín 626).

### LA RIOJA
**Banco de Galicia** (✉ S. Nicholas de Bari and Buenos Aires) has an ATM.

### SALTA
**Banco de la Nación** (✉ Mitre and Belgrano) has an ATM, as do most banks in Salta. **Cambio Dinar** (✉ Mitre 101 on the Plaza 9 de Julio) changes cash and travelers checks, though the rates are unfavorable.

### SAN SALVADOR DE JUJUY
**Banco de la Provincia** (✉ Lamadrid) changes dollars and will give you cash on your MasterCard only. **Banco Quilmes** (✉ Belgrano 904) charges 1% for cashing traveler's checks. **Cambio Dinar** (✉ Belgrano 731) and **Horus** (✉ Belgrano 722) change traveler's checks and cash for a small percentage.

### TUCUMÁN
**Maguitur** (✉ Mitre and Belgrano) charges 2% to change money.

## Emergencies
**Ambulance/Medical Assistance** (☎ 107). **Fire** (☎ 100). **Police** (☎ 101).

### CATAMARCA
**Hospital San Juan Bautista** (✉ Av. Illia and Mariano Moreno, ☎ 3833/423964). **Federal Police** (✉ San Martín 224, ☎ 3833/425522). **Local Police** (✉ Tucumán 835, ☎ 101). **Pharmacy: Farmacia Minerva** (✉ Sarmiento 599, ☎ 3833/422415); **Farmacia Rivadavía** (✉ Rivadavía 740, ☎ 3833/423126).

### LA RIOJA
**Nuevo Hospital Presidente Plaza** (✉ Av. San Nicolás de Bari Este 97, ☎ 3822/427814).

### SALTA
**Hospital San Bernardo** (✉ Tobís 69, ☎ 387/4224255). **Fire** (✉ Gral. Gúsemes 425, ☎ 387/4212222). **Police** (✉ Gral Gúsemes 750, ☎ 387/4319000).

### SAN SALVADOR DE JUJUY
**Hospital Pablo Sorias** (✉ Güsemes y Patricias Arg., ☎ 388/4221256 or 388/4222025).

TUCUMÁN
**Hospital Angel C. Padilla** (✉ Alberdi 550, ☎ 381/4219139). **Farmacia Centro** (✉ San Martín 1051, ☎ 381/4215494).

## Telephones, the Internet, and Mail

Making calls from your hotel room is very expensive all over Argentina. *Locutorios* or Telecom offices are plentiful in all the provincial capitals and even small towns; they generally have fax service and in some instances Internet access as well. If you're calling from outside the area code, add a 0 (0387 for Salta, for instance).

In Salta, **ISH** (Internet Service Home; ✉ Caseros 225, ☎ FAX 387/421-4805) has internet access; it's open Monday–Saturday 9–1 and 4–8. In Catamarca, **CEDECCO** (✉ Esquiú 418, ☎ FAX 3833/4433335) is the source for the internet; it's open daily 8–1 and 2–7.

POST OFFICES (CORREOS)
**Catamarca** (✉ San Martín 753). **La Rioja** (✉ Av. Perón 764). **Salta** (✉ Dean Funes 140). **San Salvador de Jujuy** (✉ Lamadrid and Independencia). FedEx and Western Union services are available in San Salvador de Jujuy at **J. Storni & Associates** (✉ Av. Senador Pérez 197 P.A., ☎ FAX 388/4230103). **Tucumán** (✉ 25 de Mayo and Córdoba).

## Tour Operators and Travel Agencies

CATAMARCA
**Yocavil** (✉ Rivadavía 922, Location 14–15, Catamaraca, ☎ 833/430066).

LA RIOJA
**Velasco Tur** (✉ Buenos Aires 253, La Rioja, ☎ 3822/426052) arranges tours to the Parque Provincial Talampaya.

SALTA
**La Veloz** (✉ Caseros 402 Salta, ☎ 387/4311010, FAX 387/4311114; Esmeralda 320, Piso 4, Buenos Aires, ☎ 11/43260126, FAX 11/43260852) runs city tours on its own fleet of buses. It also organizes trips to San Antonio de Los Cobres (by car or by the Tren a los Nubes), to Cafayate and the Calchaquís Valley, and to San Salvador de Jujuy and the Quebrada de Humahuaca.

SAN SALVADOR DE JUJUY
**NASA** (✉ Av. Senador Pérez 154, San Salvador de Jujuy, ☎ FAX 388/223838) is a family-owned and -operated travel office with two generations of experience. The company arranges airport pickups, city guides, and excursions for individuals or groups in and around San Salvador de Jujuy; English is spoken.

TUCUMÁN
**Duport Turismo** (✉ Mendoza 720, Galerí Rosario, Location 3, Tucumán, ☎ 381/4220000) runs four-hour city tours and three- to four-day excursions to Tafí del Valle and other nearby areas of interest and makes local, national, and international reservations.

## Visitor Information

**Catamarca** (✉ General Roca and Mota Botello, ☎ 3833/432647); open weekdays 7–1 and 4–9; weekends 9–1 and 5–9; it's difficult to find, so taking a taxi there is recommended. **La Rioja** (✉ Av. Perón 715, ☎ 3822/428834); open weekdays 8–1 and 4–9, Sat. 8–noon. **Salta** (✉ Buenos Aires 93, ☎ 387/4215927). **San Salvador de Jujuy** (✉ Belgrano 690, ☎ 388/428153); open daily 7–1 and 3–8; English is spoken. **Tucumán** (✉ 24 de Septiembre 484, ☎ 381/4222199).

# 6 THE CUYO

This semi-arid region was once a desert, but irrigation canals built by the Tehuelches and later improved upon by the Incas, the Spanish, and modern-day engineers transformed this "Land of Sand" into the largest irrigated area in the country. It's also good for outdoor activities: skiing on the slopes of Las Leñas and Penitentes in Mendoza Province; relaxing in the rivers, lakes, and hot thermal springs; hiking on the windswept glaciers of Aconcagua; and searching for fossils in the rich paleontological grounds of the Valle de la Luna. And in the easternmost province of San Luís, seldom traveled roads lead to historic mountain villages, lakes, and the great red-rock amphitheater of the Parque Nacional las Quijadas.

By Eddy
Ancinas

**I** **N THE CENTER OF ARGENTINA,** on the dry side of the Andes, this semi-arid region was once a desert—early indigenous people called it *Cuyum Mapu* (Land of Sand). Irrigation canals built by the Tehuelches and later improved upon by the Incas, the Spanish, and modern-day engineers, transformed this land of sand into the largest irrigated area in the country.

Today, olive oil, garlic, melons, and a cornucopia of other fruits and vegetables are shipped from the main town of Mendoza all over the country and abroad. The region is also the fourth largest wine producer in the world (grape vines were first planted by Jesuit missionaries in 1556), and its vineyards especially thrive in the hot sun and sandy soil of Mendoza and San Juan provinces.

The first inhabitants of the Cuyo were the Huarpes, Araucanos, and Pehuenches. The Incas, who came south from Peru, had great difficulty in subjugating these tribes. But by the late 1400s, they finally prevailed— extending their empire (Tahuantinsuyo) to its southernmost point (Collasuyo) in Argentina and Chile. The Huarpes lost much of their distinctive culture under the Incas, who imposed their language (Quechua) and their religion on the conquered tribes. Along the Inca roads across the Andes and north to Peru, forts and *tambos* (resting places) gave shelter to travelers, and remains of these ancient structures can still be found throughout the region.

Spanish settlers from Chile founded the city of Mendoza in 1561, followed by San Juan a year later, and San Luís in 1598. At that time, the Cuyo was part of the the Spanish Viceroyalty of Peru. Most of the area was cattle country and ranchers drove their herds over the Andes to sell in Santiago. Although the Cuyo became part of the eastern Viceroyalty of the Río de La Plata in 1776, the long hard journey across the country by horse cart to Buenos Aires kept the region economically and culturally tied to Chile until 1884, when the railroad from Buenos Aires reached Mendoza.

Today the area is not only known for its wine, but also for its outdoor offerings. One of the richest paleontological areas in the world is in the Valle de La Luna in San Juan Province. San Luís Province is home to numerous lakes and historic mountain villages as well as the immense Parque Nacional las Quijadas, with its great red-rock amphitheater—all relatively undiscovered. There's also skiing on the slopes of Las Leñas and Penitentes in Mendoza Province and hiking on Aconcagua, the highest mountain in the Americas.

## Pleasures and Pastimes

### Dining

Most of the Cuyo follows national culinary trends—beef, lamb, and pork—*a la parrilla* (grilled). You also find Italian restaurants serving old family recipes enhanced with fresh ingredients such as wild asparagus and mushrooms from Potrerillos. In fact, all ingredients in Cuyano cooking are fresh, as almost everything, including fine olive oil (look for Copisi), is produced locally. Spanish cuisine is another highlight of the region—the hearty soups, stews, and casseroles are a connection to the region's past, as is *clérico,* a white-wine version of sangria.

For a chart that explains the cost of meals at the restaurants listed throughout this chapter, *see* Dining Price Categories *in* Smart Travel Tips.

## Lodging

The city of Mendoza has many good, small hotels that are constantly being upgraded and expanded. The smaller cities of San Luís, San Juan, and San Rafael have at least one nice, modern hotel and the rest are rather run of the mill. Tourist offices can give you recommendations for all kinds of *hospedajes* (lodgings), including *residenciales* (bed-and-breakfasts), which are generally well maintained and a good bargain. In the countryside, you find everything from campgrounds to small *hosterías* (inns) to large resorts and spa hotels.

For a chart that explains the cost of a double room at the hotels listed throughout this chapter, *see* Lodging Price Categories *in* Smart Travel Tips.

## Wine Tasting

Wine tastings are a relatively new idea in the region. Although unexpected visitors are greeted cordially, it's a good idea to call first to arrange a tour. Local tours usually combine sightseeing with a visit to a *bodega* (winery). If you want a more comprehensive tasting and tour, it's best to go directly through the winery. Maipú, Luján de Cuyo, and Guaymallén are the main wine-growing areas near Mendoza. San Rafael's two major wineries, Suter and Valentín Bianchi, are just minutes by car or taxi from downtown Mendoza. For more on vineyards in the region, *see* the Close-Up Box on Argentine Wine, *below.*

# Exploring Cuyo

Mendoza, one of Argentina's prettiest cities, is a good base for exploring the Cuyo's open deserts, lush vineyards and orchards, deep river gorges, and high Aconcagua mountain. Tours to vineyards, mountain spas, or the top of Uspallata Pass can be arranged through local tour companies (☞ Tour Companies *in* The Cuyo A to Z, *below*). Distances are great between San Juan, San Luís, and San Rafael, so taking the bus between these cities makes sense. Once you've arrived, you can take a guided tour or rent a car and explore on your own.

## Great Itineraries

### IF YOU HAVE 5 DAYS

If you're driving from Buenos Aires, a stop in ▥ **San Luís** ⑨ is obligatory. From there, head northwest to ▥ **San Juan** ① and south to ▥ **Mendoza** ④ and ▥ **San Rafael** ⑦. If you're traveling by air, there's little reason to visit San Luís; but one site of interest in the area is the Parque Nacional las Quijadas, which is on the road to San Juan. The ultimate ski holiday might be to ski in Chile, fly (or if possible, drive, from Portillo over the Andes) to Mendoza, and then fly south to Las Leñas (or the reverse). If you're flying, go directly to Mendoza and spend two days exploring and visiting wineries. On day three, rise early (around 5 AM) and drive up the Panamerican Highway, stopping on your way up or down in ▥ **Potrerillos** ⑥ or Uspallata, lunching in Puente del Inca at the hostería, and continuing on to Las Cuevas on the Chilean border; return to Mendoza for the night. Take it easy in Mendoza on day four. On day five take another full-day excursion (beginning at 8 AM) to the Termas Villavicencio (Villavicencio Hot Springs), returning through the Quebrada del Toro (Bull's Canyon) and Garganta del Diablo (Devil's Throat). You could also combine the day three and five excursions with an overnight stay at the Termas Cacheuta spa.

### IF YOU HAVE 7 DAYS

Follow the five-day itinerary above. On day six, drive south through Tunuyán and the Valle de Uco, with its vineyards and orchards. Continue south 22 km (13 mi) to R40, which follows the Andes to ▥ **Malargüe** ⑧ and Las Leñas ski resort, or to R143, which goes directly to ⚏ **San Rafael** ⑦: Choose the route to Malrgüe for the drive and the sights along the way; pick the route to San Rafael for more vineyards and an excursion to the Cañon del río Atuel. Another option is to travel from Mendoza to ⚏ **San Juan** ① on day six and visit the **Valle de la Luna** ③ on day seven.

IF YOU HAVE 10 DAYS

Fly directly to ⚏ **San Juan** ① and arrange for a rental car or a tour to the Valle de La Luna. On day two drive or take the bus to ⚏ **San Agustín del Valle Fertíl** ②, spending the night. Day three, visit the Parque Nacional Provincial Ischigualasto in the **Valle de la Luna** ③ and return to San Juan. On day four, fly or take the bus to ⚏ **Mendoza** ④. After four days in Mendoza, exploring the city, the vineyards, and the mountains, follow the route in the seven-day itinerary above to ⚏ **San Rafael** ⑦ or ⚏ **Malargüe** ⑧ and Las Leñas ski resort.

## When to Tour

Ski season is June through September: July is crowded with vacationing Argentines and Brazilians; August usually has plenty of snow; and September offers spring conditions and warmer weather. Note that weather in the Andes is unpredictable, so it's a good idea to contact the ski area for current conditions. Since the Cuyo region is a desert region, summer (December–February) is very hot. Wine is harvested March through April and celebrated with grand festivities, making this the best time to visit.

# San Juan

❶ *1,140 km (708 mi) northwest of Buenos Aires, 167 km (104 mi) northeast of Mendoza via R40, 320 km (200 mi) northeast of San Luís via R20.*

In the Tulum Valley, in the foothills of the Andes, the capital of San Juan Province is an oasis of orchards, vineyards, and fields surrounded by monotonous, drab desert. The shady streets and plazas of this easygoing, gentle town are a welcome reprieve. The town was founded in 1562 as part of the Chilean viceroyalty. Under Spanish rule, the Río San Juan was directed into canals that still run beneath the streets, watering the streets and cooling the city on hot summer days.

On January 18, 1817, General José de San Martín gathered his army of 16,000 men in the town's plaza and set out on his historic 21-day march over the Andes to Chile, where he defeated the royalist army at the battles of Chacabuco and Maipú. In Chile, San Martín comandeered ships from the British and North Americans and sailed north to Lima, Peru, finally liberating Peru and all the rest of South America from the Spanish. A master of strategy, audacity, and sheer determination, San Martín proclaimed himself a liberator—not a conqueror. On returning to Buenos Aires in 1823, San Martín received little acknowledgement for his heroic feats, and he died in France, never having received the honors due him. Today, however, every town in Argentina has a street, school, or plaza named for San Martín and paintings of the general crossing the Andes on a white mule hang in public buildings all over the country. In January, 1944, an earthquake destroyed San Juan (but helped to establish Juan Perón as a national figure through his relief efforts, which won him much popularity). The city was rebuilt with the low-rise buildings, tree-lined plazas, and pedestrian walkways you see today.

The **Casa Natal de Sarmiento** (Sarmiento Birthplace) was home to Domingo Faustino Sarmiento (1811–1888), known in Argentina as the Father of Education. Sarmiento fervently believed that public education was the right of every citizen. After teaching in local schools as a

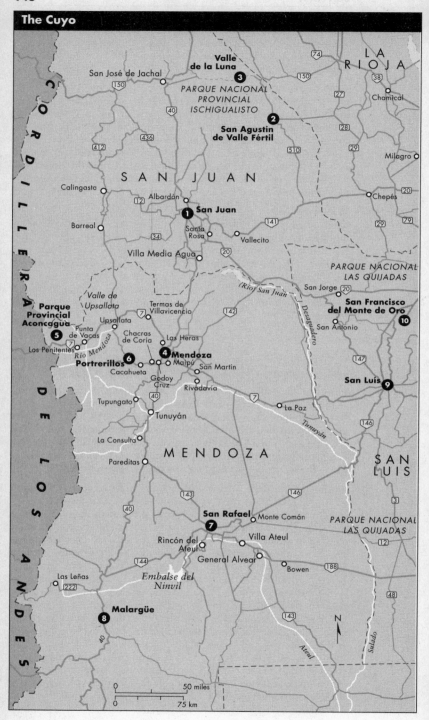

# The Cuyo

LA RIOJA

San José de Jachal

**Valle de la Luna** ③

*PARQUE NACIONAL PROVINCIAL ISCHIGUALISTO*

Chamical

② **San Agustín de Valle Fértil**

Milagro

S A N   J U A N

Calingasta

Albardón

① **San Juan**

Chepés

Barreal

Santa Rosa

Vallecito

Villa Media Agua

*PARQUE NACIONAL LAS QUIJADAS*

*(Río) San Juan*

San Jorge

*Valle de Upsallata*

Termas de Villavicencio

**San Francisco del Monte de Oro** ⑩

**Parque Provincial Aconcagua** ⑤

Upsallata

San Antonio

Punta de Vacas

*Río Mendoza*

Chacras de Coria

Las Heras

Los Penitentes

④ **Mendoza**

Maipú

**Portrerillos** ⑥

Cacahueta

San Martín

**San Luis** ⑨

Godoy Cruz

Rivadavia

Tupungato

Tunuyán

La Paz

La Consulta

S A N   L U I S

Pareditas

M E N D O Z A

*PARQUE NACIONAL LAS QUIJADAS*

**San Rafael** ⑦

Monte Comán

Rincón del Afeul

Villa Ateul

General Alvear

Bowen

Las Leñas

*Embalse del Ninvil*

⑧ **Malargüe**

N

Ateul

Sulado

0   50 miles

0   75 km

teenager, he was forced to flee to Chile, having fought against the Federalists. On returning in 1836, he founded a girl's school and a newspaper, where he could voice his opinions on education, agriculture, and government. In 1840 Sarmiento returned to Chile, once again a political exile who opposed Rosas and his nationalist Caudillo government. Threatened with extraditon back to Argentina, Sarmiento was sent by the Chilean Government to the U.S. and Europe to observe their education systems. From there he traveled to Africa. A prolific writer, Sarmiento was also a skilled diplomat and became Senator of San Juan province in 1857, Governor in 1862, and President of the nation from 1869 to 1874. During this time, Sarmiento passed laws establishing public education in Argentina. ⊠ *Sarmiento 21 (sur)*, ☎ *264/4224603.* ▧ *Admission; Sun. free.* ☉ *Dec.–June, Tues.–Thurs. and Sun. 8–1 and 3–8, Mon. and Sat. 8–1; June–Nov., Tues.–Fri. and Sun. 9–7, Mon. and Sat. 9–2.*

For more information about activities in the area, contact the **Subsecretaría de Turismo** (⊠ Sarmiento 24 Sur, ☎ 264/4227219) or **Siempre Viajes Y Turismo** (⊠ José de la Roza 237 Oeste, ☎ FAX 264/4220805).

## Dining and Lodging

Many of the town's best restaurants are on Avenida San Martín, about 15 blocks from downtown.

$$ ✕ **Castillo de Oro.** Within walking distance from many hotels, this restaurant has big windows, which are generally open to the street, revealing a peaceful, pastel green-and-white interior. Beef, lamb, chicken, and sausages are served from the outdoor grill, which is a popular spot on warm weekend nights. ⊠ *Av. J. I. de la Raza 199 Oeste*, ☎ *264/4273616. AE, DC, MC, V.*

$$ ✕ **Las Leñas.** This large, lively grill can serve up to 200 people under its high thatched roof and spinning fans. *Civita* (goat cooked asado style) is the specialty (when it's available, March–April). Otherwise, enjoy the grilled meats, sausages, and chicken, which arrives sizzling at your table, accompanied by salad, pasta, pizza, and tasty appetizers. On Sunday afternoon, families fill the long tables. ⊠ *Av. San Martín 1670 Oeste*, ☎ *264/4232100. AE, DC, MC, V.*

$$$ ▦ **Alkazar.** This modern hotel, which shines with polished glass, is in a quiet neighborhood just two blocks from the main square. Inside are plenty of gathering spaces, from the lobby bar to the café and piano bar with a panoramic view of the Andes. The modern rooms are carpeted and plain, but have every convenience you'd expect from a first-rate, big-city hotel. ⊠ *Laprida 82, Este 5400*, ☎ *264/4214965*, FAX *264/4214977. 104 rooms, 8 suites. Restaurant, bar, café, piano bar, in-room safes, minibars, pool, beauty salon, health club, sauna, airport transfer, parking. AE, DC, MC, V.*

$$ ▦ **Hotel Nogaro.** This old hotel just off the main plaza has small and adequate if somewhat dreary rooms, but is a good bargain. The pool on the second floor is surrounded by astroturf and is, unfortunately, rather uninviting. Breakfast is additional. ⊠ *Av. I. de la Raza*, ☎ *264/4227501. 100 rooms, 3 suites, 9 apartments. Restaurant, bar, pool. AE, DC, MC, V.*

## Outdoor Activities and Sports

The **Presa de Embalse Quebrada de Ullum** (Ullum Valley Dam Reservoir), 15 km (9 mi) from town, is a huge hydroelectric complex with grand views of the Río San Juan. Windsurfing, sailing, swimming, rowing, fishing, and diving keep San Juaninos cool and active on hot summer days. Equipment is available at the **Club Nautico** (Sailing Club) or the **Club Velo y Remo** (Sailing and Rowing Club) just beyond the dam.

Windsurfing equipment can be rented at the public beach, **Bahía Las Tablas,** where there's a café and a pier. White-water rafting and kayaking are possible in the San Juan and Los Patos rivers, and fishing in Las Hornillas River. Horseback riding is another option: Horses are available at **Ramón Luís Ossa** (⊠ Cabañas Doña Pipa, Mariano Moreno, ☎ 264/441004).

# San Agustín del Valle Fértil

**❷** *247 km (153 mi) northeast of San Juan, 414 km (257 mi northeast of Mendoza, 476 km (296 mi) south of La Rioja (via Villa Unión).*

In a valley formed by the Río San Juan and bordered on the west by the Sierra del Valle Fértil, the small town of San Agustín is a green and leafy surprise after miles of arid landscape, and an ideal base for exploring the Valle de la Luna.

### Dining and Lodging

Two inexpensive and tasty spots to eat are **Parrilla los Olivos** (⊠ Rioja and Santa Fe) and **Rancho Criollo** (⊠ Tucumán and Santa Fe).

**$$** 🏨 **Hostería Valle Fértil.** This low-rise, basic inn is on a hill overlooking a lake, 80 km (50 mi) from the Valle de la Luna. It's a convenient stopover on the way. ⊠ *Rivadavía,* ☎ 𝔽𝔸𝕏 2646/420015. *40 rooms. Restaurant, hiking, horseback riding, mountain biking.*

# Valle de la Luna and the Parque Provincial Ischigualisto

**❸** *80 km (50 mi) north of San Agustín via R510, 630 km (391 mi) round-trip from San Juan.*

Two-hundred-twenty-five million 'years of wind and erosion have sculpted weird rock formations in the red sandstone and pale gray volcanic ash cliffs of the Valle de la Luna (Valley of the Moon). The effects of time have also laid bare a graveyard of extinct dinosaurs from the Triassic period of the Mesozoic era. When the six-foot-long Dicinodonte roamed the valley, a large lake, surrounded by trees and shrubs, was the habitat for a variety of reptiles. Some of these fossils can be seen in the Parque Provincial Ischigualisto in the museum at the park entrance. Here you'll find a diorama explaining the paleontologic history of the area and displays of fossils, including some from the oldest predator known (230 million years old). You can take three routes through the park, one of which will take you to a petrified forest. Early morning is generally foggy, but it usually dissipates by by mid-morning. The colors of the rocks are most vivid in late afternoon. Note that roads inside the park are lonely and unpatrolled and a ranger must accompany all private cars. Tours can be arranged in San Agustín, San Juan, or Mendoza (☞ Tour Operators and Travel Agencies *in* The Cuyo A to Z, *below*).

# Mendoza

**❹** *1,040 km (250 mi) west of Buenos Aires, 340 km (211 mi) northeast of Santiago, Chile, 1,381 km (875 mi) north of Bariloche, 721 km (448 mi) southeast of Córdoba, 609 km (378 mi) south of La Rioja, 1308 km (812 mi) south of Salta, 166 km (103 mi) south of San Juan, 264 km (164 mi) west of San Luís, and 232 (144 mi) north of San Rafael.*

Mendoza, the capital of the province of the same name and the main city in the Cuyo, prides itself on having more trees than people. The result is a town with cool, leafy canopies of poplars, elms, and sycamores over its streets, sidewalks, plazas, and low buildings. Water runs in canals along the streets, disappears at intersections, and then reappears in bursts

# ARGENTINE WINE

N THE DRY, SEMIDESERT VALLEYS and foothills of Mendoza, San Juan, and San Rafael, the sun shines 300 days a year and pure mountain water from melting snow rushes down from the Andes, irrigating miles of land that produces 70% of Argentina's wine. The province of Mendoza, by far the most important wine-producing region, lies at the foot of the Andes at southern latitudes similar to the northern latitudes of the best vineyards of France, Italy, and California. With 300,000 acres of vineyards, Mendoza alone produces 65% of the nation's wine. The rest comes from the northern provinces of Jujuy, Salta, Catamarca, and La Rioja (where former President Menem's family owns a winery), and the southern province of Río Negro.

Argentina, with its 1,500 wineries, is the fourth-largest wine producer in the world, yet its fine malbecs, syrahs, cabernets, chardonnays, and chenin blancs have seldom been seen on shelves or wine lists in other countries. One reason is that Argentines have been the primary consumers of all they produced—only the French and the Italians drink more wine per capita, so there hasn't been much of a need to export. Secondly, cheap, hearty reds satisfied the beef-eating Argentines, and the white wines are sweet, which means that they haven't done well elsewhere. In 1970, for instance, Peñaflor exported an economical cabernet under the Trapiche label; though it was good enough for Argentines, it was not equal to what California was producing and it didn't impress American wine drinkers who were just beginning to consider California wines as an alternative to French or Italian vintages. Thirdly, collective marketing of Argentine wine (or collective anything) went against the grain in this land of stubborn individualists.

In the early '90s, wine consumption in Argentina declined, partly due to the economy and partly because people started drinking more beer. While Chile formed cooperative marketing groups and aggressively sold their excellent wines in the United States and elsewhere, Argentines continued their individualistic approach to marketing. When President Menem took over the government in 1989, the Argentine economy began to stabilize, and foreign investors took a new look at Argentina's potential wine industry.

One vineyard that has been changing with the times is Bodega Esmeralda, which in the 1970s was Argentina's second-largest wine producer. In 1974 Dr. Nicolas Catena, a Columbia-educated economist and former professor at the University of California at Berkeley, whose family owns Bodegas Esmeralda, visited the Napa Valley and observed the high-quality wine being produced there. Upon returning to Argentina, he decided to go for quality instead of quantity. As a result, he and other Argentine vintners are now discovering a whole new market at home and abroad.

The bold, fruit-flavored Malbec grape came to Argentina from France as a blending grape, thrived in Mendoza's soil and climate, and earned its right to be vinified as Argentina's signature red wine. Although Chardonnays and Chenin blancs are being improved and adjusted for export, Torrontés seems destined to be Argentina's signature white wine. Some of the region's best vineyards are **Bodega Escorihuela, Bodega la Colina de Oro, Bodega la Rural,** and **Villa Orfila,** just outside of Mendoza; and **Suter** and **Bodega Valentín Bianchi** in San Rafael.

of spray from the fountains in the city's 74 parks and plazas. Many of these canals were built by the Incas long before 1561, when García Hurtado de Mendoza, governor of Chile, commissioned Pedro del Castillo to lead an expedition over the Andes with the purpose of founding a city and opening the way so that knowledge could be brought back of what lay beyond.

Argentina's beloved hero, José de San Martín, resided here while preparing his army of 40,000 soldiers to cross the Andes in 1817 on the campaign to liberate Argentina from the Spaniards. In 1861, an earthquake destroyed the city, killing 11,000 people. The city of Mendoza and the Cuyo remained isolated from eastern Argentina until 1884, when the railroad to Buenos Aires was completed and the city was rebuilt. Immigrants from Italy, Spain, and France then moved here in search of good land to farm and grow grapes, and brought their skills and crafts to the region.

Avenida San Martín is the town's major thoroughfare. Between it and the Plaza Independencia, Mendoza's central square, are many shops, restaurants, and businesses. Crossing the square is Calle Sarmiento, a wide, pedestrians-only street lined with shops and outdoor cafés. Maipú, Luján de Cuyo, and Godoy Cruz (notable for their wineries), Las Heras, and Guaymallen are all suburbs of Mendoza with shopping centers, restaurants, and hotels. Take a taxi there: They're cheap and more direct than local bus service.

The **Parque General San Martín,** about 10 blocks from the city center, is a grand public space with thousands of species of plants and trees, tropical flowers, and a rose garden. A race course, golf club, tennis courts, observatory, rowing club, and museums are some of the attractions in the park. In 1995, World Cup soccer was played in the nearby stadium. Atop **Cerro de la Gloria** (Glory Hill), in the center of the park, a monument depicts scenes of San Martín's historic Andes passage.

---

NEED A
BREAK?

Day or night (the later the better) is a good time for ice cream at **Soppel** (⊠ Emilio Civit and Belgrano). Anything with *dulce de leche* (sweet caramelized milk) and *granizado* (chocolate chips) will make you want to visit every day.

---

Twice governor and later senator Emilio Civit's 1873 mansion had 26 bedrooms and four courtyards, and was the gathering place of the elite in the Belle Epoque. It's now the **Museo del Pasado Cuyano** (Museum of Cuyo's Past), a gallery and archive with paintings, antiques, manuscripts, and a library on Argentine and Chilean history. ⊠ *Montevideo 544,* ☎ *261/4241092.* ☜ *Admission.* ☼ *Tues.–Sat. 9:30–12:30.*

The **Museo Histórico de San Martín** (San Martín Historical Museum) has a token collection of artifacts from campaigns of the Great Liberator, as San Martín is known. ⊠ *Av. San Martín 1843,* ☎ *261/4257947.* ☜ *Admission.* ☼ *Weekdays 9–noon.*

The **Museo Fundacional** (Foundation Museum) is dedicated to the social and historical development of the region, with unusual attention given to indigenous cultures. Of special note is the mummified child found on Aconcagua, presumably an Inca or pre-Inca sacrifice. ⊠ *Alberdi and Videla Castillo,* ☎ *261/4256927.* ☜ *Admission.* ☼ *Tues.–Sat. 8–2 and 4:30–10:30.*

The **Bodega Escorihuela,** in the suburbs of Godoy Cruz, just five minutes from the center of Mendoza, occupies several blocks of an urban area once covered with vineyards. This huge winery was founded in

1884 by Spaniard Miguel Escorihuela Gascón. Its 63,000-liter barrel, made in France, is the largest in the province. In the old house are art exhibits and a restaurant, **1884** (☞ Dining and Lodging, *below*). Nicolas Catena, owner of Esmeralda Vineyards and a leader in the South American wine industry, bought the Bodega in 1992 and modernized the operation. ⊠ *Belgrano 1180,* ☎ *261/4242698.* ☉ *Weekdays, tours at 9, 10:30, 11:30, 12:30, 1:00, and 3:30.*

The **Bodega la Colina de Oro** (Hill of Gold Winery), formerly El Giol, was once the world's largest winery. When it was founded in 1896, an enormous oak cask, holding 75,000 litres, was imported from Nancy, France. The first wine aqueduct in the world carried wine from the production plant to the bodega. These days the **Cava Vieja** (Old Wine Cellar) is a restaurant and wine shop. It's in Maipú, a suburb of Mendoza. ⊠ *Ozamis 1040,* ☎ *261/4972090.* ☉ *Mon.–Sat. 9–7.*

The **Bodega la Rural,** also in the suburb of Maipú, was founded in 1883 by Felipe Rutini and is still family-owned and -operated. It produces San Felipe wine in its state-of-the-art winery. Not to be missed is the outsanding **Museo del Vino** (Wine Museum). ⊠ *Montecaseros,* ☎ *261/4972013.* ☉ *Tues.–Fri. 9–7, Sat. 9–1.*

The **Villa Orfila** winery, which sits on land given to José San Martín in 1818 to build a flour mill, has been owned by the Orfila family since 1905. ⊠ *Los Barriales, Junín (45 km [28 mi] east of Mendoza in San Martín),* ☎ *2623/420634.* ☉ *Weekdays 8–6.*

## Dining and Lodging

The beautiful old **Plaza Hotel,** with its broad veranda facing the Plaza Independencia, was the pride of the city until it fell into total disrepair and was finally closed in 1998. But Hyatt Hotels has bought it, and major renovation is underway, with a reopening date of 2002.

$$$ ✕ **1884 Restaurante Francis Mallman.** The soft glow of candles on the
★   patio under the maple trees at the Godoy Cruz Winery's 100-year-old Bodega Escorihuela is the perfect setting for Argentina's premier chef to show what Patagonia cuisine can be. Born in Bariloche and trained in France and Italy, this young chef is putting Argentina on the map of international *alta cocina* (haute cuisine). ⊠ *Belgrano 1188,* ☎ *261/ 4242698. AE, DC, MC, V.*

$$ ✕ **La Marchigiana.** At this cheery Italian-Argentine eatery, enjoy great pasta and the usual variety of grilled meats under the thatched roof and whirring fans. A pitcher of sangria or clérico (the white-wine version) is a cool accompaniment in summer. ⊠ *Patricias 1550,* ☎ *261/ 423075. AE, DC, MC, V.*

$$ ✕ **El Meson Español.** Tall ceilings, stained-glass windows, bullfighting posters, reproductions of works by famous Spanish artists, and a well-trodden tile floor take you right back to Spain when you enter this old colonial house. Start with a cup of garlic soup, followed by all kinds of typical Spanish fare. ⊠ *Montevideo 244,* ☎ *261/4296175. AE, DC, MC, V. No lunch.*

$$ ✕ **La Viscacha.** Come to this old, intimate white-and-green house filled with gaucho artifacts and paintings by famous cartoonist Molino Campos for pasta and grilled meats and fish. ⊠ *Sarmiento and Belgrano,* ☎ *261/4251940. AE, DC, MC, V.*

$$$ ▥ **Hotel Aconcagua.** This modern and convenient hotel with a helpful staff is predominately popular with foreign and business visitors. E-mail is accessible through the business center. ⊠ *San Lorenzo 545,* ☎ *261/4204499,* FAX *261/4202083. 159 rooms, 9 suites. Restaurant, bar, café, pool, massage, sauna, business services, meeting rooms, travel services. AE, DC, MC, V.*

**$$$** ▦ **Huentala.** This hotel—the only one right downtown—has been a standby for years, though it's looking a little aged. Rooms are modern, and some have views of the mountains. A new addition is under construction next door. ⊠ *Plaza de la Reta 1007,* ☎ *261/4200802,* FAX *261/4200664. 85 rooms, 8 suites. Bar, café, sauna, meeting rooms, parking. AE, DC, MC, V.*

**$$** ▦ **Hotel Crillon.** This efficient little hotel caters to a loyal clientele that likes the tranquil neighborhood, which is in walking distance of plazas, museums, and shops. Polished tile floors, plants, and modern chairs greet you in the lobby. The basic rooms provide all the necessaries. The staff is helpful in planning local tours or excursions into the surrounding countryside. ⊠ *Perú 1065,* ☎ *261/4298494,* FAX *261/4239658. 80 rooms. Bar, café, beauty salon, meeting rooms. AE, DC, MC, V.*

## Nightlife and the Arts

Dance the night away at **Kalatraba** (⊠ Perú 1779) or **Saudades** (⊠ Barraquero). Try your luck at the **casino** (⊠ 25 de Mayo 1123); it's open daily 9 PM–3 AM. See a movie at **Cine Arte Eisenchlas** (⊠ 9 de Julio 500), with screenings Thursday–Sunday.

## Outdoor Activities and Sports

### HIKING

Whether you hike for a day or a week in the mountains, or set out to climb Aconcagua (☞ Parque Provincial Aconcagua, *below*), many agencies and guides in town can help you. For guided hikes, maps, and information about hiking or climbing in the Aconcagua area, contact **Fernando Grajales y Associados S.R.L.** (⊠ José F. Moreno 898, Piso 6B, Mendoza, ☎ FAX 261/4293830), the best outfitter in the area (☞ Horseback Riding and White-Water Rafting, *below,* for other guides in the area).

### HORSEBACK RIDING

The hill and mountainous terrain, combined with Mendoza's tradition of fine horsemanship, makes *cabalgatas* (horseback riding) a natural way to explore the area. The grand adventure is a nine-day trip over the Andes following the footsteps (or hoof prints) of San Martín. Contact **Aymara Turismo** (⊠ 9 de Julio 983, ☎ FAX 261/42000607).

### MOUNTAIN BIKING

Many of Mendoza's back roads lead through the suburbs and into vineyards and foothills for more casual biking. More serious mountain biking can be done on your own or with organized outfitters (☞ Horseback Riding, *above*, and White-Water Rafting, *below*). Every February, **La Vuelta Ciclista de Mendoza,** a bicycle race around Mendoza Province, attracts cycling enthusiasts from all over.

### SKIING

**Las Leñas** ski area, open June–October (in a good year), is seven hours from Mendoza by car, or less by charter plane south to the town of Malargüe (☞ *below*). **Los Penitentes,** another ski area, is 153 km (95 mi) northwest of Mendoza on the Panamerican Highway. Various lifts transport skiers up to 10,479 ft. With 20 runs for all abilities and cross-country skiing, this ski area attracts daytrippers from Mendoza and weekending Argentines from all over. Note that in spite of the elevation, the snow is often thin and when it does snow a lot, the danger of avalanches is severe. At the base of the ski area are hotels, restaurants, ski rentals, day care, a first-aid clinic, and a disco. **Vallecitos,** an even smaller resort, is 80 km (49 mi) from Mendoza and 21 km (13 mi) from Potrerillos (☞ *below*). Between the Andes and the Cordon de Plata, a range that reaches 20,000 ft, the area attracts not only skiers (mostly local families on day trips), but also hikers and mountaineers in summer who come to train for an assault on Aconcagua. The **Valle Manantiales,** 150 km (93 mi) south of Mendoza near the town of Tunuyán, has great potential, when and if it ever opens as a ski resort.

WHITE-WATER RAFTING

Numerous adventure tour companies organize rafting or kayaking trips on the Río Mendoza for two days to a week (if combined with horseback treks). **Aymara Turismo** (☞ Horseback Riding, *above*) and **Betancourt Rafting** (✉ Ruta Panamericana and Río Cuevas, Trapiche G. Cruz, ☎ 𝐅𝐀𝐗 261/4390229) arrange these kind of trips.

## Shopping

Good leather and gaucho apparel can be found in the shops on the side streets off pedestrians-only Sarmiento and along Avenida Heras. The **Mercado Central** (✉ Av. Heras and Patricias Mendocinas) has more of the same, plus ponchos and Indian weavings; it's open from early in the morning to 1:30 and again from 4:30 to 9.

# Parque Provincial Aconcagua

★ ❺ *390 km (242 mi) roundtrip, northwest of Mendoza via R7.*

The Parque Provincial Aconcagua extends for 165,000 acres over wild, high country with few trails other than those used by climbing expeditions up the impressive Cerro Aconcagua (Aconcagua Mountain). Organized tours on horse or foot can be arranged in Mendoza (☞ Outdoor Activities and Sports *in* Mendoza, *above*) or at the Hostería Puente del Inca (☞ Lodging, *below*).

The drive up the Uspallata Pass to the Parque Provincial Aconcagua is as spectacular as the mountain itself. Tours can be arranged, but renting a car is well worth it as there are many sights to stop and photograph along the way. You can make the trip in one long, all-day drive or stay a night en route. Note that driving in winter on the icy roads can be treacherous and that you should be aware of the change in altitude from 2,500 ft in Mendoza to 10,446 ft at the top.

Leaving Mendoza early in the morning, head south on Av. San Martín to the Panamerican Highway (R7) and turn right. Green vineyards soon give way to barren hills and scrub brush, as you follow the river for 30 km (19 mi) to the **Termas Cacheuta** (☞ Dining and Lodging, *below*). If you're still engulfed in fog and drizzle, don't despair: When you reach the **Potrerillos Valley** (☞ Potrerillos, *below*), 39 km (24 mi) away, it's likely that you'll break through into brilliant sunshine. The road follows the fast flowing Río Mendoza and an abandoned railroad track that once crossed the Andes to Chile. In 1934 an ice dam broke and sent a flood of mud, rocks, and debris down the canyon, carrying off everything in its path. Evidence of this natural disaster is still visible all along the river.

At **Uspallata,** the last town before the Chilean frontier, excursions into the mountains by 4x4 or on horseback lead to abandoned mines, a desert ghost town, and spectacular mountain scenery where the movie *Seven Days in Tibet* was filmed. After passing Uspallata, the road goes through a wild, barren landscape of rolling hills and brooding black mountains. Along the way, the Río Blanco and Río Tambillos rush down from the mountains into the Rio Mendoza, and remnants of Inca *tambos* (resting places) remind you that this was once an Inca route. At **Punta de Vacas,** the corrals that once held herds of cattle on their way to Chile lie abandoned alongside now defunct railway tracks. Two km (1 mi) beyond the army barracks and customs office, three wide valleys converge. Looking south, you can see the second highest mountain in the region, **Cerro Tupungato** (22,304 ft). The mountain is accessible from the town of the same name, 73 km (45 mi) southwest of Mendoza.

After passing the ski area at Los Penitentes (named for the rock formations on the southern horizon that resemble penitent monks), you arrive at **Puente del Inca** (9,000 ft), a natural bridge of red rocks, saturated and encrusted with yellow sulphur, spanning the river. The hot springs below are slippery to walk on, but fine for soaking tired feet. Once a splendid hotel was here; but it, too, was a victim of the 1934 flood. A few miles farther west, after passing the customs check (for Chile), is the entrance to the park and a cabin where the park ranger lives. About 15 km (9 mi) beyond the park entrance, the highway passes Las Cuevas, a settlement where the road forks right—to a tunnel and the new road to Chile, or left—to the statue of **Cristo Redentor** (Christ the Redeemer) on the Chilean border (13,800 ft), commemorating the peace pact of 1902 between the two countries.

The main attraction of the Parque Provincial Aconcagua is **Cerro Aconcagua** itself. At 22,825 ft, it's the highest mountain in the world outside of Asia and it towers over the Andes, with its five gigantic glaciers gleaming in the sun. More than 400 expeditions have attempted the summit and Aconcagua has taken 37 fatal victims and dozens partially frozen. Nevertheless, every year hundreds of mountaineers arrive, ready to conquer the "giant of America." A trail into the park begins at the the ranger's cabin and follows the **Río Horcones** past a lagoon and continues upward to the **Plaza de Mulas** base camp at 14,190 ft, where there's a hotel (☎ 261/4231571 in Mendoza for reservations).

## Dining and Lodging

**$$$$** 🏨 **Hotel Termas Cacheuta.** Stop at this mountain spa for a sauna in a natural grotto, a volcanic mud bath, a hydromassage, and a soak in a hot tub or the large swimming pool filled with water from the hot springs that has been curing devotees since 1902. The disastrous 1934 flood that swept through the valley destroyed the original buildings, baths, and the railroad station where guests arrived from Buenos Aires in the 1920s: Old photos in the hotel and ruins along the river tell the story. The bright, airy rooms with pine furnishings look out over the lawn and swimming pool. The restaurant serves healthy, natural cuisine using vegetables from its own garden. You're welcome to turn on the lobby TV (there's none in rooms). Rates include three meals, two thermal baths, and one massage per day; hiking, river rafting, and mountain biking can be arranged. ✉ *R7, Km 38, Cacheuta*, ☎ *2624/482082; Rodriquez Peña 1412, Godoy Cruz*, ☎ *261/4316085*, FAX *261/4316089; Tucumán 672, Buenos Aires*, ☎ *11/43228340*, FAX *11/43225672. 16 rooms. Restaurant, massage, sauna, bicycling, boating. FAP. AE, DC, MC, V.*

**$$** ✕🏨 **Hostería Puente del Inca.** Mountaineers gather here to assemble equipment before climbing Aconcagua, and return here after to tell the tales of their adventure. The hostel's history as a mountaineering outpost is told in vintage photos of past climbs on the dining room walls. Guides and mules can be arranged. ✉ *Off R7, Puente del Inca 5555*, ☎ *261/4380480 for reservations or 261/4294124. 82 beds in doubles and 4- to 6-person dorms. Dining room. MC.*

## Outdoor Activities

To climb Aconcagua, you must first get a permit in Mendoza (☞ *above*) at the **Direccion de Recursos Naturales Renovables** (✉ in Parque General San Martín, ☎ 261/4252090) or at the tourist office. The best time to climb is from mid-January to mid-February. Fernando Grajales, the world-renowned climber, runs a tour company and guide service, **Fernando Grajales y Associados S.R.L.** (✉ José F. Moreno 898, Mendoza, ☎ 𝐅𝐀𝐗 261/4293830).

## Potrerillos

**❻** *53 km (33 mi) west of Mendoza.*

The little town of Potrerillos, in the Potrerillos Valley, is protected from the elements by high mountains. With its agreeable microclimate and rushing Río Mendoza running through it, the town makes an ideal adventure and sports center. Numerous rafting companies, mountain-bike rental shops, stables where you can hire horses, and hiking and camping guides have made this town their headquarters.

### Lodging

**$–$$** 🏨 **Hotel Potrerillos.** This Spanish-style, stucco- and tile-roofed building is perched on a hill overlooking the foothills and is surrounded by lawns, gardens, and sports facilities. Originally built by the government, public spaces were made to accommodate large groups. But tasteful wooden furnishings and woven rugs give it a more personal appeal. ✉ *R7, Km 50 (from Mendoza), 5549,* ☎ *2624/482010,* 𝐅𝐀𝐗 *2624/ 4233000. Restaurant, bar, café, tea room, pool, tennis, volleyball, meeting rooms.*

## San Rafael

**❼** *240 km (150 mi) south of Mendoza, 1,000 km (620 mi) northwest of Buenos Aires.*

A series of dams along the Río Ateul and the Río Diamante has created an agricultural oasis surrounding the second-largest city in Mendoza Province. Cold winters, warm summers, and late frosts guarantee high-quality grapes for the area's major vineyards, such as Suter and Valentín Bianchi, not to mention the many fine, smaller, family-owned operations such as Simonassi Lyon and Jean Rivier.

It's easy to get around in the town. Two avenues, Hipólito Irigoyen and Bartolomé Mitre, meet head on in the center of town at the intersection with Avenida San Martín. The siesta here is sacred and lasts from lunch until 4:30, at which time shops reopen and people go back to work. Plenty of restaurants, sports stores, raft and kayak companies, and horse stables offer many recreational options. Campsites and picnic spots along the river have swimming holes and raft launchings. The Hotel Valle Grande (☞ Dining and Lodging, *below*) has it all: mountain biking, horseback riding, rafting, and kayaking.

**Suter,** which produces fine wine and champagne, is owned by the fourth generation of its Swiss founders. A tour through this spotless, showcase winery leads you through a labyrinth of underground caves where wines mature at a constant temperature. ✉ *H. Yrigoyen 2900 (near the airport),* ☎ *2627/421076,* 𝐅𝐀𝐗 *2627/430135.* ☉ *Weekdays 8– 3:30, Sat. and holidays 9–5.*

**Bodega Valentín Bianchi,** on R143 near the airport, is a high-tech *champañera* (champagnery) sparkling with stainless steel vats, pipes, and walkways. The bodega has extensive underground tunnels and a vaulted tasting room. ✉ *Ortiz de Rosas and Comandante Torres,* ☎ *2627/422046,* 𝐅𝐀𝐗 *2627/430131.* ☉ *Tours at both locations: hourly 9– 11 and 2:30–4:30.*

A nice excursion out of town is a drive through the **Cañón del Ateul** (Ateul Canyon), 160-km (102-mi) roundtrip on R173. The canyon follows the Río Ateul through a labyrinth of red-, brown-, and gray-sandstone rock formations. Just as the canyon narrows, promising a winding river beneath dramatic rock walls, the river disappears underground—the unfortunate result of the demand for hydroelectric power.

## Dining and Lodging

$$ ✕ **Cabana Dos Amigos.** At this restaurant 6 km (4 mi) from town, you're greeted by the owner-chef. Dinner starts with little bowls of appetizers, followed by salad, homemade prosciutto with melon, homemade empanadas, chorizos fresh off the grill, and your choice of meat. Dessert and coffee complete the meal. ⊠ *Off R143,* ☎ *2627/441017. No credit cards. Closed Mon. No dinner Sun.*

$ ✕ **A Mi Manera.** Two tall doors open into this colonial-era building where the Spanish Club, a holdover from colonial days, has met since 1910. With its 18-ft-high ceilings, soft gold tones, wood trim, and Spanish *escudos* (emblems of Spanish and Argentine provinces) on the walls, the atmosphere is traditional. So is the food: roasted and grilled meats, marinated vegetables, pasta, and paella. ⊠ *Comandante Salas 199 and Colonel Day,* ☎ *2627/423597. AE, DC, MC, V.*

$ ✕ **Friends.** This popular local café is good for a coffee or a light lunch. Try the *barroluco* sandwich: steak, ham, cheese, and tomato compressed between thin slices of white bread. ⊠ *Hipólito Yrigoyen and San Martín,* ☎ *no phone. No credit cards.*

$$$$ ⊡ **Finca los Alamos.** When this 150-year-old estancia was established by the great-grandparents of César and Camilo Aldao Bombal in 1820, San Rafael was still a fort. The Bombal brothers inherited the vineyards and ranch from their mother who grew up here. One of the few buildings to survive the 1861 earthquake, the ranch house is filled with an eclectic collection of art and artifacts from around the world. Prices include all meals plus tea on the veranda, open bar, wine, and conversations (in English) with the owner. Horses are available for an extra charge. ⊠ *Bombal (R165), mailing address: P.O. Box 125, 5600 (10 km [6 mi] from town).* ☎ ℻ *2627/442350. 6 rooms. Dining room, bar, pool, horseback riding. FAP. No credit cards.*

$$$ ⊡ **Hotel Valle Grande.** The large stone and glass structure with a green metal roof main is the center of activities at this resort on the Río Ateul. Small cabins with the same architecural style are clustered by the river and around the ample lawns. The look is modern, with wood trim and large windows overlooking the river and the rocky landscape. Activities such as soccer, paddle tennis, minigolf, and children's games keep you occupied between forays into the river or the surrounding countryside by foot, horse, four-wheel-drive vehicle, or mountain bike. ⊠ *R173, Km 35, 5600 (35 km [22 mi] west of San Rafael in the Cañón de Ateul),* ☎ *2627/427064,* ℻ *2627/423541. 32 rooms, 10 6-person cabins. Restaurant, bar, grill, pool, sauna, shops. AE, DC, MC, V.*

$$ ⊡ **Hotel Kalton.** Polished floors and a hall lined with local photographs lead you back to the quiet, leafy lobby. Rooms are plainly furnished in somber colors and have large windows. Lunch and dinner can be arranged for large groups such as wine tours. ⊠ *Ortíz de Rosas 198, 5600,* ☎ *2627/422776,* ℻ *262/742276. 20 rooms. Minibars, laundry service. AE, DC, MC, V.*

$$ ⊡ **Hotel San Rafael.** Just off busy Avenida San Martín, this half-old and half-new hotel has views of the Andes and vineyards from the top floor, where it's quiet. There's a nicely designed reception area with plants, native stone floors, and wood trim. The newer half of the hotel has carpeted rooms with sparse but adequate decor in soft pastels. ⊠ *Colonel Day 30, 5600,* ☎ ℻ *2627/430127. 60 rooms. Café, air-conditioning, minibars, parking. AE, DC, MC, V.*

### Nightlife

**La Bodega** (⊠ H. Yrigoyen 5469, ☎ 262/429946) is a disco for all ages; it's open Friday, Saturday, and holiday nights.

### Outdoor Activities and Sports

Hiking, horseback riding, rafting on the Río Ateul, and windsurfing or kayaking on Lago Valle Grande can be arranged by local tour operators, including: **Ateul Travel** (⊠ Commandante Torres 67, ☎ 262/429282); and **Bessone Viajes** (⊠ H. Yrigoyen 423, ☎ 262/436439).

### Shopping

**Oregano** (⊠ Pellegrini 184) has a selection of handmade items for the home; it's open daily 9:30–12:30 and 4:30–8:30.

## Malargüe and Las Leñas

**8** *193 km (120 mi) south of San Rafael via R40.*

In the southwestern part of Mendoza Province, the small town of Malargüe was populated by the Pehunche until the Spanish arrived in 1551, followed by ranchers, miners, and petroleum companies. In 1981, an airport was built to accommodate skiers headed for the nearby Las Leñas ski area, and since then Malargüe has made earnest strides toward becoming a year-round adventure tourism center.

The Las Leñas ski area, 430 km (600 mi) west of Buenos Aires by air, 70 km (43 mi) from Malargüe, 445 km (276 mi) south of Mendoza (7 hrs by car or less by charter plane), and 200 km (124 mi) south of San Rafael, is the biggest and the highest ski area in Argentina. In fact, with a lift capacity of 9,200 skiers per hour, Las Leñas is the largest ski area served by lifts in the western hemisphere—bigger than Whistler/Blacomb in British Columbia, and Vail and Snowbird combined. From the top, at 11,250 ft, a treeless lunar landscape of lonely white peaks extends in every direction. Numerous long runs (the longest is a 8-km [5-mi] drop, 4,000 ft) extend over the 10,000 acres of skiable terrain. There are steep, scary, 2,000-ft vertical chutes for experts, machine-packed routes for beginners, and plenty of intermediate terrain in between.

### Outdoor Activities and Sports

In a good year, the ski season runs from June to October. Most South Americans take their vacation in July, the month to avoid. August has the most reliable snow conditions, September the most varied—a blizzard one day, sunshine the next. Seven-night ski packages are sold through travel offices in the U.S., Buenos Aires, Mendoza, and San Rafael (☞ Tour Companies *in* The Cuyo A to Z, *below*). Lift ticket prices are lowest mid-June–early July and mid-September–early October, highest mid- to late July, and in moderate mid-July and August. For information, contact the **Valle de Las Leñas–Chapelco S.A.** (⊠ Reconquista 559, Piso 4, Buenos Aires, ☎ 11/4313–1300, FAX 11/4315–2070). For reservations, contact a travel agent such as **Badino** (⊠ Paraguay 930, Buenos Aires, ☎ 11/4326–1351, FAX 11/4393–2568).

### Dining and Lodging

At the ski resort are a number of hotels. Besides Piscis and Aries (☞ *below*), try **Acuario** and **Escorpio,** which are both close to the slopes and each have 40 rooms (doubles and quads) plus bars and restaurants. **Gemini,** a time-share apart-hotel, has 114 beds in various configurations from doubles to quadruples. Shuttle buses take you around the resort from lifts to hotels, restaurants, and shops. The least expensive lodging is in the nearby hot springs resort town of Los Molles, 19 km

(12 mi) away; there's bus service from here to the ski area. For more lodging information, call ☎ 2627/471100.

You'll most likely dine slopeside during the day or at the central **El Brasero** (cafeteria by day, grill at night) or at the two restaurants in the **Pirámide** shopping center. The snack bar/pub **Innsbruck** is a popular hangout where you can order pizza and take-out food.

🏨 **Piscis.** Piscis is the most deluxe of the ski resort hotels and is closet to the slopes. Come back in the afternoon after a day of skiing for complimentary hot wine and hot chocolate. Airport transfers can be arranged. ⊠ *At Las Leñas ski resort,* ☎ *2627/471100. 99 rooms. 2 restaurants, bar, indoor/outdoor pool, beauty salon, bar, casino, babysitting. AE, MC, V.*

✕🏨 **Aries.** Though it's a little farther from the center of activities, it's close to the slopes. Skiers gather at its congenial slopeside restaurant, Shuzz, from noon to closing. ⊠ *At Las Leñas ski resort,* ☎ *2627/471100. 72 rooms. Restaurant. AE, MC, V.*

# San Luís

❾ *820 km (509 mi) northwest of Buenos Aires, 258 km (160 mi) east of Mendoza via R7.*

In the northeast corner of Las Pampas (☞ Chapter 3), the busy capital of the San Luís Province (founded in 1594) has been the crossroads between the Northwest, Mendoza, and Buenos Aires for for centuries. A growing petroleum industry, national investment in manufacturing, government tax incentives, and a university attract a lively mix of businesspeople, students, and visitors. Los Puntanos, as locals call themselves, are noticeably friendly, helpful, and polite.

In the center of town, surrounded by by shady sidewalks, is the **Plaza Pringles,** a good place to start a half-day walk. The square is named for Colonel Juan Pascual Pringles, a soldier in the battle for independence, whose statue is in the center of the plaza and whose tomb is in the cathedral across the street. Begun in 1883 and finished in 1944, the monumental **cathedral** has a lovely interior, decorated with green onyx, marble, and dark *algarrobo* (carob) wood from the region.

The **Colegio Nacional Juan Crisóstomo Lafinur** (Juan Crisóstomo National High School; ⊠ across from the plaza at Junín and San Martín), a school built nine years before the cathedral in 1869, is the finest example of colonial architecture in the city and reflects the educational ideals of Domingo Sarmiento (☞ San Juan, *above*). Its interior patio is surrounded by halls and galleries and it has a splendid vesitibule and theater. Ask permission to enter.

The Parque Nacional las Quijadas, 120 km (74½ mi) northwest of San Luís via R154, is off the beaten path, so you might find yourself all alone—but for a few gray foxes, snakes, and passing condors—staring into the colossal red-rock amphitheater called the **Potrero de la Aguada** (named for a corral with a watering hole). You can follow the semi-marked trail (it has no guard rails or carved steps for protection) through the canyon on your own or go with a guide, which is much easier. Note that in spring and summer, torrential rains and intense thunderstorms occur. In summer, the couple who lives in a camper at the end of the road into the park manages the campground and a small kiosk where soft drinks, beer, and snacks are sold. The couple's son is a guide with **Daniel Rodriquez Guía Turístico** (☎ 2652/155473328).

## Dining and Lodging

$$ ✕ **Sofia.** By 10:30 PM on Saturday night all the tables are filled with families in their Sunday best. They come for the supreme steaks, baby goat, lamb, fresh trout from the neighboring hills, and chicken cooked in a variety of sauces. For starters, the roast pig on a platter—stuffed and coiffed with fruits and vegetables—is paraded around the room on a cart accompanied by tempting appetizers. ✉ *Colón and Bolívar,* ☎ *2652/427960. AE, DC, MC, V.*

$ ✕ **La Ragazza.** At this small, street-side café close to most hotels, you can enjoy Argentine home cooking made with loving care by the owner-chef. Outstanding empanadas, pizzas, and pastas are served with fresh vegetables. ✉ *Av. Pte. Arturo Illia 210,* ☎ *2652/433732. No credit cards.*

$$$ 🏨 **Hotel Potrero de los Funes.** Only 15 km (9 mi) from San Luís on R18, this large (bordering on grandiose) resort complex built by the government during Perón's time caters to company meetings and groups. Some rooms have antiques and others are slightly antiseptic, though all are comfortable. ✉ *R18, Km 16, Potrero de los Funes (15 km [9 mi] from San Luís),* ☎ FAX *2652/495001. 94 rooms, 7 suites. Restaurant, bar, café, 5 tennis courts, exercise room, sauna, canoeing, horseback riding, windsurfing, soccer, casino, business services, meeting rooms. AE, D, MC, V.*

$$$ 🏨 **Quintana Hotel.** This cheerful, modern, clean hotel is on a wide, quiet boulevard within walking distance of downtown. The staff is attentive and well informed. Sunlight shines through tall windows into the interior garden where breakfast, drinks, and snacks are served. The spacious rooms are done in desert colors with light wood and have photographs of mountain villages. ✉ *Av. Pte. Arturo Illia 546, 5700,* ☎ FAX *2652/438400. 84 rooms, 12 suites. Restaurant, bar, café, pool, room service, massage, sauna, laundry service, business services, car rental, travel services, parking. AE, DC, MC, V.*

$$ 🏨 **Gran Hotel San Luís.** Rooms are adequate if small, dark, and drab at this conservative, business traveler's hotel. The business center with a fax machine and computers with Internet access is a significant asset in this part of the country. ✉ *Av. Pte. Arturo Illia 470, 5700,* ☎ *2652/425049,* FAX *2652/430148. 63 rooms, 2 suites. Laundry service, parking, business services. AE, DC, MC, V.*

## Outdoor Activities and Sports

Nine km (5 mi) northeast of San Luís on R20 is a sports complex called **Avenida Fénix en Koslay** (also the address), with a swimming pool, tennis courts, five soccer fields, ping-pong tables, and a picnic area with grills. Farther along the same direction, in the **Sierra de San Luís,** are dams that have been built to store precious water. Two of these dams, the **Embalse de Cruz de Piedra** (16 km [21 mi] northeast of San Luís on R20) and the **Embalse Potrero de los Funes** (18 km [11 mi] northeast of San Luís on R20 and R18), are good for fishing, sailing, swimming, and canoeing. Canoes can be rented at the hotel Potrero de los Funes (☞ Dining and Lodging, *above*). For fishing licenses and information, contact the **Dirección de Ecología y Forestación** (✉ Falucho 815, ☎ *2652/425029*), open weekdays 8–8.

## Shopping

At the **Mercado Artesanal** (✉ 25 de Mayo), facing the Plaza Independencia, local artisans sell handwoven rugs, ponchos, baskets, and objects made of onyx. Next to the tourist office, a shop also called the **Mercado Artesanal** (✉ Av. San Martín and Av. Pte. Arturo Illia) sells a more selective collection of the same handcrafted items.

## San Francisco del Monte de Oro

**❿** *112 km (69½ mi) northeast of San Luís via R146.*

At the foot of the Sierra de Michilingue, San Francisco del Monte de Oro is split in two by the Río San Francisco. Colonial buildings line the narrow streets of the southern portion of the town. **El Ranchito de Sarmiento** is an adobe house where in 1826, at age 15, Domingo Sarmiento taught adults to read and write in a school founded by his uncle.

Fourteen km (8 mi) from town, deep gorges cut through by crystal streams entice both trout fishermen and rock climbers. Look for **Salto Escondido** (Hidden Falls), a waterfall that drops 243 ft into a pool suitable for bathing and fishing.

### Lodging

$ 🏨 **Hostería del Valle de San Francisco.** This family-run inn in a remodeled country home has flowery guest rooms and a blue-and-yellow-tiled restaurant-bar. Vacationing Argentine families come here to horseback ride, go to nearby waterfalls, bird-watch, stargaze, mountain bike, and fish. You can arrange tours of the area at the inn. ⊠ *San Francisco del Monte de Oro 5705,* ☎ *2652/426137. 24 rooms. Restaurant, pool. No credit cards.*

# THE CUYO A TO Z

## Arriving and Departing

### By Airplane

MENDOZA

Mendoza's **Aeropuerto Internacional Plumerillo** (☎ 261/4307837) is 6 km (4 mi) from town on R40. **Aerolíneas Argentinas/Austral** (⊠ Sarmiento 82, ☎ 261/4204185) has daily flights from Mendoza to San Juan, Córdoba, and Santiago, Chile; three flights a day to Buenos Aires; and three flights a week to San Rafael. Thursday and Saturday the airline flies nonstop to Río de Janiero, Brazil. **Dinar** (⊠ Sarmiento 69, ☎ 261/4204520) flies from Buenos Aires to Mendoza and San Juan. **Ladeco** (⊠ Sarmiento 144, ☎ 261/4291868) has five flights a week to Santiago, Chile, with connections to Miami and New York. **Southern Winds** (⊠ Catamarca 63, ☎ 261/4293200) has flights to Córdoba with connections to Buenos Aires and other cities in northern Argentina. **TAN** (⊠ España 1012, ☎ 261/4340240) has five flights a week to Neuquén with a connection to Bariloche and two flights a week to San Rafael and Malargüe.

SAN JUAN

**Dinar** (⊠ Rivadavía 240 Oeste, ☎ 264/4214816) flies from San Juan to Mendoza and Buenos Aires.

SAN RAFAEL

**Aerolíneas Argentinas** (⊠ Day 95, ☎ 2627/430036 ).

### By Bus

Mendoza's big and busy **Terminal del Sol** (⊠ avenidas Gobernador Videla and Acceso Oeste) is in Guaynallén, a suburb east of downtown. Buses go from Mendoza to every city in Argentina. Some major transport companies are: **Andesmar** (☎ 261/4313953) with service to Bariloche, Salta/Jujuy, and San Juan; **Chevallier** (☎ 261/43143900) with daily service to Buenos Aires; **La Cumbre** (☎ 261/4380177) with daily service to San Juan and Córdoba along a scenic route; **La Estrella** (☎ 261/4311324) with buses via San Juan to La Rioja, Tucumán, and Jujuy, and to Buenos Aires via San Luís; **Jocoli** (☎ 261/4314409) has a

**WITHOUT KODAK MAX**
photos taken on 100 speed film

Ever see someone

waiting for the sun to come out

while trying to photograph

a charging rhino?

### *New!*
### Kodak Max film:

*Now with better color,
Kodak's maximum
versatility film gives
you great pictures in
sunlight, low light,
action or still.*

**WITH KODAK MAX**
photos taken on Kodak Max 400 film

## It's all you need
## to know about film.

**www.kodak.com**

# Fodor's

Distinctive guides packed with up-to-date expert advice and smart choices for every type of traveler.

**Fodor's.** For the world of ways you travel

sleeper via San Luís to Buenos Aires; **El Rápido** (☏ 261/4314094) with daily buses to Buenos Aires and Santiago, Chile, and three trips weekly to Lima, Peru; and **T.A.C.** (☏ 261/4311039) with service to Bariloche, Buenos Aires, and Córdoba.

### By Car

The trip from Buenos Aires to Mendoza is 1,060 km (664 mi) along lonely, paved R7. From Santiago, Chile, it's 250 km (155 mi) east (the road is sometimes closed in winter due to avalanches) on R7.

## Getting Around

### By Bus

Every town has local buses and if you can express where you want to go and understand the reply, you can travel cheaply (but slowly). A number in brackets on the bus indicates the route. Almost every tour agency runs minivans to local sights. In Mendoza, try **Mendoza Viajes** (☞ Tour Operators, *below*), which has its own buses for local tours.

### By Car

Driving around the Cuyo is easy—the roads are good if monotonous. Outside the major cities, there's very little traffic. Mendoza locals, however, are known for their cavalier attitude toward traffic rules. Though you can take a tour bus to sights around all the Cuyo towns, having a car to visit the wineries at your leisure or experience the high Andean villages on the highway to Chile is worth the expense. If you fear getting lost or breaking down in remote areas, hire a *remise*—a car with a driver. Usuallly less expensive than taxis, remises are a good value for groups sharing expenses. Arrangements can be made through your hotel or at the airport or bus station.

CAR RENTAL AGENCIES
Mendoza: **aiAnsa International** (⊠ San Juan 1012, ☏ 261/4202666); **Andina Rent A Car** (⊠ Sarmiento 129, ☏ 261/4380480, FAX 261/438065); and **Dollar Rent A Car** (⊠ Primitivo de la Reta 936, ☏ 261/4294435). San Rafael: **A. Sanchez** (⊠ Rodoviária, Local 4, ☏ 2627/428310).

REMISES
Mendoza: **Class Remis** (for local guided tours, ☏ 261/4318238; for airport transfers, ☏ 261/4318244; for business trips, ☏ 261/4315810; FAX 261/4319264); and **Imperio Remises** (⊠ at the bus station, Local D23, ☏ 261/4322222, 800/433368).

### By Taxi

Taxis in the region are inexpensive, metered, and plentiful. Usually there's a taxi stand near the central plaza and you can always have one called for you at hotels and restaurants. For tips—give the fare rounded up. Although drivers are generally honest, it's a good idea for long trips to agree upon the fare before you go.

## Contacts and Resources

### Banks and Currency Exchange

Banks in the region are generally open weekdays 10–4. Dollars are interchangeable with pesos in larger cities, and ATMs are increasingly popular in even the remotest towns. Hotels and sometimes travel agencies will also change dollars to pesos. Traveler's checks are the least convenient, as you must go to the bank, wait in line, and pay a fee.

MENDOZA
**Banco Mendoza** (⊠ San Martín and Gutierrez, ☏ 261/4234500; ⊠ at bus terminal). **Citibank** (⊠ San Martín 1098, ☏ 261/4204211), which

has an ATM and changes money. **Exprinter** (⊠ San Martín 1198, ☎ 261/4380309).

**Citibank** (⊠ Av. J. I. de la Raza 211 Oeste, ☎ 264/4276999). and **Lloyd's Bank** (⊠ General Acha 127 Sur, ☎ 264/4206480). ATMs: **Banco de Boston** (⊠ Laprida and Mendoza); and **Banco de Galicia** (⊠ General Acha and Rivadavía).

**Banco de Galicia** (⊠ Rivadavía and Belgrano).

**Banco Mendoza** (⊠ El Libertador and Mitre, ☎ 2627/422265). **Banco Nación** (⊠ H. Yrigoyen 113, ☎ 627/43009). ATMs: **Banco de Boston, Banco Francés,** and **Banco Galicia,** all on Calle H. Yrigoyen.

## Emergencies
**Ambulance/Medical Emergencies** (☎ 107). **Fire Department** (☎ 100). **Police** (☎ 101).

**Hospital Central** (⊠ José F. Moreno and Alem, ☎ 261/4248657), near the bus terminal. **Farmacia del Puente** (⊠ Av. San Martín 1288, ☎ 261/4258181). **Local Police** (⊠ Belgrano and Peltier).

**Hospital Dr. G. Rawson** (⊠ General Paz and E.E.U.U., ☎ 264/4222272). **Fire Department** (⊠ San Luís and Aberastain, ☎ 264/4213280). **Local Police** (⊠ Entre Ríos 579 Sur, ☎ 264/4214050).

**Hospital Materno Infantil** (⊠ Av. Republica Oriental del Uruguay 150, ☎ 2652/422627). **Fire Department** (☎ 2652/429444). **Local Police** ☎ 2652/425025). **Regional Police** (☎ 2652/422330).

**Hospital Schestakow** (⊠ Emilio Civit 151 and Corrientes, ☎ 2627/424290 or 2627/424291).

## English-Language Bookstores
In Mendoza, books in English are available at **Librerís Y** (⊠ upstairs in the Mendoza Plaza Shopping Center, Av. Acceso Este 3280, Guaymallen) and at **Y Libros** (⊠ Av. San Martín 1252, ☎ 261/4252822).

## Health and Safety
Good water and fresh fruit and vegetables are part of Cuyano culture. Though if you have doubts, bottled water is available in bars, stores, restaurants, and kiosks. If you're heading into high altitudes, precautions should be taken to acclimatize yourself. Also, carry aspirin for headaches and drink plenty of water. Herbal teas such as té de boldo, coca tea, and cachimay soothe upset stomachs. Sunscreen is a must wherever you go in this hot, dry, sunny climate.

## Telephone, the Internet, and Mail
**Correo central** (central post office; ⊠ San Martín and Colón, ☎ 261/4293050). **American Service Pack** (⊠ Casa Central, O'Brien 508 and San José, ☎ 261/4453178) is a private postal service in Guaymallén. **Telefónica Argentina** (⊠ Chile 1574).

**Correo** (⊠ Av. José I. de la Raza 259 Este, ☎ 264/4224430). **Telefónica** (⊠ Laprida 180 Oeste). Internet service is available at **Casino Cyber**

**Café** (✉ Rivadavía 12 Este, ☎ 264/4201397) and **Interredes** (✉ Laprida 362 Este, ☎ 264/4275790).

SAN RAFAEL
**Correo** (✉ San Lorenzo and Barcala, ☎ 2627/421119). **Telefónica Argentina** (✉ San Lorenzo 131). Fax and E-mail service is available at **Locutorio I** (✉ Avellaneda 76, FAX 2627/43016); and **Locutorio III** (✉ Terminal de Omnibus Location 35, FAX 2627/435809). The town has two **cybercafés** (✉ in gallería on Av. San Martín 120; ✉ upstairs at 71 H. Yrigoyen and Av. San Martín).

## Tour Operators and Travel Agencies
For ski tours all over Argentina and Chile, contact **Badino** (✉ Paraguay 930, Buenos Aires, ☎ 11/4326–1351, FAX 11/4393–2568).

MENDOZA
**Mendoza Viajes** (✉ Paseo Sarmiento 129, ☎ 261/4380480) is the most experienced, efficient, and convenient travel agency for local tours and travel arrangements of all kinds. For adventure travel (hiking, river rafting, horseback riding, and mountain biking), contact: **Aymará Turismo** (✉ 9 de Julio 938, ☎ FAX 261/4200607); and **Betancourt Rafting** (✉ Ruta Panamericana and Río Cuevas, Godoy Cruz, ☎ FAX 261/4390229).

SAN JUAN
**En.Pro.Tur** (✉ Sarmiento 24 Sur, ☎ 264/4210004). **Sempre Viajes** (✉ José I de la Roza 237 Oeste, ☎ FAX 264/4220805) can make local, national, and international hotel and airline reservations, arrange car rentals, and organize guided tours.

SAN LUÍS
**Dasso Viajes** (✉ Rivadavía 615, ☎ 2652/426616) rents cars and makes foreign, domestic, and local travel arrangements.

SAN RAFAEL
**Ateul Travel** (✉ Commandante Torres 67, ☎ FAX 2627/429282). **Bessone Viajes y Turismo** (✉ H. Yrigoyen 423, ☎ FAX 2627/436439).

## Visitor Information
**Cámara de Turismo de la Provincia de Mendoza** (✉ San Lorenzo 156, Mendoza, ☎ FAX 261/4294202). **Mendoza** (✉ Av. San Martín 1143, ☎ 261/4202800). **San Juan** (✉ Sarmiento 24 Sur, ☎ 264/421000, FAX 264/4225778). **San Luís** (✉ Avs. Presidente Arturo Illía and San Martín, ☎ 2652/423057). **San Rafael** (✉ Av. H. Yrigoyen 745, ☎ 2627/424217 or 800/2222555).

# 7 PATAGONIA

Rugged and romantic, Patagonia's mysteries have stirred the fantasies of travelers ever since 16th-century European explorers like Magellan first set foot here. Nature spared no expense on Patagonia: Imposing glaciers, petrified forests, some of the hemisphere's highest mountain peaks, and an abundance of wildlife has made the region a mecca for enjoying the outdoors. History, too, has played a part in shaping Patagonia's character: The blending of the cultures of the Mapuche and the descendants of Spanish, Welsh, Scottish, English, Italian, and Yugoslav immigrants has created a rich heritage that is still apparent today in the food, language, and customs of the region.

By Eddy
Ancinas and
Robert P.
Walzer

**P**ATAGONIA, THAT FABLED LAND of endless, empty open space at the end of the world, has humbled the most intrepid explorers. Many have described it as a cruel and lonely windswept land unfit for humans. Darwin called Patagonia "wretched and useless," yet he was deeply moved by its desolation and forever attracted to it. Today, the 800,000 sq km (308,000 sq mi) that are Argentine Patagonia continue to challenge and fascinate explorers, mountaineers, nature lovers, sports enthusiasts, and curious visitors from around the world.

From the Río Colorado (Colorado River) in the north to Cape Horn, 2,000 km (1,200 mi) south, this vast territory may seem monotonously devoid of life—uninhabited and inhospitable—but these very characteristics make it one of the most amazing natural preserves on earth. Because the population in Patagonia is small relative to its land mass, a staggering variety of plants and wildlife exists in pristine habitats, from the Andes to the great plains and deserts to the coast.

Patagonia has vast stretches of brush desert, lush mountainous areas, and artificially greened areas from water-channeling systems such as those used in the Chubut Valley around Gaiman. Micro-weather systems are scattered about, such as the one around the dry hills of the petrified forest of Sarmiento, where the wind can blow up to 220 kph (136 mph). The fossil-rich cliffs along the banks of the Río Negro, the pine forests of the Andes, and the Tierra del Fuego are some of the more dramatic settings. The trout-rich lakes of Tierra del Fuego and the northern Lake District, from Lago Alumine in the north to Lago Amutui Quimei in the south, provide more relaxing settings.

The snow-clad Andean peaks on the western border with Chile form a natural barrier to Pacific storms. The runoff from their eternal snows pours into lakes and streams, eventually spilling into major rivers that wind their way for hundreds of miles across the great arid plateau, until finally flowing into the Atlantic. Farther south, the continental ice cap spreads over 13,500 sq km (8,400 sq mi), forming the only glacier (Perito Moreno) in the world that is still growing after 30,000 years.

Ushuaia, on the Canal del Beagle (Beagle Channel) in Tierra del Fuego, prides itself on being the southernmost city in the world. Puerto Madryn, on the Atlantic coast in the province of Chubut, is the gateway to the Península Valdés and its unending show of marine life. San Carlos de Bariloche, at the foot of the Andes in the northern Lake District, is by far the largest and most frequently visited city in Patagonia and is undeniably picturesque. Yet its beauty lies outside the city limits—on a mountain road, by a lake or stream, in the forest, and on top of the surrounding mountains.

# Pleasures and Pastimes

## Dining

Lamb is not only Patagonia's commercial king but also its culinary pride. Beef, too, is featured on almost every menu. Often cooked on a *parrilla* (grill) before your eyes in an open kitchen or at your table, the beef and lamb are enhanced by a spoonful of *chimichurri* sauce (made of olive oil, garlic, oregano, and sometimes chopped tomatoes and onions), which is good on everything from meat and chorizos (homemade sausages) to bread. On ranches and in some restaurants, you may have the opportunity to try *carne asado* (barbecued meat), gaucho style, where the meat is attached to a metal cross placed in the ground aslant hot coals. The heat is adjusted by raking the coals as the meat cooks, and the fat runs down to create a natural marinade. Lamb and goat cooked in this manner are delicious, and the camaraderie of standing around the fire sipping *maté* (a traditional Argentine drink) or wine while the meat cooks is part of the gaucho tradition.

Throughout the northern or Andean Lake District, local trout, salmon, and hake are grilled, fried, baked, smoked, and dried. Wild game such as hare, venison, and boar are prepared in a variety of marinades and sauces. Smoked fish and game from the region are a popular appetizer throughout Argentina. Pasta is another ubiquitous and tasty Patagonian dish. You're usually charged one price for pasta and another for the sauce on top; make sure they're *casera* (homemade).

If the 10 PM dinner hour seems too great a gap, tea is a welcome break around 4 PM. Patagonia's Welsh teahouses, a product of Welsh immigration in the 19th century, serve delicious cakes, tarts, and cookies from recipes that have been handed down for generations. Jams made from local berries, spread on homemade bread, and scones provide a cozy escape from a blustery day.

Reservations are seldom needed except during school and summer holidays (July, January, and February). Attire is informal, and tipping is the same as in the rest of the country (about 10%). For a chart that explains the cost of meals at the restaurants listed under Dining, *below, see* Dining *in* Smart Travel Tips.

### Lodging

Argentina is investing heavily in new hotels in Patagonia—in idyllic lake-view settings and in towns near the major attractions. *Estancias* (ranches) are another option, as are inexpensive *hosterías* (hostels) where backpackers squeeze five to a room. Fishing lodges on the lakes near Bariloche, San Martín de los Andes, and Junín de los Andes are not only for fishermen; they make a pleasant headquarters for hiking, boating, or just getting away. In cities, avoid rooms on lower floors that face the street. Besides hotels, one option is *apart-hotels*; these are small, furnished apartments with kitchenettes. The local tourist offices are most helpful in finding anything from a room in a residence to a country inn or a downtown hotel. Patagonia has become such a popular tourist destination that advance reservations are highly recommended if you're traveling during peak times (December–March and July–August for the ski resorts).

The **Estancias de Santa Cruz, Patagonia** publishes an excellent booklet with information on the location, accommodations, and activities at the region's ranches. For information and reservations, contact the **Centro de Información de la Provincia de Santa Cruz** (⊠ Suipacha 1120, Buenos Aires, ☎ FAX 11/43253098); or the **Subsecretaría de Turismo de Santa Cruz** (⊠ Av. Roca 1551, Río Gallegos, ☎ FAX 2966/422702).

For a chart that explains the cost of double room at the hotels listed under Lodging, *below, see* Lodging *in* Smart Travel Tips.

### Outdoors Activities

Opportunities to experience the great outdoors abound in some of the most wild and remote places left on earth. Many ranches near Bariloche, El Calafate, and Chaltén have horseback riding *(cabalgatas)* as well as organized excursions. Horses are also available to rent for a day or a week through tour operators in Bariloche, Esquel, San Martín de los Andes, and El Calafate. Horses are well trained and so much a part of Argentine culture that horseback-riding trips are a natural way to explore the mountains, forests, and lakes of Nahuel Huapi, Lanín, Los Alerces, and the Parque Nacional los Glaciares.

Hiking trails are well marked in all the national parks of the Lake District as well as in the area around Chaltén in southern Patagonia, where Monte Fitzroy and Cerro Torre attract serious mountain climbers from the world over. Trail maps are available at park offices. Fishing in the remote lakes and streams of the Andes, from Bariloche all the way south to Tierra del Fuego, is legendary and lodges devoted to fishing enthusiasts are booked well in advance. River rafting on the Río Limay (Limay River) or on the more rapid Manso, which runs west into Chile, can be arranged with outfitters in Bariloche. The Hua-Hum also flows into Chile from San Martín de los Andes. Mountain biking, whether on the slopes of the ski runs at Cerro Bayo in Villa Angostura or Chapelco in San Martín, or over high mountain passes, through deep forests, and along rocky streams can be enjoyed for a day or a week anywhere in the Andes. Rentals and excursions can be arranged in Bariloche, San Martín, Esquel, Villa Angostura, El Bolsón, and El Calafate.

## Wildlife

Along the Atlantic coast, at Península Valdés, countless species of marine life cavort in the sea and on land. In January sea lions breed in rookeries, followed by killer whales, elephant seals, and sperm whales. At the world's largest penguin rookery, in Punta Tomba, half a million little Magellanic penguins waddle back and forth on "penguin highways." On land you'll see foxes, hares, lizards, armadillos, llamas, alpacas, and guanacos, a herbivore and relative of the camel. Though the hunting of guanacos—done for centuries for their fur and meat—has depleted their numbers, there are still about 550,000 left in Patagonia. There are also all kinds of birds: condors, hawks, black eagles, peregrine falcons, turkey vultures, parakeets, snowy sheathbills, cormorants, gulls, sandpipers, and oystercatchers.

# Exploring Patagonia

The combination of great distances, unpredictable weather, and inconvenient flight schedules makes travel in Patagonia challenging. Patience, flexibility, and a sense of humor are the only antidotes. To cover the distances between Bariloche, in the north, Ushuaia, in the south, and El Calafate/Río Gallegos and Trelew/Puerto Madryn, in the middle requires time and good planning; air travel is essential. You may have to stay overnight in Buenos Aires between destinations in Patagonia, which adds to costs and travel time. If that happens, you might as well stay a few days in the capital and enjoy it, eliminating days spent on your arrival or departure. Tours to popular sights along the Atlantic Coast, to the glaciers, or in and around Bariloche can be arranged in Buenos Aires or in each destination. If you want to see it all, packaged tours do make the whole trip easier.

## Great Itineraries

IF YOU HAVE 5 DAYS

Fly to ⚏ **Bariloche** ① and make it your base for five days. In the afternoon of the day you arrive, visit the Museo de la Patagonia and take in the view from the Civic Center. Contact local tourist offices or your hotel to set up excursions out of town. On day two (your first full one), follow the Circuito Chico, with a side trip to Cerro Otto or the ski area at Cerro Catedral. The third day, take a boat trip to Isla Victoria and the Península Quetrihué to see the Arrayanes forest. On day four, consider going hiking, fishing, horseback riding, river rafting, or mountain biking in the surrounding area; or you might just want to stay and shop in Bariloche. Yet another option is to take an overnight trip to ⚏ **Esquel** ⑦, stopping in **El Bolsón** ⑥ and the Parque Nacional los

Alerces along the way. A less-ambitious two-day outing is to follow the Circuito Grande from Bariloche, with an extension along the Circuito de los Siete Lagos to ⊞ **San Martín de los Andes** ⑤. Or you could go to El Bolsón or the Circuito Grande in one day, leaving time on your last day to take a spectacular lake cruise to Puerto Blest and Laguna Frías at the foot of Mt. Tronodór. (Note: If you're arriving or leaving Bariloche via the Chilean lake crossing, you'll have traveled this route.)

If you visit Bariloche in winter (June–September) for a ski vacation, arrange, upon arrival at your hotel, to take the bus the next morning to the ski area at Cerro Catedral. To add some variety to your ski week, you can do the Circuito Chico on your return trip from the ski area, stopping at a tea house en route. Or take a day off for the lake excursion mentioned above. Across the lake, **Villa La Angostura** ② has a smaller ski area, Cerro Bayo.

If you'd prefer to spend five days in the Tierra del Fuego, fly to ⊞ **Ushuaia** ⑪ and spend three days exploring the national park, taking a boat to the wildlife preserve on Isla Redonda, and visiting the Maritime Museum at the Almirante Berisso Naval Base. Fly on the fourth day to ⊞ **El Calafate** ⑩ and take two days to see the impressive glaciers in the Parque Nacional los Glaciares.

IF YOU HAVE 7 DAYS

Armed with your Aerolineas Argentinas' "Visit Argentina Pass" (☞ Arriving and Departing by Plane *in* Patagonia A to Z, *below*), spend four days in and around ⊞ **Bariloche** ①, as described in the five-day itinerary. On the afternoon of day four or early day five, fly to **Río Gallegos** ⑨ and take a bus (four hours) or fly (40 minutes), when weather permits, to ⊞ **El Calafate** ⑩. Allow one day for excursions to see the Glaciar Upsala and at least half a day for the Glaciar Moreno. Your plane schedule will determine in which order you visit the glaciers.

Another seven-day option, depending on the season and your preference for wildlife versus glaciers, would be to spend four days in Bariloche as described above, then fly via Buenos Aires to **Trelew** ⑱ and transfer to ⊞ **Puerto Madryn** ⑲, leaving two days to view wildlife along the coast.

A third possibility is to spend three days in ⊞ **Ushuaia** ⑪ exploring the Tierra del Fuego, and then two days in ⊞ **El Calafate** ⑩ seeing the glaciers, as described in the five-day itinerary. Fly to ⊞ **Bariloche** ① on the sixth day and spend your last two days in this area.

IF YOU HAVE 10 DAYS

Fly from Buenos Aires to ⊞ **Bariloche** ① and spend two days there, as described in the five-day itinerary. An enjoyable three-day (two-night) excursion in good weather is the lake crossing from Bariloche to Puerto Montt, Chile. On day six, fly from Bariloche to **Río Gallegos** ⑨ and travel on to ⊞ **El Calafate** ⑩. Spend all of day seven seeing the Glaciar Upsala and the following morning at the Glaciar Moreno. Return to Río Gallegos in the afternoon in time to fly to ⊞ **Trelew** ⑱. Make Trelew or ⊞ **Gaiman** ⑰ your base for the last three days, taking time to visit **Península Valdés** ⑳ or **Punta Tomba** ⑯.

If you thrive on mountain scenery, hiking, and mountain climbing, you could extend your time in El Calafate in order to include an overnight visit to Chaltén at the foot of Monte Fitzroy, with its famous Cerro Torre. If you're an avid angler, use Bariloche as your headquarters and hire a guide to take you to nearby lakes and streams. Or go on a real fishing odyssey to Lago Traful (Traful Lake), and then spend three days in ⊞ **San Martín de los Andes** ⑤ and three days at the Paimún Lodge north of ⊞ **Junín de los Andes** ④. If that's not enough fishing for you, drive south to the Nacional Parque los Alerces for a week of fishing in the streams and lakes around Lago Futalaufquen.

## When to Tour

January and February are some of the peak months in Patagonia and for good reason: The wind dies down and long (the sun sets at 10 PM), warm days ensure plenty of time to enjoy a multitude of activities. Hotel and restaurant reservations are necessary in popular destinations, and campgrounds get crowded. March and April are still good months to visit, although rainy, cloudy days and cold nights might curtail some activities. But the rewards are fewer crowds and the great colors of fall. Many hotels close from May through September, as few want to brave the knock-down winds, rain, sleet, and snow of Patagonian winters. In Bariloche and the northern Lake District, however, it's ski season. The snow-covered mountains reflected in the blue lakes are spectacular, and the weather is typical of any Alpine region—tremendous snowstorms, rain, and fog punctuated by days of brilliant sunshine. August and September are the best overall months for skiing. July is the time to avoid, as the slopes and restaurants are mobbed with vacationing schoolkids and their families.

December is spring in Patagonia. The weather might be cool, breezy, overcast, or rainy, but the rewards for bringing an extra sweater and rain gear are great: an abundance of wildflowers and very few other tourists. The period December–June is the best time to visit Peninsula Valdés—this is when you can see the whales. Tierra del Fuego has different charms year round: In summer it's warm during the day and cool at night, which is ideal for outdoor activities but also means big crowds; in winter it's great for skiing, sledding, visiting dog-sledding camps, and hiking through beautifully desolate woods. If you want to whale-watch and do winter sports, consider combining a trip to Tierra del Fuego and Puerto Madryn sometime between June and September. Tierra del Fuego winters are not as harsh as you might think: The average temperature in August, the dead of winter, is about 36°F.

# ANDEAN PATAGONIA

High, snow-packed peaks, a perfect white volcano mirrored in a still lake, chalk-white glacial streams cascading over polished granite, meadows filled with chin-high pink and purple lupine, fast-flowing rivers, and thousands of lakes, with no houses, no piers, no boats: Could this be paradise on earth?

Andean Patagonia's northern lake district seems like one big national park: The Parque Nacional Lanín, just north of San Martín de los Andes in Neuquén Province, combined with the neighboring Parque Nacional Nahuel Huapi, in Río Negro Province, with Bariloche as its headquarters, adds up to 2.5 million acres of natural preserve—about the size of New England. South of the Cholila Valley and northwest of Esquel is the Parque Nacional los Alerces, named for its 2,000-year-old *alerces (Fitzroya cupressoides)*, which are similar to California redwoods. The park covers 1,610 sq km (1,000 sq mi) of true wilderness, with only one dirt road leading into it.

Along the eastern edge of the northern Lake District, mountain streams flow into rivers that have carved the deep canyons with fertile valleys. Welsh farmers have been growing wheat and raising sheep in the Chubut Valley since 1865. Rain diminishes as you move eastward, and the land flattens into a great plateau, running eastward into dry, desolate Patagonia. This is sheep-breeding country and Benetton owns a large portion of it. In summer (December–March), the towns of El Calafate and El Chaitén, in the southern Lake District, come alive with the influx of visitors to the Parque Nacional los Glaciares and climbers headed for Cerro Torre and Monte Fitzroy.

## Bariloche

**❶** *1,615 km (1,001 mi) southwest of Buenos Aires (2 hrs by plane), 432 km (268 mi) from Neuquén on R237, 1,639 km (1,016 mi) from Rio Gallegos, 876 km (543 mi) from Trelew, 357 km (221 mi) from Puerto Montt, Chile.*

In 1620, the Governor of Chile sent Captain Juan Fernández and his troops across the Andes in search of the *Enchanted City of the Caesars,* a mythological city alleged to be somewhere in Patagonia. The Jesuits established a mission on the shores of the lake, near what is now Isla Huemúl. Until the 1720s they attempted to convert the Tehuelches, who were very warlike and ultimately massacred the missionaries, including the missions' founder, Father Mascardi. No Europeans again visited the area until the next century, when Captain Cox arrived by boat from Chile in 1870, and later in 1876 *perito* (expert) Francisco Moreno led an expedition from the Atlantic, thus becoming the first explorer to arrive from the East.

Most of the indigenous people of the area were brutally massacred during the infamous Campaña del Desierto (Desert Campaign, 1879–1883). Settlers then felt safe to colonize and a fort (called Chacabuco) was built at the mouth of the Río Limay in 1883. Many were German farmers immigrating from Chile, such as Karl Wiederhold, who built the first house in Bariloche in 1895. Swiss, German, Scandinavian, and northern Italians found a rugged and relatively unexplored land similar to their Alpine homelands. They skied and climbed the mountains, fished in nearby lakes and streams, and built chalets in town and along the shore of Lago Nahuel Huapi.

Bariloche's first tourists stayed in a hotel by Carlos Wiederhold called La Cuchara Sucia (the Dirty Spoon). By 1924 tourists traveled two days from Buenos Aires by train, then drove 560 km (350 mi) on dirt roads. The railway finally reached Bariloche in 1934, and by 1938 people from all over the world came to ski on the slopes at nearby Cerro Catedral (☞ *below*).

These days Bariloche has all the comforts and conveniences of a resort town, and is the gateway to the recreational and scenic splendors of the northern lake district. Though planes, buses, trains, boats, and tour groups arrive daily, once you're away from town, you can generally find a spot where you seem to be the only person in the world. The best way to escape into the stunning wilderness of clear blue lakes, misty lagoons, rivers, waterfalls, mountain glaciers, forests, and flower-filled meadows is by mountain biking, horseback riding, or hiking. Or by going fishing in one of the 40 nearby lakes and countless streams. It's possible to get around on your own with a rented car or to go on a planned excursion with a local tour company (☞ Tour Companies *in* Patagonia A to Z, *below*).

For information on mountain climbing, trails, *refugios* (refuges or mountain cabins), and campgrounds, visit the **Intendencia de Parques Nacionales** at the Civic Center (✉ Av. San Martín 24, Bariloche, ☎ 2944/23111). Another source of information on local activities, excursions, lodging, and private and public campgrounds is the **Oficina Municipal de Turismo** (✉ in the Civic Center, Av. Bartolomé Mitre, across from the clock tower, Bariloche, ☎ 2944/423022), open daily 8:30 AM–

# Patagonia

Valdivia

*Parque Nacional Lanín*

NEUQUEN

Neuquen

BUENOS AIRES

**Junín de los Andes**

**4**

**5** **San Martín de los Andes**
Lago Hermosa

**3** **Villa Traful**

San Antonio Oeste

**Carmen de Patagones**

**23**

**22** **Viedma**

La Lobería
*Reserva Turística Prov.*

Balneario
El Condo

**Villa La Angostura**

**2** **1**
Puerto
Blest

**Bariloche**

Ingeniero
Jacobacci

RÍO NEGRO

Puerto Montt

*Parque Nacional Nahuel Huapi*

**6**

**El Bolsón**

**Sierra Grande** **21**

*Golfo San Matías*

*Cerro Catedral*

Cholila

Gastre

Puerto Piramide

**20** **Península Valdés**

Castro

**7** **Esquel**

**8** **Trevelin**

**Puerto Madryn** **19**

**Trelew** **18**

**Gaiman** **17**

Chaiten

*Parque Nacional Los Alerces*

CHUBUT

Rawson

**16** **Punto Tomba**

ANDES

25

25

3

LOS

**Camarones**

**15**

29

30

**14** **Sarmiento**

20

27

Puerto Aisen

Colhalque

40

Río
Mayo

26

*Golfo San Jorge*

**13** **Comodora Rivadavia**

DE

CHILE

43

Las Heras

Caleta Olivia

*Cabo Tres Puntas*

Perito
Moreno

CORDILLERA

*Deseado*

281

**12** **Puerto Deseado**

*P. N.
F. P. Moreno*

*Monumento
Natural Bosques
Petrificados*

40

3

SANTA CRUZ

*L. San Martín*

25

*Fitzroy*

El Chaiten

**Co Terre**

*L. Viedma*

Tres Lagos
Punta del Lago

288

Puerto
San Julián

*Parque Nacional los Glaciares*

**El Calafate**

**10**

9

Puerto
Santa Cruz

*Reserva
Tehuelche*

*Bahía Grande*

40

*Cabo Buen Tiempo*

Río Turbio
Yacimiento

*Gallegos*

**9** **Río Gallegos**

Puerto
Natales

*Bahía Lomas*

ATLANTIC OCEAN

PACIFIC OCEAN

TO FALKLAND
ISLANDS (LAS
MALVINAS)

*Bahía
Felipe*

TIERRA DEL
FUEGO

Punta
Arenas

Porvenir

3

Río Grande

*Estrecho Magallanes*

*Tierra del Fuego*

*Canal Beagle*

N

*Parque Nacional
Tierra del Fuego*

**11**

3

*Peninsula
Mitre*

*Isla de
los Estados*

**Ushuaia**

Puerto
Williams

0        50 miles

0        75 km

*Cape Horn*

9 PM. Alejandro Bustillo, the architect who designed the rustic, grey-green stone-and-log buildings of the Civic Center also designed the Llao Llao Hotel (☞ Dining and Lodging, *below*). His Andean-Swiss style is recognizable, too, in lodges and buildings throughout the lake district. The spacious square in front of the Civic Center, with an equestrian statue of General Roca (1843–1914) and a wide-angle view of the lake, is a good place to begin exploring the town. Note that the Civic Center is Km 0 for measuring points from Bariloche.

The **Museo de la Patagonia** (Patagonia Museum) tells the social and geological history of northern Patagonia through displays of Indian and Gaucho artifacts and exhibits on regional flora and fauna. The history of the Mapuche and the Conquista del Desierto (Conquest of the Desert) are also explained in detail. ☒ *In Centro Cívico, next to the arch over Bartolomé Mitre,* ☎ *2944/422309.* ☒ *Admission.* ☉ *Weekdays, 10–12:30 and 2–7, Sat. 10–1.*

The **Parque Nacional Nahuel Huapi,** created in 1943, is Argentina's oldest national park, and **Lago Nahuel Huapi** is the sapphire in its crown. The park extends over 2 million acres along the eastern side of the Andes in the provinces of Neuquén and Río Negro, on the frontier with Chile. It contains the highest concentration of lakes in Argentina. The biggest is Lago Nahuel Huapi, a 897-sq-km (557-sq-mi) body of water, whose seven long arms (the longest is 96 km [60 ft] long, 12 km [7 mi] wide) reach deep into forests of *coihué* (a native beech tree), cyprés, and *lenga* trees. Intensely blue across its vast expanse and aqua green in its shallow bays, the lake meanders into distant lagoons and misty inlets where the mountains, covered with vegetation at their base, rise straight up out of the water to lofty heights. Participating in every water sport invented and tours to islands and other extraordinarily beautiful spots can be arranged through local tour offices, outfitters, and hotels (☞ Outdoor Activities and Sports, *below*). Throughout the park are also information offices where you can get help in exploring the miles of mountain and woodland trails, lakes, rivers, and streams.

The most popular excursion on Lago Nahuel Huapi is by boat to **Isla Victoria** (Victoria Island), the largest in the lake. A grove of redwoods transplanted from California thrives in the middle of the island. After a walk on trails that lead to enchanting views of emerald bays and still lagoons, the boat crosses to the tip of the **Quitruihué Peninsula** for a visit to the **Parque Nacional los Arrayanes** (☞ Villa La Angostura, *below*).

The renowned ski area at **Cerro Catedral** (Mt. Cathedral) is 46 km (28½ mi) west of town on Avenida Ezequiel Bustillo (R237); turn left at Km 8½ just past Playa Bonita. The mountain was named for the Gothic-looking spires that crown its peaks. Though skiing is the main activity here (☞ Outdoor Activities and Sports, *below*), the view from the top of the chairlift at 6,600 ft is spectacular any time of year. Looking northwest, the intense blue of Lago Nahuel Huapi meanders around islands into invisible bays and disappears beneath mountains and volcanoes miles away, with Lanín Volcano (☞ San Martín de los Andes, *below*) visible on the horizon.

You can reach the summit of **Cerro Otto** (Mt. Otto; 4,608 ft), another fine ski area, by hiking, mountain-biking, or driving 8 km (5 mi) up a gravel road from Bariloche. Hiking to the top of the mountain takes you through a forest of lenga trees to Argentina's first ski area at Piedras Blancas. Here Herbert Tutzauer, Bariloche's first ski instructor, won the first ski race by climbing the mountain, then skiing down it through the forest in one hour and 30 minutes. Or you can take the **Teleférico Cerro Otto** (☒ Av. de Los Pioneros), 5 km (3 mi) west of town; a free shuttle bus leaves from the corner of Mitre and Villegas, and Perito Moreno and Independencia; the ride to the top takes about 12 minutes. All proceeds go to local hospitals. At the top, a revolving cafeteria with a 360-degree panorama takes in Mt. Tronador, lakes in every direction, and Bariloche. In winter, skis and sleds are available for rent at the cafeteria. In summer, hiking and mountain biking are the main activities. For a real thrill, try soaring out over the lake with the condors in a paraplane. For information on schedules and sled or ski rentals, call ☎ 2944/41031.

A visit to **Monte Tronador** (Mt. Thunderer) requires an all day outing of 170 km (105 mi) round trip from Bariloche. The 12,000-ft extinct volcano, the highest mountain in the northern lake district, sits astride the frontier with Chile, with one peak on either side. Take R258 south along the shore of **Lago Gutiérrez**; from here you can see Cerro Catedral. The road continues along the shore of **Lago Masacardi**. Between the two lakes the road crosses from the Atlantic to the Pacific watershed. At Km 35, turn off onto a road marked TRONADOR AND PAMPA LINDA and continue along the shore of Lago Mascardi, passing a village of the same name. Just beyond the village, the road forks and you continue on a gravel road, R254. Near the bridge the road branches left to **Lago Hess** and **Cascada Los Alerces** (☞ *below*)—a detour you might want to take on your way out. Bearing right after crossing Los Rápidos Bridge, the road narrows to one direction only: It's important to remember this when you set out in the morning, as you can only go up the road before 2 PM and down it after 4 PM. The lake ends in a narrow arm (Brazo Tronador), at the lovely Hotel Tronador, which has a dock for tours arriving by boat. The road then follows the **Río Manso** (Manso River) to **Pampa Linda**, which has a lodge, restaurant, park ranger's office, campsites, and the trailhead for the climb up to the **Refugio Otto Meiling** at the snowline. Guided horseback rides are organized at the lodge. The road ends 7 km (4 mi) beyond Pampa Linda in a parking lot that was once at the tip of the now receding **Glaciar Negro** (Black Glacier). As the glacier flows down from the mountain, the dirt and black sediment of its lateral moraines is ground up and covers the ice. At first glance, it's hard to imagine the tons of ice that lie beneath its black cap. The detour to **Cascada Los Alerces** (Los Alerces Falls), 17 km (10 mi) from the turnoff at the bridge, follows the wild Río Manso, where it branches off to yet another lake, **Lago Hess**. At this junction you find a campground, refuge, restaurant, and a trailhead for the 1,000-ft climb to the falls. The path through dense vegetation over wooden bridges crossing the rushing river as it spills over steep rocky cliffs is a grand finale to a day of viewing nature at its most powerful and beautiful. For more information about excursions to and activities on Mt. Tronador, ☞ Outdoor Activities and Sports, *below,* and ☞ Tour Operators *in* Patagonia A to Z, *below.*

Another excursion from Bariloche is the **Circuito Chico** (Small Circuit), a half-day, 70-km (43½-mi) scenic trip along the west shore of Lago Nahuel Huapi. You can do it by car, tour bus, or mountain bike. First head west on Avenida Bustillo (R237) toward Península Llao Llao. At Km 20, you can take a brief side trip to the **Península San Pedro**, a 11-km-long (7-mi-long) appendage running parallel to the coastal road; this dirt road passes some fine homes set back in the woods. At the **Ahumadero Familia Weiss** (Weiss Family Smokehouse), along the way, you can buy smoked fish and game. Back on the main road, continue west to **Puerto Pañuelo** (Km 25½) in a little bay on the right; it's the embarkation point for lake excursions and for the boat crossing to Chile. Across from the port, a long driveway leads up a knoll to the Hotel Llao Llao (☞ Dining and Lodging, *below*), which is worth a visit even if you're not staying there. The Circuito Chico now follows R77 to Bahía Lopez, winding along the lake's edge through a forest of ghostly, leafless lenga trees. After crossing the bridge that links **Lago Moreno** (Lake Moreno) and Lago Nahuel Huapi at Bahía Lopez, the road crosses the Arroyo Lopez (Lopez Creek). Here you can stop for a hike up to a waterfall and then climb above Lago Moreno to **Punto Panoramico**, a scenic overlook well worth a photo stop. Just before you cross Lago Moreno, an unmarked dirt road off to the right leads to the rustic village of **Colonia Suiza**, a good spot to stop for tea or lunch. After passing **Laguna El Trebol** (a small lake on your left), R77 joins R237 from Bariloche.

| | |
|---|---|
| NEED A BREAK? | The window of the **Bellevue Casa de Te** holds the mirrored image of Mt. Tronador, framed by a forest of cypress and lenga trees. It's hard to say which is better—the view, the rich chocolate cake, the fruit tarts, or the garden. ⊠ *At Km 25 on Av. Bustillo (R237); just before Puerto Pañuelo, turn away from the lake down a dirt road; a sign will direct you.* ☎ *2944/448389. No credit cards. Closed Mon.–Tues. No lunch.* |

The **Circuito Grande** (Large Circuit), a more ambitious excursion, which is particularly lovely in spring or fall, covers 250 km (155 mi). Along the way there are plenty of spots to stop and enjoy the view, have a picnic lunch, or even stay overnight. Leaving Bariloche on R237, follow the **Río Limay** into the **Valle Encantado** (Enchanted Valley), with its magical red-rock formations. Before crossing the bridge at **Confluéncia** (where the Río Traful joins the Limay), turn left onto R65 to Lago Traful. Five km (3 mi) beyond the turnoff, on a dirt road heading toward Cuyín Manzano, are some astounding formations. As you follow the shore of Lago Traful, a sign indicates a *mirador* (lookout) on a high rock promontory, which you can climb up to on wooden stairs. At **Villa Traful** (☞ *below*), you can buy picnic supplies. In Villa Traful, stop for a break at Ñancu-Lahuen, a teahouse and restaurant with a luscious garden; it's also a good place to get travel and fishing information. From here the road dives into a dense forest until it comes to the intersection with the Seven Lakes Circuit (☞ *below*); turn left, following the shore of **Lago Correntoso** to the paved road down to the bay at **Villa La Angostura** (☞ *below*).

The **Circuito de los Siete Lagos** (Seven Lakes Circuit) is an all-day trip of 360 km (223½ mi) round-trip, which could be extended to include an overnight in San Martín de los Andes. Drive north on R237 for 21 km (13 mi), and turn left on R231 to **Villa La Angostura**, 65 km (40 mi) from Bariloche. About 11 km (7 mi) farther along the same road is the Seven Lakes Road (R234), which branches right, and along the way passes **Lago Correntoso, Lago Espejo, Lago Villarino, Lago Falkner,** and **Lago Hermoso.** After lunch or tea or an overnight in **San Martín de los Andes** (☞ *below*), head south to Bariloche on the dirt road over Paso Cordoba, passing **Lago Meliquina** on the way. At Confluéncia, the road joins R237, following the Río Limay through Valle Encantado to Bariloche.

A longer, less traveled, all-day boat excursion to **Puerto Blest** leaves from Puerto Pañulo on the Península Llao Llao (accessible by bus, auto, or tour). The boat heads west along the shore of Lago Nahuel Huapi to Brazo Blest, a 1-km-long (¾-mi-long) fjordlike arm of the lake. Along the way, waterfalls plunge down the face of high rock walls. A Valdivian rainforest of coihués, cypress, lengas, and *arrayanes* (myrtle) covers the canyon walls. After the boat docks at Puerto Blest, a bus transports you over a short pass to Puerto Alegre on **Laguna Frías** (Cold Lagoon), where a launch waits to ferry you across the frosty green water to **Puerto Fríos** on the other side. Mt. Tronador towers like a great white sentinel. The launch returns to the dock at Puerto Alegre, where you can return by foot or by bus to Puerto Blest. A trail through the forest and up 600 steps to **Cascada Los Cántaros** (Singing Waterfalls) is worth the effort. After lunch in **Puerto Blest** at its venerable old hotel, the boat returns to Bariloche. Note: this is the first leg of the Cruce a Chile por Los Lagos (☞ *below*).

★ The **Cruce a Chile por Los Lagos** (Chile Lake Crossing) is a unique excursion by land and lakes that began in the 1930s when ox carts used to haul people. These days you can do this tour in one day or two. Follow the itinerary above, stopping for lunch in **Puerto Blest** and then continuing on to **Puerto Fríos** on **Laguna Frías**. After docking at Puerto Fríos and clearing Argentine customs, another bus climbs through a lush rainforest over a pass, then descends to **Peulla**, where Chilean customs is cleared (bring your passport). A little farther on is a comfortable lodge by **Lago Todos los Santos**. Early the next morning a catamaran sets out across the lake, providing views of the volcanoes **Putiagudo** (which lost its *punto* in an earthquake) and **Osorno**. The boat trip ends at the port of **Petrohué**. Another (and final) bus skirts **Lago Llanquihue**, stopping for a visit at the rockbound Petrohué waterfalls, passing through the town of **Puerto Varas** (famous for its roses) and arriving, at last, at the Chilean port town of Puerto Montt. Catedral Turismo (☞ Tour Operators and Travel Agencies *in* Patagonia A to Z, *below*) specializes in this trip and can arrange a one-day return by bus to Bariloche.

## Dining and Lodging

Accommodations range from family-run *residenciales* (pensions) to superluxurious resort hotels. If you don't have a car, it's better to stay in town. But if you're looking for more serenity, stay at one of the country inns or resort hotels outside town. Addresses for out-of-town dining and lodging are measured in kilometers from the Civic Center, and signposts along the road denote these distances. The most crowded time of the year, and the best time to avoid, is during school vacations (July and January). August is best for skiing; February, the height of summer; May, for fall colors. Of the many fine restaurants, most are casual and open noon–3 for lunch and 8–midnight for dinner. Note: All lodging prices include tax and Continental breakfast.

**$$$** ✕ **La Marmite.** If there's a Euro-Argentine cuisine, this is it: wild boar
★ in wine with local mushrooms served with cabbage and elderberry jam; and venison, trout, and lamb prepared with equal imagination. Argentina's famous malbecs or cabernets are the perfect companion for this international fare. ⊠ *Mitre 329,* ☎ *2944/423685. AE, DC, MC, V. No lunch Sun.*

**$$$** ✕ **El Patacón.** On a bluff overlooking the lake, this restaurant, con-
★ structed of local stone and wood, hosted President Clinton and Argentine President Menem when they visited Bariloche in 1998. The ranch-style interior displays gaucho tools, local art, and weavings. Leather and sheepskin furniture creates a warm atmosphere. An organic garden with fresh herbs, berries, and vegetables enhances the menu of meats, game, and fish. ⊠ *Av. Bustillo, Km 7,* ☎ *2944/442898. AE, DC, MC, V.*

**$$** ✕ **El Boliche de Alberto.** This popular lunch spot serves typical Argentine cuisine with a Patagonian accent. Just point at a slab of beef, chicken, or lamb and have it grilled per your instructions (if you don't speak enough Spanish, there's always pasta). Sausages, empanadas, and chimichurri sauce accompany all of the above. ⊠ *Villegas 347,* ☎ *2944/ 431433. AE, DC, MC, V.*

**$$** ✗ **El Boliche Viejo.** Next to the Río Limay, under the *alamos* (poplars), is this 100-year-old tin-and-wood structure that was once part of the Jones Ranch. In its rustic atmosphere, enjoy quintessential meat-and-potato dishes served from a giant grill. ⊠ *R237, Km 17 (18 km [11 mi] north of town)*, ☎ *2944/425977. DC, MC, V.*

**$$** ✗ **Jauja.** Big, friendly, and casual, this spot is a favorite with locals and families for its variety of meats, fish, and game dishes. Good salads and fresh vegetables are always available, as are pasta dishes. The nonsmoking section is a plus. ⊠ *Quaglia 366,* ☎ *2944/422952. AE, DC, MC, V.*

**$$$$** ✗▣ **Hotel Edelweiss.** Three blocks from the Civic Center, and walk-
★ ing distance from tour offices, restaurants, and shops, is this excellent medium-size hotel. Fresh flowers from the owner's nursery are arranged throughout. The modern, spacious rooms and suites have lake views from their bay windows. Breakfast includes eggs, bacon, sausages, fresh fruits, and juices—unusual in this country of *medias lunas* (croissants) and coffee. Both lunch and dinner consist of good salads, grilled fish, fowl, game, and beef prepared with fresh vegetables and tasty sauces. Most ski and tour buses, whether arranged through the hotel or other travel agencies, pick up passengers at this hotel. ⊠ *Av. San Martín 202,* ☎ *2944/426165,* FAX *2944/425655. 94 rooms, 6 suites. Restaurant, bar, in-room safes, indoor pool, beauty salon, massage, sauna, exercise room, meeting rooms, travel services, parking. CP. AE, DC, MC, V.*

**$$$$** ✗▣ **Llao Llao Hotel & Resort.** This masterpiece by architect Alejandro Bustillo sits on a grassy knoll surrounded by three lakes with a back-drop of sheer rock cliffs and snow-covered mountains. Local wood—alerce, cypress, and hemlock—has been used for the walls, and wicker furniture upholstered with native weavings makes the lobby feel like an elegant hunting lodge. Along the 100-yard hallway, paintings by local artists are displayed between fine boutiques. Activities abound: chil-dren's supervised play activities, tango and salsa lessons, a full spa pro-gram, tennis courts, a superb 18-hole golf course ($25 fee for guests), windsurfing, mountain-bike rentals, and walking tours around the peninsula. ⊠ *Av. Ezequiel Bustillo, Km 25 (25 km [15½ mi] west of Bariloche),* ☎ *2944/448530,* FAX *2944/445781. 162 rooms, 8 suites. Restaurant, bar, café, piano bar, in-room safes, minibars, no-smoking rooms, indoor pool, beauty salon, hot tub, massage, sauna, spa, 18-hole golf course, tennis courts, aerobics, archery, exercise room, pad-dle tennis, dock, windsurfing, boating, skiing, children's programs, convention center, meeting rooms, travel services. AE, DC, MC, V.*

**$$$$** ▣ **El Casco.** Outside town, just off the busy road to Llao Llao, El Casco is tucked away behind carefully tended gardens and trees. A fine view of Isla Huemul and the lake brightens every room, each decorated with different antiques. In the oldest part of the original house, the three-room apartment has a private entrance and a sitting room with a fire-place. ⊠ *Av. Ezequiel Bustillo, Km 11 8400 (11 km [7 mi] west of Bariloche),* ☎ FAX *2944/461032 or 2944/461088. 23 rooms, 1 apart-ment. Restaurant, bar, café, beauty salon, massage, sauna, dock. AE, DC, MC, V.*

**$$$$** ▣ **Hotel Nevada.** Right in the middle of town, this traditional hotel is a favorite of business travelers and tourists. Rooms are well above street-noise level, and although the hotel is old, rooms are well fur-nished in a pleasant mountain style. Breakfast, snacks, and tea are served in the bar/café. The business center with fax and Internet access is a rare amenity in this recreation-minded town. ⊠ *Rolando 250, 8400,* ☎ *2944/422778,* FAX *2944/427914. 74 rooms, 14 suites. Bar, café, sauna, business services, parking. CP. AE, DC, MC, V.*

$$$$ 🏨 **Hotel Tunquelen.** Surrounded by 20 acres of woods and gardens, this châteaulike hotel outside Bariloche is visible from the lake, but not from the busy road to Llao Llao. An uninterrupted view across the water to distant peaks—even from the indoor pool—has a tranquilizing effect. From the minute you step into the lobby/living room, sink into the soft cushions in front of the fireplace, and look out on the lake, you feel at home. Rooms are neat, with whitewashed stucco and native wood, and open onto the garden or overlook the lake. A downstairs dining room serves breakfast and dinner, and cocktails are served in the garden, weather permitting. ⊠ *Av. Bustillo, 8400 (22 km [13 mi] west of Bariloche on the road to Llao Llao),* ☎ FAX *2944/48400 or 2944/48600. 31 rooms, 1 suite, 8 apartments. Restaurant, piano bar, indoor pool, tennis court, paddle tennis, beach, boating, ski shuttle, meeting rooms, travel services.* AE, DC, MC, V.

$$$–$$$$ 🏨 **Hotel Catedral.** The handsome stone and wood Hotel Catedral sits on a hill just beyond the tram building across the road from the Cerro Catedral ski area. Its dining room windows frame a perfect postcard view of the lake and surrounding mountains. Rooms are furnished with simple, white fabrics and solid wood furnishings; the apartments are done in quiet earth tones and modern furnishings. In winter, Argentines and Brazilians book well in advance. ⊠ *Cerro Catedral ski area; mailing address in Buenos Aires: Av. Córdoba 1345,* ☎ *11/4816– 8811 in Buenos Aires. 60 rooms, apartments. 2 restaurants, bar, pool, 2 tennis courts, sauna, shops, travel services.* AE, DC, MC, V. *Closed Apr.–May and Oct.–Nov.*

$$ 🏨 **Casita Suiza.** Swiss owned and -operated since 1961, this charming downtown chalet exudes old-world hospitality. Rooms are immaculate, and rates include a hearty breakfast with homemade wheat bread, jams, and juices. In summer and spring the street-side terrace explodes with blossoming pansies and violets. ⊠ *Quaglia 342, 8400,* ☎ FAX *0944/23775 or 0944/26111. 13 rooms. Restaurant, bar, laundry service.* CP. AE, DC, MC, V.

$$ 🏨 **Patagonia Sur.** This tall, slender seven-story structure is Bariloche's newest hotel; it's high on a hill overlooking the town and the lake, just five blocks from town. The view of the church spire, rooftops, and blue lake make the climb up the stairway from town worth the effort. Inside and out it's thoroughly clean and modern, from the new softly upholstered chairs in the lobby to the sparsely furnished rooms—an appropriate treatment, as the view dominates the decor. ⊠ *Elfleín 340, 8400,* ☎ *2944/422995,* FAX *2944/424329. 55 rooms. Café, parking.* CP. AE, DC, MC, V.

$ 🏨 **Quime Quipan.** This congenial wood and white-stucco *hostería* (inn) is surrounded by a garden in a quiet neighborhood within walking distance of the Civic Center. Rooms are small, simple, and tidy. ⊠ *Av. Los Pioneros, Km 1, 8400 (1 km [¾ mi] west of downtown),* ☎ FAX *2944/425423. 18 rooms, 1 apartment. Dining room, snack bar, parking.* CP. DC, MC, V.

## Nightlife and the Arts

Three of the town's most popular *discotecas* (discos) are all on the same street, Avenida J. M. de Rosas. All open at 10 PM and cost about $10– $20 plus the purchase of a drink. Whole families—from children to grandparents—go to discos, though on Saturday night only people 25 years and older are admitted. The clubs are especially busy during school holidays and ski season. Try **Cerebro** (⊠ 405 Av. J. M. de Rosas, ☎ 2944/424965); **El Grisu** (⊠ 574 Av. J. M. de Rosas, ☎ 2944/422269); and **Rocket** (⊠ 424 Av. J. M. de Rosas, ☎ 2944/420549 day and 2944/431940 night). Around the corner from the Avenida J. M. de Rosas strip of clubs is the **Casino Española** (⊠ España 476, ☎ 2944/424421); it's open 10 PM–4 AM.

## Outdoor Activities and Sports

### FISHING

Lago Nahuel Huapi and the Gutiérrez, Masacardi, Correntoso, and Traful lakes are just a few of the many in the northern Lake District that attract fishing fanatics from all over the world. If you're seeking the perfect pool or secret stream for fly-fishing, you may have to do some hiking, particularly along the banks of the Chimehuín, Limáy, Traful, and Correntoso rivers. Near Junín de los Andes, the Río Malleo (Malleo River) and the Currihué, Huechulafquen, Paimún, and Lácar lakes are also good fishing grounds (☞ Villa Traful and Junín de los Andes, *below*). Near El Bolsón and in the Parque Nacional los Alerces, many remote lakes and streams are accessible only by boat or seldom-traveled dirt roads (☞ Esquel, *below*). Fishing lodges offer rustic comfort in beautiful settings; boats, guides, and plenty of fishing tales are usually included. Make reservations early, as they're booked well in advance by an international clientele of repeat visitors. Fishing season runs November 15–April 15; guides are available to take you fishing for a day or a week.

Fishing licenses allowing you to catch brown trout, rainbow trout, perch, brook trout, and *salar sebago* (landlocked) salmon are easy to get at Bariloche's **Direcciones Provinciales de Pesca** (⊠ Elfleín 10, ☎ 2944/425160), in the Nahuel Huapi National Park office (☞ *above*) and at most tackle shops. Boats can be rented at **Charlie Lake Rent-A-Boat** (⊠ Av. Ezequiel Bustillo, Km 16.6, ☎ FAX 2944/448562). For information about fly-fishing in the area, contact the following guides: Oscar Baruzzi at **Baruzzi Deportes** (⊠ Urquiza 250, ☎ 2944/424922, FAX 2944/428374); **Martín Pescador** (⊠ Rolando 257, ☎ 2944/422275, FAX 2944/421637); or **Ricardo Almeijeiras** (⊠ Quinchahuala 200, ☎ FAX 2944/441944). For trolling or spinning contact: **Jorge Lazzarini** (☎ 2944/294411), **Luís Navarro** (☎ 2944/066855044), or **Pedro Fernándes** (☎ 2944/468290).

### MOUNTAIN BIKING

The entire Nahuel Huapi National Park is ripe for mountain-biking. Whether you're a beginner or an expert, you can find a trail to suit your ability. One favorite descent is from the parking lot at the Cerro Catedral ski area to Lago Gutiérrez. Bike rental, helmet, guide, and transport for this half-day excursion costs about $45. Local tour agencies can arrange guided tours by the hour or day and even international excursions to Chile. Rental agencies provide maps and suggestions and sometimes recommend guides. All of the following rent bikes and organize tours: **Adventure World** (⊠ Quaglia 262, Local 23, ☎ FAX 2944/427264); **La Bolsa del Deporte** (⊠ Elfleín 385, ☎ FAX 2944/423529); **Cumbres Patagonia** (⊠ Villegas 222, ☎ 2944/4232646, FAX 2944/431835); and **Dirty Bikes** (⊠ Vice Almirante O'Conner 681, ☎ FAX 2944/425616).

### PARAGLIDING

*Parapente* (paragliding) gives you the exciting opportunity to soar with the condors through mountains and out over lakes, lagoons, and valleys. Cerro Otto and Cerro Catedral (both accessible by ski lifts) are popular launch sites. For equipment and guide information, contact **Tacul Viajes** (⊠ San Martín 430, ☎ 2944/426321).

### WHITE-WATER RAFTING

With all the interconnected lakes and rivers in the national park, there's something for everyone—from your basic family float down the swift-flowing, scenic Río Limay, to a wild and exciting ride down Río Manso (Class II), which takes you 16 km (10 mi) in three hours. If you're really adventurous, you can take the Manso all the way to Chile (Class IV) through spectacular scenery. Some tour companies organize a trip down the Manso with return by horseback and a cookout at a ranch. Both **Adventure World** and **Cumbres Patagonia** (☞ Mountain Biking, *above*) arrange white-water rafting trips along the Manso. Cumbres Patagonia also arranges trips along the Río Limay, as does **Bariloche Rafting** (✉ Mitre 86, Room 5, ☎ 2944/424854).

## Shopping

Along Bariloche's main street, Calle B. Mitre, and its cross streets, from Quaglia to Rolando, and in *gallerías* (shopping malls), you can find shops selling sportswear and sports equipment, leather goods, hand-knit sweaters, and local food items such as homemade jams. **Ahumadero Familia Weiss** (✉ Palacios 401) makes pâtés, cheeses, smoked fish, and wild game. You can't avoid the chocolate shops on both sides of Mitre: **Abuela Goya** (✉ Mitre 258), **Del Turista** (✉ Mitre 239), and **Fenoglio** (✉ Mitre and Rolando). Items for the discerning equestrian or modern gaucho, such as fine leather belts, jackets, boots, and bags; silver buckles; jewelry; and accessories are artfully displayed at **Cardon** (✉ Villegas 216), with shops at Hotel Llao Llao and the Catedral Ski Area. **Cerámica Bariloche** (✉ Mitre 112) has been creating fine ceramics inspired by colorful local flora and fauna for 50 years (you can also visit the factory at ✉ Anasagasti 1515). **Cultura Libros** (✉ Elfleín 78) has books in English and coffee-table books with superb photos of the Lake District and Patagonia, as well as local guidebooks. **El Establo** (✉ Mitre 22) sells gaucho knives, maté gourds, leather clothing, and silver accessories. **Fitzroy** (✉ Mitre 18), just past the Civic Center, has a good selection of ponchos, Mapuche blankets, and gaucho articles.

# Villa La Angostura

❷ *81 km (50 mi) northwest of Bariloche (a 5-hr drive on R237 around the east end of Lago Nahuel Huapi); also accessible by boat from Bariloche; 90 km (56 mi) southwest of San Martín de los Andes.*

Thoughtful planning and strict adherence to building codes have made this lakeside hamlet an attractive escape from the bustle of Bariloche. Log art abounds—over doorways, under window sills, on signposts, and on fences—there's even a large hand-carved wooden telephone on the street in front of the telephone office. Most shops and restaurants are on Avenida Arrayanes (R231), in a commercial area called El Cruce (the Crossing—the name refers to the crossing of R231, which goes from Bariloche to the Chilean border, with the road to the port, Nahuel Huapi and the Seven Lakes Road, R234, to San Martín de los Andes). The **Secretariat de Turismo y Cultura** (✉ Av. Siete Lagos 93, ☎ 2944/494121) is at the southern end of Avenida Arrayanes. At the intersection of Avenida Arrayanes and Avenida Siete Lagos, turn left onto Bv. Nahuel Huapi to get to the original **Villa Angostura** (Narrow Village) on the lake—so named because it occupies a narrow isthmus connecting it to the Península Quetrihué.

The **Parque Nacional los Arrayanes** (12 km [7½ mi] along a trail from the Península Quetrihué) is the only forest of arrayanes in the world. These native trees absorb so much water through their thin skins that they force all other vegetation around them to die, leaving a barren forest of peeling cinnamon-color trunks. You can make this excursion by boat from Bariloche (☞ Bariloche, *above*) or from the pier at Bahía Brava in Villa La Angostura; or walk (three hours) or ride a bike or horse across the isthmus. A nice combination is to go by boat and return by bicycle (it's all downhill that way).

The ski area at **Cerro Bayo** (Bay-colored Mountain), named for the dirt-brown color) is 9 km (5½ mi) northeast of town. Multiple lifts carry skiers and snowboarders in winter and mountain bikers in summer to the top (☞ Outdoor Activities and Sports, *below*). The reward for hiking, biking, or skiing the long trail around the mountain is a panoramic view of Lago Nahuel Huapi.

## Dining and Lodging

$$ ✕ **Grünswald.** It's easy to mistake this dark-timbered log house with a sod roof for Hansel and Gretel's. The interior is a riot of hearts and flowers and Swiss canton shields. It's a good spot for tea as well as for a lunch, or for a dinner of fondue and Patagonian lamb served on rough-hewn tables. ⊠ *Av. Arrayanes 6431 (R231),* ☎ *2944/495123. AE, DC, MC, V. Closed Mar.–June.*

$ ✕ **La Casita de la Oma.** This tea house between the main street and the bay serves homemade soups, sandwiches, salads, and a tempting array of cakes, pies, and scones. Jars of jams line the shelves. ⊠ *Inacayal 303,* ☎ *2544/494602. MC, V. Closed May.*

$ ✕ **El Esquiador.** A *tenedor libre* (salad and appetizer bar) makes for easy pickings at this simple family-run café and restaurant one block from Avenida Arrayanes. Photos of local skiers and fishing conquests add local color. ⊠ *Las Retamas 142,* ☎ *2944/49433, AE, DC, MC, V.*

$$$$ ✕🏨 **Las Balsas.** A short drive down a secluded road brings you to this Relais & Chateaux hotel right at the edge of Lago Nahuel Huapi. A country manor house painted bright blue shows off the white-wicker furniture on the lovely veranda. It has a raft for swimming to and a pier from which lake excursions come and go. Natural wood, wicker, and photographs of the area decorate the walls; straw hats for guests hang on pegs, and blue umbrellas wait by the door—they've thought of everything. All rooms have views into pine woods or out to the lake, but each looks different, from wildflower prints on pine walls to plump white comforters and handwoven rugs. An award-winning Mapuche chef prepares fresh trout and game accompanied by vegetables and spices grown in the hotel's organic garden; dinner reservations are advised if you're not a guest. ⊠ *Bahía las Balsas, 8407,* ☎ 𝔽𝔸𝕏 *2944/494308. 13 rooms, 2 suites. Restaurant, bar, pool, beach, dock, baby-sitting, laundry service, meeting room. CP. AE, DC, MC, V.*

$$$ 🏨 **Hostería la Posada.** A broad green lawn slopes to a long, low white building on a hillside above Lago Nahuel Huapi. From inside you can look out onto the terraced lawns and gardens, the pool, the beach, and across the emerald-color bay to distant mountains. There's no reason to close the flowery curtains in the bay windows of the simple wood-trimmed rooms, as there's nothing out there but forest, lake, and stars. The hotel has its own pier and boats and bicycles for rent. ⊠ *Box 12, 8407,* ☎ 𝔽𝔸𝕏 *2944/494450 or 2944/494368. 18 rooms, 2 suites. Restaurant, bar, pool, beach, bicycles, boating, dock. CP. AE, DC, MC, V.*

$$ 🏨 **Pichi Rincón.** Just outside town in a grove of trees is the Little Corner, a modern two-story inn. Enter through the two columns of gray river rock to the light and airy interior. There's a comfortable sitting area with a fireplace, couches, and chairs. From the spacious lawn is access to a path into the woods. ⊠ *Off Av. Quetrihué, 8407 (3 km [2 mi] south of town on R231; just before Correntoso, turn left on Av. Quetrihué),* ☎ 𝔽𝔸𝕏 *2944/494186. 19 rooms. Dining room. MC, V.*

$$ 🏨 **Los Tres Mosqueteros.** At the port on the lake, 3 km (2 mi) from Villa La Angostura, this complex of whitewashed cabins and simple rooms has its own pier, a yard in front, and a beach in back. A bike

rental shop is next door. The French owners also run Cerro Bayo, the ski area. ✉ *Nahuel Huapi 84, [the road by the pier], 8407,* ☎ FAX *2944/ 494217. 9 apartments in 3 cabins. CP. AE, MC, V.*

## Outdoor Activities and Sports

### FISHING

The bays and inlets of Lago Nahuel Huapi are ideal for trolling and spinning, and the mouth of the Río Correntoso (Correntoso River) is famous for its brown trout. For information on guides, fly-fishing school, and equipment rental or purchase, contact the **Banana Fly Shop** (✉ Av. Arrayanes 282, ☎ 2944/94634).

### HORSEBACK RIDING

Most trails used for hiking and mountain biking are also used for horse-back riding (☞ Mountain Biking, *below*). Horses are available from **El Establo** (✉ R231, Km 3, ☎ 068301084).

### MOUNTAIN BIKING

In and around the village are more bike rental shops than gas stations. You can easily ride from the village to such places as Laguna Verde, near the port, or off the Seven Lakes Road to Mirador Belvedere and on to the waterfalls at Inacayal. The tourist office (☞ *above*) has a brochure, *Paseos y Excursiones,* with maps, distances, and descriptions (in Spanish) of mountain biking, hiking, and horseback-riding trails throughout the area. Maps, information, and rentals are available in Las Cruces at **Free Bikes** (✉ Las Retamas 159, ☎ 2944/495047); and **IAN Bikes** (✉ at Topa Topa 102 and Las Fucsias, ☎ 2944/495005). Bikes are also available at the base of Cerro Bayo, at **Mountain Bike Cerro Bayo** (☎ 2944/494189), or down by the pier next to **Los Tres Mosqueteros** (☞ Dining and Lodging, *above*).

### SKIING

**Cerro Bayo** (for information call ☎ FAX 2944/494189), 9 km (5½ mi) from El Cruce via R66, is good for skiing from July through September. Get a ride on four surface lifts and two chairlifts, one of which takes you to the top (5,000 ft), where a 5-km (3-mi) panoramic trail wends its way around the mountain. Runs are easy to intermediate, with shorter, more direct descents from the top down to a midstation, where a café, El Tronador, serves local jams on waffles among other fare. El Refugio Chalten, at the base of the mountain, serves goulash, lamb stew, snacks, and beverages. Children five and under and adults 65 and older ski free, and all-day rates are less than most ski areas. Rental equipment and lessons are available at the base facility.

## Shopping

Shops along Avenida Arrayanes carry products that are typical of the area—chocolate, smoked meats, dried mushrooms, handicrafts, sporting goods, and knitwear. Delicious homemade jams (*dulces caseros*) are found in nearly every shop, at roadside stands, and at tea houses.

*En Route*    Just beyond El Cruce, R231 crosses the world's shortest river (according to locals), between lakes Nahuel Huapi and Correntoso. Eleven km (7 mi) from El Cruce, R65 goes north past Lago Espejo, then turns east for 22 km (14 mi), when it meets R234 to San Martín de los Andes. Continuing on R65, the road (sometimes closed in winter) goes over a pass and descends through a forest of coíhues to Lago Traful.

# Villa Traful

❸    *60 km (37 mi) north of Villa La Angostura on R231 and R65; 100 km (60 mi) northwest of Bariloche on R234 and R65.*

Small log houses built by early settlers peek through the cypress forest along the way to Villa Traful, a village on Lago Traful. The town consists of about 50 log cabins, horse corrals, two fishing lodges, shops for picnic and fishing supplies, and a park ranger's office. The town is much less touristed than other neighboring villages, and it has some fine ranches and private fishing lodges tucked back in the surrounding mountains. By day swimmers play on sandy beaches on the lake, a lone water skier cuts the still blue water, and divers go under to explore the mysteries of a submerged forest. Night brings silence, thousands of stars, and the glow of a lakeside campfire. The **Oficina Municipal de Turismo** (⊠ across from municipal pier, ☎ 2944/479020) can assist you with planning excursions.

Only 3 km (2 mi) from the village is **Arroyo Blanco,** a waterfall that cascades 66 ft over the rocks into a natural pool. You can walk or ride (a bike or a horse) through 1,000-year-old forests above and beyond the village to this waterfall as well as to nearby caves and mountain lookouts.

### Dining and Lodging

Besides the resorts outside town, you can also pitch a tent and throw your sleeping bag down just about anywhere along the lake. Good campsites, however, with restrooms, benches, tables, and fire pits are plentiful along the southern shore of the lake. For exquisite beauty, look for Puerto Arrayanes at the western end of the lake. A large campground near the village is **Camping Vulcanche** (☎ 2944/479061).

$$ × **Ñancu-Lahuen.** The carved-wood sign says TEAHOUSE, but it's much more. Sandwiches, omelets, homemade ice cream, tarts, pies, and anything chocolate are served from noon until sundown, when salmon, trout, and steak dinners are served in an adjacent log house with a hand-hewn thatched roof and a floor of trunk rounds. ⊠ *Right in town,* ☎ FAX *2944/49017. AE, DC, MC, V.*

$$$ ×▦ **Rincón del Pescador.** This long, low white lodge in the middle of an ample lawn attracts fishing and outdoor enthusiasts. Enjoy dinners of fresh-caught fish and afternoon tea. Fishing guides are available. ⊠ *On R65, 9006,* ☎ FAX *2944/479028. Restaurant, fishing.*

$$ ×▦ **Hostería Villa Traful.** Across the road from the lake is this large log house, which is more than 50 years old. You can stay in the house or rent one of the cabins. Afternoon tea is served as are dinners of trout and salmon; breakfast is included. The hotel can arrange fishing guides and lake tours. ⊠ *Across the road from the lake, 9006,* ☎ FAX *2944/ 479005. Rooms and cabins. Restaurant, fishing, mountain bikes.*

### Outdoor Activities and Sports

The most popular activity around here is fishing and the area is especially famous for its land-locked salmon. Trout fishing in Lago Traful and the Laguna Las Mellizas (the Twins Lagoon), 5 km (3 mi) from town on the northern coast, is also exceptional. The fishing season runs November 15–April 15.

## Junín de los Andes

❹ *41 km (25 mi) northeast of San Martín on paved R234; 219 km (136 mi) north of Bariloche on paved R237 and R234.*

The quickest route between Bariloche and San Martín de los Andes (☞ *below*) is the paved road that runs through this typical Andean agricultural town, where gauchos can be seen riding along the road, with dogs trotting faithfully behind. Once a fort in a region inhabited by the Mapuche, Junín de los Andes became a town during the last phase (1882–1883) of the Conquista del Desierto, making it the oldest town in Neuquén Province. For centuries the valley where the town lies was the trading route of the Mapuche between mountainous Chile and the fertile plains of Argentina. Today Mapuche descendents sell their handicrafts and weavings in local shops and fairs, and the town's main attraction is its proximity to the Río Chimehuín (Chimehuín River), lakes Huechulafquen and Paimún, the Parque Nacional Lanín, and Lanín Volcano (☞ San Martín de los Andes, *below*).

### Dining and Lodging

The **Dirección Municipal de Turismo** (✉ Coronel Suárez y Padre Milannensio, ☎ FAX 2972/491160) has information on lodging, dining, campgrounds, and nearby fishing lodges, which are open November–April. The best restaurants are in hotels, except for Ruca Hueney (☎ 2972/49113) on Suárez and P. Milanesia.

## San Martín de los Andes

**❺** *260 km (161 mi) northwest of Bariloche on R237 via Junín de los Andes; 160 km (99 mi) northwest of Bariloche on R237 over the Cordóba Pass (69 km [42 mi] of it is paved); 184 km (114 mi) northwest of Villa La Angostura on R234 (the Seven Lakes Road, only 66 km [41 mi] of which is paved).*

San Martín de los Andes lies nestled in a natural basin surrounded by mountains, lakes, and dense forests. It's the major tourist center in the Neuquén Province and is the jumping-off point for exploring the Parque Nacional Lanín. San Martín was founded in 1898 by General Rudecindo Roca, who moved the original fort, built in 1883, from Vega de Maipú, 3 km (2 mi) north, to the present city. With a population of 20,000, San Martín is much like Bariloche was 30 years ago but without the traffic or nonstop commercial activities. Wide, flat streets run from the town pier on the eastern shore of Lago Lacar, along tree-lined sidewalks to a four-block commercial area of shops and chalets. Private gardens, stores, and the town square all display a colorful profusion of native flowers and roses from spring until the snow first falls in June. Early Patagonian houses built with local timber and covered with corrugated metal to keep the wind out are still visible around the Plaza San Martín. The Obeid Family mansion (✉ at Roca and Coronel Perez) one house of note, was built in 1903 with materials brought from Valdivia (Chile). For information on tours, lodging, and other services, contact the **Dirección Municipal de Turismo** (✉ Av. San Martín y Rosas 790, ☎ 2972/427347); it's open summer, daily 7AM–10 PM, and winter, daily 8 AM–9 PM.

The **Museo Pobladores** (Pioneer Museum), next to the tourist office, gives you an idea of what life was like for the early pioneers. ✉ J. M. de Rosas 700. ☉ *Weekdays 8–2 and 4–8.*

The **Parque Nacional Lanín** (Lanín National Park), north of Nahuel Huapi National Park, runs north–south for 150 km (93 mi) along the Chilean border and covers 3,920 square km (1,508 square mi) of mountain lakes, rivers, and ancient forests. Giant *Araucaria araucana* (monkey puzzle trees) grow in thick groves in the northern region of the park. These spiky conifers, also known as *pehuén* to the Mapuche and Pehuenche, were so named because the Pehuenche depended on the nutritious *piñon* nuts as a dietary staple during long winters. Towering over the entire park and visible from every direction, **Volcán Lanín** (Lanín Volcano), rises 12,378 ft in solitary snow-clad splendor—an imposing white cone on the western horizon.

The **Intendencia de Parques Nacionales** (National Park Office) building is a classic example of Andean-alpine architecture in the style of

Bustillos, who did the Civic Center in Bariloche and the Llao Llao Hotel. Here you can get maps and information on all the parks and trails in the region. ⌧ *E. Frey 749*, ☎ *2972/427233*. ☉ *Weekdays 7–2.*

From town you can walk, mountain-bike, or drive to the **Mirador de las Bandurrias** (Overlook of the Bandurrias), a distance of 7 km (4 mi), where you get a magnificent view of the town and the lake. To walk there, take Calle San Martín to the lake, turn right, cross the bridge over Puahullo Creek, and then head uphill on a path around the mountain.

The rather long (200 km [124 mi] round-trip) but infinitely rewarding excursion to **Lago Huechulafquen** can be made from San Martín de los Andes. From town take R234 north to Junín de los Andes (☞ above), and then take the dirt road (R61) to **Lago Paimún** (Paimún Lake). As you speed across the open range following the **Río Chimehuín** toward the lake, Lanín Volcano beckons in the distance. This is serious fishing country. Numerous beaches and campsites along the lakeshore make good picnic stops.

## Dining and Lodging

Restaurants in San Martín are mostly parrillas, pizzerias, and simple cafés. There's more variety in lodging—cabins, campgrounds, estancias, hotels, inns, and B&Bs. Rates are highest in July, when Argentine families take ski vacations, lower in August, and even lower December–March, which is summer and perhaps the best time to visit. There are campgrounds at the **Playa Catrite** (⌧ R234, Km 4, ☎ 2972/428820); and at **Quila Quina** (⌧ R108, Km 12, ☎ 2972/426919).

$$$ ✕ **La Fondue Betty.** At this restaurant in an unassuming little house, Betty Casanova specializes in wild game, fondue, and trout. This long-standing favorite is especially popular with skiers. ⌧ *Villegas 568*, ☎ *2972/428792. DC, MC, V.*

$$ ✕ **Picis.** Probably the best parrilla in the area, this spot serves all the usual grilled beef and chicken dishes as well as fish from local lakes and streams. ⌧ *Villegas 598*, ☎ *272/427601. AE, DC, MC, V.*

$$ ✕ **La Tasca.** It may look Swiss or Tyrolean on the outside, but inside the food is pure Patagonia. Regional dishes, such as homemade pastas, smoked meats, and local cheese, are served. ⌧ *M. Moreno 866*, ☎ *2972/428663. AE, DC, MC, V.*

$$$$ ✕🏠 **Hostería Paimún.** Upon arriving at this unique fishing lodge on
★ the shore of Lago Paimún, you look through a screen of lupine to a low-lying building surrounded by rosebushes and shaded by an immense *Araucaria araucana* (monkey puzzle tree). Inside, tables in the sitting room/bar are littered with fishing magazines, and photos of famous catches hang on the log walls. Rooms are small, cozy, and lodgelike (everything is made of wood). Besides fishing and exploring the wild shorelines by boat, you can rent horses or go hiking to a waterfall or up to the volcano. Meals (three are included in the price) and tea in the sunny dining room are simple affairs of home-cooked meat dishes, vegetables from the garden, and fresh (just caught) fish (perhaps your own catch). ⌧ *R61, Camino al Lago Paimún*, ☎ *2972/491201,* FAX *2972/491211. Dining room, fishing, horseback riding. FAP. Closed May–Sept.*

$$$$ 🏠 **Hotel la Cheminée.** Two blocks from the main street is this homey inn with pink-floral chintz and lace curtains. Plump pillows, fresh flowers, and fireplaces in some rooms enhance the coziness. A sumptuous breakfast and an afternoon tea of homemade breads, scones, cakes, cookies, and jams are served. ⌧ *M. Moreno and Gral. Roca, 8370*, ☎ FAX *272/427617. 15 rooms, 3 suites. Bar, café, heated pool, sauna, parking. CP. AE, DC, MC, V.*

$$$   🏨 **Hotel Caupolican.** In season, flowers cascade from the wooden window boxes of this hotel on the main street. In the reception/sitting area, locally carved wooden chairs are covered with sheepskin. The simple, comfortable rooms, done in deep red and blue tones, are off the street in back and thus quiet. A game room with a fireplace, two meeting rooms, and the reception/bar area face the street. ✉ *Av. San Martín 969, 8370,* ☎ *272/427658,* FAX *272/427090. 42 rooms, 2 suites. Bar, café, sauna, meeting rooms, parking. CP. AE.*

$$   🏨 **Hosteria Anay.** *Anay* means "friendship," and that's what you feel when you step inside this small, white stucco-and-log house. You can gather around the fireplace in the cozy sitting area or in the bright, cheerful breakfast room, where breakfast and tea are served. Rooms have simple whitewashed walls, beamed ceilings, and carpeted floors—no frills, except for the flowery print curtains. ✉ *Capitán Drury 841, 8370,* ☎ FAX *2972/427514. 13 rooms. Breakfast room, baby-sitting, laundry service, parking. CP. No credit cards.*

## Outdoor Activities and Sports

### BEACHES

**Playa Catrite,** 4 km (2½ mi) from San Martín on R234, on the south side of Lago Láar, is a sandy beach with a campground, a store with picnic items, and a café. **Playa Quila Quina,** 18 km (11 mi) from San Martín, is reached by turning off R234 2 km (1 mi) before the road to Catrite and then going on to R108. On the 12-km (7-mi) drive to the lake you'll pass through Mapuche farm lands and forests. The soft, sandy beach and clear water attract day users and campers as well as residents with vacation homes. Both beaches can be reached by boat.

### FISHING

During the fishing season (November 15–April 15), local guides can take you to their favorite spots on Lácar, Lolog, Villarino, and Falkner lakes and on the Caleufu, Quiquihue, and Hermoso rivers. Permits are available at the **provincial tourist office** (✉ Rosas and Av. San Martín, ☎ 2972/42347) or any licensed fishing stores along Avenida San Martín. Most stores can suggest guides. Or contact **Tiempo Patagónico** (✉ Av. San Martín 950, ☎ 2972/427113, FAX 2972/427113).

### HORSEBACK RIDING

Horseback riding is a great way to see country that you can't get to by car or boat. Organized rides with a guide last two hours, all day, or even a week (camping trips). Some rides include a ranch visit and even an asado. At **Abuelo Enrique** (✉ Callejón Ginsgins V. Maipú, ☎ 972/426465), beginners and experts can rent horses for guided rides. Take Av. Dr. Koessler (R234) toward Zapala, turn left at the polo field and head toward Lago Lolog, and then take a right past the military barracks to Callejón Ginsgins V. Maipú. **Tiempo Patagónico** (☞ Fishing, *above*) also organizes tours by horseback.

### MOUNTAIN BIKING

San Martín is flat, but everything goes up from it. Dirt and paved roads and trails lead through forests to lakes, waterfalls, and higher mountain valleys. In town you can rent at **HG Rodados** (✉ Av. San Martín 1061, ☎ 2972/427345) and **MTB Rodados Ecologicos** (✉ Villegas 970, ☎ 2972/429229). **Chapelco Ski Area** (☞ *below*) has bike rentals, good trails, and mountain-biking lessons.

### SKIING

The ski station and summer resort of **Cerro Chapelco** (San Martín information office: ✉ San Martín and Elordi, ☎ FAX 2972/427845; Buenos Aires office: Tucumán 540, ☎ 11/4332–73650, FAX 11/4322–0605) is 15 km (9 mi) above town along a dirt road. Ideal for families and beginning and intermediate skiers, it has modern facilities and all kinds of lifts. Visible from the top (6,534 ft) are almost all the runs plus Lanín Volcano. The summer Adventure Center has mountain biking for experts and classes for beginners, horseback rides, hiking, paragliding, a swimming pool, an alpine slide, and numerous children's activities.

WHITE-WATER RAFTING

A day-long white-water rafting trip to Chile on the Río Hua Hum can be arranged by **Tiempo Patagónico** (☞ Fishing, *above*).

## Shopping

San Martín has shops selling chocolate, regional handicrafts, and fishing and camping gear. Next to the tourist office, **Artesanías Neuquinas** (✉ J. M. de Rosas 790, ☎ 2972/428396) carries Mapuche ceramics, weavings, and wood carvings; authenticity is guaranteed.

# El Bolsón

**❻** *131 km (80 mi) south of Bariloche via R258.*

El Bolsón (The Purse), in southwestern Río Negro Province, is so named because it's surrounded by high mountain ranges. This narrow mountain valley was first settled by Chilean farmers in the late 1800s and remained isolated until the 1930s, when a long, winding dirt road (often closed in winter) connected it to Bariloche. Even the new highway seems to hold many of Bariloche's tourists at bay, leaving this valley and its nearby parks less traveled. Basque, Spanish, Polish, Arab, English, Swiss, and American hippies, attracted by the bucolic setting, a pleasing (for Patagonia) microclimate, and the productive land have all contributed to the cultural identity of the community. The first in Argentina to declare their town a non-nuclear zone, the forward-thinking populace has preserved the purity of its air, water, and land, creating an environment where the country's largest crops of hops thrive along with strawberries, raspberries, gooseberries, boysenberries, cherries, and plums. Canneries export large quantities of jams and syrups.

Traveling here from Bariloche, the road passes Lago Gutiérrez and enters the Pacific watershed. Lago Mascardi flows into Lago Guillelmo just before the road climbs gently to a pass. At Km 66 from Bariloche, the first glimpse of the valley below comes as a surprise after the mountain and lake scenery around Bariloche. As you drive onward, looking south and west, the frozen glaciers of Perito Moreno and Hielo Azul (both more than 6,500 ft) appear on the horizon as you descend into the valley. If you need a break as you're driving, stop in the town of El Foyel, 88 km (54½ mi) south of Bariloche and 43 km (27 mi) north of El Bolsón at Tacuifi, a little log house with a red-metal roof where lunch, tea, and snacks are available all day. Note that in El Bolsón and all of Chubut Province to the south, gas costs 50% less than elsewhere. The **Secretaría de Turismo** (✉ Plaza Pagano and Av. San Martín, ☎ 2944/492604) has all kinds of information about activities and excursions in the area.

The **Cascada de la Virgen** (Waterfall of the Virgin), 18 km (11 mi) north of El Bolsón (and 113 km [70 mi] south of Bariloche), is visible from the road. Nearby is a campground (for information call ☎ 2944/492610) with cabins, grills, and a restaurant.

The **Cascada Mallín Ahogado** (Drowned Meadow Waterfall), 10 km (6 mi) north of El Bolsón on R258, makes a grand picnic spot. The ski area at **Cerro Perito Moreno** (☞ Outdoor Activities and Sports, *below*) is farther up the gravel road from the Cascada Mallín Ahogado.

A 39-km (24-mi) round-trip (mostly on dirt roads) to the **Parque Nacional Lago Puelo** (Puelo Lake National Park) is a good all-day excursion from El Bolsón. Information is available at the **park ranger's office** (☎ 2944/499183) and picnic and fishing supplies can be purchaseed at the roadside store, 4 km (2½ mi) before you reach the sandy beach at **Lago Puelo (Puelo Lake)**. Three launches, maintained by the Argentine navy, wait at the dock to take you on one- to three-hour excursions on the lake. The trip to **El Turbio**, an ancient settlement at the southern end of the lake on the Chilean border, is the longest. On the return trip, a branch to the right leads down a narrow arm to a river connecting Lago Puelo with **Lago Epuyén** (Epuyén Lake). A cruise along the shore of the Brazo Occidental (Western Arm) ends at the Chilean border, where the lake runs into a river bound for the Pacific Ocean. A return by horse or foot adds variety. One side of the lake is inaccessible, as the Valdivian rain forest grows on steep rocky slopes right down into the water. Campgrounds are at the park entrance by the ranger's station, in a bay on the Brazo Occidental and at the Turbio and Epuyén river outlets.

## Dining and Lodging

Many campgrounds line the banks of the Río Los Repollos (Los Repollos River), just before you enter town. More hotels and restaurants are being renovated or constructed along the rose bush–lined main street. Note that many restaurants give a 5%–10% discount if you pay cash. Lodges in the surrounding mountains open for fishing season from November through April (summer) and close in winter. Information about hotels and campgrounds is available at the **Secretaría de Turismo** (☞ *above*).

$$ ✕ **Arcimboldo.** Right on the main street, this basic family restaurant has good pastas and steak and fries. In summer you can dine on the front patio. ⊠ *Av. San Martín 27,* ☎ *2944/492137. DC, MC, V.*

$$ ✕ **Don Diego.** At this spot you can get beef, trout, and fresh vegetables cooked any way you like. Also available are fresh pasta, pizzas, and a good fixed-price menu. ⊠ *Av. San Martín, next to Hotel Amancay,* ☎ *2944/492222. AE, MC, V.*

$$ ✕ **El Viejo Maitén.** Locals and tourists fill this popular spot next to the bus station. The specialties are roast pork, trout, and a mixed grill of lamb, pork, beef, sausages, tripe, and kidneys cooked right at your table ⊠ *Roca 359,* ☎ *2944/492412. DC, MC, V. Closed Mon.*

$$ ▥ **Cordillera.** The large lobby, big dining room, and open garden with a big lawn make this a good choice for families and groups. Rooms are simple, with cheerful prints on beds and windows; many have balconies. ⊠ *Av. San Martín 3210, 8430,* ☎ *2944/492235. 64 rooms. Restaurant, café. MC, V.*

$ ▥ **Hotel Amancay.** A rose garden and masses of flowers greet you outside the door of this pretty white-stucco hotel with a tile roof three blocks from the center of town. The warm, casual lobby, with its tile floors and dark wood furniture with bright cushions, looks Spanish. Adjoining is the excellent Don Diego restaurant (☞ *above*). ⊠ *Av. San Martín 3217, 8430,* ☎ *2944/492222,* FAX *2944/492374. 15 rooms. Restaurant, café, parking. AE, DC, MC, V.*

## Outdoor Activities and Sports

Fishing is exciting and rewarding all over this area; local tour operators can arrange fishing trips. Hiking, rock climbing, mountain biking, and horseback riding (sometimes all combined in one trip) lead you to waterfalls, high mountain huts, deep canyons, and hidden lakes; trips can last a day or a week. Often you'll encounter a little tea house or an asado at the end of your day. The tourist office (☞ *above*) can supply maps and directions or direct you to local outfitters. Both cross-country and downhill skiing are winter options at Cerro Perito Moreno, 22 km (13½ mi) north of town on R258. At the base is a refuge belonging to the Club Andino Piltriqitrón, as well as a restaurant and a rental shop. Three lifts service the trails for downhill skiing (3,000 ft–10,000 ft). To help you arrange your trip, *see* Tour Operators and Travel Agencies *in* Patagonia A to Z, *below.*

## Shopping

Every Saturday (and Tuesday and Thursday in summer) a local market is held on the main plaza. Stands display ceramics, leather goods, wood handicrafts, objects made from bone and clay, and agricultural products. Music and folk dancing enliven the scene.

*En Route*     If you're heading south from El Bolsón to the Parque Nacional los Alerces (☞ Esquel, *below*) on R71, just north of Cholila, take the turnoff for the Casa de Piedra teahouse. Before crossing the Arroyo Blanco (White Creek), you pass a gate and a path to the small log house where Butch Cassidy, Etta Place, and the Sundance Kid lived and ranched between 1901 and 1905. Here they kept a low profile until they attended a Governor's Ball in Esquel. The governor so enjoyed their company, he asked to pose with them in a photograph that later appeared in a Buenos Aires newspaper, where Pinkerton detectives, after years of searching, saw the pictures. After robbing the bank in Río Gallegos, they fled to Bolivia, where they were finally shot.

# Esquel

❼ *193 km (120 mi) southeast of El Bolsón via R258 and R71; 285 km (177 mi) south of Bariloche via R259 and R40.*

In 1906 Esquel was a small village where sheep ranchers, many of them Welsh, came to buy supplies and visit with seldom-seen neighbors from the huge ranches, which still operate on the endless steppes east of the Andes. In 1910 the British owners of the approximately 980,000-square-mi Leleque Ranch (now owned by Benetton) brought merino sheep from Australia to the region, establishing this breed forever in Patagonia. Although Esquel is now the most important town in northern Chubut Province and the gateway to unlimited recreational activities, it retains much of its frontier-town feeling. Along the roads outside town, for instance, you often see gauchos herding their sheep or "riding the fences" (checking to see that they aren't broken) of their vast ranches. For information about activities in the area, go to the **tourist office** (✉ Alvear and Sarmiento, ☎ FAX 2945/451927).

In 1905, when Patagonia was still a territory, a railway project was conceived to facilitate the transport of wool, cattle, and lumber from the far-flung villages of El Maitén, Trevelín, and Esquel to Ingeniero Jacobacci, where it would link up with the national railway and the rest of the country. German and American companies worked with the Argentine railroad from 1922 until 1945, when the last section was completed. Today, **El Trocha Angosta,** known as La Trochita or the Great Patagonia Express, puffs clouds of steam and toots its horn as its 1922 Belgian Baidwin and German Henschell engines pull the vintage wooden cars 402 km (249 mi) between Esquel and Ingeniero Jacobacci (194 km [120 mi] east of Bariloche). Inside the cars, passengers gather around the wood stoves to add wood, sip maté, and discuss the merits of this rolling relic. The entire one-way trip takes 14 hours, averaging an agonizing 30 kph (19 mph) around hundreds of curves and through mountains and valleys and across wide-open plateaus. Add to that six scheduled stops, nine whistle stops, unscheduled stops for repairs or passengers, and stops every 45 km (28 mi) to refill the water tanks. The tourist-oriented trip from Esquel to the first stop at **Nahuel Pan** (20 km [12 mi] round-trip), which runs Monday–Wednesday and weekends, is one option. Another is the train to **El Maitén** (165 km [102 mi] one way) on Tuesday and Saturday; this leg is primarily filled with train buffs. You can return more quickly by bus from both of these trips. Note that schedules are subject to drastic changes and cancellations. For current schedules and reservations, contact the Estación Esquel (Esquel Train Station; ⊠ Brown and Roggero, ☎ 2945/495190) or the tourist office (☞ *above*).

The **Parque Nacional los Alerces** (Los Alerces National Park) is 50 km (30 mi) west of Esquel on R258 (and 151 km [94 mi] south of El Bolsón). The park is named for its 2,000- to 3,000-year-old *alerces* (*Fitzroya cupressoides*), which are similar to redwoods. Covering 2,630 square km (1,012 square mi) of lakes, rivers, and forests, most of the park is accessible only by boats and trails. Wild, rugged, and achingly beautiful, this park is mostly untouched. The dirt road (the only one) into the park takes you to **Villa Futalaufquen** (Futalaufquen Village), on the lake of the same name. The park has only four small hotels (☞ Dining and Lodging, *below*) and a few cabins; most people camp or come from Esquel or El Bolsón for the day. For camping and fishing information, visit the **park information office** (☎ 2945/471020) in Villa Futalaufquen. Fishing in the 14 lakes and connecting rivers is legendary; licenses are available in the village at two small shops, Kiosco and Almacén, at the fishing lodges, and the campgrounds at Bahía Rosales.

A boat excursion from Puerto Limonao, the principal port on Lago Futalaufquen, takes you to **Lago Menendez** (Menendez Lake). Along the way you see the glaciers of the **Cerro Torrecillos**, and you stop at a grove of giant alerces. Tour operators in Esquel (☞ Tour Operators and Travel Agencies *in* Patagonia A to Z, *below*) and lodges in the park can arrange lake excursions.

En route to the **Cañadon de Los Bandidos** (Bandit Canyon) on the way to La Hoya Ski Area (☞ Outdoor Activities and Sports, *below*), you see evidence of gold mines and prospectors' broken dreams abandoned on the rocky mountainside. Butch Cassidy and the Sundance Kid mined for gold here and bought a ranch in the nearby Cholila Valley (103 km [64 mi] north toward El Bolsón on R258; ☞ *above*).

## Dining and Lodging

Besides downtown hotels and nearby hosterías, there are many inns, cabins, and campgrounds in the surrounding countryside. For information contact the tourist office (☞ *above*).

$$$ ✕ **Cassis.** Formerly chef at such swank resorts as Las Leñas and Punte
★ del Este, Mariana Müsller has returned with her husband to her hometown and given it one of the best restaurants in Argentina. Trout carpaccio, pork rolled around nuts and vegetables, and chicken with almonds and rhubarb are just a few examples of "*la nueva cocina Patagónica*" (new Patagonian cooking). Dessert is an extravaganza of such dishes as red berries served with homemade ice cream and meringue. ⊠ *Sarmiento 120*, ☎ *2945/450576. AE, DC, MC, V.*

$$ ✕ **De Maria Parrilla.** This is a typical grill with better-than-average dishes. The owner, also a ski instructor, studied cooking in Buenos Aires and returned home to open this restaurant. The local lamb, pork, and game dishes are all prepared with a personal touch. ⊠ *Rivadavía 1024*, ☎ *2945/454247. AE, DC, MC, V.*

$ ✕ **Vestry.** The two great-granddaughters of founder William Freeman carry on the tradition begun in 1904 at the best Welsh tea house in the area. ⊠ *Rivadavía 1065. No credit cards.*

$$$$ ✕🏠 **Hostería Futalaufquen.** From this stone-and-log lodge on top of a hill, you can look through tall alamo trees across miles of blue lake. Six-foot-tall lupines almost hide the little log cabins across the lawn. Inside, worn leather, wicker furnishings, and wooden beams evoke a rustic elegance, reminiscent of an English hunting lodge. The rooms are simple—whitewashed walls, wood trim, a chair, and a bed—all you need because the place to be is outside. Mountain-bike rentals, fishing, hiking, horseback riding, waterskiing, and lake excursions can all be arranged. ✉ *Villa Futalaufquen, 9200 (4 km [2 mi] from the village),* 🕿 FAX *2945/471008. 12 rooms, 3 cabins. Restaurant, bar, horseback riding, waterskiing, bicycles, fishing. CP. AE, DC, MC, V.*

$$$ 🏠 **Hostería Cumbres Blancas.** What a delight to find this clean, modern hotel with large rooms and all the comforts of home right in Esquel. After a day of skiing, hiking, or exploring the nearby parks, a little luxury is much appreciated. The top-floor suite has a mountain view, balcony, fireplace, and dining room. All the other rooms are big, carpeted, and exude a feel of unexpected luxury as you look beyond the ample lawn to windswept plains and lonely mountains. ✉ *Av. Ameghino 1683, 9200,* 🕿 *2945/455100,* FAX *2945/455400. 19 rooms, 1 suite. Restaurant, bar, game room, room service, sauna, playground, parking. CP. AE, DC, MC, V.*

$$ ✕🏠 **Hostería Cume Hué.** There are two ways to get to this inn known as the "Place of Peace" from Esquel (70 km [43 mi] away): After entering the park bear right on the dirt road (R71) along the eastern shore of the lake for 27 km (17 mi); from El Bolsón R71 follows the shore of Lago Rivadavia, Laguna Verde, and the Río Arraynes to Lago Futalaufquen. Owner Camilo Braese was born here in his family's stucco-and-wood inn overlooking the lake. Having hiked and fished the area since he was a boy, Braese is much sought after as a guide. Breakfast, lunch, and tea are served in the homey living room, and dinner is eaten in the *quincho* (a room with a walk-in fireplace for asados); in the evening, music and wine accompany chorizos, homemade bread, and salad. Rooms are comfortable though basic, with small beds and lots of blankets; the ones in front have a lake view; some share a bath. There's no telephone and no electricity, except by generator at night. Behind and below the inn, good campsites are scattered along the river; sign up at the inn for a site; you can use the hotel's facilities. Lake excursions and an English-speaking fishing guide can be arranged. ✉ *Off R71 on Lago Futalaufquen (70 km [43½ mi] from Esquel),* 🕿 *2945/453693,* FAX *no fax. 10 rooms. FAP. No credit cards. Closed May–Oct.*

$$ 🏠 **Hostería los Tulipanes.** On a quiet side street in Esquel but close enough to the center of town is this family-run *residenciál* (pension) where the owners make you feel like a guest in their home. There's a small sitting room with a fireplace and dining rooms. Guest rooms are small but neat. ✉ *Av. Fontana 365, 9200,* 🕿 *2945/452748,* FAX *no fax. 7 rooms, 1 apartment. No credit cards.*

$ 🏠 **Hotel Sol del Sur.** This large brick building right in downtown Esquel was a casino until 1987, when the top floor was converted to a large dining area and a meeting room and guest rooms were added on the floors in between. The building is still old and austere, as are the rooms. The convenience of having an adjoining tour agency and ski retail/rental shop makes up for the plain furnishings. ✉ *9 de Julio y Sarmiento, 9200,* 🕿 *2945/452189,* FAX *2945/452427. 50 rooms and 2 5-person apartments. Restaurant, bar. CP. AE, DC, MC, V.*

## Outdoor Activities and Sports

**FISHING**

Fishing fanatics from the world over come to battle with the stubborn brown trout in the Río Grande or catch and release the wily rainbow in the rivers of the Los Alerces National Park and the Río Futaleufú (Futaleufú River), near Chile. Guide information and permits are available in Esquel at the **Dirección de Pesca Continental** (✉ Alte Brown and 9 de Julio, ☎ 2945/451226). Also *see* Tour Operators and Travel Agencies *in* Patagonia A to Z, *below,* for information about fishing tours.

SKIING

Only 13 km (8 mi) from Esquel and generally blessed with the longest ski season (July–mid-November) and more snow than anywhere else in the country, **La Hoya** is a popular ski resort for its reasonable prices and uncrowded slopes. Three chairlifts and two surface lifts take you up 39,500 ft. From here runs are long (some 13,200 ft) and all above the tree line. With 2,220 acres of skiable terrain, $20 for an all-day ticket is hard to beat. The company that handles lift ticket sales and information is **CAM La Hoya** (☎ 2945/454946); the tourist office (☞ *above*) is also a resource.

WHITE-WATER RAFTING

For organized white-water rafting trips to the Río Corcovado (Corcovado River), near the Chilean border, contact **Outworker** (✉ 9 de Julio 1080, ☎ 2945/450516); or **Travesis** (✉ Rivadavía 1650, ☎ FAX 2945/454690).

## Shopping

At **Casa los Vascos** (✉ 25 de Mayo and 9 de Julio) you can outfit yourself in gaucho attire: black hat, scarf pulled through leather knot, *bombachas* (baggy, pleated pants, gathered at the ankle), and boots. **Braese** (✉ 9 de Julio 1540) has the best selection of jams, cakes, chocolates, and smoked meats. Local dried flowers, hand-knit sweaters, and handicrafts are for sale at **Ramos Generales** (✉ 25 de Mayo 528).

# Trevelín

**❽** *25 km (15½ mi) south of Esquel on R259.*

The Welsh came to Trevelín in 1888, when 30 men were sent out to explore the region. Their ancestors, beginning in 1865, set sail across the Atlantic to seek a better life and to escape the economic, religious, and social oppression in their homeland. Expecting to find the Promised Land, they instead found a windswept empty expanse with little or no arable land—nothing like the fertile green valleys they had left behind. Undaunted, these hardy pioneers settled in the Chubut Valley. As the population grew while land for farming grew scarce, they looked westward toward the Andes. They found their *cwn hyfryd* ("beautiful valley" in Welsh) between the present towns of Esquel and Corcovado. Fifty families settled in the area, building their town around a flour mill—*Trevelín* in Welsh means "mill town." Today the town is still a pleasant and quiet place.

The **tourist office** (✉ Plaza Coronel Fontana, ☎ 2945/480120) has information on the history of the region and can arrange an interview with descendants of the first settlers. Hardworking, honest, faithful, and as proud to be Argentine as they are of their own traditions, many descendents of those first families still live here.

Now a regional museum, the four-story brick mill, **El Molino Viejo,** houses agricultural tools, photos, a Welsh bible, and artifacts from everyday life during the early settlement years. ✉ *25 de Mayo,* ☎ *2945/480145.* ☺ *Dec.–Mar., daily 11–8:30; Apr.–Nov., Wed. 10–4 and Thurs.–Sun. 2–8.*

## Dining and Lodging

**$** ✕ **Casa de Te Nain Maggie.** *Nain* (grandma) Maggie (1878–1981) handed down the old family recipes to her granddaughter who, with her daughter, continues to make the same fruit tarts, cakes, breads, and scones with current or gooseberry jam that are just a few of the confections you'll find in this typical Welsh tea house. ⊠ *Perito Moreno 179,* ☎ *2945/480232. No credit cards. No lunch.*

**$** ✕ **Küsimey Ruca.** The name of this restaurant means "beautiful house" in Mapuche. Look for the log tower across from the tourist office. With 36 kinds of pizzas and nine kinds of empanadas created by owner-chef Hugo Molares, it's easy to eat well. Molares's fine photographs decorate the walls under the imposing log ceiling. ⊠ *28 de Julio, at the plaza,* ☎ *2945/480088. DC, MC, V. Closed Mon.*

**$** 🏨 **Hotel Estefania.** This small, neat hotel is in the center of town, next door to an ice cream parlor/restaurant. Rooms are small but adequate, with utterly plain furnishings. ⊠ *P. Moreno, 9203,* ☎ *2945/480148,* FAX *2945/480445. 8 rooms. Restaurant. CP. DC, MC, V.*

**$** 🏨 **Residencial Trevelin.** This B&B on a quiet side street is no frills—it has clean, comfortable rooms and a good breakfast. ⊠ *San Martín and Jhon Evans, 9203,* ☎ *2945/480102. 5 rooms. CP. No credit cards.*

# Río Gallegos

**❾** *2,640 km (1,639 mi) south of Buenos Aires, 1,034 km (640 mi) south of Comodoro Rivadavía via R3, 319 km (197 mi) south of El Calafate, 596 km (370 mi) north Ushuaia, and 187 km (115 mi) east of Puerto Natales, Chile via R40.*

The administrative and commercial capital of Santa Cruz Province and perhaps the windiest town in the world (from September to November), Río Gallegos was founded in 1885 and served as a port for coal shipments from Río Túrbio (Túrbio River), on the Chilean border. Wool and sheepskins were its only other economic factors. Now, as the gateway city to southern Patagonia and the Parque Nacional los Glaciares (☞ *below*), tourism presents a new commodity. A desk at the airport has information on all the tourist attractions in the area, and the helpful attendants can make suggestions and hotel reservations. More information is available at the **tourist office** (⊠ Av. Roca 1551, ☎ 2966/42595) in town.

If you're into dinosaurs, the **Museo Regional Provincial Padre Manuel Jesus Molina** (Provincial Museum) has exhibits of reconstructed skeletons excavated at sites in Patagonia. Exhibits on biology, geology, history, paleontology, and Tehuelche ethnology are displayed in different sections of the museum. ⊠ Ramon y Cajal 51, ☎ 2966/423290. ☉ *Weekdays 10–5, weekends 11–7.*

## Dining and Lodging

**$$** ✕ **El Horreo.** A well-heeled clientele begins to fill this rather classy Spanish-looking restaurant around 10:30 PM. Complimentary Pisco sours (a delicious drink of Pisco brandy from Chile, whirred in a blender with lemon, egg whites, and sugar) begin your repast. It's hard to beat the local spring lamb, the steaks, or the mountain trout, crab, and seafood cooked a variety of ways—grilled or in homemade sauces. Service is slow but attentive. ⊠ *Av. Roca 862,* ☎ *2966/426462. MC, V.*

**$** ✕ **Trattoria Diaz.** This big, open, family-style café in the center of town has been serving grilled lamb and beef, homemade pastas, seafood, and fish since 1932. ⊠ *Av. Roca 1157,* ☎ *2966/420203. DC, MC, V.*

**$$$** 🏨 **Costa Río.** Flags flutter above the entrance to this modern white-brick "apt-hotel" (hotel with apartments, similar to small condominiums) on a quiet side street. For business travelers and families in

# Finally, a travel companion that doesn't snore on the plane or eat all your peanuts.

When traveling, your MCI WorldCom Card is the best way to keep in touch. Our operators speak your language, so they'll be able to connect you back home—no matter where your travels take you. Plus, your MCI WorldCom Card is easy to use, and even earns you frequent flyer miles every time you use it. When you add in our great rates, you get something even more valuable: peace-of-mind. So go ahead. Travel the world. MCI WorldCom just brought it a whole lot closer.

You can even sign up today at www.mci.com/worldphone or ask your operator to make a collect call to 1-410-314-2938.

## EASY TO CALL WORLDWIDE

1 **Just dial the WorldPhone access number of the country you're calling from.**
2 **Dial or give the operator your MCI WorldCom Card number.**
3 **Dial or give the number you're calling.**

| **Argentina** | |
|---|---|
| To call using Telefonica | 0-800-222-6249 |
| To call using Telecom | 0-800-555-1002 |
| **Brazil** | 000-8012 |
| **Mexico** | |
| Avantel | 01-800-021-8000 |
| Telmex ▲ | 001-800-674-7000 |
| Collect access in Spanish | 980-9-16-1000 |
| **Morocco** | 00-211-0012 |

For your complete WorldPhone calling guide, dial the WorldPhone access number for the country you're in and ask the operator for Customer Service. In the U.S. call 1-800-431-5402.

▲ When calling from public phones, use phones marked LADATEL.

## EARN FREQUENT FLYER MILES

**AmericanAirlines**
**AAdvantage**

**Continental Airlines**
*OnePass*

▲**Delta Air Lines**
**SkyMiles**

**MILEAGE PLUS.**
United Airlines

**U·S AIRWAYS**
DIVIDEND MILES

MCI WorldCom, its logo and the names of the products referred to herein are proprietary marks of MCI WorldCom, Inc. All airline names and logos are proprietary marks of the respective airlines. All airline program rules and conditions apply.

**MCI WORLDCOM**

# The first thing you need overseas is the one thing you forget to pack.

## FOREIGN CURRENCY DELIVERED OVERNIGHT

Chase Currency To Go® delivers foreign currency to your home by the next business day*

It's easy—before you travel, call 1-888-CHASE84 for delivery of any of 75 currencies

Delivery is free with orders of $500 or more

Competitive rates— without exchange fees

You don't have to be a Chase customer—you can pay by Visa® or MasterCard®

 CHASE

**THE RIGHT RELATIONSHIP IS EVERYTHING.®**

## 1•888•CHASE84
www.chase.com

town for an extended stay, having a room with chairs, sofas, and tables makes this slightly expensive hotel (for this region) worth the extra money. A kitchenette and eating area offer an alternative to going out for every meal. All rooms are carpeted and have comfortable, contemporary furnishings. ⊠ *Av. San Martín 673, 9400,* ☎ FAX *2966/ 423412. 54 apartments. Café, kitchenettes, minibars, laundry service and dry cleaning, baby-sitting, parking. AE, DC, MC, V.*

$$ ⊞ **Hotel Santa Cruz.** This hotel looks old, but rooms are comfortable though they have no frills. Intimate seating areas, plants, and a friendly staff make the lobby bar a pleasant retreat on a windy day. Avoid rooms on the Avenida Roca side, as they can be noisy. ⊠ *Av. Roca 701, 9400,* ☎ *2966/420601,* FAX *2966/420603. 53 rooms, 1 suite. Restaurant, sauna, parking. AE, DC, MC, V.*

### Shopping

**Monte Aymond** (⊠ Maipú 1320, ☎ 2966/438012) is a factory outlet for sheepskin and leather coats; the children's jackets, hats, and little sheepskin booties make great gifts. There's also a shop at the airport.

# El Calafate and the Parque Nacional los Glaciares

**⑩** *300 km (186 mi) north of Río Gallegos via R5, 253 km (157 mi) east of Río Turbio on Chilean border via R40, 213 km (123 mi) south of El Chaltén via R40.*

Founded in 1927 as a frontier town, El Calafate is the base for all excursions to the Parque Nacional los Glaciares (Glaciers National Park), which was created in 1937. Because of its location on the southern shore of Lago Argentino, the town enjoys a microclimate much milder than the rest of southern Patagonia. During the long summer days between December and February (when the sun sets around 10 PM), thousands of visitors come to see the glaciers and fill the hotels and restaurants (be sure to make reservations well in advance if you plan on coming during this time). October, November, and March are less crowded, less expensive periods to visit. March through May is the rainy season, followed by cold winter weather through September.

Getting here may seem like a daunting task, but the experience of seeing the glaciers more than compensates for any difficulties you may encounter. Every year airlines and tour companies are making it easier. From Río Gallegos, the trip can take up to six hours by land across desolate plains filled with more sheep than you can count in a lifetime of sleepless nights. But the journey is occasionally enlivened by the sight of *ñandú* (rheas), llamalike guanacos, silver-gray foxes, and fleet-footed hares the size of small deer. A shorter option is a 45-minute flight from Río Gallegos to El Calafate on Kaiken Airlines.

Avenida del Libertador San Martín (known as Libertador or San Martín) is the only paved street with sidewalks; along it are shops selling sportswear, camping and fishing equipment, souvenirs, and food (☞ Shopping, *below*). A staircase in the middle of San Martín ascends to Avenida Julio Roca, where you'll find the bus terminal and a very busy **tourist office** (⊠ Av. Julio Roca 1004, ☎ FAX 2902/491090) with a board listing available accommodations and campgrounds; you can also get brochures and maps and there's a multilingual staff that can help you plan excursions. It's open October–April, daily 7 AM–10 PM. You can also get information at the **national park office** (⊠ Av. Libertador 1302, ☎ 2902/491005), open weekdays 7–2.

Approximately 1.5 million acres of the *hielo Continental* (Continental ice cap), which spreads its icy mantle from the Pacific Ocean across Chile and the Andes into Argentina and covers an area of approximately

21,700 sq km (8,400 sq mi), are contained in the **Parque Nacional los Glaciares,** a UNESCO World Heritage Site. Extending along the Chilean border for 350 km (217 mi), the park is 40% covered with ice fields that branch off into 47 major glaciers that feed two lakes—the 15,000-year-old **Lago Argentino** (Argentine Lake, the largest body of water in Argentina) in the southern end of the park and **Lago Viedma** at the northern end near **Monte Fitzroy** (Fitzroy Mountain Range), which rises 11,138 ft. Visits to the park are usually by tour, though you could rent a car and go on your own. Travel agents in El Calafate or Buenos Aires can book tours if you haven't made arrangements from home. Plan on a minimum of three days to see the glaciers and enjoy the town—more if you plan to visit El Chaitén, Cueva de los Manos (Cave of the Hands), or any of the lakes.

★　One of the few glaciers in the world still growing after 3,000 years, the **Glaciar Moreno** (Moreno Glacier), 80 km (50 mi) and a two-hour drive on R11 from El Calafate, is generally the first destination in the national park. After entering the park, the road winds through hills, until suddenly the startling sight of the glacier, descending like a long white tongue for 80 km (50 mi) through distant mountains, abruptly ends in a translucent blue wall, 3 km (2 mi) wide and 165 ft high. A viewing area, wrapped around the point of the **Península de Magallanes,** allows you to wander back and forth, looking across the **Canal de los Tempanos** (Iceberg Channel). Here you listen and wait for the cracking sound—when tons of ice break away and fall with a thunderous crash into Lago Argentino—nature's number one ice show. Sometimes water even splashes onlookers across the channel! As the glacier creeps across this narrow channel and meets the land on the other side, an ice dam builds up between **Brazo Rico** on the left and the rest of the lake on the right. As the pressure on the dam increases, everyone waits for the day it will rupture. The last time was in 1986, when the whole thing collapsed in a thunderous finale that lasted hours and could be heard in El Calafate. Videos of this event are still sold locally.

**Glaciar Upsala** (Upsala Glacier), the largest glacier in South America, is 60 km (37 mi) long and 10 km (6 mi) wide. Accessible only by boat, daily cruises depart from **Puerto Banderas** (40 km west of El Calafate via R11) for a 2½-hour trip. Along the way, the boats dodge floating islands of ice as they maneuver as close as they dare to the wall of ice rising up from the aqua-green water of Lago Argentino. The seven glaciers that feed the lake deposit their debris into the runoff, causing the water to cloud with minerals ground to fine powder by the glacier's moraine (the accumulation of earth and stones left by the glacier). Condors and black-chested buzzard eagles build their nests in the rocky cliffs above the lake. When the boat stops for lunch at **Onelli Bay,** you can walk behind the restaurant into a wild landscape of small glaciers and milky rivers carrying chunks of ice from four glaciers into Lago Onelli (Onelli Lake).

For a jaw-dropping view of the Glaciar Viedma (Viedma Glacier) and **Monte Fitzroy,** drive north 213 km (123 mi) to the northern limits of the park. The Fitzroy range is visible for hundreds of miles (weather permitting); the Tehuelche called it *Chaltén* (Mountains of Smoke), which is the name of the village of **Chaltén,** a hiking mecca, at the base of the range. From this little town, founded in 1985, you can do many great hikes to lakes, glaciers, and stunning viewpoints. Expert mountaineers from every corner of the globe come to Chaltén to plan their ascent of **Cerro Torre,** that most illusive peak; sometimes they camp for weeks (even months) at Laguna Torre, waiting for the wind to die down, the rain to stop, or the clouds to disperse so that they can climb. For maps, hiking, and lodging information, contact the **Comisión de Fomento** (✉ Av. M. de M. Güemes 25, Chaltén, ☎ FAX 2962/493011) or the **national park office** (✉ before you cross the bridge to town over Río Fitzroy, ☎ FAX 2962/93004). Information is also available at the Río Gallegos and El Calafate tourist offices. To reach this area, drive east from El Calafate on R11 (toward Río Gallegos) until it meets R40 (35 km); then take R40 north (a dirt road), crossing Río Santa Cruz and Río La Leona, which connects with Lago Viedma. At this point, stop and look at **Viedma Glacier** descending into the lake, with the the Fitzroy massif towering on the horizon. The **Laguna del Desierto** (Lake of the Desert), a lovely lake surrounded by forest, is 37 km (23 mi) north of Chaltén on R23, a dirt road. The **Posada Lago del Desierto** (☎ FAX 2962/93010) has a restaurant and a few rooms in a small lodge as well as cabins without hot water or indoor bathrooms.

## Dining and Lodging

$$ ✕ **Michelangelo.** This 22-year-old establishment won a gold medal for "International Gastronomy" in 1995. The low wooden ceilings, white stucco walls, and wooden floors create a friendly dining-hall atmosphere. Sizzling steaks prepared with a variety of sauces, grilled chicken and fish, homemade pasta, and lamb cooked in tarragon and mustard sauce are some of the local specialties. ✉ *Moyano 1020,* ☎ *2902/491045. AE, DC, MC, V.*

$ ✕ **La Cocina.** This casual café on the main shopping street serves great food made with cheese—quiches, crepes, pastas, and hamburgers. Homemade ice cream and delicious cakes make a good snack any time of the day. ✉ *Av. Libertador 1245,* ☎ *2902/491758, MC.* ☾ *Closed 2–7:30.*

$$$$ ✕▥ **Hostería los Notros.** Forty km (25 mi) west of El Calafate on the road (R11) to the Moreno Glacier, this simple wooden structure clinging to the mountainside, looks across at the astounding mass of ice. Rooms are large, with simple country furnishings, gold and terra cotta walls, and the glacier framed in every window; some also have fireplaces. A short stroll through the garden, over a bridge spanning a canyon with a waterfall, connects rooms to the main lodge. Appetizers and wine are served in full view of sunset (or moonrise) over the glacier, followed by dinner featuring roast beef, venison, wild boar, and trout—all enhanced by fresh vegetables and homegrown herbs. An in-house coordinator arranges tours with multilingual guides and box lunches. ✉ *Reservations in Buenos Aires: Arenales 1457, 7th floor,* ☎ *11/48143934 in Buenos Aires, 2902/491437 in El Calafate,* FAX *11/48157645 in Buenos Aires, 2902/491816 in El Calafate. Restaurant, bar, room service, travel services, airport shuttle. 20 rooms. AE, DC, MC, V. Closed June–Aug.*

$$$$ ✕▥ **Hotel Kau-yatun.** A short drive from town, this former ranch house at the foot of the mountains exemplifies traditional Patagonian hospitality. The large living room, with picture windows looking out on a spacious lawn, is pleasantly cluttered with books, games, and magazines. Comfortable furniture, a well-stocked bar, and an open fireplace encourage mingling. Guest rooms vary in size, shape, and decor, but mostly follow the casual ranch theme, with flowery curtains and simple furnishings. Country cuisine—meat, pasta, and vegetables—are served in the dining room, and more exotic fare—trout, venison, and wild boar—are available at *La Brida.* On weekends, in the *quincho* (combination kitchen/grill/dining room), steaks and *chorizos* (sausages) sizzle on a large open grill, while lamb or beef cooks gaucho style on an *asador* (a skewer stuck in the ground to cook meat over hot coals). Folk music and dancing provide entertainment. ✉ *Estancia 25 de*

*Mayo,* ☎ *2902/491059,* 🅵🅰🆇 *2902/491045. 45 rooms. Restaurant, bar, shops, town shuttle. AE, MC, V.*

$$$$  ✕🅷 **Posada los Alamos.** Surrounded by tall, leafy alamo trees and constructed of brick and dark *quebracho* (ironwood), this attractive country manor house is a model of tasteful luxury. The rich tones of wood, leather, and handwoven fabrics in the lobby, bar, and sitting areas; the plush comforters and chairs in every room; and a staff ready with helpful suggestions make this a top-notch hotel. Lovingly tended gardens surround the building and line a walkway through the woods to the shore of Lago Argentino. ✉ *Moyano 1355,* ☎ *2902/491144,* 🅵🅰🆇 *2902/ 491186. 140 rooms, 4 suites. Restaurant, 2 bars, tennis court, 3-hole golf course, shops, travel services. AE, MC, V. Closed June–Aug.*

$$$  🅷 **El Quijote.** Sun shining through picture windows onto polished slate floors and high beams gives this modern hotel, on a quiet side street in town, a light and airy feel. The carpeted rooms with plain white walls and wood furniture provide peaceful comfort. It's right next to to El Molino restaurant and a few blocks from the main street. ✉ *Gregores 1155, 9405,* ☎ *2902/491017,* 🅵🅰🆇 *2902/491103. 80 rooms. Bar, café, travel services. AE, DC, MC, V.*

$$$  🅷 **Michelangelo.** This very reasonably priced hotel is two blocks from the town center and next to the restaurant of the same name (☞ *above*). Bright red and yellow native flowers line the front of the low log and stucco building with its distinctive A-frames over rooms, restaurant, and lobby. A fine collection of local photographs are displayed on the walls next to a sunken lobby, where a banquette covered with flower print cushions, and easy chairs surround the fireplace. Some rooms have beamed ceilings, and all are simply furnished with floral prints. ✉ *Moyano 1020, 9405,* ☎ *2902/491045,* 🅵🅰🆇 *2902/ 491058. 20 rooms. Restaurant, café. AE, MC, V. Closed June–Aug.*

## Outdoor Activities and Sports

### HIKING

You can hike anywhere in the national park. Short excursions to and along Lago Argentino, in the hills south and west of town, or to some rather overrated caves with restored paintings, 8 km (5 mi) east of town at Punta Gualichó, are the hiking options close to El Calafate. El Chaltén, the village in the northern part of the park, is a good base for many excellent hikes to lakes and glaciers and up mountain peaks like **Cerro Torre.** On the way to Lago del Desierto, the 5 km (3 mi) hike to **Chorillo del Salto** (Trickling Falls) is a good warm-up walk. The six-hour hike to the base camp for Cerro Torre at **Laguna Torre** guarantees (weather permitting) dramatic views of torres Standhart, Adelas, Grande, and Solo. The eight-hour hike to the base camp for **Monte Fitzroy** passes Laguna Capri, which mirrors the granite tower framed by ghostly lenga trees. Other hikes to and around Lago del Desierto are described in brochures and maps obtainable at the tourist office in El Chaltén (☞ *above*) or at the tourist office or national park office in El Calafate (☞ *above*).

### HORSEBACK RIDING

Short rides along Lago Argentino, day trips to the caves of Gualichó, and weeklong camping excursions into the mountains can all be arranged in El Calafate by **Gustavo Holzman** (✉ J.A. Roca 2035, ☎ 2902/ 491203) or through the tourist office and some hotels in El Calafate. In Chaltén, most of the hiking trails can also be done on horseback, as mountaineering equipment is transported to basecamps in this manner. Make arrangements through local outfitters and guides: **Rodolfo Guerra** (✉ northwest of town at the Fitzroy trailhead, ☎ 2962/ 493020); and **Thomás Fernandez** (✉ Lago del Desierto, ☎ 2962/ 493009). At some *estancias turisticas* (tourist ranches), you can go horseback riding and participate in ranch activities for a day. For a list of ranches and activities, go the tourist offices in El Calafate or Río Gallegos and ask for the book, *"Estancias Santa Cruz Patagonia."*

### ICE TREKKING

A two hour minitrek on the Moreno Glacier involves transfer from El Calafate to Brazo Rico by bus, and a short lake crossing to a dock and refugio, where you set off into the woods with a guide through the treacherous terrain. Crampons, provided, are attached over hiking boots and the climb commences. The entire outing lasts about five hours. Most hotels arrange minitreks as does **Hielo y Aventura** (⊠ Av. Libertador 935, ☎ FAX 2902/491053), which also organizes much longer, more difficult trips of 8 hours to a week to other glaciers.

### MOUNTAIN BIKING

Opportunities for mountain biking are numerous, including along the dirt roads and mountain paths that lead to the lakes, glaciers, and ranches. Rent bikes and get information at **Alquiler de Bicicletas** (⊠ Av. Libertador and Cmte. Espora, ☎ 2902/491496).

### MOUNTAIN CLIMBING

Lionel Terray and Guido Magnone were the first to climb **Monte Fitzroy** in 1952. Terray remarked, "Of all the ascents in my life, Fitzroy was the one that took me closest to my limits of strength and endurance. Climbing it is mortally dangerous; its ascent more complex, risky, and difficult than anything in the Alps." **Cerro Torre** is also known as one of the most difficult climbs in the world. The best time to climb is February through March. Climbing permits are available at the national park office (☞ *above*). Alberto del Castillo, owner of **E.V.T. Fitzroy Expeditions** (⊠ Av. San Martín, ☎ 2962/493017, FAX 2962/49136) has English-speaking guides and organizes both glacier and mountain treks.

## Shopping

Along Avenida Libertador are mainly sporting good shops and some crafts shops. **Mercado Artesanal** (⊠ Av. Libertador 1208) has books about the area and Patagonia memorabilia. The **Patagonia Supermercado** (⊠ Libertador and Perito Moreno) also has all kinds of Patagonia-related items.

# ATLANTIC PATAGONIA

From the immense whales at Península Valdés to the one million penguins of Punto Tomba, traveling through Atlantic Patagonia is like being on an adventure aboard Jacques Cousteau's boat. There are also giant dinosaur bones, fossils, and petrified forests, witnesses to an era extinct for millions of years but displaying a continuity with the current species on the beaches and in the waters. Experiencing Atlantic Patagonia means crossing vast, flat, windswept deserts to reach oases of isolated population centers. It means traveling to the "end of the world"—Tierra del Fuego, with its dramatic Alps-like scenery and picturesque lakes, streams, mountains, and wildlife. It means being embraced by independent, pioneering souls just beginning to understand the importance of tourism because the traditional industries—wool, livestock, fishing, and oil—are drying up.

The culture of Atlantic Patagonia, like other parts of the region, stems from a hybrid of the culture of immigrants, primarily from Europe, who came here in the 19th century, and the culture of the indigenous peoples, mainly the Mapuche. Its history is in large part the fascinating story of the Welsh who left Great Britain in 1865 for reasons of religious persecution and came to Patagonia to establish a colony of their own in Chubut Province. It's also a tale of rugged, pioneering Italians, Spanish, Croats, Germans, Lebanese, and Portuguese, among others, who staked a claim in inhospitable, uncharted territories upon invitation from the Argentine state beginning in the mid-19th century. Argentina, in an effort to thwart Chilean and European ambitions for the land and to quell the indigenous population, sought to settle the territory by actively courting European immigration, instituting customs and tax incentives, and even shipping hundreds of prisoners as colonizers. The settlers who came built water channels, ports, and chapels, while baking the breads and planting the crops of their homelands; today these cultural traditions remain.

The communities of the descendents of immigrants are still such an important force in Patagonia that they are called "VIQs," or "*venida y quedada*," which basically means "came and stayed" (as opposed to the "NICs," or "*nacida y creadad*," those born and raised here). The indigenous populations are long gone; they were wiped out by the four-year military campaign (1879–1883) led by General Roca and known as the Conquest of the Desert. To their credit, the Welsh didn't participate in the massacre of the native populations, though the campaign did open up the territory to further settlement and colonization.

## Ushuaia and the Tierra del Fuego

⑪ *230 km (143 mi) south of Río Grande, 596 km (370 mi) south of Río Gallegos, 914 km (567 mi) south of El Calafate, 3,580 km (2,212 mi) south of Buenos Aires.*

Ushuaia—which at 55 degrees latitude south is closer to the South Pole (2,480 mi) than to Argentina's northern border with Bolivia (2,540 mi)—is the capital and tourism base for Tierra del Fuego, an island at the southernmost tip of Argentina. Although its physical beauty is tough to match, Tierra del Fuego's historical allure is based more on its mythic past than on reality. The island was inhabited for 6,000 years by Yamana, Haush, Selk'nam, and Alakaluf Indians. But in the late 19th century, after vanquishing the Indians in northern Patagonia, the Argentine Republic was eager to populate Patagonia to bolster its territorial claims in the face of European and Chilean territorial ambitions. An Anglican mission had already been established in Ushuaia in 1871, and Argentina had seen Great Britain claim the Falklands, a natural Argentine territory. Thus, in 1902 Argentina moved to initiate an Ushuaian penal colony, establishing the permanent settlement of its most southern territories and, by implication, everything in between.

At first, only political prisoners were sent to Ushuaia. But later, fearful of losing Tierra del Fuego to its rivals, the Argentine state sent increased numbers of more dangerous criminals. When the prison closed in 1947, Ushuaia had a population of about 3,000, mainly former inmates and prison staff. Another population boom occurred after Argentina's 1978 industrial incentives law, which attracted electronics manufacturers like Philco and Grundig to Ushuaia. In recent years many of these television and home-appliance factories have shut down because they weren't able to compete in the global marketplace. But the children those boom times produced now roam Ushuaia's streets.

Today the Indians of Darwin's "missing link" theory are long gone—wiped out by disease and indifference brought by settlers—and the 45,000 residents of Ushuaia are hitching their star to tourism. Ushuaia feels a bit like a frontier boom town, with noisy, smelly, circa-1970s cars clogging the streets, and restaurants and hotels opening on once-empty lots. In the late '90s the local government completed an airport that has the capacity to handle direct flights from abroad and finished a deep-water pier that welcomes cruise ships stopping for provisions in Ushuaia on their way to the Antarctic. Unpaved portions of R3, the last stretch of the Panamerican Highway, which connects Alaska to Tierra del Fuego, are finally, albeit slowly, being paved.

The town of Ushuaia itself can be called picturesque at best. Parts of it resemble an oversize mining camp awaiting the next strike. Wooden shacks, precariously mounted on upright piers and ready for speedy displacement to a different site, look like entrants in a contest for most original log cabin. A chaotic and contradictory urban landscape includes a handful of luxury hotels amid some of the world's most unusual public housing projects—one monstrous, corrugated-tin development has a highway running right through it. Town planning has never been a strong point in Ushuaia; instead, irregular rows of homes sprout with the haphazardness of mushrooms in a moist field.

And yet, as you stand on the banks of the Canal del Beagle (Beagle Channel) near Ushuaia, as Captain Robert Fitzroy—the captain who was sent by the English government in 1832 to survey Patagonia, including Tierra del Fuego—must have done so long ago, the spirit of the farthest corner of the world takes hold. What stands out is the light: At sundown it casts the landscape in a subdued, sensual tone; everything feels closer, softer, more human in dimension despite the vastness of the setting. The snowcapped mountains of Chile reflect the illumination of the setting sun back onto a stream rolling into the channel, as nearby peaks echo their image—on a windless day—in the still waters.

Above the city, the last mountains of the Andean Cordillera rise, and just south and west of Ushuaia they finally vanish into the often stormy sea. Snow dots the peaks with white well into summer. Nature is the principal attraction here, with trekking, fishing, horseback riding, and sailing among the most rewarding activities, especially in the Parque Nacional Tierra del Fuego (Tierra del Fuego National Park). In winter, when most international tourists stay home to enjoy their own summer, the adventurous have the place to themselves for cross-country and downhill skiing, dog sledding, and snowmobiling across the powdery dunes. In an effort to attract more tourists in winter (presently summer is the busiest season), the government built a new ski resort, Cerro Castor, and began actively promoting winter sports.

The **tourist office** (✉ Av. San Martín 674, ☏ 2901/432000 or toll free 0800/3331476) is a good resource for information on the town's and Tierra del Fuego's attractions. It's open weekdays 8 AM–midnight and weekends and holidays 8 AM–11 PM. Several people on the cheerful staff speak English.

The **Antigua Casa Beben** (Old Beben House), built in 1913, is one of Ushuaia's original houses. It was initially a branch office of Banco Nacion, then a house owned by the Croatian Beben family, and was finally moved to its current location and restored in 1994. It's now a cultural center where art exhibitions are mounted. ✉ *Maipú and Pluschow.* ☏ *Free.*

Rainy days are a reality in Ushuaia, but two museums give you an avenue for urban exploration and a glimpse into Tierra del Fuego's fascinating past. Part of the original penal colony, the Presidio was built to house political prisoners, street orphans, and a variety of other social undesirables from the north. Today it houses the **Museo Marítimo** (Maritime Museum), within Ushuaia's naval base, with exhibits on the town's extinct indigenous population, Tierra del Fuego's navigational past, Antarctic explorations, and life and times in an Argentine penitentiary. You can enter cell blocks and read the fascinating stories of the prisoners who lived in them while gazing upon their eerily lifelike effigies. Well-presented tours, in English and Spanish, are conducted at 5 PM daily. ⊠ *Gobernador Paz and Yaganes,* ☎ *2901/437481.* ◨ *Admission.* ⊙ *Daily 10–3 and 5–8.*

At the **Museo del Fin del Mundo** (End of the World Museum), you can see a scarily large stuffed condor, among other native birds, indigenous items, maritime instruments, and such seafaring-related artifacts as an impressive mermaid figurehead taken from the bowsprit of a galleon. In addition, there are photographs and histories of El Presidio's original inmates, such as Simon Radowitzky, a Russian immigrant anarchist who received a life sentence for killing an Argentine police colonel. The museum also has the best existing library and bookstore devoted to Tierra del Fuego as well as a snack bar. ⊠ *Maipú 173 and Rivadavía,* ☎ *2901/421863.* ◨ *Admission.* ⊙ *Daily 10–3 and 5–8.*

The **Tren del Fin del Mundo** (Train of the End of the World) takes you to the Parque Nacional Tierra del Fuego (☞ *below*), 12 km (7½ mi) away. The train ride is a simulation of the trip on which El Presidio prisoners were taken into the forest to chop wood. Though it's pricey at $30, the 2¼-hour ride is a pleasant trip in which a good deal of Ushuaia history is detailed. Try to get on the more quaint and realistic steam train rather than the smelly diesel one. ⊠ *Train departs from a stop near the entrance to the national park,* ☎ *2901/431600,* FAX *2901/437696.*

For a trip along the **Canal del Beagle,** contact tour operators in Ushuaia (☞ Tour Operators and Travel Agencies *in* Patagonia A to Z, *below*). On the tour you can get a startling close-up view of all kinds of sea mammals and birds on **Sea Lion's Island** and near **Les Eclaireurs Lighthouse.**

One good excursion in the area is to picturesque **Lago Escondido** (Hidden Lake) and Lago Fagnano (Fagnano Lake). On the way you pass through deciduous beech-wood forest and past beavers' dams, peat bogs, and glaciers. The lakes have campsites and fishing and are good spots for a picnic or a hike. A rougher, more unconventional tour of the lake area goes to **Monte Olivia** (Mt. Olivia), the tallest mountain along the Canal del Beagle, rising 4,455 ft above sea level. You also pass the **Five Brothers Mountains** and go through the **Garibaldi Pass,** which begins at the Rancho Hambre, climbs into the mountain range, and ends with a spectacular view of Lago Escondido. From here you continue on to Lago Fagnano through picturesque countryside past sawmills and lumberyards. To do this trip in a four-wheel-drive vehicle with an excellent bilingual guide, contact Canal Fun & Nature; for a more conventional tour in a comfortable bus with a bilingual guide and lunch at Valle de los Huskies, try All Patagonia (☞ Tour Operators and Travel Agencies *in* Patagonia A to Z, *below*).

**Estancia Harberton** (Harberton Ranch) consists of 50,000 acres of coastal marshland and wooded hillsides. The property was a late-19th-century gift from the Argentine government to Reverend Thomas Bridges, officially considered the Father of Tierra del Fuego. Today the ranch is managed by Bridges's great-grandson, Thomas Goodall, and his American wife, Natalie, a scientist who has cooperated with the National Geographic Society on conservation projects; most people visit as part of organized tours (☞ Patagonia A to Z, *below*), but you'll be welcome if you stray by yourself onto the couple's spread. They serve up a solid and tasty tea in their home, the oldest building on the island. For safety reasons, exploration of the ranch can only be done through a guide. Lodging is not available, but you can arrange to dine at the ranch by calling ahead for a reservation (☎ 2901/422742). Most tours reach the estancia by boat, offering a rare opportunity to explore the **Isla Martillo** penguin colony, in addition to a sea lion refuge on **Isla de los Lobos** (Island of the Wolves) along the way.

If you've never butted heads with a glacier, the mountain range just above Ushuaia is home to the **Glaciar Martial.** Named after Frenchman Luis F. Martial, a 19th-century scientist who wandered this way aboard the warship *Romanche* to observe the passing of planet Venus, the glacier is reached via a panoramic ski lift. Take the Camino al Glaciar (Glacier Road) 7 km (4 mi) out of town until you reach the Glaciar Martial ski lodge (☞ Outdoor Activities and Sports, *below*). A 15-minute skyline ride brings you to the beginning of a 1-km (½-mi) trail that winds its way over lichen and shale straight up into the mountain. After a strenuous 30-minute hike, you can cool your heels in one of the many gurgling, icy rivulets that cascade down water-worn shale shoots, or enjoy a picnic while you wait for an early sunset. When the sun drops behind the glacier's jagged crown of peaks, brilliant rays beam over the mountain's crest, spilling a halo of gold-flecked light on the glacier, valley, and channel below. Moments like these are why this land is so magical. However, temperatures drop dramatically after sunset, so come prepared with warm clothing.

The pristine **Parque Nacional Tierra del Fuego,** 12 km (7½ mi) west of Ushuaia, offers you a chance to wander through peat bogs, stumble upon hidden lakes, trek through native *canelo,* lenga, and wild cherry forests, and experience the wonders of Tierra del Fuego's rich flora and fauna. Visits to the park, tucked up against the Chilean border, are commonly arranged through tour companies. Trips range from bus tours to horseback riding to more adventurous excursions, such as canoe trips across Lapataia Bay. Another way to get to the park is to take the Tren del Fin del Mundo (☞ *above*). Or you could take a bus run by **Transporte Kaupen** (☎ 2901/434015) or several other private bus companies (☞ Getting Around by Bus *in* Patagonia A to Z, *below*); the Transporte Kaupen buses travel through the park, making several stops within it; so you can get off the bus, explore the park, and then wait for the next bus to come by or trek to the next stop. Yet one more option is to drive to the park on R3 (take it until it ends and you see the last sign on the Panamerican Highway, which starts at Alaska and ends here). Trail and camping information is available at the park entrance ranger station or at the tourist office (☞ *above*). A nice excursion in the park is by boat from lovely **Ensenada Bay** to **Isla Redonda** (Redonda Island), a wildlife refuge where you can follow a footpath to the western side and see a wonderful view of the Canal del Beagle. While on Isla Redonda, you can send a postcard and get your passport stamped at the world's southernmost post office. Tours are run by **Isla Verde,** represented by Yishka Turismo y Aventuras (☞ Tour Operators and Travel Agencies *in* Patagonia A to Z, *below*).

## Dining and Lodging
Dotting the perimeter of the park are five free campgrounds, none of which has much more than a spot to pitch a tent and a fire pit. Call the **park office** (☎ 0800/231476) or consult the ranger station at the park entrance for more information. **Camping Lago Roca** (✉ Lago Roca, 20 km [12 mi] from Ushuaia, ☎ no phone), also within the park, charges $5 a day and has bathrooms, hot showers, and a small market. Of all the campgrounds in the area, **Camping Río Pipo** is the closest to Ushuaia (it's 10 km [6 mi] away).

**$$** ✕ **Café Ideal.** This casual local hangout has become popular by serving good, light food and providing solid service. Try the homemade pastas, the local trout, or the pizza. Its also open all day long, unlike most Argentine restaurants. And come weekend summer evenings, the place gets funky with live music performed by local groups. ⊠ *Av. San Martín 393,* ☎ *2901/437860. AE, DC, MC, V.*

**$$** ✕ **La Estancia.** For lamb and other typical Patagonian meats, try this restaurant in the center of town. Sit by the glass wall to see the chef artfully coordinate the flames, the cooking, and the cutting of tender pieces of lamb and parrilla-styled meats. Don't be bashful about requesting more lamb if you're still hungry; there's no extra charge. ⊠ *Av. San Martín 253,* ☎ *2901/421241. AE, DC, MC, V.*

**$$** ✕ **Hotel Albatros.** Your best bet is the weekday, fixed-price menu, which includes appetizer, main course, and dessert; at other times it's much more expensive and it always costs more if you order à la carte. The food is reasonably well prepared, including such dishes as steak, ravioli with red sauce, baked chicken with french fries, and hake with mashed potatoes. Best of all, tables overlook the Canal del Beagle with the Isla Navarino in the distance. The restaurant only gets crowded when tour groups are staying at the hotel (☞ *below*). ⊠ *Av. Maipú 505,* ☎ *2901/430003. AE, DC, MC, V.*

**$$$$** 🏨 **Hotel y Resort Las Hayas.** In the wooded foothills of the Andes, this massive hotel serves as a lordly lookout over the town and the channel below. Not a single detail has been left out in the meticulous design and decor, making it one of Argentina's finest hotels. From the Portuguese linen to the oak furnishings and fabric-padded walls, luxurious amenities abound. A suspended glass bridge connects the hotel to a complete health spa, where you can bathe in a heated indoor pool or rekindle your hiker's spirit with aromatherapy or a lymphatic massage. The hotel is outside the town center, but frequent shuttle buses can take you there. ⊠ *Camino Luis Martial, Km 3, 9410,* ☎ *2901/ 430710, 1/4499808 in Buenos Aires,* FAX *2901/430710 or 2901/430719. 102 rooms, 8 suites. Restaurant, bar, coffee shop, in-room safes, indoor pool, hot tub, massage, sauna, golf privileges, health club, squash, laundry service, convention center, 2 meeting rooms, travel services. AE, DC, MC, V.*

**$$$** 🏨 **Hotel Albatros.** The best part about this hotel is the view from the restaurant and bar; aside from that, services are solid but unremarkable. Originally constructed of lenga, a local hardwood, the Albatros burned to the ground in 1982 and was rebuilt of wood but without the same charm. Rooms are clean and standard issue: reasonably comfortable beds, plain wood furniture, and TVs; some have views of the dock and channel. ⊠ *Av. Maipú 505, 9410,* ☎ *2901/430003,* FAX *2901/430666. 73 rooms, 4 suites. Restaurant, bar, café, minibars, laundry service, travel services. AE, DC, MC, V.*

**$$$** 🏨 **Hotel del Glaciar.** Just above the Hotel Las Hayas (☞ *above*), in the Martial Mountains, this spot is owned by the same people as the Albatros (☞ *above*). It's comparable in price and amenities, though it feels fresher and more up to date. However, you should be aware that a sizable native forest was razed to make room for the Glaciar and its carefully maintained lawns. Hourly shuttle buses take you to the town center. ⊠ *Camino Glaciar Martial, Km 3½, 9410,* ☎ *2901/430640,* FAX *2901/430636. 73 rooms, 4 suites. Restaurant, bar, café, minibars, laundry service, tourist services. AE, DC, MC, V.*

**$$** 🏨 **Hostería Petrel.** At this small, isolated lodge along the shores of Lago Escondido, fishing, hiking, and relaxing are the order of the day; the hotel can arrange for guides. Its oversize restaurant serves tour buses stopping on their way to visit Escondido and Fagnano lakes. Ask for one of the upstairs rooms if you'd like a pleasant balcony over the lake, or for a lower room if you'd prefer a large Jacuzzi but no balcony. ✉ *R3, Km 3,086, 9410 (50 km [31 mi] from Ushuaia),* ☎ ℻ *2901/433569. 9 rooms. Restaurant, snack bar. No credit cards.*

**$$** 🏨 **La Posada.** This family-run hotel in the middle of town is a decent, lower-cost alternative to the bigger, more costly hotels. It has rooms facing the mountains on one side and the bay and mountains on the other; all have telephones and TVs. The owners are eager to please: With their own minivan, they'll pick you up at the airport and take you on excursions to nearby sites (for an additional fee). ✉ *Av. San Martín 1299, 9410,* ☎ ℻ *2901/454901 or 2901/433330. 17 rooms. Breakfast room. AE, MC, V (10% discount if you pay with cash).*

## Nightlife and the Arts

Ushuaia has a lively nightlife scene in summer, with its casino, discos, and cozy cafés where you can have coffee or a beer. The biggest and most popular disco is **Kronos. Barney's** is a more intimate dance club. Try your luck at the only full-fledged casino, **Casino Club S.A.** (✉ Av. San Martín 638), where roulette minimums are $2 and blackjack table minimums are $5; there's a $3 entrance fee in the evening. **El Pueblo** (✉ Av. Gobernador Campo and Av. Rivadavia) has free, live folk music Wednesday–Sunday. For more traditional Argentine entertainment, see the Tango show at the **Hotel del Glaciar** (☞ Dining and Lodging, *above*) on weekends; shows start at 9 PM.

## Outdoor Activities and Sports

### FISHING

The rivers of Tierra del Fuego are home to a variety of trophy-size freshwater trout—including browns, rainbows, and brooks—making the area a sportsperson's paradise. Both fly and spin casting are available. The fishing season runs November 1–March 31; fees range from $10 a day to $40 for a month. Fishing expeditions are organized by the following companies: **Asociación de Caza y Pesca** (✉ Av. Maipú 822, ☎ 2901/423168); **Rumbo Sur** (✉ Av. San Martín 342, ☎ 2901/422441 or 2901/223085); and **Yishka Viajes y Aventuras** (✉ Gobernador Godoy 115, Piso 1, Oficína 7, ☎ 2901/431230).

### MOUNTAIN BIKING

A mountain bike is an excellent alternative in Ushuaia, giving you the freedom to roam without the exorbitant fee of a rental car. Good mountain bikes normally cost about $5 an hour and $15–$20 for a full day. They can be rented at **D. T. T. Cycles Sport** (✉ Av. San Martín 1258); **Firpo** (✉ Sebastian El Cano 176, ☎ 2901/24424) or **Seven Deportes** (✉ Av. San Martín and Av. 9 de Julio). Guided bicycle tours (including rides through the national park), for about $50 a day, are organized by **All Patagonia** (✉ Fadul 26, ☎ 2901/430725); **Licatur** (✉ Av. San Martín 880, ☎ 2901/22337, ℻ 2901/23551); **Pretour** (✉ Tekenika 119, ☎ 2901/422150); and **Rumbo Sur** (✉ Av. San Martín 342, ☎ 2901/422441).

### SKIING

Ushuaia is the cross-country skiing center of South America, thanks to enthusiastic Club Andino members who took to the sport in the 1980s and made the forested hills of a high valley about 20 minutes from town a favorite destination for skiers. From Hostería Tierra Mayor and Hostería Los Cotorras, two places where you can ride in dog-pulled sleds, rent skis, go cross-country skiing, get lessons, and eat; contact the tourist office (☞ *above*) for more information. **Glaciar Martial Ski Lodge** (☎ 2901/2433712), open year-round, Tuesday–Sunday 10–7, functions as a cross-country ski center from June to October. Skis can also be rented in town, as can snowmobiles.

For downhill skiers, Club Andino has bulldozed a couple of short, flat runs directly above Ushuaia. A new downhill ski area, **Cerro Castor,** 26 km (16 mi) northeast of Ushuaia on R3, was scheduled to have opened by 1999, with 15 trails and four high-speed ski lifts. Supposedly it will rival the slopes of Bariloche but with a longer ski season. More than half the trails are at an intermediate level, a fifth are for beginners, and another few are for experts. You can rent skis and snowboards and take ski lessons here.

### Shopping

**El Globo** (⊠ Av. San Martín 991) carries an array of antique Patagonian furnishings and paintings, maritime antiquities, wood carvings, and picture frames. For typical regional chocolates, head for **Laguna Negra** (⊠ Av. San Martín 513); or **Ushuaia** (⊠ Av. San Martín 785). **Mascaras Aborigenes Fueguinas** (⊠ Piedrabuena 25) has masks made from local lenga—copies of aboriginal masks used for the *hain* ceremony, in which adolescents were initiated into sexual life. **Temaukel** (⊠ Av. San Martín 1051) sells some interesting local artisan goods. **Tierra de Humos** (⊠ Av. San Martín 861) and **Ushuaia Drugstore** (⊠ Av. San Martín 638) have leather and ceramic handicrafts, postcards, T-shirts, and Patagonian jams.

## Puerto Deseado

**⑫** *742 km (460 mi) north of Río Gallegos, 292 km (181 mi) south of Comodoro Rivadavía, 140 km (87 mi) southeast of Fitzroy.*

Puerto Deseado, once a Spanish whaling station, is now a quiet town of about 9,000 slowly being discovered as a jumping-off point for nearby nature reserves. It's also the base for a number of ships that fish the waters of the western South Atlantic. The center of activity in town is around the intersection of avenidas Almirante Brown and San Martín. Of note here is the **Vagon Histórico,** a circa 1898 cargo and passenger train that once carried wool and lead from Chilean mines in Pico Truncado and Las Heras, 280 km (174 mi) northwest. Of interrest, too, is the **Museo del la Corbeta Swift** (Corbeta Swift Museum), which houses relics of a ship that sunk off the coast of Puerto Deseado in 1776 and was discovered in 1984.

The **Reserva Natural Ría Deseado,** a nature reserve near Puerto Deseado, is the only place in the world where five species of cormorants coexist. You can also see spectacular black-and-white Commerson's dolphins and sharks. Magellan penguins, another big attraction, are present from October through April on the islands of Quiroga, Punta del Paso, de los Pájaros, and Chaffers, all part of the reserve.

### Dining and Lodging

**$** ⊡ **Los Alcantilados.** The views from here are great, but the hotel has seen better days. ⊠ *Pueyrredon and Espana, 9050,* ☎ 𝔽𝔸𝕏 *297/4872167 or 297/4872007.*

**$** ⊡ **Hotel Isla Chaffers.** This hotel is Puerto Deseado's best. ⊠ *San Martín and Moreno, 9050,* ☎ *297/4872246 or 297/4870476.*

## Comodora Rivadavía

**⑬** *1,854 km (1,149 mi) south of Buenos Aires, 1,726 km (1,070 mi) north of Ushuaia, 945 km (586 mi) north of Río Gallegos, and 397 km (246 mi) south of Rawson.*

Argentina's answer to Houston, Comodoro Rivadavía is the town that oil built. Argentina's first oil discovery was made here in 1907 during a desperate search for water because of a serious drought. It was an event that led to the formation of Yacimientos Petroliferos Fiscales (YPF), among the world's first vertically integrated oil companies. After YPF's privatization in 1995, however, thousands were laid off, and record low oil prices prompted a halt in drilling, which has brought hard times to Comodoro's 145,000 residents. Even as authorities hope for a comeback in oil prices, they are counting on the city's proximity to natural wonders, including the Petrified Forest in Sarmiento, to attract tourists and help compensate for the lost petroleum business. As Patagonia's second-biggest city after Bariloche, Comodoro Rivadavía is a regional center. Comodoro is also a jumping-off point for the reserves of Camarones, to the north, and Puerto Deseado's natural attractions, to the south (☞ Puerto Deseado, *above*).

Surrounded by dry hills and sheer cliffs off the Golfo San Jorge (San Jorge Gulf), Comodoro looks dramatic from a distance. But up close it's frayed around the edges. Comodoro's main commercial streets, also where restaurants and bars can be found, are San Martín and Comodoro Rivadavía. A relative urban newcomer, Comodoro has little of the old-world charm found in colonial Latin American cities, and it lacks a main central plaza with a traditional church. Residents congregate around the port, with its promenade, park, and basketball and volleyball courts. In many ways it's a typical Patagonian city, with flat roofs, tall buildings, fisheries, textile factories, and the ever-present wind.

You can learn more about petroleum than you probably ever wanted to know—from the big-bang theory, which helps explain oil's geological origins, to the dramatic story of Argentina's first oil discovery in Comodoro and its subsequent exploitation—at the **Museo Nacional de Petroleo** (National Petroleum Museum). It's well worth a visit, though unfortunately English-language information is scant. ⊠ *San Lorenzo 250,* ☎ *0297/4559558.* ☞ *Admission.* ☉ *Summer hours, weekdays 9–2 and 4–9, Sat. 4–9; winter, weekdays 8–6.*

Another interesting sight is the tangle of windmills at the **Parque Eolicó,** a 20-minute drive east of the city. The windmills, which are some of the world's most efficient and modern, generate electricity for the country, taking advantage of the windy conditions in this area.

## Dining and Lodging

$$$     ✕ **Tunet.** Though it's Comodoro Rivadavía's best seafood restaurant, the fish, ironically, is mostly imported, owing to the lack of a consistent supply of good-quality local fish. Nonetheless, the food is very good, the service attentive, and the ambience elegant if not too formal. Weekdays it's filled with oil executives on company accounts, and weekends it's filled with families. ⊠ *In Austral Hotel, Av. Rivadavía 190,* ☎ *0297/4472200. AE, DC, MC, V.*

$$       ✕ **La Estancia.** This restaurant—made to look like a typical Argentine ranch—has been serving finely prepared, traditionally-cooked meats for 34 years and is the city's oldest. Try the *cordero* (lamb) with chimichurra sauce and mashed potatoes, the seafood, or the homemade pasta. Desserts are extravagant, especially the pancakes with *dulce de leche* (sweet milk). The owners, the friendly Dos Santos family, provide excellent service. Unlike other restaurants, it has a menu in English. ⊠ *Urquiza 863,* ☎ *0297/4474568 or 0297/4479864. AE, DC, MC, V.*

$$$     🛏 **Luciana Palazzo Hotel.** The newest and most luxurious hotel in town, the Luciana is also blessed with the best waterfront views. Large white pillars, marble floors, and cushy white-leather chairs in the lobby lend to its appearance. The spacious suites, with corner views on both sides, are particularly attractive, and other rooms are a cut above everywhere else, too. ⊠ *Moreno and Rufino Rivera, 9000,* ☎ FAX

0297/4460100. 79 rooms. Sauna, exercise room, meeting rooms, business services, parking. AE, DC, MC, V.

$$ 🏨 **Austral Hotel.** It's really two hotels in one: a 42-room luxury hotel with marble floors and thick towels completed in late 1998 and a modest 108-room hotel adequate for its class. The older portion has the advantage of being cheaper while allowing access to some of the newer portion's amenities, such as fax and Internet services. The Austral also has perhaps the city's finest seafood restaurant, Tunet (☞ *above*). ⊠ *Av. Rivadavia 190, 9000,* ☎ *0297/4472200,* 🖷 *0297/4472444. 150 rooms. Restaurant, sauna, exercise room, business services, parking. AE, DC, MC, V.*

$$ 🏨 **Comodoro Hotel.** Among the city's oldest lodgings, this hotel is also one of the most reliable. Rooms are clean and unremarkable, though those higher up have lovely views. Have trouble finding it? Just look for the biggest Coke advertisement you've ever seen, which is on one of its side walls. ⊠ *Av. 9 de Julio 770, 9000,* ☎ *0297/4472300,* 🖷 *0297/4473363. Cafeteria. AE, DC, MC, V.*

### Outdoor Activities
The **beach** at Rada Tilly is about 8 km (5 mi) south of Comodoro. You can get a bus there or drive.

### Shopping
Comodoro has some shops selling regional artisan items, many carrying baby clothes—a holdover from the population explosion during the oil boom days—and other general stores, but little out of the ordinary. **Doris Hughes Decoraciones** (⊠ Av. San Martín 282), has regional paintings and international artisan goods.

*En Route*    From Comodoro a two-hour drive through a monotonous landscape of desert punctuated by oil derricks brings you to the unique Bosque Petrificado José Ormaechea.

---

## Sarmiento and the Bosque Petrificado José Ormaechea

⑭ *220 km (136 mi) west of Comodoro Rivadavia.*

Sarmiento is a sort of one-horse town, with small, low structures—primarily houses, dirt and paved roads, a couple of churches, a gas station, a few small restaurants, and some no-frills hotels. It's also the jumping-off point for the Bosque Petrificado José Ormaechea (José Ormaechea Petrified Forest), about 30 km (19 mi) from Sarmiento on R26, where you can see trunks of petrified wood 65 million years old, with their colorful stratifications, and feel the overpowering wind. Let the park's resident attendant and self-professed "Patagonia fanatic," Juan José Balera, give you a whirl through the eerily lonely landscape in his Mercedes Benz bus (just show up, he's usually there). This forest, like several others in Patagonia, tells much of the geological past of the land, which long ago was covered in trees or by water. If you rent a car, make it a four-wheel-drive vehicle, since you'll have to drive a half hour on a rough, unpaved road once you leave Sarmiento. For more information about the park, contact the **tourist office** (☎ 2965/4893401) in Sarmiento. While you're in the area, stop at **Lago Musters** (Musters Lake), 7 km (4 mi) from Sarmiento, and **Lago Olhue Huapi** (Olhue Huapi Lake), a little farther on. In Lago Musters you can take an isolated swim or drop in a fishing line.

### Dining and Lodging
$ ✕ **Restaurant Heidy's.** About a mile off the main highway in Sarmiento is this restaurant owned by Luis Kraan, who is of Dutch heritage, and his German-descended wife, Kathy Mueller. Enjoy delicious vegetable

broth, called *puchero,* homemade pasta, and steak. And don't skip the delicious chimichurra sauce. ✉ *Perito Moreno and Patagonia,* ☎ *2965/4898308. No credit cards.*

$ 🏨 **Hotel Ismar.** If you're en route through the Andean region and want an inexpensive stopover, this hotel is the best in Sarmiento. Rooms are clean and have simple wood furnishings and cable TV. ✉ *Right in town, 9020,* ☎ *2965/4893293,* FAX *no fax. Parking. No credit cards.*

# Camarones

**15** *252 km (156 mi) south of Trelew, 105 km (65 mi) south of Punto Tomba, and 258 km (160 mi) north of Comodoro Rivadavia.*

Camarones is a tiny and dilapidated but charming fishing town whose main attractions are the particular blueness of the sea and the nearby nature reserve. Every year, on the second weekend in February, the town celebrates the Fiesta Nacional de Salmon (National Salmon Festival) with all kinds of events and a fishing contest. Camarones is difficult to reach by public transportation, though at least one bus company, Don Otto (☞ Getting Around by Bus *in* Patagonia A to Z, *below*), passes through here on its 3½-hour trip from Trelew. The **Cabo Dos Bahías Fauna Reserve,** 30 km (19 mi) southeast of town, has all kinds of wildlife, including penguisn, sea lions, all kinds of birds, seals, guanacos, rheas, and foxes.

## Lodging

Camping is free in the municipal campgrounds that front the Bay of Camarones; call the Chubut Province tourism agency for more information (☞ Visitor Information *in* Patagonia A to Z, *below*).

# Punto Tomba

**16** *120 km (74 mi) south of Trelew, 132 km (81 mi) north of Camarones.*

The **Reserva Faunística Punto Tomba** (Punto Tomba Reserve) has the largest colony of Magellanic penguins in the world and one of the most varied seabird rookeries. Over a million penguins live here from the middle of September until March. You can walk among them (along a designated path) as they come and go along well-defined "penguin highways" that link their nests with the sea, and you can see them fishing near the coast. Other wildlife found here in abundance includes cormorants, guanacos, seals, and Patagonian hares. Although December is the best month to come—that's when the adult penguins are actively going back and forth from the sea to feed their newborns—anytime is good, except from April through August when the penguins feed at sea. Other than driving, the easiest way to get to Punto Tomba is with a tour guide from Trelew, Rawson, Gaiman, or even Puerto Madryn (☞ Tour Operators and Travel Agencies *in* Patagonia A to Z, *below*).

# Gaiman

**17** *17 km (10½ mi) west of Trelew.*

The most Welsh of the Atlantic Patagonian settlements, Gaiman is far more charming than nearby Trelew and Rawson—other stopover points for the Punto Tomba Reserve (☞ *above*). The Welsh colony's history is lovingly preserved in museums and private homes, Welsh can still be heard on the streets, and there continues to be a connection to Wales, with teachers, preachers, and visitors going back and forth frequently. Even the younger generation has had a renewed interest in Welsh culture and language.

Gaiman was founded in 1874, a few years after the Welsh arrived in Patagonia seeking escape from religious persecution in Britain. Since then, Welsh, German, and British immigrants, the indigenous population, and, more recently, Bolivians, who have renewed the agriculture industry, have made Gaiman home. Seeing the Celtic-looking faces of of second- or third-generation Welsh Argentines makes you feel like you're in Great Britain, but hearing them speak accentless Spanish reminds you that you're in Latin America. Yet Gaiman has a number of tea houses, some small wooden chapels, and a cemetery with tombstones engraved in Welsh.

The **Museo Histórico Regional de Gaiman** (Gaiman Regional Historical Museum) has photographs of Gaiman's original 48 settlers, stock certificates from the Companía Unida de Irrigación del Chubut (United Company for Chubut Irrigation), which was nationalized by Perón in the '40s, and other interesting memorabilia. Tegai Roberts, the octogenarian who gives tours here, is the great-granddaughter of Michael Jones, one of the authors of the Patagonian colony. Ask her about her grandfather, who in 1910 was killed by members of Butch Cassidy's Wild Bunch. ⊠ *Av. Sarmiento and Av. 28 de Julio.* ▨ *Admission.* ☉ *Jan.–Feb., daily 10–1:30 and 3–8; Mar.–Dec., daily 3–8.*

The **Parque Desáfio** is a unique park; it's filled with recycled goods—80,000 bottles, 15,000 tin cans, and the remains of several automobiles as well as thousands of other pieces of refuse. Its mastermind is Joaquín Alonso, an eccentric octogenarian and a self-professed anarchist who made his way into the *Guinness Book of World Records* for the feat of using tens of thousands of pieces of refuse to create the park. ⊠ *Brown, just before the Na Petko restaurant.* ▨ *Admission (negotiable).* ☉ *Dawn–dusk.*

At night, visit the **Capilla Bethel,** a chapel that is central to Gaiman life. Townspeople gather here to celebrate Welsh traditions with song, poetry, and dance below its wooden vaulted ceilings. In fact, throughout the Chubut Valley are three dozen or so other chapels—where the Welsh went to school; held meetings, trials, and social events; sang religious hymns; and even had their tea—some of which are still functioning.

The **Parque Paleontológico Bryn Gwyn** (Bryn Gwyn Paleontology Park), outside of town, is the companion to the Museo Paleontológico Egidio Feruglio in Trelew (☞ *below*). Here you can see 40 million years of geological history in a natural setting. Tour guides can be arranged. ⊠ *11 km (7 mi) from town,* ☏ *call the Museo Paleontológico Egidio Feruglio in Trelew to make arrangements for getting into the park and having a tour there: 2965/435464.* ▨ *Admission.*

## Dining and Lodging

For a small town, Gaiman has an array of culinary offerings, from parrilla to pizza. Not to be missed is a visit to one of Gaiman's six tea houses, which all serve pretty much the same thing for about the same price (around $14) but have different atmospheres: Ty Gwyn, Plas-y-Coed, Ty Nain, Ty Cymraeg, Ty Draw Avon, and Ty Te Caerdydd.

**$$** ✕ **El Angel.** This delightful restaurant is run out of the house of Gustavo Durante and Antonio Zappia, two interior designers and furniture restoration specialists. It's only open on Friday and Saturday nights and is usually filled with patrons from nearby towns or tour groups, especially October–March. After dinner you can sit on the plush couches in the cozy living room amid photos of past guests, concrete angels, and candles. Expect a French, international-style dinner of beef, chicken, or pork. ⊠ *M. D. Jones 591,* ☏ *2965/491460. Reservations essential. Closed Sun.–Thurs.*

$ ✕ **Ty Gwyn.** This circa-1974 wood-and-brick tea house is run by a woman of Spanish descent, Maria Elena Sanchez Jones, but nonetheless serves delicious scones, breads, jams lovingly made from local fruits, and other elaborate sweets, including the classic Argentine-Welsh tea accompaniment, *torta negra* (black Welsh cake), a kind of fruit cake. ✉ *Av. 9 de Julio 111,* ☎ *2965/491009. No credit cards.*

$ ✕ **Gustos Pizzeria y Confitería.** Surprisingly good pizza can be found at Gustos. Besides the usual, toppings include Roquefort cheese, ham, hard-boiled egg, red pepper, onion, and tuna fish. ✉ *Av. Eugenio Tello 156,* ☎ *2965/491828. No credit cards.*

$ ✕ **Na Petko.** It's worth seeking out this bar and restaurant, creatively put together using pieces of farm equipment and local artifacts—the bathroom doors are culled from a jail, the windows are made from old cart wheels, and a rusty Model T sits in the yard. Owner Pedro Osvaldo Teodoroff runs it like it's his own parlor—you can even see the headboard of the bed in which he was born. Especially good is the *tarta de pescado* (fish tart) as well as other fish dishes and the steak. ✉ *Brown 100,* ☎ *2965/491650. No credit cards. No lunch.*

$ ☷ **Hosteria Gwesty Tywi.** This cozy, comfortable, clean bed-and-breakfast is in the home of Welsh- and English-speaking Gwyn and Monica Jones. The Joneses are great hosts—they pick you up at the bus station, serve you maté, tell you all the history you would want to know, and even, perhaps, give you a spin around town. ✉ *M. D. Jones 342, 9105,* ☎ ⟨FAX⟩ *2965/491292. 6 rooms. No credit cards.*

$ ☷ **Hotel-Restaurant Unelem.** Despite its 109-year-old history, this hotel is fairly standard. It was recently restored and reopened after being shut for 10 years because of financial difficulties. Rooms are rustic and spacious, though a bit dark; a couple of the suites have fireplaces. The wood-floored dining room and courtyard are charming, with Gaiman memorabilia and other mementos on the walls. Tours of nearby points of interest, including the Península Valdés, the penguin reserve at Punto Tomba, and the region's chapels in Dolavan and elsewhere are organized by the hotel (tours are open to nonguests as well). ✉ *Av. E. Tello and Av. 9 de Julio, 9105,* ☎ ⟨FAX⟩ *2965/491663. Restaurant.*

## Shopping

Gaiman isn't really a place to shop, though you can get tortas negras, cheeses, jams, chocolate, T-shirts, and leather, wood, and ceramic crafts at **Paseo Artesanal** (✉ Av. 9 de Julio, ☎ 2965/491134 or 2965/491700).

# Trelew

**⑱** *17 km (10½ mi) east of Gaiman, 250 km (155 mi) north of Camarones, 1,800 km (1,116 mi) north of Ushuaia, and 67 km (41½ mi south of Puerto Madryn.*

Trelew is a commercial, industrial, and service hub with hotels, restaurants, gas stations, mechanics, and anything you else you might need as you travel from point to point. Its biggest attractions are its paleontology museum and its proximity to the Punto Tomba Reserve (☞ *above*) and Península Valdés (☞ *below*). Like Gaiman (☞ *above*), Trelew has a strong Welsh tradition. If you come in the spring (the second half of October), you can participate in the Eisteddfod, a Welsh literary and musical festival, first held in Patagonia in 1875. The town itself was founded in 1886 as a result of the construction of the Chubut railway line, which joined the Chubut River valley with the Atlantic coast. It's named after its Welsh founder, Lewis Jones (Tre means "town" in Welsh, and Lew represents Lewis), who fought to establish the rail line. Trelew gained another kind of infamy in 1974 for the massacre of political prisoners who had escaped from the local jail. For more information about the town, contact the **tourist office** (✉ San Martín 171, ☎ 2965/ 420139, 2965/435797, or 2965/435941).

At the **Museo Paleontológico Egidio Feruglio,** the paleontology museum, the most modern display is 2 million years old. This wonderful and educational museum has exhibits on extinct dinosaurs from Patagonia, one of the world's three most important territories for such work. Other prizes are a fossil of a 290-million-year-old spider with a 3-ft leg span and the 70-million-year-old petrified dinosaur eggs of a Carnotaurus. But the tour de force is the bones of a 100-ton, 120-ft-long dinosaur. The museum received a $4 million grant and was set to have moved into new quarters by 1999. ✉ *Fontana and Lewis Jones,* ☎ *2965/435464.* ▣ *Admission.* ☉ *Daily 9–8. Tours in English available.*

To find out more about the history of the Welsh settlement in Chubut Province, and Trelew in particular, visit the **Museo Regional Pueblo de Luis** (Lewis's Town Regional Museum). Built in the original train station, which is no longer operating, the museum has a mishmash of displays on the European influence in the region, the indigenous populations of the area, and wildlife. ✉ *Avs. 9 de Julio and Fontana,* ☎ *no phone.* ▣ *Admission.* ☉ *Dec.–Feb., weekdays 7–1 and 3–9; Mar.–Nov., weekdays 7–1 and 2–8.*

The **Teatro Verdi** (Verdi Theater; ✉ San Martín between Belgrano and Rivadavía) was built by the city's Italian immigrants in the early 1900s. At press time it was undergoing restoration to convert it into a movie theater showing old classics. The **Teatro Español** (Spanish Theater), constructed by the city's Spanish immigrants in 1918, is today a cultural center.

## Dining and Lodging

$ ✗ **El Quijote.** Two blocks off the main plaza is this spot serving homemade pasta, as tasty as it gets outside Tuscany, and good fish dishes, which can sometimes be a bit oversalted. Meat is also available, but there's no parrilla in sight, so you're better off sticking with the seafood and pasta. ✉ *Av. 25 de Mayo 90,* ☎ *2965/434564. AE, DC, MC, V.*

$$ ▥ **Hotel Libertador.** This hotel is centrally located—it's three blocks from the central square—and rooms are clean and reasonably modern and light (and all have cable TV and phones). If you're in town on business, its has all kinds of services, such as fax and Internet access. ✉ *Av. Rivadavía 31, 9100,* ☎ FAX *2965/420220. 70 rooms. Restaurant, snack bar, laundry service, business services, car rental, parking. AE, DC, MC, V (you get a 10% discount with cash).*

$ ▥ **Rayentray.** The nicest, and most expensive, hotel in Trelew is the Rayentray, a 22-year-old lodging that is part of an Argentine chain. Rayentray, which means "stream of flowers" in Mapuche, has more amenities than any other local hotel. But judging from the worn rugs and slightly drab appearance of the rooms, it could definitely use a renovation. ✉ *Av. Libertador and Av. Belgrado, 9100,* ☎ *2965/434702. Restaurant, pool, massage, sauna, business services. AE, DC, MC, V.*

$ ✗▥ **Touring Club.** This classic, old hotel and confitería, a cafeteria where you can get coffee, drinks, and sandwiches, was founded in 1907 by the Chubut Railway Company as a restaurant and became Chubut's first hotel in 1926. In its heyday it was one of Patagonia's most luxurious options, particularly since it had hot water and private bathrooms. It was the choice of Argentine presidents Juan Perón and Arturo Frondizi, both of whose photos grace the restaurant walls. Now, the hotel's a bit musty and worn, but not bad for the price (and you get cable TV and a phone). ✉ *Av. Fontana 240, 9100,* ☎ *2965/433997. Restaurant, bar, cafeteria, parking. AE, DC, MC, V.*

### Shopping

**Jaguel** (✉ 25 de Mayo 140) has good-quality leather jackets and belts, regional artisan goods and some touristy items. Classic Welsh fruit-cakes are for sale at **La Tienda del Sol** (✉ Pasaje La Ríoja) and **Torta Típica Galesa** (✉ A. P. Bell 315).

## Puerto Madryn

**❶❾** *67 km (41½ mi) north of Trelew, 450 km (279 mi) north of Comodoro Rivadavía, 104 km (64 mi) west of Puerto Pirámides, and 1,380 km (856 mi) south of Buenos Aires.*

The Welsh people who came to Patagonia seeking refuge from religious persecution in Great Britain landed first in Puerto Madryn in 1865. You can still find many of their descendants today, but there isn't much evidence of the natives who helped the Welsh survive and become the first foreigners to unveil the secrets of Patagonia's interior. If you find yourself in Puerto Madryn or any of the other main Chubut towns on July 28, be prepared to celebrate the anniversary of the Welsh's arrival to Patagonia.

Puerto Madryn's history of economic rises and falls is tied to local industry. Its first boom came in 1886, when the Patagonian railroad was introduced, spurring the town's port activities and the salt and fishing industries. Customs taxes were removed in the 1960s, attracting manufacturers (mainly of salt) to the town, but many folded within a decade or so because of inefficient operations and low international commodity pricing for salt. The construction of Argentina's largest aluminum plant, Aluminios Argentinos S.A., however, prompted a population explosion in the 1970s and at press time was expanding its operations. The fishing and mining industries, too, continue to provide jobs. But most recently Puerto Madryn residents have been riding the tourism boom because of the town's proximity to the nature reserves at Península Valdés (☞ *below*). So these days there's evidence that Puerto Madryn's 55,000 residents are prospering; new, stately houses in areas such as Barrio Sur are being constructed, and branches of national banks are opening up.

Puerto Madryn's main hotels and residences are on or near the 3½-km-long (2-mi-long) Las Ramblas, the shore road that hugs Golfo Nuevo; it's also a favorite place for joggers and strollers. In high whale-watching season—from September to December—the city's nearly 5,000 hotel rooms and its campgrounds usually fill up.

The **Museo Oceonográfico y Sciencias Naturales** (Oceanographic and Natural Science Museum) is worth a visit if you have the time. Housed in a lovely 1917 colonial building once owned by the Pujol family, some of the original settlers, the museum focuses on marine life. You can see a giant squid preserved in formaldehyde, learn how fish breathe, and find out more about colonial times. ✉ *Domecq García and Menéndez,* ☏ *2965/451139.* ⊡ *Admission.* ⊙ *Tues.–Sun. 9–noon and 4:30–8:30.*

### Dining and Lodging

**$$$** ✕ **Placido.** For an elegant dining experience and nouveau cuisine, head to this glass-ringed restaurant, overlooking the water and the bay's fishing ships. It specializes in seafood but also has pasta, chicken, and meat dishes. ✉ *Av. Roca 506,* ☏ *2965/455991. AE, DC, MC, V.*

**$$** ✕ **Cantina El Nautico.** Owned and operated since 1970 by three generations of an immigrant French Basque family, this restaurant is a local favorite. It feels like a town institution, with its framed photographs of semifamous visitors, including a Hemingway (one of his daughters) and Juan Manuel Fangio (a Formula One race-car driver). The homemade pasta and the fresh seafood are especially good, as is the "butter"—a mixture of mayonnaise with garlic, parsley, and pepper—that accompanies the bread. Your best bet is the "executive menu," a very reasonably priced, all-inclusive buffet. ⊠ *Av. Roca 790,* ☎ *2965/471404. AE, DC, MC, V.*

$$ ✕ **Restaurant Estella.** Owner Estella Yachowsky, who is of Ukrainian descent, has learned salutary phrases in quite a few languages. She offers menus in English, German, French, and Italian and hangs up maps and postcards from all over Europe, Asia, Africa, and the Americas sent by many of her dinner guests. The food, however, is strictly Argentine—lamb and beef on the parrilla and good fresh fish. ⊠ *R. S. Pena 27,* ☎ *09265/451573. AE, MC, V. Closed Mon.*

$$ ✕ **El Restaurant Pequeño.** This restaurant does it all pretty well: pastas, beef, and fresh fish. Try the delicious salmon or perhaps the *lenga* (tongue) in a tasty sauce of onions, chives, peppers, and other herbs. ⊠ *Av. Roca 822,* ☎ *2965/472807. AE, DC, MC, V.*

$$ ✕🏠 **Estancia San Guillermo.** If you want to experience a Chubut farm, filled with snorting pigs, overfriendly guanacos, and strutting roosters, head for Estancia San Guillermo. Just a few miles outside Puerto Madryn, owners Alfredo and Cristina Casado make you feel at home with their 1,200 sheep, which roam on their 7,400-acre fossil-filled farm. Watch Alfredo sheer a sheep (from September through December only) or his helpers prepare the parrilla. Stay in roomy, comfortable villas with their own kitchens and bathrooms; rates include meals. The estancia has a dining room, too, if you're just coming for the day. ⊠ *Contact info in Puerto Madryn: Av. Roca 1909 in Puerto Madryn,* ☎ *2965/473535 or 2965/452150,* 𝐅𝐀𝐗 *no fax. Dining room.*

$$ 🏠 **Bahía Nueva Hotel.** One of the newest lodgings in town is this pleasing hotel on the bay front. Clean and spacious rooms, open and pleasant common areas, a great location, and friendly service make this a good option. ⊠ *Av. Julio A. Roca, 9120,* ☎ 𝐅𝐀𝐗 *2965/451677, 450045, or 450145. 40 rooms. Bar, library, video games, business services, parking. AE, DC, MC, V .*

$$ 🏠 **Hotel Aguas Mansas.** This four-year-old hotel is just one block from the beach in a residential neighborhood and a few blocks from the center of town. It's nothing fancy—just clean, quiet rooms and good, personable service. It's one of the few lodgings with a pool, especially in this price range. ⊠ *José Hernandez 51, 9120,* ☎ *2965/456626,* 𝐅𝐀𝐗 *2965/473103 . Restaurant, bar, pool, parking. AE, DC, MC, V.*

## Nightlife and the Arts

**La Oveja Negra** (⊠ Irigoyen 144) is a small, cozy bar and literary café; Thursday through Sunday nights you can attend poetry readings or hear good local bands. For a totally different experience, try your hand at the **Casino Puerto Madryn** (⊠ Av. Roca 639).

## Outdoor Activities and Sports

You can do all kinds of sports in and around Puerto Madryn, ranging from bicycling and fishing to sand-boarding, which is basically surfing on the sand. Puerto Madryn is also considered Argentina's scuba-diving capital. In an effort to further boost interest in scuba diving by giving divers something else to explore, town officials recently sunk the *Albatros,* a large fishing vessel, off the coast in Golfo Nuevo. Several scuba shops rent equipment and arrange dives of the *Albatros,* Puerto Piramides, and other spots: **Abismo** (⊠ Av. Roca 550, ☎ 2965/451483); **Patagonia Buceo** (⊠ at Balneario Rayentray, ☎ 2965/452278); and **Safari Submarino** (⊠ Complejo Solana, ☎ 2965/474110). Several companies rent bicycles for about $20 a day, including: **Hi Adrenaline** (⊠ Humphreys 85, ☎ 2965/471475), which also arranges sand-boarding on some nearby dunes; and **XT Mountain Bike** (⊠ Av. Roca 742,

☎ 2965/472232). **Costas Patagonicas** (☎ 2965/451131) and **Jorge Schmid** (☎ 2965/451511) organize fishing trips.

## Shopping

Puerto Madryn is one of the better shopping cities on the eastern coast of Patagonian. The best shopping is found on the streets that intersect with Las Ramblas, such as **Avenida 28 de Julio,** which is the town's mini version of Madison Avenue. For some regional culinary goodies, such as torta *galetas,* chocolates, jellies made from wild Patagonian fruits, and teas, try **Con Buen Gusto** (⊠ Av. 28 de Julio 10). **Taller de Ceramica Mag** (⊠ off Av. 28 de Julio on Av. Roca 1082) makes its own pots and craft items from a local white clay known as *arcilla*; it also sells leather goods, hand-drawn postcards, and unique knives.

# Península Valdés

**㉑** *Puerto Piramides is 104 km (64 mi) northwest of Puerto Madryn.*

The Península Valdés is one of Argentina's most important wildlife reserves. Its biggest attractions are the 1,200 southern right whales that feed, mate, give birth, and nurse their offspring here. One unique characteristic of these whales is that they have two external blow holes on top of their heads, and when they emerge from the water, they blow a V-shape water blast that can be seen for miles away. The protected mammals attract some 100,000 visitors every year from September through December, when people crowd into boats small and large to observe at close range the 30- to 35-ton whales leap out of the water and blow water from their spouts. The worldwide population of these giant mammals is only 4,000, down from 100,000 before hunters killed the majority for their blubber and oil.

Off-season the peninsula is still worth visiting: you find sea lions, elephant seals, Magellanic penguins, egrets, and cormorants as well as land mammals like guanacos (a relative of the llama), gray fox, and Patagonian *mara,* a harelike animal. Discovered by Spanish explorer Hernando de Magallanes in 1520 and named after Don Antonio Valdés, minister of the Spanish navy in the late 18th century, Península Valdés is a protected zone. So valued is the peninsula's animal population that UNESCO is considering declaring it a site of universal patrimony. It's also the lowest point on the South American continent, at 132 ft below sea level.

To get to the peninsula, you must drive along desolate, unpaved roads surrounded by vast estancias dotted with sheep and a handful of cows. The biggest landholder since the late 19th century, the Ferro family owns one-quarter of Península Valdés—3,625 sq km (5,850 sq mi), with five airstrips from which they can visit their property. You also pass abandoned salt mines, an important industry in the early 1900s, and a boon industry for Puerto Madryn, the shipping point for the salt. But the salt is a reminder of the at least 260,000 sea lions killed in the peninsula between 1917 and 1953, at which point hunting was prohibited: salt was used to preserve the sea lions' blubber. Today only about 20,000 sea lions remain. For information about tours of the peninsula, *see* Tour Operators and Travel Agencies *in* Patagonia A to Z, *below.*

**Puerto Pirámide,** the only village on Península Valdés, is a more tranquil, isolated base than Puerto Madryn from which to explore the area's natural attractions. Only 150 people are allowed to live there for ecological reasons, but there are a handful of campsites, hotels, and restaurants. Aside from lounging around with a beer in hand and looking out on the sheer pyramid-shape cliffs of Valdés Bay, the only activities in town are scuba diving and surfing. Just about every little five-and-dime rents out scuba equipment.

### Dining and Lodging

**$$**  ✗🏨 **Paradise Hotel.** This hotel has the best reputation in town, and a double, including breakfast, isn't as inexpensive as you'd expect. Rooms are clean and no frills. The restaurant serves seafood and steaks. The hotel can organize scuba-diving and bicycling tours for you. ✉ *In Puerto Pirámide,* ☎ 𝔽𝔸𝕏 *2965/495030 or 2965/495003. 12 rooms. Restaurant, gift shop, business services.*

### Outdoor Activities and Sports

Scuba-diving equipment can be rented at Puerto Pirámide from **Jorge Schmid** (☎ 𝔽𝔸𝕏 2965/295012 or 2965/295112), who also organizes whale-watching tours, Visa and MasterCard are accepted; and from the **Paradise Hotel** (☞ Dining and Lodging, *above*).

## Sierra Grande

🔞 *70 km (43 mi) north of Sierra Grande.*

"Mining tourism" is the main attraction of this town, which is worth a stop if you're interested in hiking 300 ft beneath the earth's crust, rappelling, rafting in underground waters, and learning something about iron mining. Iron was first discovered here in 1944 by a local shepherd; the government started mining it in 1970 to supply the military with iron for armaments. In 1991, the mine was closed, a victim of costly production, low international iron prices, and other financial difficulties. Said to be South America's largest underground iron mine, it still has among the world's biggest reserves, with only 18% of its potential exploited.

A tour of the mine costs $15 to $25 per person; contact **Area Natural Recreativa Movil 5** (☎ 2934/4810212 or 2934/481333, 𝔽𝔸𝕏 2934/481095) for information. Besides visiting the mine, another option is to take a combination mountain biking and hiking trip up a nearby mountain. If you're interested in doing this, ask for Claudio Hinacayal Paz at Area Natural Recreativa Movil 5; he's a descendant of the original native inhabitants of the area. Lodging in the peaceful, poplar-ringed, summer camplike setting that Movil 5 has craftily transformed from a former military camp into its base of operations; cabins go for $60 and sleep up to five.

## Viedma

🔞 *528 km (327 mi) north of Puerto Madryn, 176 km (109 mi) south of Bahía Blanca, 662 km (410 mi) east of Neuquen, and 960 km (595 mi) south of Buenos Aires.*

Landing amid the desert thistle that surround's Viedma's airport, you might think that you've made an unscheduled stopover. But within minutes of the airport, you get to the vibrant, albeit small, provincial city of Viedma whose 50,000 residents go about their daily routines unaware of the tourism boom that their Patagonian neighbors are undergoing. The quarter-mile wide Río Negro (Black River), which separates Viedma from its sister city, Carmen de Patagones (☞ *below*), is the heart of town. By day people swim and boat in it and picnic and play ball by it; by night people stroll along it and fill the restaurants and bars lining it. Aside from La Costanera (The Coastal Area), as the river is known, the other center of activity in town is Avenida Buenos Aires, along which are hotels, restaurants, shops, and the Cathedral Cardenal Cagliero.

In 1779, Francisco de Viedma y Narvaez, with his men dying of fever amid a critical water shortage in Península Valdés, decided to anchor along the shores of the Río Curru Leuvu, now the Río Negro. Viedma, who was aiming to claim Patagonia for Spain, was attracted by the lush conditions and abundance of fresh water. The date of which the town's residents are the most proud, however, is the victorious 1885 battle against Portuguese settlers from Brazil who were seeking to claim this strategic site along the river. In 1879 Viedma became the administrative and political capital of all of Patagonia. Five years later Patagonia was divided into five separate provinces, at which point Viedma became simply the capital of the Río Negro Province, which it still is today. In the mid-1980s, Viedma was slated by President Raúl Alfonsín to become the new capital of the Argentine Republic—the Argentine Brasília—but the plan was abandoned because of the cost. Although legislation for such a move is still floating around Buenos Aires, the plan appears mortally wounded for the moment.

At Viedma's unusual **Museo Technologico del Agua y del Suelo** (Museum of Water and Soil Technology; ⊠ Colón and Rivadavía), you can meet its founder and caretaker, Osvaldo Casamiquela, a 75-year-old engineer and retired bureaucrat with a passion for water. It's an important subject in a province that is 95% arid and where only 345,000 of 55 million acres are under agricultural production because of a lack of irrigation. On display are hydrological maps and surveys and models of irrigation equipment; there's also a library of related materials. At press time a drought had led to forest fires on Río Negro's western forested side and clarify: to at least one island not longer being surrounded by water. ⊠ *Av. Colon 498, 1st floor,* ☎ *2920/431569.* ⊠ *Admission.* ⊙ *Weekdays 9–11.*

The **Golfo San Matías,** 30 km (19 mi) south of Viedma, is a stretch of coast favored by Viedma and Carmen de Patagones residents for its beaches and wildlife. **Balneario El Cóndor,** a nice beach area, is bordered by sheer cliffs and has a number of small hotels, restaurants, campgrounds, and even a little casino. It's also home to the first lighthouse in Patagonia, the **Faro Río Negro,** built in the 1880s to aid ships coming into Río Negro; climb the 64 steps to the top for a good view of the coast. It has a small apartment at its base for the caretaker, who will give you a little tour in Spanish for a small fee.

Another 30 km (19 mi) south is the **Reserva Faunística de Punta Bermeja** (Point Bermeja Fauna Reserve), more commonly known as La Lobería (Seal Home), for the 3,500 sea lions that line its shores in high season. Bring binoculars (if you can) to better observe from the breezy bluffs the sea lions and the striking scenery (it's prohibited to go down to the beach). Binoculars can be rented at the small visitor center on the way to the cliffs, or you can use the coin-operated ones. If you're here from May to November, you might even see a sea lion being pursued—or even eaten—by an orca whale, their only natural predator. Look out for the *loros barranqueros,* a type of parakeet that nests in the soft cliff rocks. You'll see the holes of the parakeets' nests and possibly the black eagles, peregrine falcons, and turkey vultures that prey on them. Other birds commonly seen in the reserve are snowy sheathbills, cormorants, gulls, sandpipers, and oystercatchers. Land-based wildlife includes guanacos, rheas, maras, wildcats, skunks, foxes, armadillos, and small reptiles. You can also bathe in the natural-stone tidal pools and walk on the black, iron-tinged sand at the beach at **La Lobería,** which is about a mile down the road. Here there are lifeguards in summer, showers, bathrooms, and a restaurant. After La

Lobería, the highway is no longer paved, and the farther you go, the more desolate it gets.

## Dining and Lodging

For information about campsites and other lodging options in the area, contact the Viedma **tourist office** (⊠ on the Costanera between Colón and Alvaro Barros, ☎ FAX 2920/427171 or 2920/422287).

**$$**  ✕ **La Balsa Restaurant.** Like many good restaurants, the bread and butter at this local favorite are exceptional—though it's not really butter, but an artery-hardening yet delicious mixture of Roquefort cheese, cream, olive oil, and a drop of whiskey. The food is fresh and good—steak, mashed potatoes, fish, and pasta. It's on the Río Negro in a breezy, pleasant spot. ⊠ *Villarino 51, at Av. Costanera,* ☎ *2920/431974. AE, DC, MC, V.*

**$$**  ✕ **Catamaran de la Comarca.** At 4 PM daily you can take a guided, catered tour (drinks and snacks, or even lunch) down the Río Negro on this 90-person catamaran. At night, when the catamaran is docked in front of the Hotel Austral (☞ *below*), you can sit overlooking the water, feasting on pasta, seafood, and steak. It's quite nice. ⊠ *Muelle de las Lanchas,* ☎ *2920/426421. AE, DC, MC, V.*

**$**  ✕ **Dragon Restaurante Chino.** For a cheap meal, and not a bad one, try this restaurant, which isn't really Chinese, but Argentine. There's an all-you-can-eat buffet with steak, parrilla, pork, chicken, pasta, side dishes, fruit, and dessert in a cafeterialike setting. ⊠ *Av. Buenos Aires 366,* ☎ *no phone. No credit cards.*

**$$**  🏨 **Hotel Austral.** Though it's a tad shabby for a hotel in this category, it's the best in town (and rooms have cable TV and are light). It's location is also excellent: across the street from the Río Negro, with great northward views of Carmen de Patagones and its cathedral (ask to be lodged on this side) and of Viedma to the south. The tiny boat that takes you to Carmen de Patagones for 50¢ is just steps from the hotel, as are most of the town's other attractions. The large lobby is comfortable, and there's a full-service restaurant with Argentine basics: steak, chicken, and pasta. ⊠ *Av. 25 de Mayo and Av. Villarino, 8500,* ☎ *2920/ 422615, 2920/422616, 2920/422617, or 2920/422618,* FAX *2920/ 422619. 100 rooms. Restaurant, air-conditioning, laundry service and dry cleaning, business services, meeting rooms, parking. MC, V.*

**$**  🏨 **Hotel Comahue.** On a quieter, less-trafficked side of the town park, this hotel has unspectacular but clean rooms for a good price. It also has a popular restaurant and a cybercafé where you can use the Internet for a modest hourly fee. ⊠ *Colon 385, 8500,* ☎ *2920/424291,* FAX *2920/423092. Restaurant, air-conditioning, parking. No credit cards.*

**$**  🏨 **Hotel Peumayen.** Though it's nothing out of the ordinary, this hotel is a good value for the money. Rooms are on the small side, with basic wood furniture; all have TVs. It's in front of a pleasant tree-lined park on the main drag and just three blocks from the river. The staff is helpful. ⊠ *Av. Buenos Aires 334, 8500,* ☎ *2920/425234 or 425222,* FAX *2920/425243. Bar, air-conditioning, in-room safes, parking. No credit cards.*

## Nightlife

On weekends Viedma can get lively, with youngsters and families walking and playing alongside the riverfront, and processions of cars with blasting music heading down the main streets. One popular stop is **Fiore Helados,** an ice cream shop where throngs of people line up for such Italian-styled delights. A young (teens to mid-twenties) smart set heads to the **Eclipse Discoteque** to drink, primp, and dance the night away. Another option is Viedma's little casino, the **Salon de Juegos**

(✉ Belgrano and Av. Buenos Aires). Don't expect Las Vegas–style croupiers; this casino uses plastic smart cards with cash credits (no cash is laid down on tables), and a computer keeps track of your wins and losses on the roulette tables. There are also slot machines. It's open daily 1:30 PM–3:30 AM (you must be at least 18 to enter).

## Outdoor Activities and Sports

Kayaking, canoeing, fishing, and swimming in the Río Negro are the main outdoor activities in Viedma. You might even be able to join in a soccer game being played in the street alongside the river. If you can get hold of a bike (they are hard to come by), the tree-lined promenade along the river makes for a lovely ride. You may be able to rent a bike (though they primarily sell them) at the **Bike Shop del Vecchio** (☎ 2920/424466). For kayaking (both rentals and tours), contact Mauricio Vergauben at **Aquaventura** (☎ 2920/ 428229) or the **Club Nautico** (☎ 2920/431110), which also rents fishing gear. Every year during the second week of January is the **Regatta Río Negro,** when dozens, if not hundreds, of boats strut their stuff down the Río Negro.

# Carmen de Patagones

**㉓** *On the north bank of the Río Negro across from Viedma; it can be reached from Viedma by taking the five-minute ferry ride across the river; service ends at about 10 PM. If going by car or taxi, there are two bridges on the town's outskirts.*

The southernmost city in the Buenos Aires Province, Carmen de Patagones is the gateway to Patagonia. More picturesque and quieter and smaller than its neighbor Viedma, Carmen de Patagones still conserves much of the early 19th-century colonial heritage that Viedma lost in a early 1900s flood. It was founded, with Viedma, in 1779 with the construction of a fort. For four decades the early settlers lived in caves, one of which is preserved in the Museo Histórico Regional Francisco de Viedma. Residents are sometimes called Maragatos, a reference to the many settlers who came from the Spanish area of Maragateria, in the Leon Province. The town is oriented around its cathedral, which is fronted by a park and a bench-lined waterfront, where kids can often be found jumping off an old pier into the water. For more information about activities in the area, contact the **tourist office** (✉ Comodoro Rivadavía 193, ☎ 2920/262053).

At the **Museo Histórico Regional Francisco de Viedma** (Francisco de Viedma Historical Regional Museum) the biggest attraction is the *craneo fletchado,* the skull of an 18th-century Tehuelche Indian, with a Mapuche Indian arrow in place of its nose; it will give you more appreciation for the struggles of indigenous people even before the arrival of the colonizers. Also here is one of the actual caves in which the earliest settlers lived before moving into houses. ✉ *J. J. Biedma 64, in front of the ferry landing.* 🎟 *Free (donations accepted).* ☼ *Weekdays 9–noon and 7–9.*

The early 19th-century adobe-walled **Casa Historica La Carlota** (La Carlota Historical Home) last belonged to Dona Carlota, a stern-looking Spanish immigrant seen in a hallway photo, who died in the early 1900s. The city's early immigrants built houses like this one from their earnings from working in the salt mines; this is one of the three earliest remaining houses. Still standing are the well, the wheat-grinding stones, the stone oven used for baking bread, and other rudimentary tools. In preparation for Indian attacks, which never happened, the house is ringed with thick cacti and outfitted with a secret compartment where the children were to hide. ✉ *Bynon 112.* ☼ *Weekdays 9–noon and 7–9, by* *guided tour only (tours can be arranged by request at the Museo Regional Francisco de Viedma).*

In 1827 the locals fought off a Brazilian invasion headed by the Portuguese. To understand the importance of this battle to residents on both sides of the Río Negro, visit the **Iglesia Parroquial** (Parochial Church), built by Salesan priests and inaugurated in 1885. You can't miss the two immense Brazilian flags on either side of the main altar, which were captured in the battle. ⊠ *Av. Comodoro Rivadavía and Av. 7 de Marzo.*

### Dining and Lodging

$ ✕ **Rigolleto.** A favorite local spot, this restaurant and bar feels like a Western saloon, with lots of dark wood. Come here for good oven-baked pizza, light snacks, and the location overlooking the water; on a hot day you can stroll with your cool Quilmes beer out to the waterfront. ⊠ *J. J. Biedma 2. No credit cards.*

$ ✕ **Tío Pepe.** Owned by a third-generation Basque and longtime restaurant man, Carlos Gaztelu, this spot is simple and unadorned; usually there's a soccer game going on the tiny TV. Built on the site of a 1920s building that housed Patagonia's first Ford dealership, it has typical regional food, including *churrasco* (barbecued beef), *milanesa* (thinly cut steak), parrillas, salads, and pastas. The service is good, and the food is reasonably well prepared. ⊠ *Biynon and Alsina. No credit cards.*

$ ▦ **Hotel Percaz.** Like it or not, this hotel is the only game in town. Rooms are simple but clean and have cable TV, and you get breakfast. And it's only a few short blocks from the central square. ⊠ *Comodoro Rivadavía and Irigoyen, 8504,* ☏ *2920/254104,* FAX *no fax. 20 rooms. Breakfast room, snack bar. AE, DC, MC, V.*

### Nightlife and the Arts

Every year on March 7 begins the weeklong **Fiesta de Soberanía y la Tradición** (Sovereignty and Tradition Festival) celebrating the city's defense against the incursion by Brazil in 1827. Events include live music, regional foods, and crafts for sale.

# PATAGONIA A TO Z

## Arriving and Departing

### By Airplane

The best way to get to Patagonia is to fly from Buenos Aires. **Aerolíneas Argentinas** (☏ 11/4317–3000 or 11/4340–7800 in Buenos Aires; ☏ 800/333–0276 in the U.S.), the country's major airline, flies from Buenos Aires to Trelew, Comodoro Rivadavia, Ushuaia, Río Gallegos, and Bariloche. Some smaller airlines fly from Buenos Aires to other towns in the region and fly between towns; generally, however, to get around the region, you have to fly back to Buenos Aires and then fly to another town. Though flying to Patagonia is costly—for instance, Aerolíneas Argentina's least expensive one-way fare between Buenos Aires and Ushuaia is $260—you don't have much choice, especially if you're short on time. One money-saving option is Aerolineas Argentina's "Visit Argentina" pass, which allows you to fly to multiple destinations at a discount; it must be purchased outside of Argentina.

**Kaiken** (☏ contact Almafuerte Travel in Buenos Aires, 11/4331–0191 or 11/4331–0191, FAX 11/4342–6447; ☏ 2944/420251 in Bariloche; Av. San Martín 880, Piso 2, Ushuaia, ☏ 2901/432963) flies between Buenos Aires and Bariloche, Trelew, Comodoro Rivadavia, Río Gallegos, and Ushuaia; request the *banda negativa* fare for cheaper tickets sold subject to availability. In summer, **LADE** (☏ 11/4361–7071 or

11/4361–7174 in Buenos Aires, FAX 11/4362–4899; ☎ 2944/423562
in Bariloche), the Air Force transport line, flies from Buenos Aires to
Bariloche and Viedma and between Comodoro Rivadavía and Puerto
Deseado. **Lapas Líneas Aereas** (☎ 11/4819–5272 or 11/4819–6200 in
Buenos Aires, FAX 11/4814–2100; ☎ 2944/423714 in Bariloche) flies
between Buenos Aires and Bariloche, Trelew, Comodoro Rivadavía,
and Ushuaia. If you're coming from Chile, **ALTA** (☎ 562/3345872 in
Santiago) and **LanChile** (☎ 562/6323211 in Santiago) make the 50-
minute flight from Punta Arenas regularly.

### BARILOCHE

The 1,935-km (1,200-mi) trip between Buenos Aires and Bariloche takes
two hours by plane. **Aerolíneas Argentinas** (⊠ Quaglia 238, ☎ 2944/
422425) flies daily from Buenos Aires to Bariloche. **Kaiken** (⊠ Palacios 266, ☎ 2944/420251); **LADE** (⊠ ☎ 2944/423562); and **Lapas** (⊠
Villegas 121, ☎ 2944/423714) have less expensive but fewer flights
between Buenos Aires and Bariloche. Several flights a week depart from
Bariloche for Trelew and Esquel. **Southern Winds** (⊠ Villegas 145, ☎
2944/423704) has flights to northern cities, with a stopover in Córdoba.

### COMODORO RIVADAVÍA

Flights between Buenos Aires and Comodoro Rivadavía are available
on: **Dinar** (☎ 11/4327–1111 or 11/4819–5272 in Buenos Aires); **Kaiken**
(☞ *above*); **Lapas** (☞ *above*); and **Transporte Aereas Neuquen** (☎ 11/
4311–2699 or 11/4312–8520 in Buenos Aires). In summer, **LADE** (☞
*above*) flies between Comodoro Rivadavía and Puerto Deseado.

### RÍO GALLEGOS AND EL CALAFATE

**Río Gallegos Aeropuerto** (☎ 2966/442059). **Aerolíneas Argenti-
nas/Austral** (⊠ Av. San Martín 545, ☎ 2966/422020) has daily flights
between Buenos Aires and Río Gallegos. **Kaiken** (⊠ at the Río Gallegos Aeropuerto, ☎ 2966/442062 or Zapiola 63, ☎ 2966/437177) has
daily flights to El Calafate, weather permitting.

### SAN MARTÍN DE LOS ANDES

**Austral** (☞ Aerolíneas Argentinas, *above*) flies from Buenos Aires to
San Martín's **Aeropuerto Chalpeco** (☎ 2972/428388).

### USHUAIA

**Aerolíneas Argentinas** (☞ *above*), **Kaiken** (☞ *above*), and **Lapas** (☞
*above*) fly between Buenos Aires and Ushuaia.

### VIEDMA

**Austral** (☞ Aerolíneas Argentinas, *above*) flies between Buenos Aires
and Viedma. In summer, **LADE** (☞ *above*), the Air Force transport line,
flies from Buenos Aires to Viedma.

## By Boat

Traveling between Bariloche and Puerto Montt, Chile by boat is one
of the most popular excursions in Argentina. It requires three lake cross-
ings and various buses and can be done in a day or overnight (☞ Bariloche, *above*). Travel agents and tour operators in Bariloche and Buenos
Aires can arrange this trip and many foreign tour companies include
it in their itineraries (☞ Tour Operators and Travel Agents, *below*).
Cruises to Antarctica and the Malvinas (Falkland Islands) rarely stop
at Ushuaia nowadays; they call instead at Punta Arenas, Chile.

## By Bus

Every Patagonian town, no matter how small or insignificant, has a
bus station; and it's not uncommon for buses to stop and pick up a
passenger standing by the road where there's nothing in sight for hundreds of miles. Buses arrive in Bariloche from every corner of Ar-

gentina—from Jujuy in the north, Ushuaia in the south, and everywhere in between as well as from Puerto Montt, Osorno, Valdivia, and Santiago in Chile. Several companies have daily service to Buenos Aires.

BARILOCHE

**Bariloche's Terminal de Omnibus** (Bus Station; ✉ Av. 12 de Octubre, ☎ 2944/432860) is in the Estacíon de Ferrocarril General Roca (Railroad Station) east of town, where all bus companies have offices. Most have downtown offices, too, but your best bet is to go directly to the terminal. The following bus companies run comfortable and reliable overnight buses between Buenos Aires and Bariloche (the trip takes 22 hours): **Chevallier** (✉ Moreno 107, Bariloche, ☎ 2944/423090 in Bariloche, 11/4314–0111 or 11/4314–5555 in Buenos Aires); **El Valle** (✉ Mitre 321, Bariloche, ☎ 2944/429012 in Bariloche, 11/4313–3749 in Buenos Aires); and **Via Bariloche** (✉ Av. 12 de Octubre 1884, Bariloche, ☎ 2944/422217 in Bariloche, 11/4663–8899 in Buenos Aires). Buses also depart daily from Bariloche for Chile (Osorno, Puerto Montt, Valdivia, and Santiago) via the Puyehue Pass; contact **Tas–Choapa** (✉ Bariloche Bus Terminal, ☎ 0944/26663 in Bariloche, 562/6970062 in Santiago).

RÍO GALLEGOS AND EL CALAFATE

The following bus companies connect Buenos Aires to Río Gallegos and El Calafate: **Don Otto** (Mitre 161, ☎ 2944/323269); **Interlagos** (✉ Av. San Martín 1175, El Calafate, ☎ 0902/91018; ☎ 0966/22614 in Río Gallegos); **El Pingüino** (☎ 11/4315–4438 in Buenos Aires); and **TAC** (☎ 11/4313–3627 or 11/4313–3632 in Buenos Aires). In summer, **Bus Sur** (☎ FAX 5661/411325); and **Turismo Zaahj** (☎ 5661/412260, FAX 5661/411355) make the five-hour run from Puerto Natales, Chile, to El Calafate.

USHUAIA

You'll probably want to fly to Ushuaia to make the most of your time in the Tierra del Fuego, but direct bus service between Buenos Aires and Chile and Ushuaia exist. **Trans los Carlos** (✉ Av. San Martín 880, Ushuaia, ☎ 0901/22337); and **Turismo Ghisoni** (✉ Lautaro Navarro 975, Punta Arenas, ☎ 5661/223205, FAX 5661/222078) make the 12-hour run to and from Punta Arenas, Chile.

## By Car

Driving to any of the towns in Patagonia from Buenos Aires is a long haul (1,593 km ; 2–3 days) of interminable stretches without motels, gas stations, or restaurants. Fuel in Argentina is expensive and if you break down in the hinterlands, it's unlikely that you'll find anyone who speaks much English. Note, too, that places on the map may just be estancias and when you arrive all you may find is a gate and a road leading off to the horizon. But roads are paved all the way to Bariloche, and if you're a more adventurous traveler driving exposes you to the heart of the country. Planning is essential, and **ACA** (Automóvil Club Argentina; ☞ Driving *in* Smart Travel Tips A to Z) can provide maps and advice. To get to Bariloche from Buenos Aires: Take R5 to Santa Rosa (615 km ), then R35 to General Acha (107 km ), then R20 to Colonia 25 de Mayo, then R151 to Neuquen (438 km ), and then R237 to Bariloche (449 km ).

Driving to **Río Gallegos** (2,504 km from Buenos Aires) is even more daunting, more isolated, and more monotonous. The most sensible solution is to fly and rent a car at your destination. Roads between towns and sights in both the northern and southern Lake Districts are mostly paved, and if not, generally kept in good condition.

### By Train

Direct train service between Buenos Aires and Bariloche is not an option. Trains do, however, make a 20-hour haul to Viedma, leaving twice a week from Bariloche. For information, contact **Servicios Ferroviarios Patagónicos** (✉ in the train terminal, ☎ 2944/23172 in Bariloche, 2920/22130 in Viedma).

## Getting Around

Traveling the length of Patagonia is a formidable task, especially if you're short on time. To put its size in perspective, Patagonia is 1,930 km (1,200 mi) long, a bit more than the distance from New York City to Miami. No single airline flies everywhere in the region, nor is there a system that links them all. Some towns, such as Puerto Deseado, has no air service whatsoever and infrequent and inconvenient bus service. Most likely you'll find yourself taking a mishmash of planes and buses.

### By Bus

Andesmar Autotransportes and La Puntual are two of the main regional bus companies. They stop at almost every major and minor city along the coast and also cross Patagonia between Bahía Blanca and Neuquen. To the west, they reach Chile's cities of Los Andes and Santiago, among others. And they go as far south as Río Gallegos. Bus schedules can be picked up at bus stations.

#### BARILOCHE

To travel from Bariloche south to El Bolsón and Esquel, contact **Don Otto** (✉ Mitre 161, ☎ 2944/323269. **Andesmar** (✉ Palacios 246, ☎ 2944/422140 or 2944/430211 at the bus terminal); and **TAC** (✉ Villegas 147, ☎ 2944/432521). For travel north to Villa Angostura, Traful, and San Martín de los Andes, contact TAC.

#### RÍO GALLEGOS AND EL CALAFATE

**Pinguino** (✉ Zapiola 445, ☎ 2966/423338) has daily service to El Calafate (✉ Terminal de Omnibus, Julio Roca 1004, ☎ 2902/491273) as well to Trelew and Puerto Madryn and to Bariloche with a change in Comodoro Rivadavía.

### By Car

Renting a car is the most satisfactory way to explore Patagonia; it gives you the freedom to travel when and where you want, to stop for photographs, and to enjoy a picnic in the woods whenever you want. Although rental rates are high, gas is expensive ($4 a gallon at press time), and the distances between cities are extensive, the rewards may justify the expense and the time it takes to travel. Almost all hotels have off-street parking, some in locked yards, which is a good idea to use, especially at night. In an effort to attract tourists and new residents to El Bolsón and Chubut Province, the government has lowered the price of gas 50% in this region.

A number of U.S. car rental agencies can be found in Patagonia's major cities and tourist centers: **Avis** (☎ 11/4326–5542 in Buenos Aires; ✉ Av. 9 de Julio 687, Comodoro Rivadavía, ☎ 0297/4476382; ✉ Paraguay 105, Trelew, ☎ 2965/234634); **Budget** (☎ 11/4313–9870 in Buenos Aires; ✉ Mitre 106, Bariloche, ☎ 2944/422482); **Dollar** (☎ 11/4315–8800 in Buenos Aires; ✉ Av. San Martín 491, inside the Hotel Panamericano, Bariloche, ☎ 2944/430358); and **Hertz** (☎ 11/4312–1317 in Buenos Aires).

**Ai-Ansa International** (✉ Av. San Martín 235, across from Edelweiss Hotel, Bariloche, ☎ 2944/422582, FAX 2944/427494; ✉ Av. San Martín 866, Paseo del Maiten, local #3, ☎ 2972/427997, FAX 2972/428482) is locally owned and recommended for its good rates and knowledgable agents who can help you plan excursions, suggest hotels, even make reservations. Local chains include: **Aonik'Enk de Patagonia** (✉ Av. Rawson 1190, Comodoro Rivadavía, ☎ 0297/4466768); **Duma** (✉ Belgrano and Rosales, Ushuaia, ☎ 2901/231914); **Localiza** (☎ 11/4816–3999 or 11/4815–6303 in Buenos Aires; Av. Julio Roca, El Calafate, ☎ 2966/491446; ✉ Av. Rivadavía 190, Comodoro Rivadavía, ☎ 0297/4460334; ✉ Av. Rivadavía 1168, Esquel, ☎ 2945/453276; ✉ Av. Roca 536, Puerto Madryn, ☎ 2965/256300; ✉ Sarmiento 237, Río Gallegos, ☎ 2966/42441; ✉ Urquiza 310, Trelew, ☎ 2965/253344; ✉ Av. San Martín 1222, Ushuaia, ☎ 2901/230739); **Patagonia** (✉ Av. Roca 31, Puerto Madryn, ☎ 2965/255106); **Rent-A-Car** (✉ Av. Roca 277, Puerto Madryn, ☎ 2965/250295; ✉ Av. San Martín 125, Trelew, ☎ 2965/220898; ✉ Belgrano and Ameghino, Ushuaia, ☎ 2901/230757); **Unidas** (☎ 11/4315–0777 in Buenos Aires); and **Visita Rent-a-Car** (✉ Maipú, Ushuaia, ☎ 2901/235181).

If you don't like dealing with traffic and tour buses don't fit your schedule, a *remise* (car with driver) is a good option; it costs about the same as a taxi, but is bigger and the rate is set before you depart on your trip. In Bariloche: **Remises Auto Jet** (✉ España 11, ☎ 2944/422408); and **Remises Bariloche** (✉ Villegas 282, ☎ 2944/430222). In Esquel: **Nevada** (☎ 2945/453622). Río Gallegos: **Centenario** (✉ Maipú 285, ☎ 2966/422320). In San Martín: **Del Bosque** (✉ Villegas 971, ☎ 2972/429109); and **Los Andes** (✉ Villegas 945, ☎ 2972/429110).

### By Taxi

Since taking a taxi doesn't cost much and drivers know their way around, arranging tours or quick trips by taxi to sights near Bariloche, Calafate, Esquel, or other locales makes sense. If you're in El Calafate and have a sudden urge to see the Moreno Glacier, for instance, or you missed the bus to a boat departure on Lago Nahuel Huapi, taking a taxi is a good solution. In Bariloche, there are taxi stands at the Civic Center and at calles Mitre and Villegas. In other towns, taxis line up at the airport, the bus terminal, and at main intersections. You're hotel can also call a taxi for you.

## Contacts and Resources

### Banks and Currency Exchange

Hardly anyone changes dollars to pesos these days since the rate is equal; in fact, you often get change in both. In smaller towns, such as El Bolsón and Esquel, pesos are preferred. Torn or marked dollars may not be accepted. Banks are open 10–4 in most towns.

#### BARILOCHE

ATMs (Banelco, Link, Cirrus) can be found at **Banco Frances** (✉ Av. San Martín 336, ☎ 2944/430325); and **Banco Quilmes** (✉ Mitre 433, ☎ 2944/423675).

#### EL CALAFATE

Look for **Provincia de Santa Cruz** (✉ Av. Libertador 1285, ☎ 2902/491168).

#### COMODORO RIVADAVÍA

Head for **Banco Almafuerte** (✉ Av. Rivadavía 202, ☎ 0297/4465883); **Banco Nación** (✉ Av. San Martín 102, ☎ 0297/4472700); or **Lloyds Bank** (✉ Av. Rivadavía 266, ☎ 0297/4474814).

#### ESQUEL

Try **Banco de la Nación** (✉ Alvear and Roca, ☎ 2945/452105).

PUERTO MADRYN

In Puerto Madryn, look for **Banco Almafuerte** (⊠ Roque Sanez Pena and 25 de Mayo, ☎ 2965/2521941); or **Banco Nación** (⊠ 9 de Julio 117 ☎ 2965/250465).

SAN MARTÍN

There are ATMs at **Banelco** (⊠ Av. San Martín 687 ☎ 2972/427292); and **Banco de la Nación** (⊠ Av. San Martín 687 ☎ 2972/427292).

RÍO GALLEGOS

Look for **Bancos de Galicia, Nazionale de Lavoro,** and **Hipotecario Nacional** (⊠ all on Fagnano off of Av. Roca). **Banco de Santa Cruz** (⊠ Roca and Errázuri) changes travelers' checks.

TRELEW

Try **Banco Nación Argentina** (⊠ Fontana and 25 de Mayo, ☎ 2965/235956); or **Lloyds Bank** (⊠ 9 de Julio 102, ☎ 2965/234264).

## Emergencies

**Coast Guard** (☎ 106). **Fire** (☎ 100). **Forest Fire** (☎ 103). **Hospital** (☎ 107). **Police** (☎ 101).

BARILOCHE

**Hospitals: Hospital Ramon Carillo** (⊠ Moreno 601, ☎ 2944/42117 or 426119); **Sanatorio del Sol** (20 de Febrero 640, ☎ 2944/432094, 2944/433111 for emergencies). **Local Police** (⊠ in Civic Center, ☎ 2944/422992). **Pharmacies: Del Centro** (⊠ Rolando 699, ☎ 2944/424422); **De Miguel** (⊠ Mitre 130, ☎ 2944/423025); and **Elustondo** (⊠ Mitre 379, ☎ 2944/422847).

EL CALAFATE

**Hospital Municipal** (⊠ Av. Roca 1487, ☎ 2902/491001).

ESQUEL

**Hospital Zon. Esquel** (⊠ 25 de Mayo 150, ☎ 2945/451074 or 2945/451224). **Local Police** (⊠ Rivadavía and Mitre, ☎ 2945/450789 or 2945/450001). **Pharmacies: Atenas** (⊠ Av. Fontana 779, ☎ 2945/451004); and **Dra. Bonetto** (⊠ 25 de Mayo 150, ☎ 2945/450662).

RÍO GALLEGOS

**Hospital Regional** (⊠ José Ingeniero 98, ☎ 2966/420025 in emergencies, ☎ FAX 2966/420641). **Local Police** (⊠ Av. San Martín and Buenos Aires, ☎ 2966/420287).

SAN MARTÍN DE LOS ANDES

**Ambulance** (⊠ P. Moreno 654, ☎ 2972/422174). **Hospital Ramon Carillo** (⊠ San Martín and Rodhe, ☎ 2972/427211). **Local Police** (⊠ Belgrano 635, ☎ 2972/427300). **Pharmacies: Farmacia Austral** (⊠ Elordi 765, ☎ 2972/427393); **Farmacia del Centro** (⊠ San Martín and Belgrano, ☎ 2972/428999).

## Health and Safety

The water in Bariloche and throughout Patagonia is generally safe. But if you're susceptible to intestinal disturbances, it's best to stick to bottled water, which is available in stores, restaurants, and at some kiosks. *Tabanas* (horse flies) are pests around horses and in the woods in summer; horse-fly repellent is more effective than general bug spray; bring enough for yourself and the horse. Car break-ins and purse snatching is on the rise late at night, so take precautions.

## Telephones, the Internet, and Mail

PHONES AND INTERNET

When calling from outside the area code within Argentina, a 0 precedes the area code. Local calls can be made from *telecabinas* (phone booths) with a phone card purchased at kiosks. Numerous *locutorios* (telephone offices) are found in all towns. They're easy to use: An attendant sends you to a booth where you can call all over the country or the world, and then pay one bill when you leave. Since hotels charge exorbitant rates for long distance calls, it's best to go to the closest locutorio.

In Bariloche, **Locutorio Quaglia** (⊠ Quaglia 220, ☎ FAX 2944/426128) has fax, Internet, E-mail, and Western Union services; it's open daily 7:30AM–1AM. **Mas** (⊠ Moreno 724, in front of the hospital, ☎ 2944/428414), in Bariloche, has fax and photcopy services; it's open daily 7 AM–4 AM. **Cyber Club Bariloche** (⊠ Galería del Sol, Location 54, 340 Mitre, ☎ 2944/421418), in Bariloche, has internet and E-mail access; it's open Monday–Saturday 9:30–9:30. In Viedma, Internet access is available at **Arnet** (⊠ Alvaro Barros 266, ☎ 2920/431616. For Internet and E-mail service in Puerto Madryn, try **Compulab** (⊠ 25 de Mayo 95). In Trelew, **Locutorio del Centro** (⊠ Av. 25 de Mayo 219) has phone and internet access. Internet and E-mail access in Trelew are available at **Arnet** (⊠ San Martín and Mitre). In Ushuaia, you can make calls and access the internet at **Locutorio Cabo de Hornos** (⊠ Av. 25 de Mayo 112) and **Locutorio Fin del Mundo** (⊠ Av. San Martín 957).

### POST OFFICES (CORREOS)

**Bariloche** (⊠ in the Centro Civico) is open daily 8–8; stamps can also be purchased at kiosks around town. **El Calafate** (⊠ Av. Libertador 1122). **Carmen de Patagones** (⊠ Paraguay 38). **Esquel** (⊠ Alvear 1192, across from bus station, ☎ 2945/451865). **Río Gallegos** (⊠ Avs. Julio Roca and San Martín). **San Martín de los Andes** (⊠ at the Civic Center, General Roca and Pérez, ☎ 2972/42720). **Viedma** (⊠ Moreno and 25 de Mayo; ⊠ Av. Rivadavía 151; ⊠ Oca and Zatti 545).

## Tour Operators and Travel Agencies

If you want a comprehensive tour of Patagonia, including the Parque Nacional los Glaciares, Lago Argentino, Trelew, and Bariloche, contact **Gador Viajes** (⊠ Tucumán 941, Buenos Aires, ☎ 11/43229806, FAX 11/43226344).

### BARILOCHE

The English-speaking owners of **Alunco** (⊠ Moreno 187, Piso 1, Bariloche, ☎ 2944/422283, FAX 2944/422782; Maipú 812, Piso 4, Buenos Aires, ☎ 11/43149076, FAX 11/43110675), a very professional travel office specializing in trips in and around Bariloche, are third generation Barilocheans, expert skiers, and outdoors enthusiasts who have explored the remotest regions in the area. The main focus of **Catedral Turismo** (⊠ Mitre 399, Bariloche, ☎ 2944/425443, FAX 2944/426215) is the lake crossing from Bariloche to Chile (☞ Bariloche, *above*), excursions on the Patagonian Express (☞ Esquel, *above*), and tours in around Bariloche.

### EL BOLSÓN

Guided fishing, rafting, and horseback riding trips from El Bolsón and excursions to Lago Puelho National Park can be arranged by **Patagonia Adventures** (⊠ Pablo Hube 418, El Bolsón, ☎ 2944/493280); and **Quen Quen Turismo** (⊠ Berutti, next to bus terminal, El Bolśn, ☎ 2944/493522).

### EL CALAFATE

Alberto del Castillo, owner of **E.V.T. Fitzroy Expeditions** (⊠ Av. San Martín, ☎ 2962/493017, FAX 2962/49136), has English-speaking guides and organizes both glacier and mountain treks. Most hotels arrange treks to glaciers around El Calafate as can **Hielo y Aventura** (⊠ Av. Libertador 935, El Calafate, ☎ FAX 2902/491053). Horseback riding trip of various lengths can be arranged by **Gustavo Holzman** (✉ J.A. Roca 2035, El Calafate, ☎ 2902/491203) or through the tourist office.

### ESQUEL

**Plan Mundo** (✉ Adolfo Alsina 960, Planta Abajo 2, Buenos Aires, 1088, ☎ 11/43454566; Av. Cabildo 1165, Buenos Aires, 1426, ☎ 11/47876555) organizes fishing trips in Los Alerces National Park for about $1,200. The package includes roundtrip airfare between Buenos Aires and Esquel, airport transfer on both ends, three nights with breakfast and dinner in the Hostería Futalaufquen in Esquel, and three full days of fishing, including launch, guide, permit, meals, and equipment. For organized white-water rafting trips to the Río Corcovado, near the Chilean border, contact **Outworker** (✉ 9 de Julio 1080, ☎ 2945/450516); or **Travesis** (✉ Av. Rivadavia 1650, ☎ FAX 2945/454690).

### GAIMAN

**Noria Tours** (✉ Eugenio Tello 612, Gaiman, ☎ 2965/491207 or 15670985) organizes tours from Gaiman to the nearby Punto Tomba penguin reserve as well as to farms and chapels in the Chubut Valley.

### PUERTO MADRYN AND PENINSULA VALDÉS

**Factor Patagonia** (✉ 25 de Mayo, Puerto Madryn, ☎ 2965/454990 or 2965/454991) arranges all-day tours of the Peninsula Valdés, with an abundance of explanation; reserve ahead, especially if you want an English-speaking guide. The company also organizes tours to Punta Tombo, the Dique Ameghino, and Camarones. **Jorge Schmid** (☎ 2965/495112 or 2965/495029) specializes in whale-watching tours; his boat has ample covered space (in case it rains). **Peke Sosa** (☎ 2965/495010, FAX 2965/471291) also operates whale-watching tours. **Zonotrikia** (✉ Av. Roca 536, Puerto Madryn, ☎ 2965/451427 or 2965/455888) leads treks through paleontological sites in the area.

### SAN MARTÍN DE LOS ANDES

**Chapelco Turismo** (✉ Av. San Martín 876, San Martín de los Andes, ☎ 2972/427550) runs a grand lake and volcano excursion between San Martín and Chile. **Ici Viajes** (✉ Villegas 570, San Martín de los Andes, ☎ 2972/428491, FAX 2972/427800) organizes tours in and around San Martín as well as national and international travel. **Tiempo Patagonico** (✉ Av. San Martín 540, San Martín de los Andes, ☎ 2972/427114, FAX 2972/427113) arranges extensive outdoor and adventure tours in the area around San Martín.

### RÍO GALLEGOS AND EL CALAFATE

**Interlagos Turismo** (✉ Fagnano 35, Río Gallegos, ☎ 2966/422614; ✉ Av. Libertador 1175, El Calafate, ☎ 2902/491179, FAX 2902/491241) arranges tours of Río Gallegos and El Calafate and transportation between the two. **Tur Aike Turismo** (✉ Zapiola 63, Río Gallegos, ☎ FAX 2966/424503 or 2966/422436) organizes tours in and around Río Gallegos. In El Calafate, **Cal Tur** (✉ Av. Libertador 1080, El Calafate, ☎ FAX 2966/491368) runs local tours.

### SARAMIENTO AND THE BOSQUE PETRIFICADO

**Aonik'Enk** (✉ Rawson 1190, ☎ 0297/4466768 or 0297/4461363, FAX 0297/4476349) gives tours of the city, the petrified forest, and other nearby destinations; it also rents four-wheel drive vehicles.

### USHUAIA AND THE TIERRA DEL FUEGO

**Antartur** (✉ Maipú 237, Ushuaia, ☎ 2901/23240, FAX 2901/24108); **Licatur** (✉ Av. San Martín 880, Ushuaia, ☎ 2901/22337, FAX 0901/23550); **Linéa B** (☎ 2901/441139); **Tiempo Libre** (✉ Av. San Martín 863, Ushuaia, ☎ 2901/31374, FAX 2901/21017); and **Yishka Turismo**

**y Aventuras** (⊠ Av. San Martín 1295, Ushuaia, ☎ 2901/431230 or 2901/431535, FAX 2901/437606) offer a wide variety of adventurous treks through the Parque Nacional Tierra del Fuego and around the Beagle Channel. **Tolkeyén** (⊠ Tekenika 119, Ushuaia, ☎ 2901/22150 or 2901/32920, FAX 2901/30532); and **Rumbo Sur** (⊠ Av. San Martín 342, Ushuaia, ☎ 2901/21139, FAX 2901/30699) organize tours of the Beagle Channel and bus trips that give an overview of the national park. **All Patagonia** (☎ 2901/437025, FAX 2901/430707) organizes bus trips to Lago Escondido and other spots in the area. Sailing out to sea usually means contact with wide-eyed seals, sea elephants, and sea lions sunning on the rocks. **Antartur, Rumbo Sur,** and **Tiempo Libre** (☞ *above*) all do sea excursions as well as trips to Antarctica. To charter a sailboat, head to the **Club Naútico** (⊠ Maipú 1210).

VIEDMA AND CARMEN DE PATAGONES

Gloria Rousiot de Alejandro of **Emprese Iniros** (☎ 2920/421368 or 15604009) conducts tours of Viedma and Carmen de Patagones and organizes trip to Balneario El Condor and El Lobería. **Jose Luis Breitman** (☎ 15605196) also arranges tours of Viedma, Carmen de Patagones, and nearby beaches and parks, including Balneario El Condor and La Lobería.

## Visitor Information

Provincial tourism boards include the following. **Nuequen Tourism Institute** (⊠ Felix S. Martín 182, Neuquen, 8300, ☎ 0299/4424089 or 0299/4423388, FAX 0299/4432438). **Provincial Tourism Unit of Chubut** (⊠ Av. 9 de Julio 280, Rawson, 9103, ☎ 2965/481113, 2965/484144, or 2965/485271, FAX 2965/481113 or 2965/484144). **Santa Cruz Tourism Institute** (⊠ Av. Roca 863, Río Gallegos, 9400, ☎ 2966/422702 or 2966/437447, FAX 2966/422702). **Tierra del Fuego Tourism Institute** (⊠ Av. Maipú 505, Ushuaia, 9410, ☎ 2901/421423, FAX 2901/430694). **Tourism Secretariat of Río Negro** (⊠ Gallardo 121, Viedma, 8500, ☎ 2920/422150, 2920/424615, or 2920/430996, FAX 2920/421249).

Local tourist offices (*Direcciónes de Turismo*) are generally easy to find, open all day and often into the evening, and helpful. **Bariloche** (⊠ in the Civic Center, east end of Bartolomé Mitre, ☎ 2944/423022, FAX 2944/426784). **El Bolsón** (⊠ Plaza Pagano and Av. San Martín, ☎ 2944/492604). **El Calafate** (⊠ Terminal de Omnibus, Julio A. Roca 1004, ☎ FAX 2902/49090). **Comodoro Rivadavía** (⊠ Av. Rivadavía 430, ☎ 0297/4474111). **Esquel** (⊠ Sarmiento and Alvear, ☎ FAX 2945/451927; ⊠ at train station, ☎ 2945/451403). **Junín de los Andes** (⊠ Padre Milanesio 590, ☎ 2972/491142). **Puerto Deseado** (⊠ Colón and Belgrano ☎ 0297/4870220 or 0297/4871157). **Puerto Madryn** (⊠ Av. Roca 223, ☎ 2965/453504 or 2965/452148). **Rio Gallegos** (⊠ Av. Roca 1551, ☎ FAX 2966/42595). **San Martín de los Andes** (⊠ San Martín and Rosas, ☎ 2972/427347). **Sarmiento** (☎ 2965/4893401). **Trelew** (⊠ Av. San Martín 171, ☎ 2965/420139, 2965/435797, or 2965/435941). **Trevelín** (⊠ Plaza de la Fontana, ☎ 2945/480120). **Ushuaia** (⊠ Av. San Martín 674, ☎ 2901/432000 or 0800/3331476). **Viedma** (⊠ on the Costanera between Colón and Alvaro Barros, ☎ 2920/427171 or 2920/422287). **Villa la Angostura** (⊠ Siete Lagos and Los Arrayanes, ☎ FAX 2944/494124). **Villa Traful** (⊠ in the center of town, ☎ 2944/479020).

# SPANISH VOCABULARY

## Words and Phrases

| | English | Spanish | Pronunciation |
|---|---|---|---|
| **Basics** | | | |
| | Yes/no | Sí/no | see/no |
| | Please | Por favor | pore fah-**vore** |
| | May I? | ¿Me permite? | may pair-**mee**-tay |
| | Thank you (very much) | (Muchas) gracias | (**moo**-chas) **grah**-see-as |
| | You're welcome | De nada | day **nah**-dah |
| | Excuse me | Con permiso | con pair-**mee**-so |
| | Pardon me | ¿Perdón? | pair-**dohn** |
| | Could you tell me? | ¿Podría decirme? | po-dree-ah deh-**seer**-meh |
| | I'm sorry | Lo siento | lo see-**en**-to |
| | Good morning! | ¡Buenos días! | **bway**-nohs **dee**-ahs |
| | Good afternoon! | ¡Buenas tardes! | **bway**-nahs **tar**-dess |
| | Good evening! | ¡Buenas noches! | **bway**-nahs **no**-chess |
| | Goodbye! | ¡Adiós!/¡Hasta luego! | ah-dee-**ohss/ah**-stah-**lwe**-go |
| | Mr./Mrs. | Señor/Señora | sen-**yor**/sen-**yohr**-ah |
| | Miss | Señorita | sen-yo-**ree**-tah |
| | Pleased to meet you | Mucho gusto | **moo**-cho **goose**-to |
| | How are you? | ¿Cómo está usted? | **ko**-mo es-**tah** oo-**sted** |
| | Very well, thank you. | Muy bien, gracias. | **moo**-ee bee-**en**, **grah**-see-as |
| | And you? | ¿Y usted? | ee oos-**ted** |
| **Numbers** | | | |
| | 1 | un, uno | oon, **oo**-no |
| | 2 | dos | dos |
| | 3 | tres | tress |
| | 4 | cuatro | **kwah**-tro |
| | 5 | cinco | **sink**-oh |
| | 6 | seis | saice |
| | 7 | siete | see-**et**-eh |
| | 8 | ocho | **o**-cho |
| | 9 | nueve | new-**eh**-vey |
| | 10 | diez | dee-**es** |
| | 11 | once | **ohn**-seh |
| | 12 | doce | **doh**-seh |
| | 13 | trece | **treh**-seh |
| | 14 | catorce | ka-**tohr**-seh |
| | 15 | quince | **keen**-seh |
| | 16 | dieciséis | dee-**es**-ee-**saice** |

| 17 | diecisiete | dee-**es**-ee-see-**et**-eh |
| 18 | dieciocho | dee-**es**-ee-**o**-cho |
| 19 | diecinueve | **dee-es**-ee-new-**ev**-ah |
| 20 | veinte | **vain**-teh |
| 21 | veinte y uno/veintiuno | **vain**-te-**oo**-noh |
| 30 | treinta | **train**-tah |
| 40 | cuarenta | kwah-**ren**-tah |
| 50 | cincuenta | seen-**kwen**-tah |
| 60 | sesenta | sess-**en**-tah |
| 70 | setenta | set-**en**-tah |
| 80 | ochenta | oh-**chen**-tah |
| 90 | noventa | no-**ven**-tah |
| 100 | cien | see-**en** |
| 101 | ciento uno | see-**en**-toh **oo**-noh |
| 200 | doscientos | doh-see-**en**-tohss |
| 500 | quinientos | keen-**yen**-tohss |
| 1,000 | mil | meel |
| 1,000,000 | un millón | oon meel-**yohn** |

## Colors

| | | |
|---|---|---|
| black | negro | **neh**-groh |
| blue | azul | ah-**sool** |
| brown | café | kah-**feh** |
| green | verde | **ver**-deh |
| pink | rosa | **ro**-sah |
| purple | morado | mo-**rah**-doh |
| orange | naranja | na-**rahn**-hah |
| red | rojo | **roh**-hoh |
| white | blanco | **blahn**-koh |
| yellow | amarillo | ah-mah-**ree**-yoh |

## Days of the Week

| | | |
|---|---|---|
| Sunday | domingo | doe-**meen**-goh |
| Monday | lunes | **loo**-ness |
| Tuesday | martes | **mahr**-tess |
| Wednesday | miércoles | me-**air**-koh-less |
| Thursday | jueves | hoo-**ev**-ess |
| Friday | viernes | vee-**air**-ness |
| Saturday | sábado | **sah**-bah-doh |

## Months

| | | |
|---|---|---|
| January | enero | eh-**neh**-roh |
| February | febrero | feh-**breh**-roh |
| March | marzo | **mahr**-soh |
| April | abril | ah-**breel** |
| May | mayo | **my**-oh |
| June | junio | **hoo**-nee-oh |
| July | julio | **hoo**-lee-yoh |
| August | agosto | ah-**ghost**-toh |
| September | septiembre | sep-tee-**em**-breh |

| | | |
|---|---|---|
| October | octubre | **oak-too**-breh |
| November | noviembre | no-vee-**em**-breh |
| December | diciembre | dee-see-**em**-breh |

## Useful Phrases

| | | |
|---|---|---|
| Do you speak English? | ¿Habla usted inglés? | **ah**-blah oos-**ted** in-**glehs** |
| I don't speak Spanish | No hablo español | no **ah**-bloh es-pahn-**yol** |
| I don't understand (you) | No entiendo | no en-tee-**en**-doh |
| I understand (you) | Entiendo | en-tee-**en**-doh |
| I don't know | No sé | no seh |
| I am American/British | Soy americano (americana)/inglés(a) | soy ah-meh-ree-**kah**-no (ah-meh-ree-**kah**-nah)/ in-**glehs** (**ah**) |
| What's your name? | ¿Cómo se llama usted? | koh-mo seh **yah**-mah oos-**ted** |
| My name is . . . | Me llamo . . . | may **yah**-moh |
| What time is it? | ¿Qué hora es? | keh **o**-rah es |
| It is one, two, three . . . o'clock. | Es la una. . . . Son las dos, tres | es la **oo**-nah/sohn lahs dohs, tress |
| Yes, please/No, thank you | Sí, por favor/No, gracias | **see** pohr fah-**vor**/no **grah**-see-us |
| How? | ¿Cómo? | **koh**-mo |
| When? | ¿Cuándo? | **kwahn**-doh |
| This/Next week | Esta semana/la semana que entra | **es**-teh seh-**mah**-nah/lah seh-**mah**-nah keh **en**-trah |
| This/Next month | Este mes/el próximo mes | **es**-teh mehs/el **proke**-see-mo mehs |
| This/Next year | Este año/el año que viene | **es**-teh **ahn**-yo/el **ahn**-yo keh vee-**yen**-ay |
| Yesterday/today/tomorrow | Ayer/hoy/mañana | ah-**yehr**/oy/mahn-**yah**-nah |
| This morning/afternoon | Esta mañana/tarde | **es**-tah mahn-**yah**-nah/**tar**-deh |
| Tonight | Esta noche | **es**-tah **no**-cheh |
| What? | ¿Qué? | keh |
| What is it? | ¿Qué es esto? | keh es **es**-toh |
| Why? | ¿Por qué? | pore **keh** |
| Who? | ¿Quién? | kee-**yen** |
| Where is . . . ? | ¿Dónde está . . . ? | **dohn**-deh es-**tah** |
| the train station? | la estación del tren? | la es-tah-see-**on** del **train** |
| the subway station? | la estación del Tren subterráneo? | la es-ta-see-**on** del trehn soob-tair-**ron**-a-o |
| the bus stop? | la parada del autobus? | la pah-**rah**-dah del oh-toh-**boos** |

| | | |
|---|---|---|
| the post office? | la oficina de correos? | la oh-fee-**see**-nah deh koh-**reh**-os |
| the bank? | el banco? | el **bahn**-koh |
| the hotel? | el hotel? | el oh-**tel** |
| the store? | la tienda? | la tee-**en**-dah |
| the cashier? | la caja? | la **kah**-hah |
| the museum? | el museo? | el moo-**seh**-oh |
| the hospital? | el hospital? | el ohss-pee-**tal** |
| the elevator? | el ascensor? | el ah-**sen**-sohr |
| the bathroom? | el baño? | el **bahn**-yoh |
| Here/there | Aquí/allá | ah-**key**/ah-**yah** |
| Open/closed | Abierto/cerrado | ah-bee-**er**-toh/ ser-**ah**-doh |
| Left/right | Izquierda/derecha | iss-key-**er**-dah/ dare-**eh**-chah |
| Straight ahead | Derecho | dare-**eh**-choh |
| Is it near/far? | ¿Está cerca/lejos? | es-**tah** sehr-kah/ **leh**-hoss |
| I'd like . . . a room | Quisiera . . . un cuarto/una habitación | kee-see-ehr-ah oon **kwahr**-toh/ **oo**-nah ah-bee-tah-see-**on** |
| the key | la llave | lah **yah**-veh |
| a newspaper | un periódico | oon pehr-ee-oh-**dee**-koh |
| a stamp | un sello de correo | oon **seh**-yo deh koh-**reh**-oh |
| I'd like to buy . . . | Quisiera comprar . . . | kee-see-**ehr**-ah kohm-**prahr** |
| cigarettes | cigarrillos | ce-ga-**ree**-yohs |
| matches | cerillos | ser-**ee**-ohs |
| a dictionary | un diccionario | oon deek-see-oh-**nah**-ree-oh |
| soap | jabón | hah-**bohn** |
| sunglasses | gafas de sol | **ga**-fahs deh sohl |
| suntan lotion | loción bronceadora | loh-see-**ohn** brohn-seh-ah-**do**-rah |
| a map | un mapa | oon **mah**-pah |
| a magazine | una revista | **oon**-ah reh-**veess**-tah |
| paper | papel | pah-**pel** |
| envelopes | sobres | **so**-brehs |
| a postcard | una tarjeta postal | **oon**-ah tar-**het**-ah post-**ahl** |
| How much is it? | ¿Cuánto cuesta? | **kwahn**-toh **kwes**-tah |
| It's expensive/ cheap | Está caro/barato | es-**tah** kah-roh/ bah-**rah**-toh |
| A little/a lot | Un poquito/ mucho | oon poh-**kee**-toh/ **moo**-choh |
| More/less | Más/menos | mahss/**men**-ohss |
| Enough/too much/too little | Suficiente/ demasiado/ muy poco | soo-fee-see-**en**-teh/ deh-mah-see-**ah**-doh/**moo**-ee poh-koh |

| Telephone | Teléfono | tel-**ef**-oh-no |
| I am ill | Estoy enfermo(a) | es-**toy** en-**fehr**-moh(mah) |
| Please call a doctor | Por favor llame a un medico | pohr fah-**vor ya**-meh ah oon **med**-ee-koh |
| Help! | ¡Auxilio! ¡Ayuda! ¡Socorro! | owk-**see**-lee-oh/ ah-**yoo**-dah/ soh-**kohr**-roh |
| Fire! | ¡Incendio! | en-**sen**-dee-oo |
| Caution!/Look out! | ¡Cuidado! | kwee-**dah**-doh |

## Dining Out

| A bottle of . . . | Una botella de . . . | **oo**-nah bo-**teh**-yah deh |
| A cup of . . . | Una taza de . . . | **oo**-nah **tah**-thah deh |
| A glass of . . . | Un vaso de . . . | oon **vah**-so deh |
| Ashtray | Un cenicero | oon sen-ee-**seh**-roh |
| Bill/check | La cuenta | lah **kwen**-tah |
| Bread | El pan | el pahn |
| Breakfast | El desayuno | el deh-sah-**yoon**-oh |
| Butter | La mantequilla | lah man-teh-**key**-yah |
| Cheers! | ¡Salud! | sah-**lood** |
| Cocktail | Un aperitivo | oon ah-pehr-ee-**tee**-voh |
| Dinner | La cena | lah **seh**-nah |
| Dish | Un plato | oon **plah**-toh |
| Menu of the day | Menú del día | meh-**noo** del **dee**-ah |
| Enjoy! | ¡Buen provecho! | bwehn pro-**veh**-cho |
| Fixed-price menu | Menú fijo o turistico | meh-**noo fee**-hoh oh too-**ree**-stee-coh |
| Fork | El tenedor | el ten-eh-**dor** |
| Is the tip included? | ¿Está incluida la propina? | es-**tah** in-cloo-**ee**-dah lah pro-**pee**-nah |
| Knife | El cuchillo | el koo-**chee**-yo |
| Lunch | La comida | lah koh-**mee**-dah |
| Menu | La carta, el menú | lah **cart**-ah, el meh-**noo** |
| Napkin | La servilleta | lah sehr-vee-**yet**-ah |
| Pepper | La pimienta | lah pee-me-**en**-tah |
| Please give me | Por favor déme | pore fah-**vor deh**-meh |
| Salt | La sal | lah sahl |
| Spoon | Una cuchara | **oo**-nah koo-**chah**-rah |
| Sugar | El azúcar | el ah-**thu**-kar |
| Waiter!/Waitress! | ¡Por favor Señor/Señorita! | pohr fah-**vor** sen-**yor**/sen-yor-**ee**-tah |

# INDEX

# Looking for a different kind of vacation?

**Fodor's** makes it easy with a full line of specialty guidebooks to suit a variety of interests—from adventure to romance to language help.

**Fodor's.** For the world of ways you trav